THE BEST OF THE
REJECTION
COLLECTION

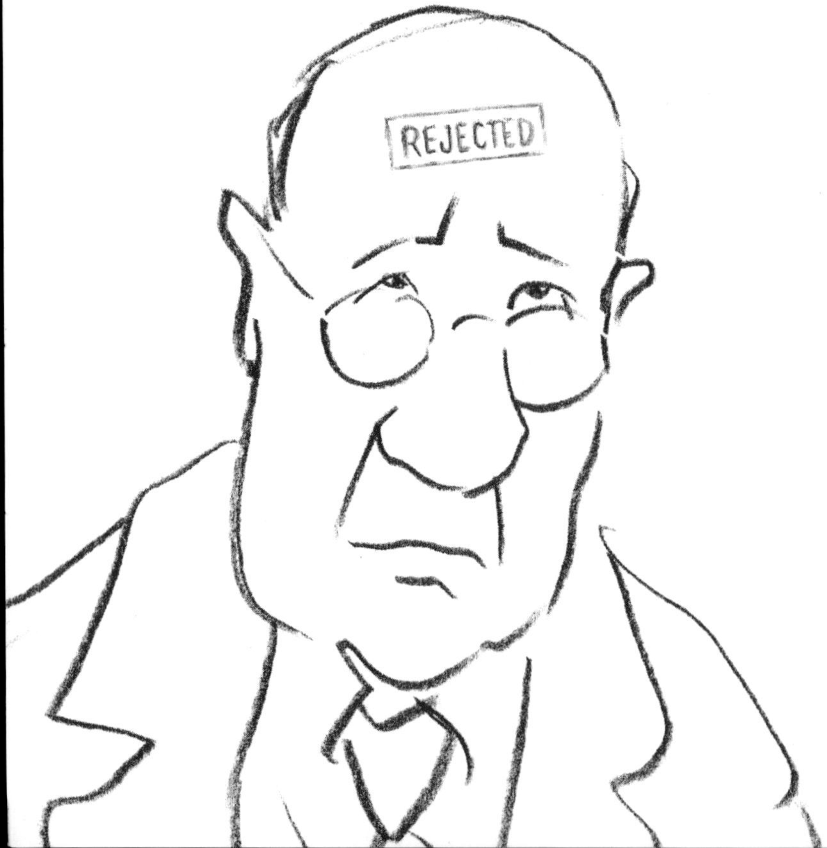
REJECTED

THE BEST OF THE
REJECTION
COLLECTION

293 Cartoons That Were Too
Dumb, Too Dark, or Too Naughty
for *The New Yorker*

Rescued by Matthew Diffee
FOREWORD BY ROBERT MANKOFF

WORKMAN PUBLISHING • NEW YORK

— DEDICATION —

In memory of
J. B. (Bud) Handelsman and Leo Cullum—
wonderful cartoonists and even better friends

This book is neither authorized nor sponsored by *The New Yorker*.

Copyright © 2011 by Matthew Diffee

All rights reserved. No portion of this book may be reproduced—mechanically, electronically, or by any other means, including photocopying—without written permission of the publisher. Published simultaneously in Canada by Thomas Allen & Son Limited.

Library of Congress Cataloging-in-Publication Data

The best of the rejection collection : 293 cartoons that were too dumb, too dark, or too naughty for the New Yorker / rescued by Matthew Diffee ; foreword by Robert Mankoff.
    p. cm.
  ISBN 978-0-7611-6578-1 (alk. paper)
1. American wit and humor, Pictorial. 2. New Yorker (New York, N.Y. : 1925) I. Diffee, Matthew. II. New Yorker (New York, N.Y. : 1925)
  NC1428.N47B47 2011
  741.5'6973--dc23
                2011024089

Design by Sue Macleod with Janet Vicario

Much of the material in this book originally appeared in *The Rejection Collection* and *The Rejection Collection, Vol. 2* by Matthew Diffee (published by Simon Spotlight Entertainment, a division of Simon & Schuster, in 2006 and 2007, respectively).

Page 323 constitutes an extension of this copyright page.

Workman books are available at special discounts when purchased in bulk for premiums and sales promotions as well as for fund-raising or educational use. Special editions or book excerpts also can be created to specification. For details, contact the Special Sales Director at the address below, or send an e-mail to specialmarkets@workman.com.

Workman Publishing Company, Inc.
225 Varick Street
New York, NY 10014-4381

www.workman.com

Printed in the United States of America

First printing September 2011

10 9 8 7 6 5 4 3 2 1

CONTENTS

FOREWORD
BY ROBERT MANKOFF

I f memory—or, more accurately, Google—serves me correctly, it was Keats who proclaimed: "Beauty is truth, truth beauty,—that is all / Ye know on earth, and all ye need to know." Well, let me tell ye, Keats was dead wrong. Certainly, he's dead; we can agree on that. But my main point is that if you want to know what makes something funny, it's not beauty. Look, the *Mona Lisa* is beautiful, but until Marcel Duchamp put a mustache and goatee on her, she was no fun at all. Funny isn't about beauty—it's about freedom. Sometimes that freedom leads to disrespect, ridicule, and outright offensiveness. To see the truth of that, you don't have to look any further than this collection of cartoons that happily exploit all that is vile for the sake of a smile.

Furthermore, if you're like me, many of the offensive, obscene, disgusting cartoons here will actually make you laugh out loud—and, in some cases, cause incontinence, nausea, and fainting. So before looking at these cartoons, ask your doctor if incontinence, nausea, and fainting are right for you.

This collection is yet more proof that bad taste and humor are not strange bedfellows but intimate partners whose down-and-dirty doings often delight us against our better judgment, our scruples, and our politically respectable attitudes.

But whereas cartoonists (at least the ones I've known, including myself) are not known for their better judgment, their scruples, and their respectability, *The New Yorker* is. And since I've been the cartoon editor of the magazine for the past ten years, a patina of *The New Yorker*'s respectability has unavoidably rubbed off on me. It's just a veneer, of course, but after a decade it's quite thick and, according to my dermatologist, very difficult to remove. Besides, the procedure isn't covered by my health plan.

But thick veneer notwithstanding, if it were really up to just me, some of these cartoons would probably have made it into *The New Yorker,* offending not only the little old lady in Dubuque but perhaps even the cross-dressing CEO in Manhattan. But none of these cartoons did, in fact, make it into *The New Yorker.* That's because others at the magazine have better judgment, more scruples, and greater respectability than I do, as evidenced by the fact that they rejected this cartoon of my own.

MANKOFF

"Hey, my eyes are up here!"

How these cartoons got into the hands of the editor of this collection, Matthew Diffee, cartoonist and former friend, I don't know, and he won't tell, even under the threat of extraordinary rendition. So there's nothing to be done but enjoy them and be damned.

INTRODUCTION

Welcome to *The Best of the Rejection Collection.* In this book you'll find a bunch of wonderfully awful and some awfully wonderful rejected *New Yorker* cartoons. They're not really *New Yorker* cartoons (after all, *The New Yorker* rejected them), but they are cartoons by *The New Yorker* cartoonists. I'm one of those cartoonists. My job is to come up with cartoons and pitch them to the magazine. The magazine's job is to reject almost all of those cartoons. What happens to those rejected ideas? Nothing, unless you count gathering dust as something. Are the rejected cartoons any good? That depends on what you mean by "good." Good for *The New Yorker*? No, probably not. Good for a laugh? Certainly. In fact, if you ask the cartoonists, some of the rejected ones are the flat-out funniest cartoons we've ever done. But they're different than what you're used to seeing from us. The ones you see in the magazine are the ones *The New Yorker* chose to show you. If we were doing the choosing you might end up with a magazine full of cartoons like this one. . . .

"I'd say my biggest influence is probably Pollock."

You might think, like I did when I submitted it, that a gag like this could totally be in *The New Yorker,* but you, like I, would be wrong. Sure, it makes a highbrow reference to an abstract expressionist painter whose work you have to know in order to get the joke, but it's also a cartoon about bird poop. Oddly, *The New Yorker* doesn't seem to go for that kind of thing. I assume that's why they passed on it. (Of course I don't really know for sure why this or any of the cartoons in this book were rejected. I have only my hunches. I've made a list of those and illustrated each with an example from my own stack of rejects. You'll find them at the end of this introduction.)

Let me take just a second here and put all this rejection business into perspective for you. The cartoons you see in *The New Yorker* are only a small percentage—the tip of the iceberg. We cartoonists are lucky if they take one of the ten ideas we pitch each week. It's a 90 percent rejection rate, but it's actually worse than that because our final ten, the ones we deem good enough to sketch up and pitch, are the tip of an even bigger iceberg. Well, it's the same iceberg, and I guess it can't technically be the tip since I just called the other part the tip. It's the next part below the tip. If it were a piece of candy corn, it would be the dark orange part. (And speaking of that, why would anyone name candy after a vegetable? Makes no sense.) Tell you what. Forget the candy corn. Stay with me on the iceberg. In fact, let me draw it. . . .

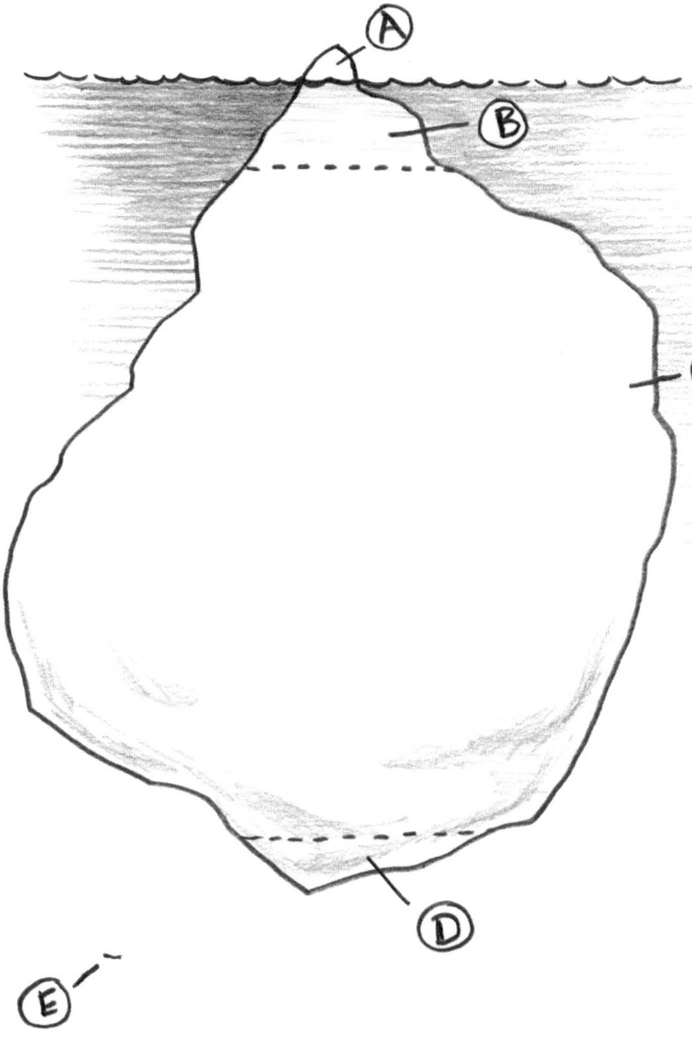
A
B
C
D
E

A. Tip of the Iceberg. The cartoons *not* rejected by *The New Yorker*. You can see these by getting yourself a subscription.

B. Top of the Iceberg. These are the cartoons that are rejected by *The New Yorker,* but not rejected by the cartoonist. See what I'm saying? These are his or her ten best ideas from a week's worth of work, what we call the "batch." You can see the best of these in the pages of this book.

C. Bulk of the Iceberg. These are cartoon ideas that the cartoonist rejected. See, in order to get ten good gags for the batch, the cartoonist comes up with a whole lot more. Probably close to 90 percent more. The theory being that the more ideas generated, the better the quality will be of the final ten that are drawn up and pitched. These are probably not good ideas. Where can you see them? Well, you're not supposed to see them. In a way, they don't even exist because they weren't good enough to draw. However, in the interest of science, I'll give you a glimpse of these on the following pages of this introduction.

D. Butt of the Iceberg. A special classification of the above category, these are cartoon ideas that the cartoonist has rejected from other people. They can come from family members, former friends, psychiatric professionals, and even complete strangers. In most cases these are the worst cartoon ideas EVER. You can see some of them at the back of this book. For real. See page 300.

E. A Blue Whale.

So that's the cold hard truth about cartoon ideas. Get it? Huh? Get it? Sorry. Now, as promised, in the interest of science, I'm going to give you a look at some of my ideas that would fall into the "bulk of the iceberg" category. Again, these are the surplus ideas that I didn't think were strong enough to get into the final ten that I sketched and sent to the magazine. Hopefully this will also take us a few steps toward answering the question cartoonists get asked more than any other: *How do you come up with your ideas?* The honest but not very satisfying answer is, *We think of them.* It's unsatisfying because people want to know *how* we think of them, and that's tough to answer and impossible to demonstrate because it happens in our heads—but I'll give it a try here.

What you're about to see on the following page is the closest I can come to showing what happens in my brain, bad ideas and all. It's a piece of paper that I used to jot my thoughts during an idea-getting brainstorm session several years ago. I can't pinpoint the date, but I think it must have been sometime in 2005. See, every day, I make a pot of coffee and then sit down with a pen in front of a blank sheet of paper and think. If things are working correctly, by the time the pot's empty, the page will be full. What it's full of is scribbling. There'll be a bunch of half ideas, false starts, and then a few actual cartoon ideas. Almost all of these, however, will be "bulk of the iceberg" ideas. I think this is what some people call a mind map. Most of the work happens in my head of course, but the notes here provide a sort of dotted line of where my mind wandered. It might not look like much, but it represents a day's work for me. And of course, when I say a day, I'm really talking about a few hours—I'm a cartoonist not a coal miner.

A DAY IN THE BRAIN OF A CARTOONIST

A
TACKLE BOX
boxing
football

wiffle ——
nerf

just because you/I ——
doesn't mean

let's just keep
this between me and you and the internet
and our facebook friends

D
A restaurant
that serves
airplane food
called ——

B Fear of flying

picket line
picket fence — fencing
dont picket fence
me in
protestors strike
say no to protests
stop the picketing

Sign next
to hot dog
vendor ?

Beware of dog
cat crap

Robin Hood steal from the rich
and give to middleclass
the wife

a penny saved is a penny earned
but which is
a penny who has accepted Jesus as his personal savior ?

its all in the wrist
offensive driving
drivers Ed guy: make
sure you keep both knee
one on the wheel

I'm trapped in
an effusive
relationship

this might be the
most important
fig newton
of my life.

some guy in a bar: you want a piece of me???

Student Driver

C Sign on air plane
tractor bicycle
zamboni

E
metal Detector = tin man
medal
man in suit of armor
"maybe its your keys."
Super man: Oh I know what it is. I'm the man of steel."
or should be clark kent.

I'm just going thru a hard
time right now
said by a guy
missing an arm
and leg
or just
a head?

cubical on fire

looking in window at a bird in a cage

Reality TV
literature

H
I need to join a
gym but I want
to get in shape first.

take a page from my book
on the same
page

The real you/me
I want to know the
real you unless the
real you is ——
isnt rich

kick the
tires.
rotate.
burn rubber

PIGEONS on a Wire
can you feel the
electricity
we met online
target practice
bomb

I
as artist: right now
I'm working on a bug
sort of an homage
to Pollock

Workaholic
need a bigger bucket
floating
belly up
little
castle

GRIM Reaper
raking leaves

Bucket
need a KFC
kick the bucket
L list

Gold fish in a bowl
bronze
silver

F
fish sticks
luck
fish out of water gas
money
phish
fileto'fish ——
fileto' ——

pillow case
guitar case — detective

kick it
again

If it aint broke...
If it aint Baroque
broken leg ?

cowboy hat
how big is it in liters?

LOST AND FOUND
I lost my Lunch.
at zoo?
at Amusement Park

man trying on
hats
do you have this in ——
—beret
do you have
anything more
pretentious
I want a beret that
says

does it make me look like an artist wannabe

Eating lunch
hm. what should
I do with this
extra boiled egg

Shallow girl: I just dont want
to be alone for the
rest of my week
weekend

G
Sometimes I'm afraid
I'll end up...

Construction workers
up on an i beam
dropped tool?

sign: men working on their tans
men talking
scared of Heights
(widths)

Here's a guide to a few points of interest:

A. This is a topic. Nothing going on with it really, but when I first sit down, I often start by just jotting down the first random things that come to me. It helps to get rid of some of the scary white space. You gotta start somewhere.

B. This is a topic too, but not as random as the other. It's a topic that I had a funny feeling about. A topic I thought I'd be able to wring some humor from. As you can see by the lack of additional notes, I was mistaken.

C. "The old switcheroo." Here, I started with a thing, in this case a "student driver" sign that you'd see on top of a Driver's Ed car. Then I just tried to come up with a funny alternative vehicle to replace the car. Sometimes this works. Here it didn't. Clearly the funniest vehicle option is a Zamboni. There's just something funny about a Zamboni, but that by itself isn't an idea. It needed more, and apparently I didn't come up with anything to nudge that notion into an actual cartoon idea. Thinking now, the obvious thing would be to have the Zamboni with the student driver sign in some sort of bad situation: The driver's rammed it into the wall, or he's running over figure

skaters, but that's not anything really. You could go absurd with it and have him driving it out in the middle of a desert. Or, I don't know. . . . See? This is what happens. If those are ideas at all, they're easily rejected ones.

D. This is a setup that didn't lead anywhere. Hence the blank. I'm sure I thought of stuff, but nothing worth writing down. Either that or I got distracted and didn't come back to it.

E. This is just a phrase I was hearing at the time. From there I try to think of a surprising image to use with it, or some way of manipulating the phrase into a joke. You can see some of that process here. Sometimes something comes from it, but usually not.

F. This fish business is just a little riff that I got into. Trying to generate something by jotting down a bunch of things around a single topic. I'm "fishing" for ideas here. Get it? Sorry. The closest thing to an idea here is taking the phrase "fish out of water" and changing it to "fish out of money." You can imagine a few ways that one could turn that into a cartoon, but can you think of any way to turn it into a good cartoon? I couldn't. Probably wasted eleven minutes of my life trying.

G. This is an idea. It's not that great. I rejected it.

H. This is also an idea: It's circled, so I guess I thought it was okay. Good enough to consider sketching up. I don't remember how the idea came to me and you don't see any of the process here. I do remember drawing it and I remember it getting rejected, which surprises me. Not that it was rejected, but that I remember it, because the idea itself isn't very memorable.

I. This is another idea, and this is the reason I chose this sheet to show you instead of all the others. This is the germ of the idea for that Pollock pigeon cartoon I showed you a couple pages back. It looks like I got to the idea from the seemingly random starting point of "pigeons on a wire" a few lines above. You'll notice I streamlined the caption later, making it better, but this is the initial spark. At this point, I was thinking the idea would work only if the reader pictured the pigeon "splatter" landing on something Pollock-size and rectangular, thus the bus reference. Going back through the week's idea sheets a few days later and selecting this one to draw, I had a better perspective on it and realized the bus wasn't necessary.

So there you go. That pigeon idea was a "top of the iceberg" idea. Not even a "tip of the iceberg" idea. It was good enough for me, but not for *The New Yorker*. I don't know if I sold a cartoon at all that week, but I know I didn't sell that one. Sad, huh? If you multiply this sheet times six or seven, depending on whether I took a day off or not, and then add fifty percent for the ideas that didn't even make it to the page, you'll get a ballpark idea of how big the "bulk of the iceberg" was for me that week. Multiply that times the number of cartoonists in this book and then times the number of weeks in a year and suddenly we're talking about a pretty big ball of ice.

I hope you also get from this a sense of how a cartoonist—at least this one—thinks. You'll get a whole lot more of that in the following pages. Particularly in the sections between the cartoons where I asked (okay, forced) my cartooning colleagues to answer some ridiculous questions in hopes of offering you a peek at their personalities and revealing just how endlessly creative and occasionally twisted they really are.

But first, as I mentioned earlier, here's a batch of some of my own rejected cartoons along with my best guess as to why they might have been rejected. Consider this a "what not to do" list if you want to get your cartoons into a sophisticated literary magazine.

10 POSSIBLE REASONS

WHY CARTOONS GET REJECTED BY

THE NEW YORKER

---

*As Exemplified by Some of
My Own Favorite Rejects*

REASON #1:

TOO LOW-BROW

PLEASE DO NOT
FEED THE ANIMALS
CHILI.

The New Yorker shies away from anything of this sort. No poop jokes, no projectile vomiting, and certainly nothing coming in or out of noses. (I know . . . what else is there?) I, for one, have done scores of scatological jokes over the years and never sold one. But what are you gonna do? Stop doing 'em? The funny thing is, when you spend all day trying in vain to create little diamond-cut tidbits of sophisticated, highbrow humor, nothing makes you giggle at the drawing board like a good old-fashioned flatulent pachyderm gag. Alas.

REASON #2:

TOO POLITICALLY INCORRECT

GO
INDIANS

I don't know. To me this cartoon is less about Native Americans and more about people who paint their faces at ball games. And besides, you can't say the gentleman on the right isn't wholeheartedly pro-Indian. Crap, I'm gonna get letters.

REASON #3:

"Come on in. The kids are in the backyard bobbing for pinkeye."

By "too dark" I mean cartoons that are too morbid, too creepy, too sick or twisted—cartoons that are a little too "real" about dying, disease, dismemberment, drug use, bad things happening to animals or children. Surprisingly, I can't think of anything funny to say about those things.

REASON #4:

"Kids at school call us 'eight eyes.'"

I told you, it's weird.

Here's another:

"She's a weiner cat."

For some reason a lot of my rejects fall into this category. It's the flip side of having complete creative freedom. Occasionally I'm gonna do stuff that's a little too "me." I can't really explain why, but to me these are funny. I am apparently alone in that opinion, and I'm surprisingly okay with that.

REASON #5:

TOO POLITICAL

I actually don't have any examples of this one, mainly because *The New Yorker* just doesn't run things that are overtly or specifically political. Besides, there are great cartoonists doing the political thing very well in other places. Also, I don't really keep up with the news. I watched CNN once, but that was only because I couldn't get to the remote control without dislodging the catheter.

TOO DIFFICULT TO GET REASON #6:

(And when readers do get it, it isn't funny enough to justify the effort, prompting the thought, *Is there something more here that I'm missing?*)

"Sellouts."

It's a Nike symbol . . . and therefore hilarious, and no, there isn't anything else that you're missing. It's just not that funny. A swing and a miss. Or, at best, a foul ball. Get it? Foul ball—as in fowl? Which leads us nicely into the next reason. . . .

REASON #7:

HORSE-DRAWN CARRIAGE

This is one of my favorites. I'm dumb.

REASON #8:

"It's from my Swiss account."

This is a bad cartoon. Just terrible. It's a pun, the domain of amateurs. Puns are to cartooning what lip-synching into a hairbrush is to show business. I can only say that when I did this, it must have been a really slow week in my head. Notice that I didn't even bother to do a finished drawing of this one. What you see here is the "rough" used to pitch the idea to the magazine.

REASON #9:

"You say sex pervert. I say horse enthusiast."

The New Yorker does plenty of sex-related cartoons, but there are some things the magazine won't touch—mostly things that are illegal. I guess there's a good reason why you've never seen *The New Yorker Book of Bestiality Cartoons.*

REASON #10:

ALL OF THE ABOVE

BALLOON GENITALS!
$5
DIFFEE

Sorry, Mom.

THE
REJECTS

LEIGHTON

ROBERT LEIGHTON

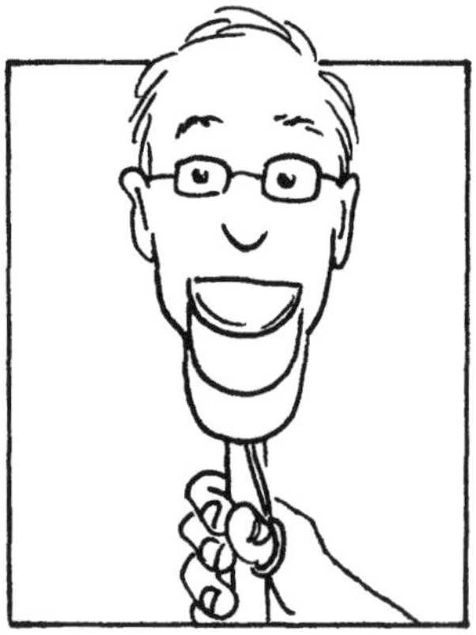

Frequently Asked Questions

- Where do you get your ideas?

  Happy Dragon Cartoon Mill, Hong Kong (trade secret).

- Which comes first, the picture or the caption?

  Usually I draw a sketch which suggests an idea/cartoon . . . which then suggests a different picture.

- How'd you get started?

  R. L. Stine published my work when he was an editor at Scholastic.

- I admire . . .

  Ayad Meyer. (Complete coincidence.)

- How do you deal with rejection?

  As a *New Yorker* cartoonist, I thrive on rejection. Imagine my disappointment on those fortunately rare occasions when they buy one of my cartoons.

- What are some things that make you laugh and why?

  Buster Keaton's *One Week*, Harvey Kurtzman's *Starchie*, *Calvin and Hobbes* Sunday strips, *The Onion's Our Dumb Century*. In each case, the humor is in the details.

- I've got a great idea for a cartoon—wanna hear it?

  Not unless you want to hear my great idea for investment banking.

Infrequently Asked Questions

- Have you mooned or *been* mooned more often in your life?

  Been mooned (1), Mooned (0).

- What would make a terrible pizza topping?

  Those stringy things you peel off bananas.

- What might one expect to find at a really low-budget amusement park?

  Bring-your-own safety bar/Walk-up Ferris Wheel.

■ What did the shepherd say to the three-legged sheepdog?

It's kind of slow around here. I'm going to have to let another one of your legs go.

And Now for a Few More Questions . . .

■ What do you hate drawing?

Mansion interiors, crowd scenes, cars.

■ Being as accurate as possible, how many desert island cartoons do you think you've come up with and submitted to *The New Yorker*?

16. (None sold.)

■ What's the funniest thing that you witnessed, overheard, or came up with that you couldn't figure out how to use in a cartoon?

Being indiscreet/Peeing in the street.

■ If you could ask Bob Mankoff, *The New Yorker* cartoon editor, one question, what would it be?

Get it?

Draw Some Sort of Doodle

. . . using the random lines below as a starting point.

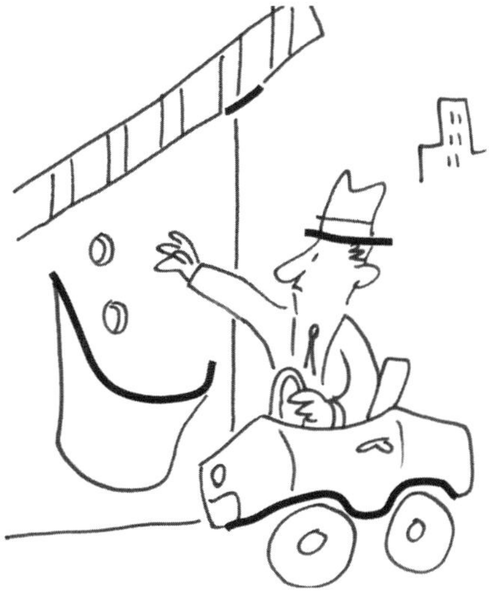

Naming Names

■ What name might you give to a mild-mannered, slightly overweight dental assistant in one of your cartoons?

Peg or Josie. (I have Steely Dan playing in the background.)

■ Other than Lance, what name would you give to a twenty-eight-year-old metrosexual entertainment lawyer who cycles on weekends?

Billy-Bob. (Playing against stereotypes here.)

■ What would be a good name for a new, commercially unviable breakfast cereal?

(I have been paid to do this.) Toback-O's/Deep Morning.

■ Come up with a name for an unpleasant medical procedure.

The Paine-Hertz procedure.

■ If you used a pen name, what would it be?

Who says I don't?

Complete the Pie Chart Below

. . . in a way that tells us something about your life or how you think.

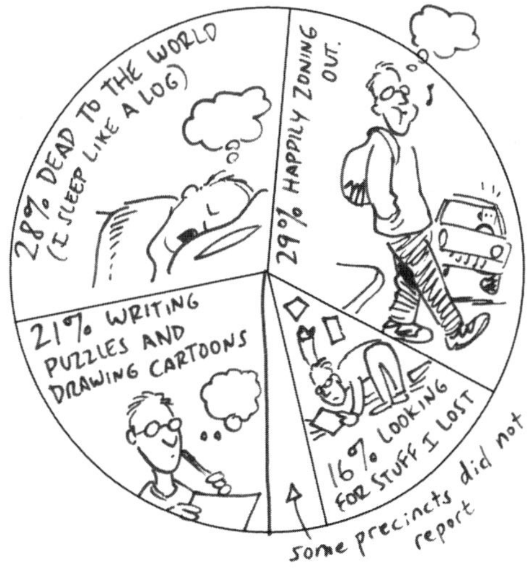
28% DEAD TO THE WORLD (I SLEEP LIKE A LOG)
29% HAPPILY ZONING OUT.
21% WRITING PUZZLES AND DRAWING CARTOONS
16% LOOKING FOR STUFF I LOST
some precincts did not report

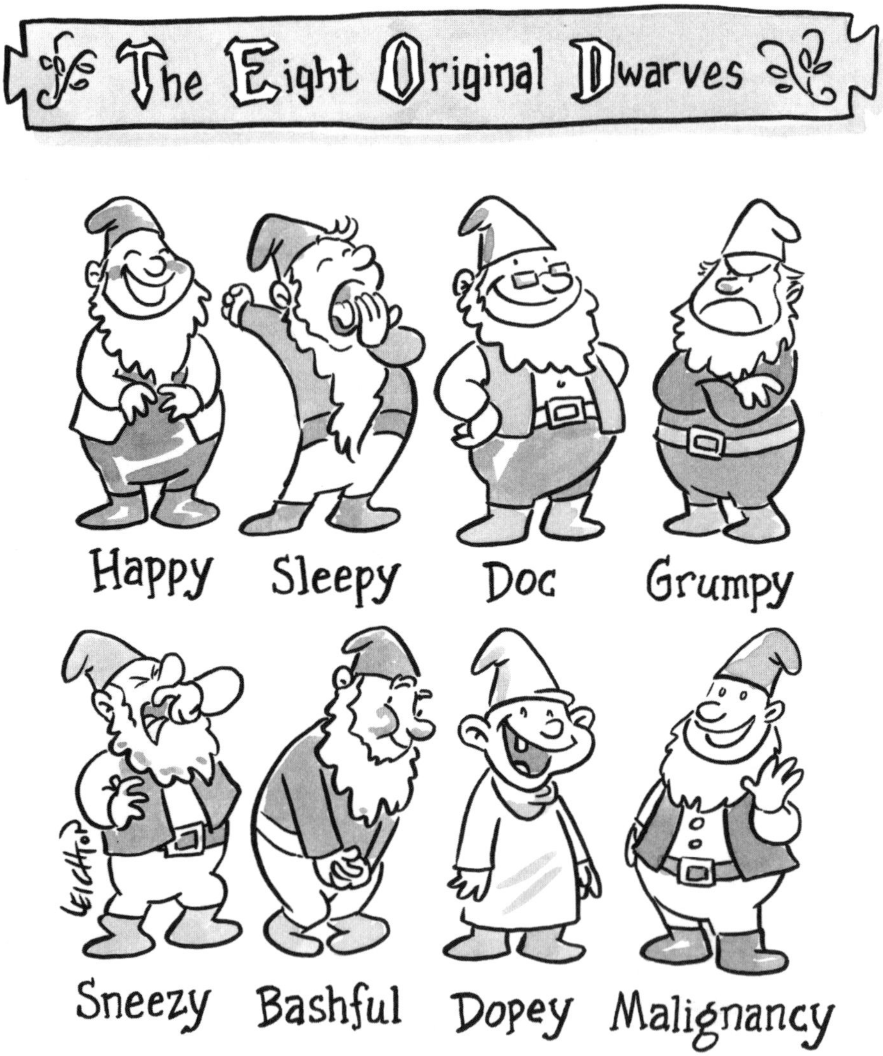
The Eight Original Dwarves
Happy
Sleepy
Doc
Grumpy
Sneezy
Bashful
Dopey
Malignancy
Leighton

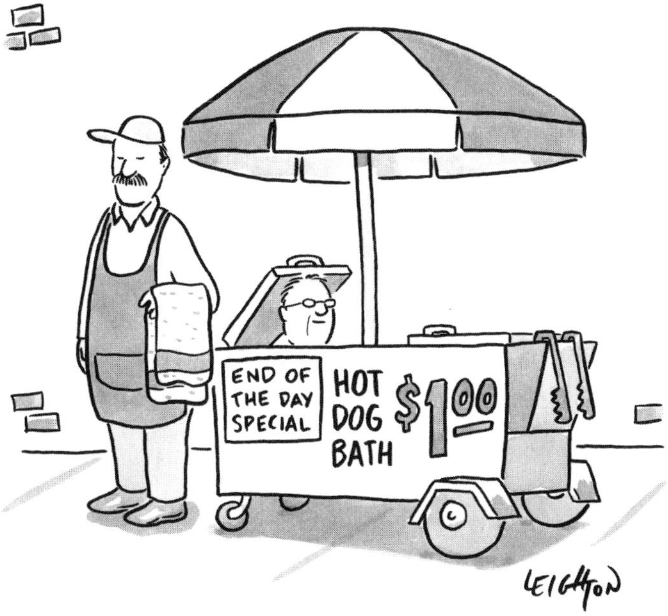
END OF THE DAY SPECIAL
HOT DOG BATH
$1.00
LEIGHTON

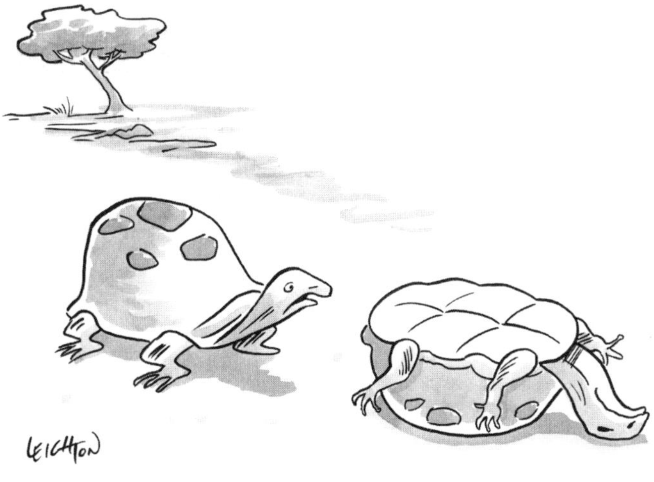
LEIGHTON

"I came as soon as I heard."

ZIEGLER

JACK ZIEGLER

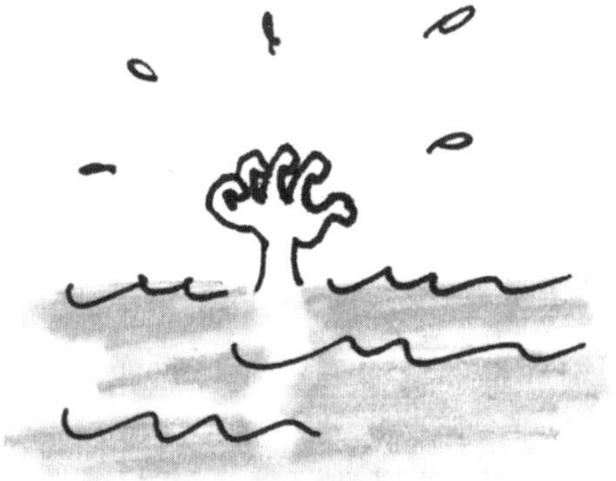

Frequently Asked Questions

- Where do you get your ideas?

  Macy's.

- Which comes first, the picture or the caption?

  Neither. Breakfast comes first.

- How~~'d~~ DO you get started?

  With lots of baby oil—and then WATCH OUT!!

- I admire . . .

  Steinberg, Picasso, Steig, Henry Miller, Geo Booth, Alan Dunn, B. Kliban, M. K. Brown, André Francois, Wayne Thiebaud, Rick Griffin, Harvey Kurtzman, Mobius, etc., etc.

- How do you deal with rejection?

  I go out and hunt down small creatures in the forest.

- What are some things that make you laugh and why?

  David Caruso in any episode of *CSI: Miami;* any *Seinfeld* rerun featuring Jerry Stiller; Dane Cook; certain friends who shall be unnamed. Why? Because they're funny.

- I've got a great idea for a cartoon—wanna hear it?

  I'm all ears.

Infrequently Asked Questions

- Have you mooned or *been* mooned more often in your life?

  Neither.

- What would make a terrible pizza topping?

  Iron filings.

- What might one expect to find at a really low-budget amusement park?

  David Caruso.

- What did the shepherd say to the three-legged sheepdog?

  FETCH! And this time more quickly please.

Draw Some Sort of Doodle

. . . using the random lines below as a starting point.

HELL'S
ANGELS
SAN BERDOO

And Now for a Few More Questions . . .

- What do you hate drawing?

  Tall people.

- Being as accurate as possible, how many desert island cartoons do you think you've come up with and submitted to *The New Yorker*?

  Hundreds. (Rejection rate: 97 percent.)

- What's the funniest thing that you witnessed, overheard, or came up with that you couldn't figure out how to use in a cartoon?

  My first lobotomy.

- If you could ask Bob Mankoff, *The New Yorker* cartoon editor, one question, what would it be?

  Where did you get that haircut?

Naming Names

- What name might you give to a mild-mannered, slightly overweight dental assistant in one of your cartoons?

  Bob.

- Other than Lance, what name would you give to a twenty-eight-year-old metrosexual entertainment lawyer who cycles on weekends?

  Bob.

- What would be a good name for a new, commercially unviable breakfast cereal?

  Fibrous Bob-o-Links.

- Come up with a name for an unpleasant medical procedure.

  The Bob Reduction.

- If you used a pen name, what would it be?

  Bob.

Complete the Pie Chart Below

. . . in a way that tells us something about your life or how you think.

SEX
DRUGS
ROCK + ROLL
MOM

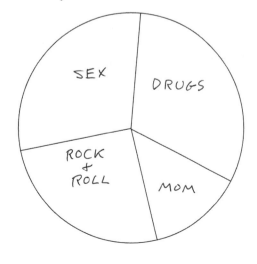

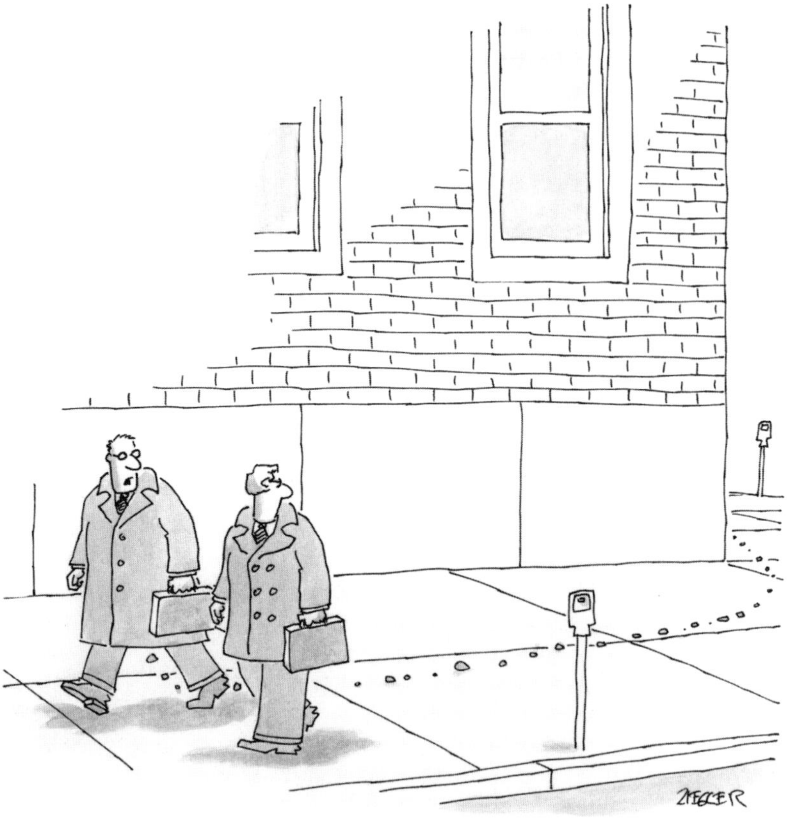
ZIEGLER

"Sorry, Ted. Generally, what happens in the pants stays in the pants."

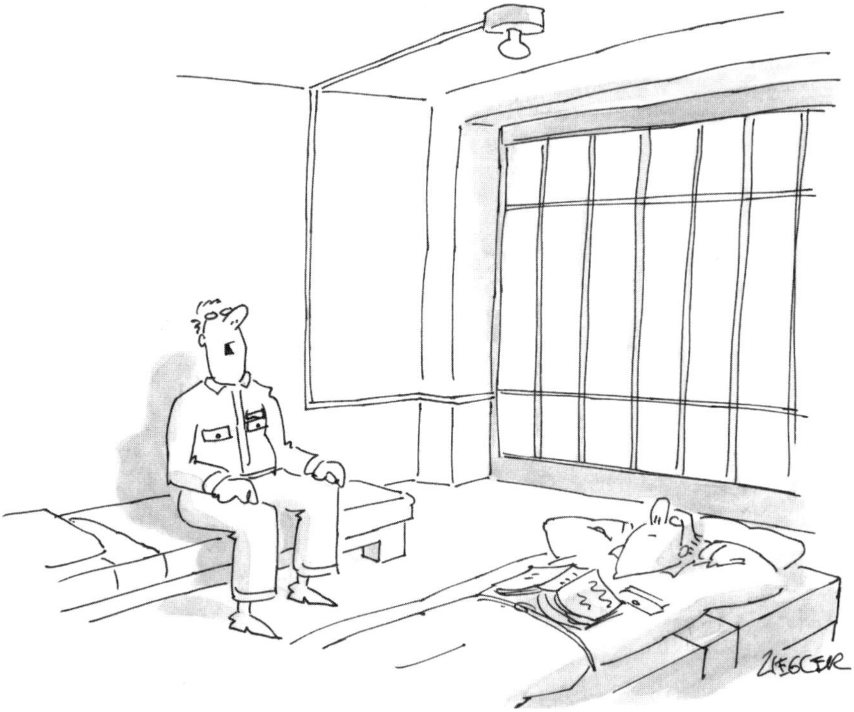
ZIEGLER

"As an ex-priest, I'm having a hard time adjusting to these noncathedral ceilings."

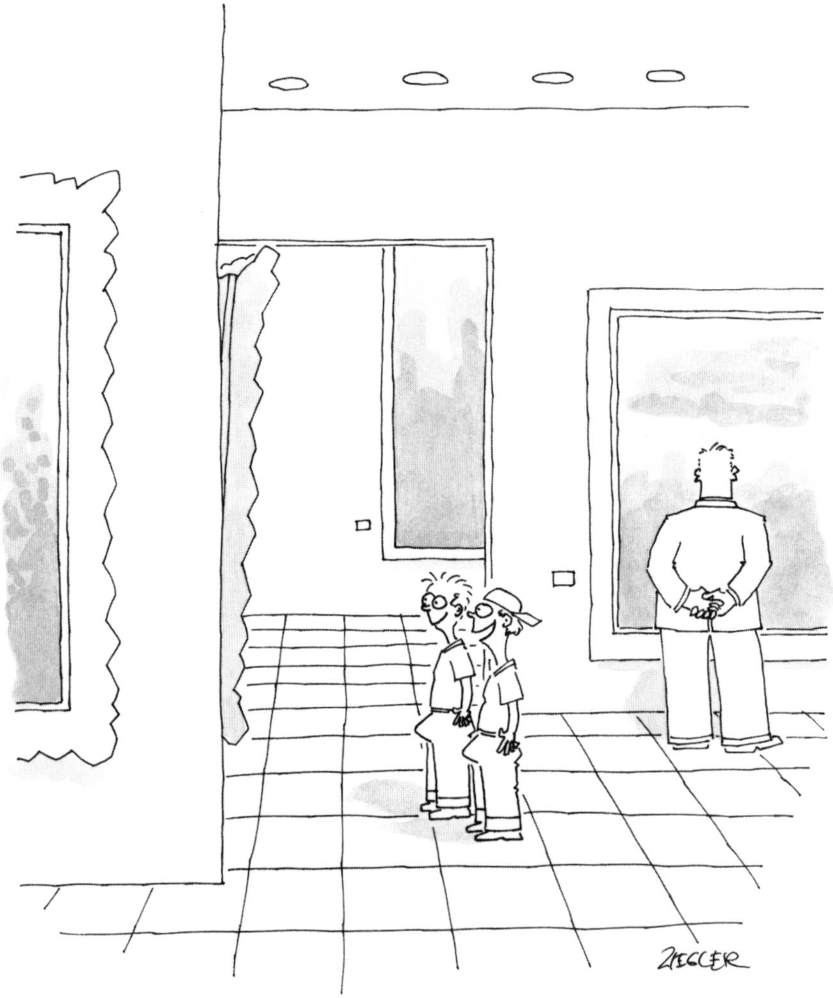
ZIEGLER

"Wow! Great Nude!"

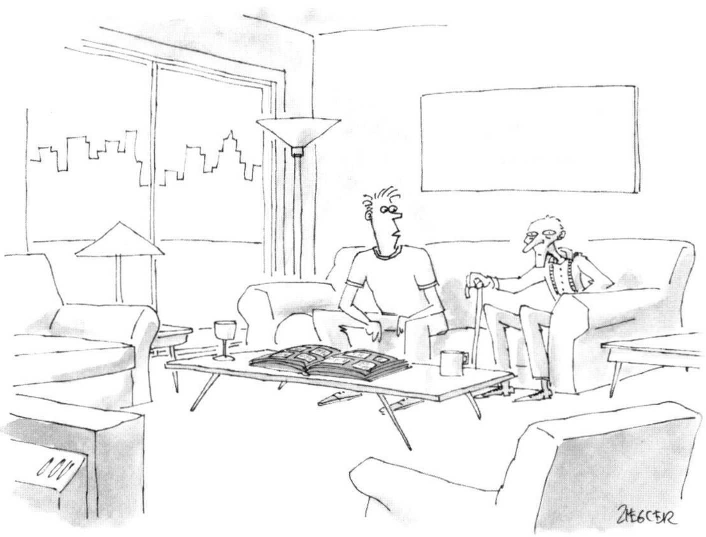
ZIEGLER

"What's the deal, Gramps? You couldn't get any color film at Auschwitz?"

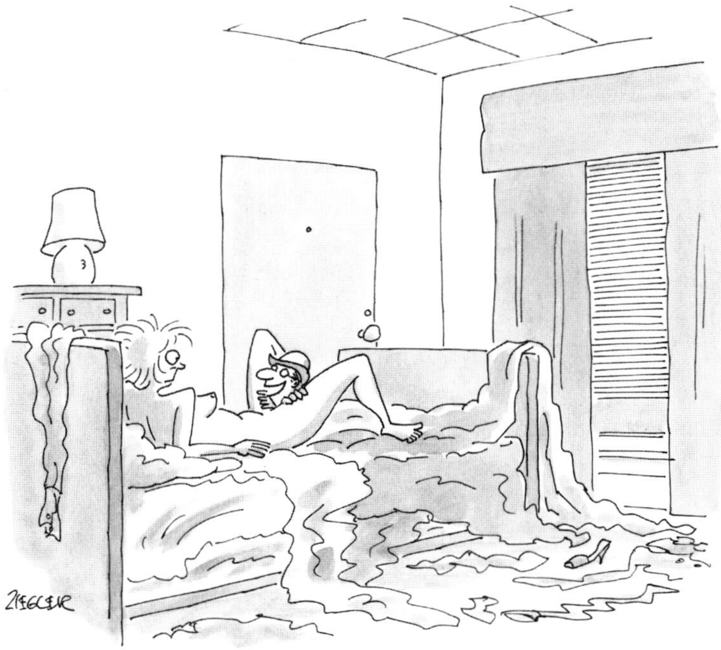
ZIEGLER

"I'm afraid I made quite a nuisance of myself in here last night."

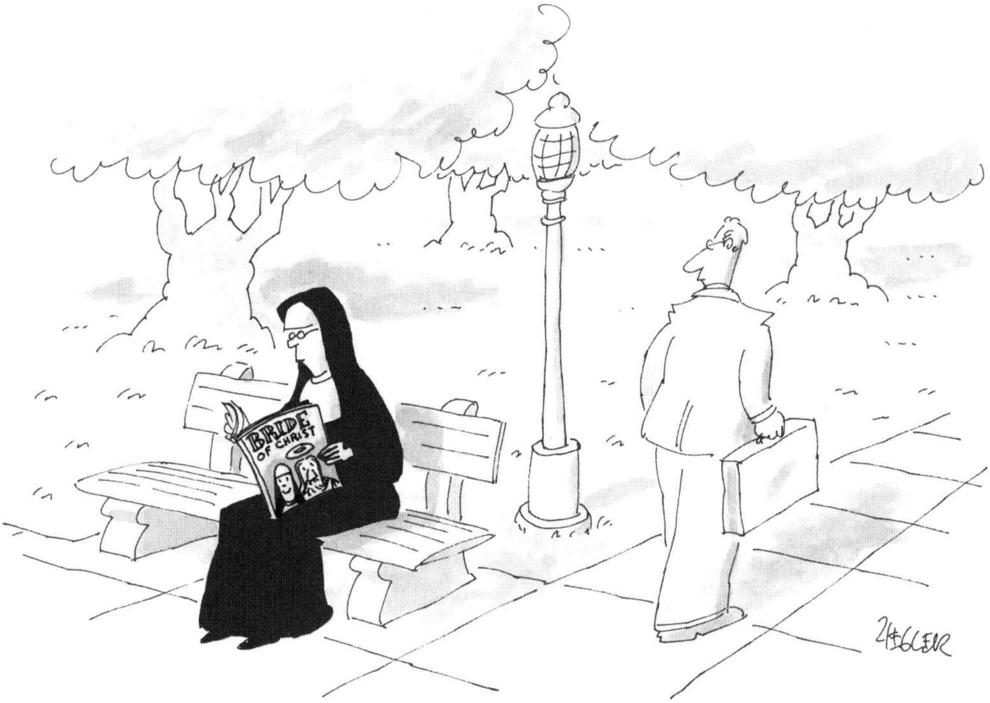
BRIDE
OF CHRIST
ZIEGLER

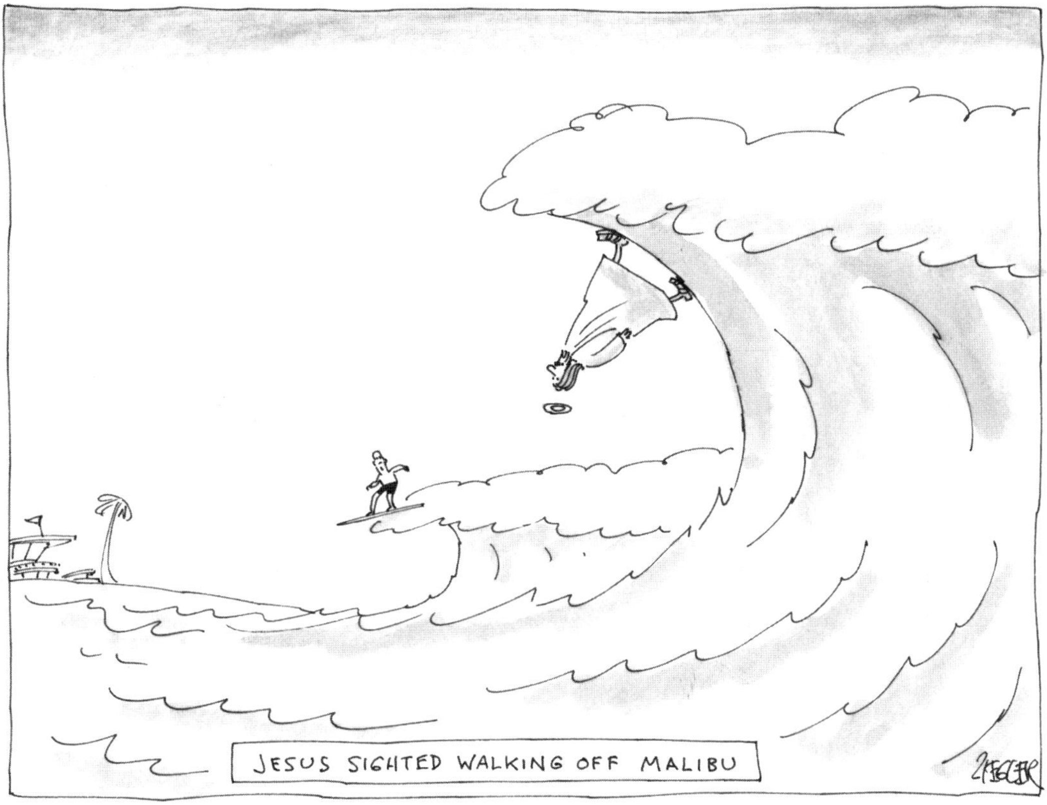
JESUS SIGHTED WALKING OFF MALIBU
ZIEGLER

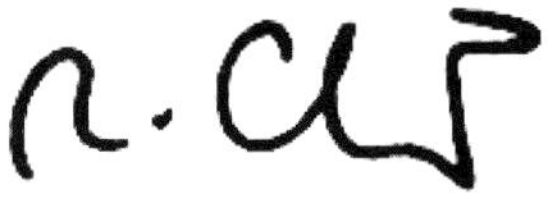

ROZ CHAST

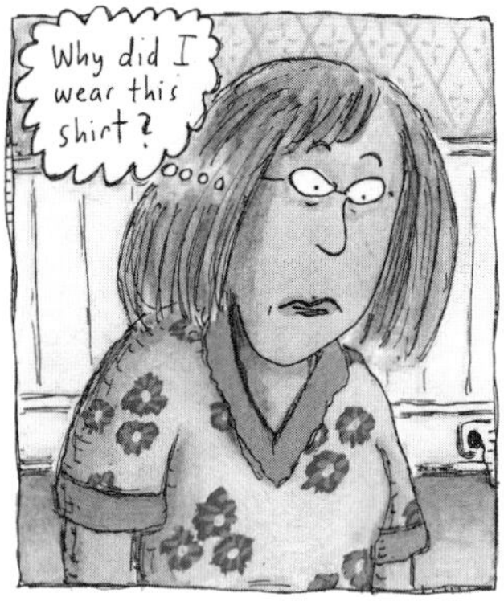
Why did I wear this shirt?

Frequently Asked Questions

- Where do you get your ideas?
  No.

- Which comes first, the picture or the caption?
  Yes.

- How'd you get started?
  Sometimes.

- I admire . . .
  Bruce Jay Friedman, Charles Portis, Thomas Mann, Charles Addams, Mary Petty, Sue Coe, Jack Ziegler, Gahan Wilson, Stephin Merritt, and about a million others. It would sicken you if I listed all of them.

- How do you deal with rejection?
  I feel very sorry for myself and sometimes get into a panic. Then I do my best to get back to work, because what else is there to do? There's only so much origami a person can fold.

- What are some things that make you laugh and why?
  Once I was at lunch with a group of cartoonists and the word "bolus" came up. A bolus is a lump of chewed food. That made me really laugh, but I don't know why. I also find *It's a Gift*, an old W. C. Fields movie, very hilarious, especially that scene when the mother and the daughter are discussing whether to buy something called Syrup of Squill. Weird, unexpected things set me off way more than scripted jokes, which sometimes just make me depressed.

- I've got a great idea for a cartoon—wanna hear it?
  Rarely.

Infrequently Asked Questions

- Have you mooned or *been* mooned more often in your life?
  Neither.

- What would make a terrible pizza topping?
  Stye ointment.

- What might one expect to find at a really low-budget amusement park?

  My family.

- What did the shepherd say to the three-legged sheepdog?

  How did you lose your leg?

And Now for a Few More Questions . . .

- What do you hate drawing?

  Forests.

- Being as accurate as possible, how many desert island cartoons do you think you've come up with and submitted to *The New Yorker*?

  Four.

- What's the funniest thing that you witnessed, overheard, or came up with that you couldn't figure out how to use in a cartoon?

  My husband told a highway tollbooth clerk that soon her job would be done by a robot.

- If you could ask Bob Mankoff, *The New Yorker* cartoon editor, one question, what would it be?

  I just found this note on my desk that says, "Call Fred! Important! 2 P.M.!!" Do you know who this Fred is?

Draw Some Sort of Doodle

. . . using the random lines below as a starting point.

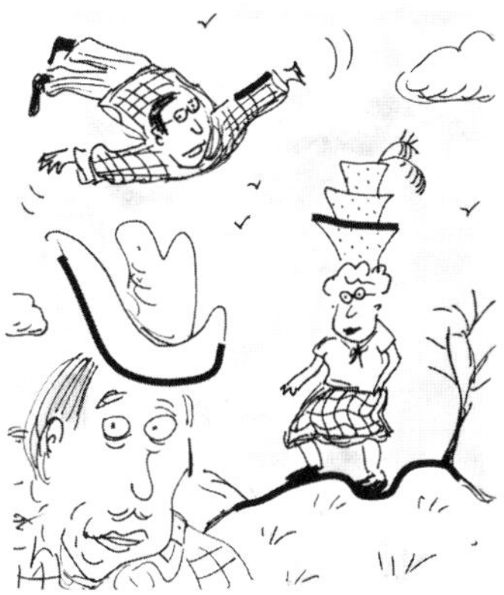

Naming Names

- What name might you give to a mild-mannered, slightly overweight dental assistant in one of your cartoons?

  Trixi.

- Other than Lance, what name would you give to a twenty-eight-year-old metrosexual entertainment lawyer who cycles on weekends?

  Mance.

- What would be a good name for a new, commercially unviable breakfast cereal?

  Kidney Chex.

- Come up with a name for an unpleasant medical procedure.

  Eyeball 'Splodofication.

- If you used a pen name, what would it be?

  Penny McPen.

Complete the Pie Chart Below

. . . in a way that tells us something about your life or how you think.

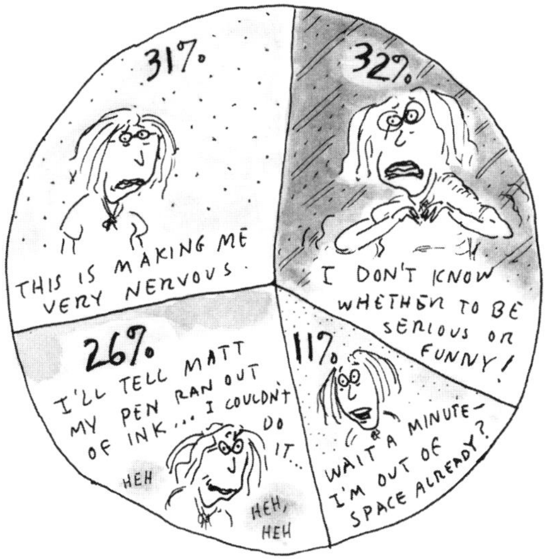
31%
THIS IS MAKING ME VERY NERVOUS
32%
I DON'T KNOW WHETHER TO BE SERIOUS OR FUNNY!
26%
I'LL TELL MATT MY PEN RAN OUT OF INK... I COULDN'T DO IT...
HEH
HEH, HEH
11%
WAIT A MINUTE— I'M OUT OF SPACE ALREADY?

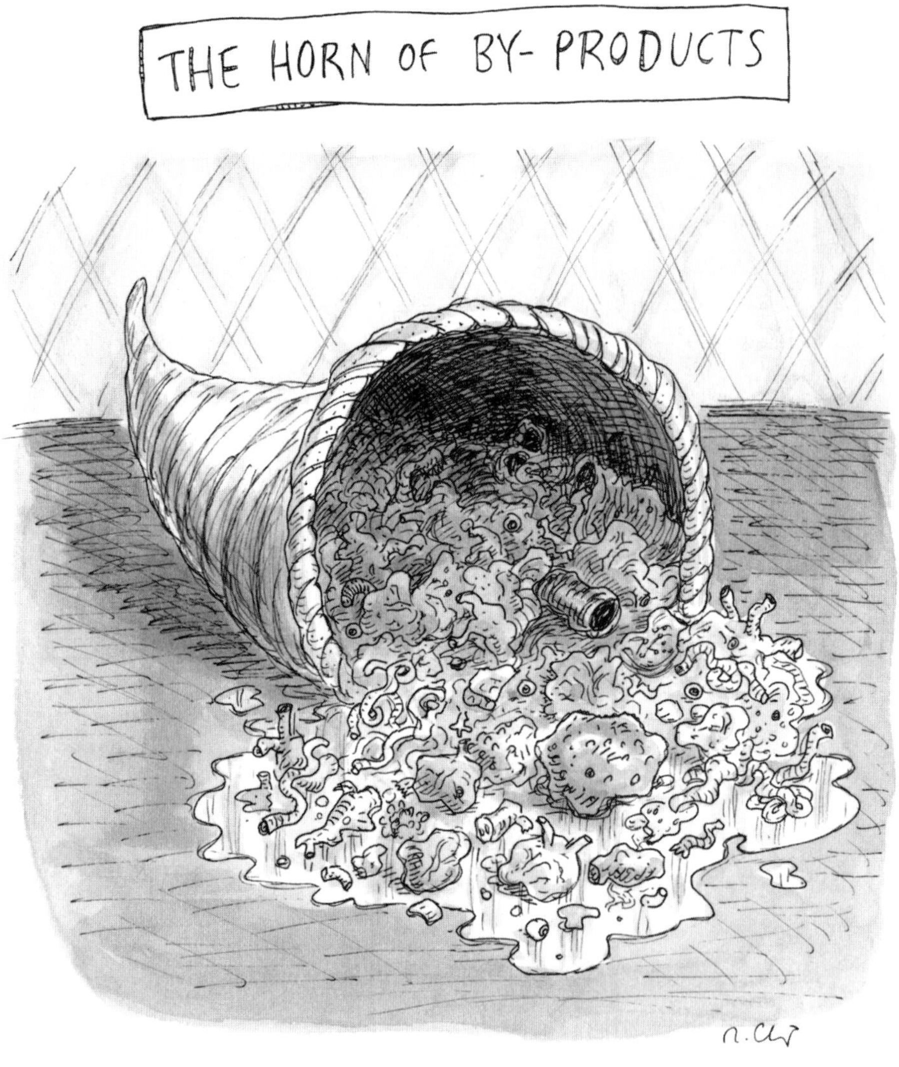
THE HORN OF BY-PRODUCTS

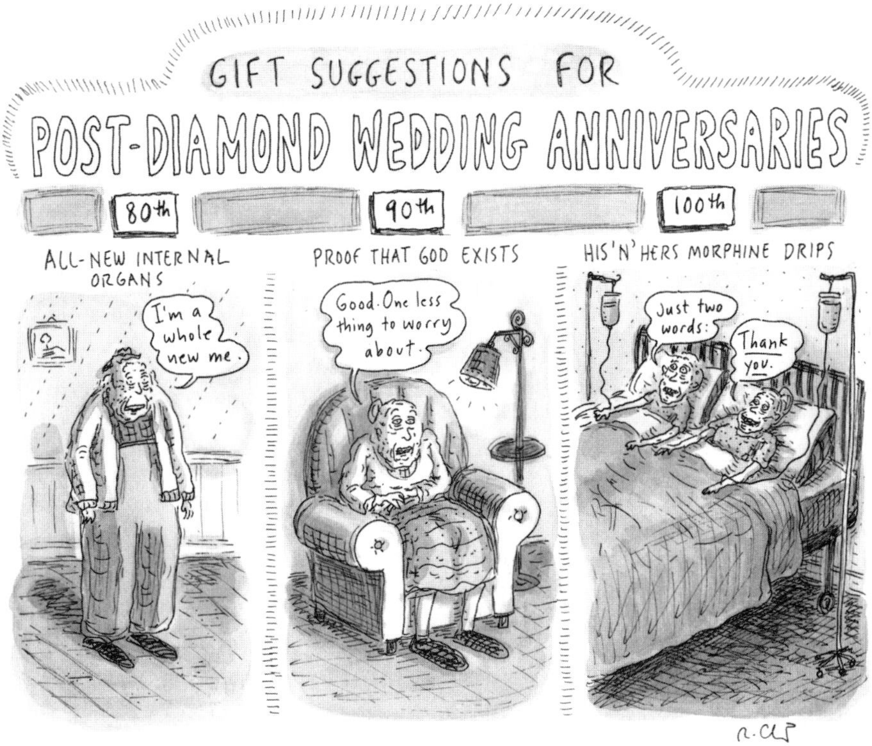
GIFT SUGGESTIONS FOR
POST-DIAMOND WEDDING ANNIVERSARIES
80th
ALL-NEW INTERNAL ORGANS
I'm a whole new me.
90th
PROOF THAT GOD EXISTS
Good. One less thing to worry about.
100th
HIS'N'HERS MORPHINE DRIPS
Just two words:
Thank you.

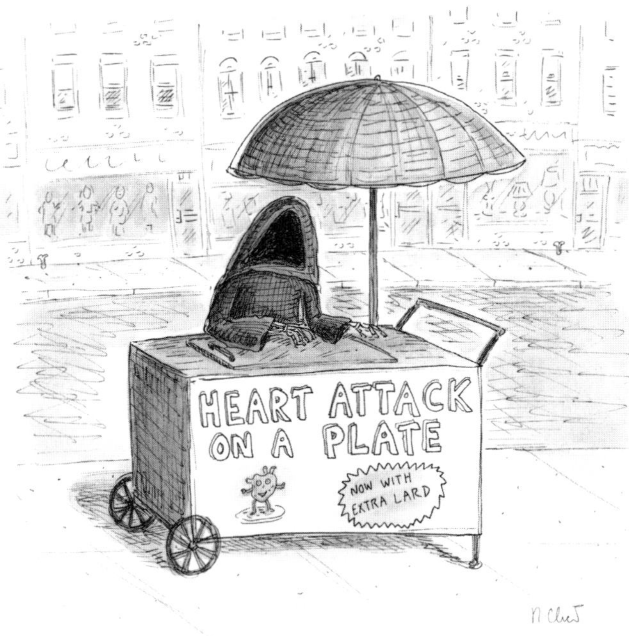
HEART ATTACK ON A PLATE
NOW WITH EXTRA LARD

SIPRESS

DAVID SIPRESS

Frequently Asked Questions

◼ Where do you get your ideas?
Barcelona.

◼ Which comes first, the picture or the caption?
The egg.

◼ How'd you get started?
God appeared to me in a vision and handed me crow quill pen points and a Bristol pad.

◼ I admire . . .
Anyone who has a regular job—how the hell do they do it???

◼ How do you deal with rejection?

◼ What are some things that make you laugh and why?

This is not an answer to this question. I can't think of an answer to this question. I just felt like drawing a dog with a guy's head.

◼ I've got a great idea for a cartoon—wanna hear it?
Are you from Barcelona?

Infrequently Asked Questions

◼ Have you mooned or *been* mooned more often in your life?
This question is asinine.

◼ What would make a terrible pizza topping?
Stool softener.

◼ What might one expect to find at a really low-budget amusement park?
Poor children.

■ What did the shepherd say to the three-legged sheepdog?

Yum—that was delicious. I think I'll go ahead and eat the other three.

Draw Something in This Space

. . . that will help us understand your childhood.

"You're a loser."
"You're a failure."
"You'll never amount to anything."

"It's a motivational technique I learned from my father."

And Now for a Few More Questions . . .

■ What do you hate drawing?

Anything complicated.

■ Being as accurate as possible, how many desert island cartoons do you think you've come up with and submitted to *The New Yorker*?

Ten thousand.

■ What's the funniest thing that you witnessed, overheard, or came up with that you couldn't figure out how to use in a cartoon?

Two people stuck on a desert island.

■ If you could ask Bob Mankoff, *The New Yorker* cartoon editor, one question, what would it be?

Have you no sense of decency, sir? At long last, have you no sense of decency?

Naming Names

■ What name might you give to a mild-mannered, slightly overweight dental assistant in one of your cartoons?

I don't give people in my cartoons names. They come up with them themselves.

■ Other than Lance, what name would you give to a twenty-eight-year-old metrosexual entertainment lawyer who cycles on weekends?

See above.

■ What would be a good name for a new, commercially unviable breakfast cereal?

Nukes.

■ Come up with a name for an unpleasant medical procedure.

Check up.

■ If you used a pen name, what would it be?

Bic.

Complete the Pie Chart Below

. . . in a way that tells us something about your life or how you think.

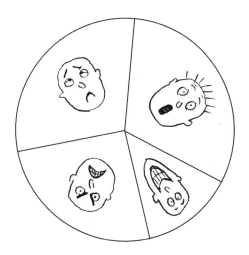

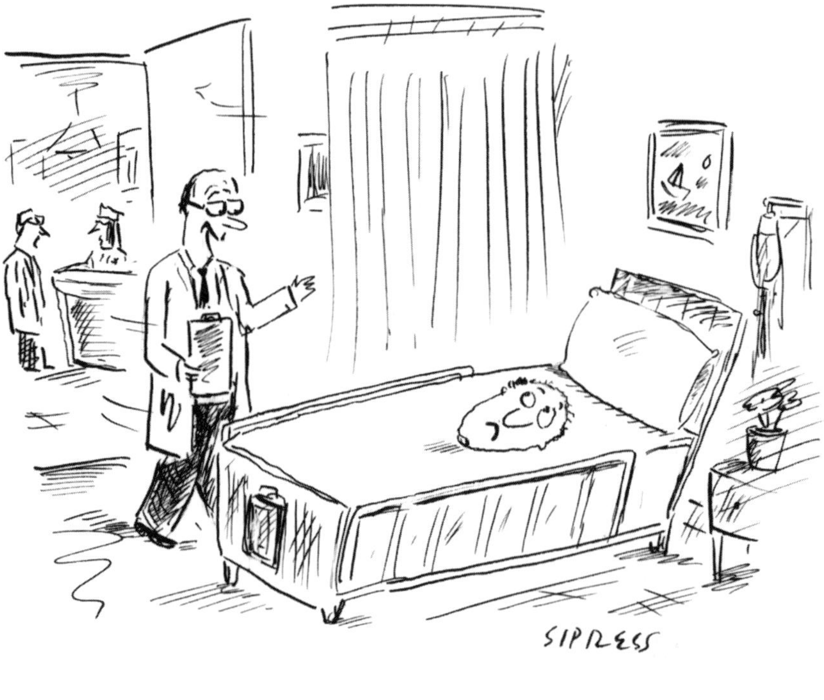
SIPRESS

"Congratulations! I think we got it all."

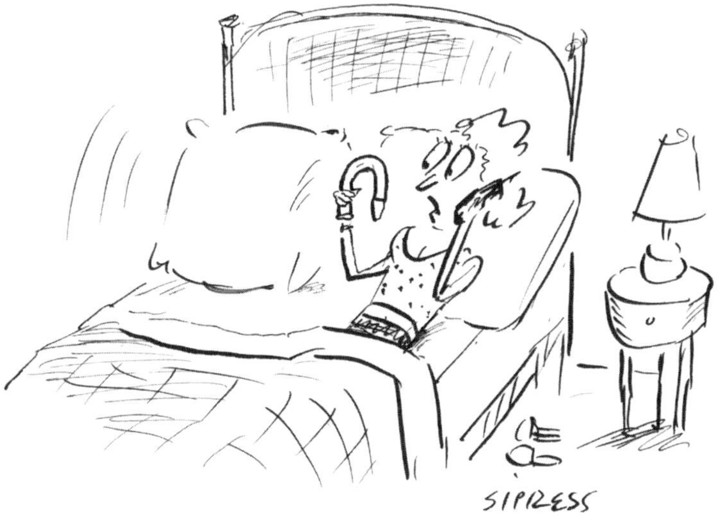
SIPRESS

"Hello . . . technical support?"

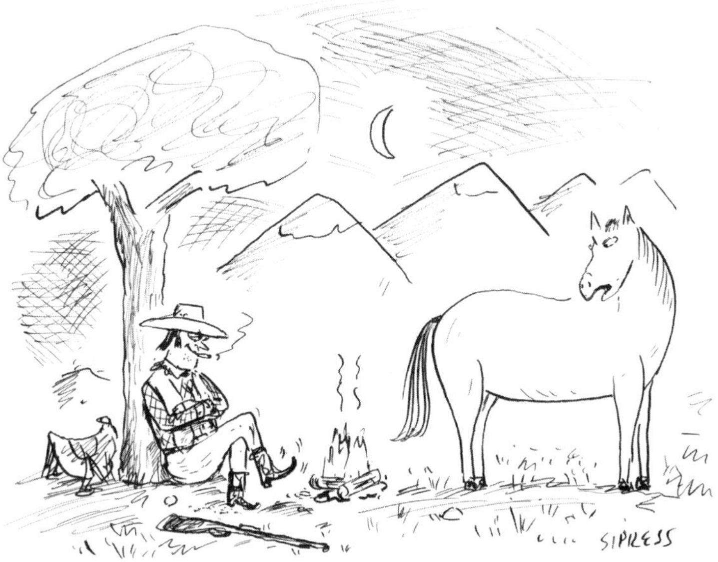
SIPRESS

"Don't even think about it, cowboy."

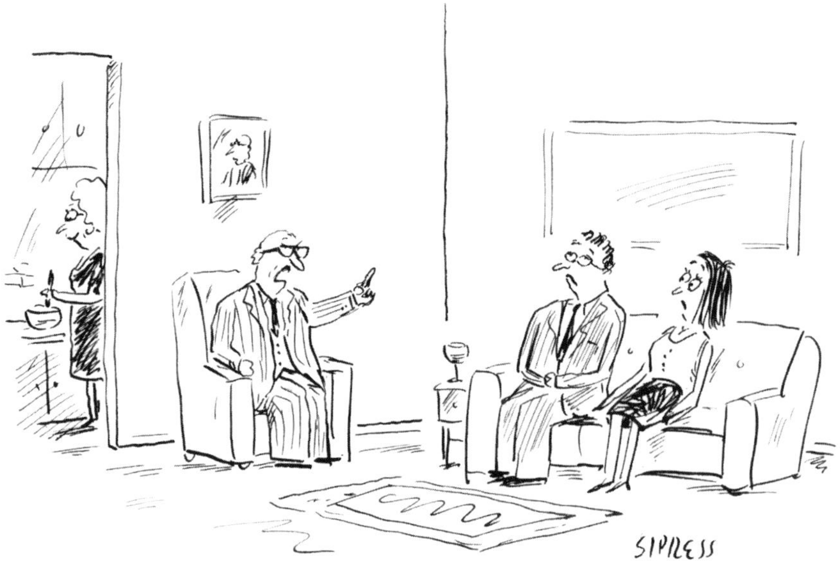
SIPRESS

"I came to this country with nothing but the hair on my back."

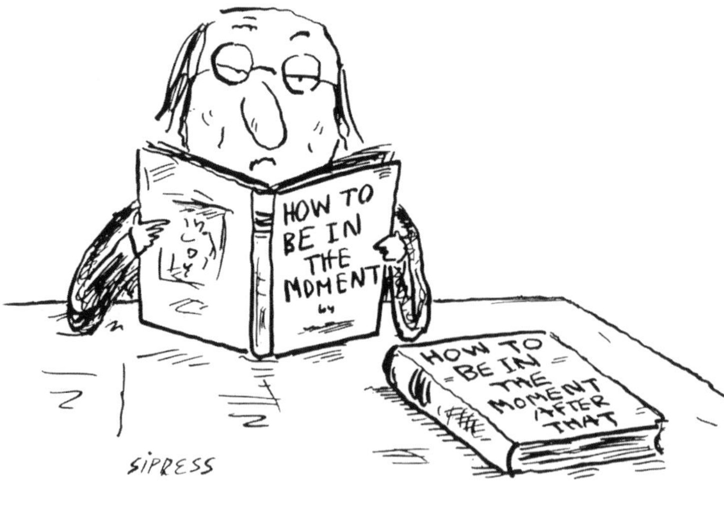
HOW TO BE IN THE MOMENT
HOW TO BE IN THE MOMENT AFTER THAT
SIPRESS

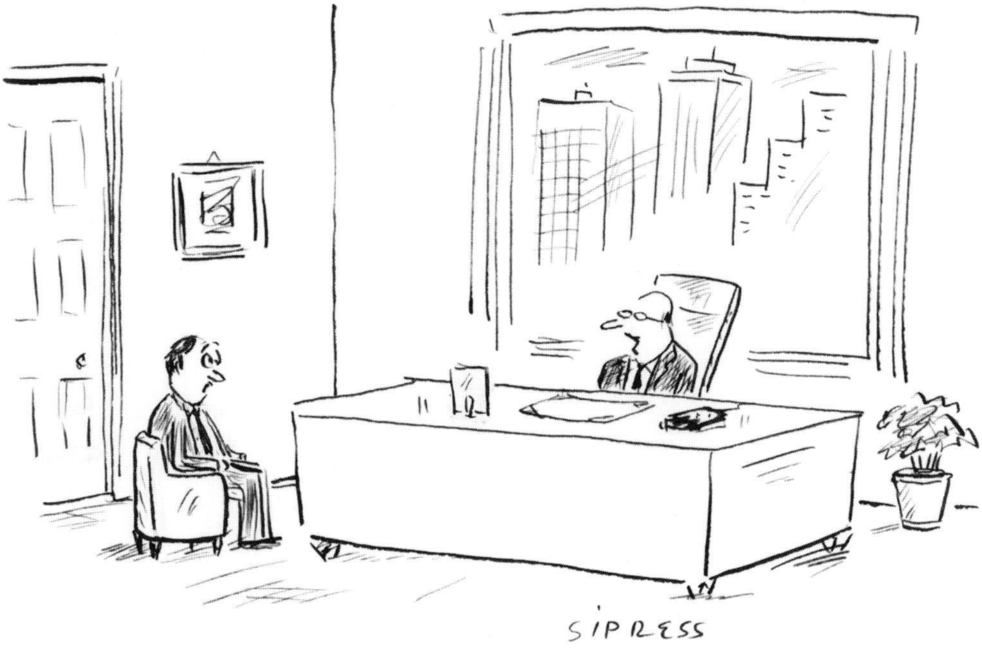
SIPRESS

"Corporate Diversity would like you to get a sex change."

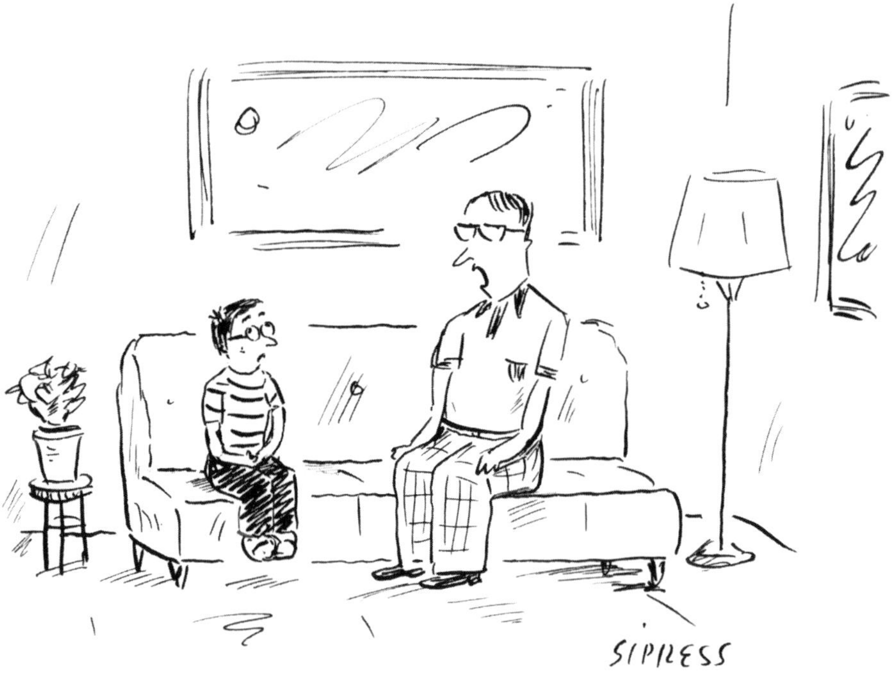
SIPRESS

"From everything you're describing, son, it sounds to me like you've just had your first boner."

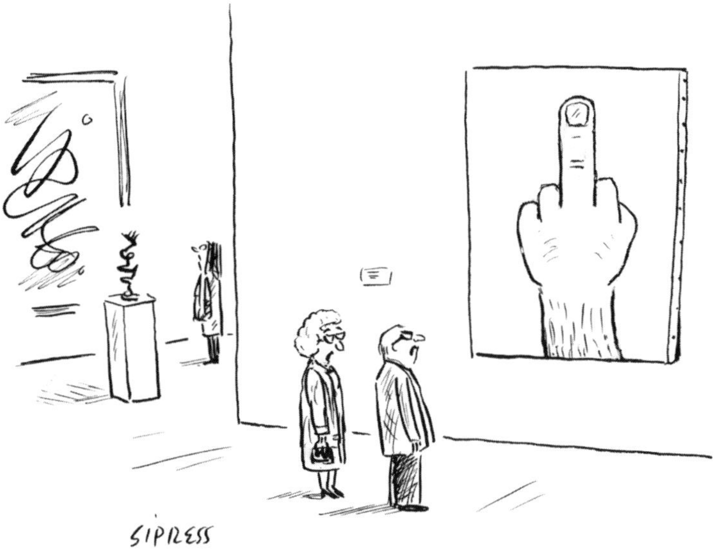
SIPRESS

"I don't think you're supposed to like it."

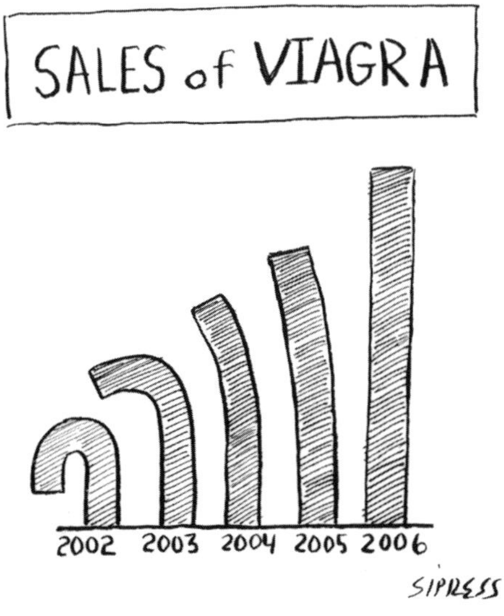
SALES of VIAGRA
2002
2003
2004
2005
2006
SIPRESS

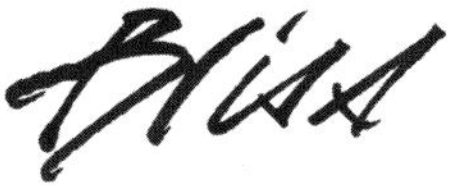

HARRY BLISS

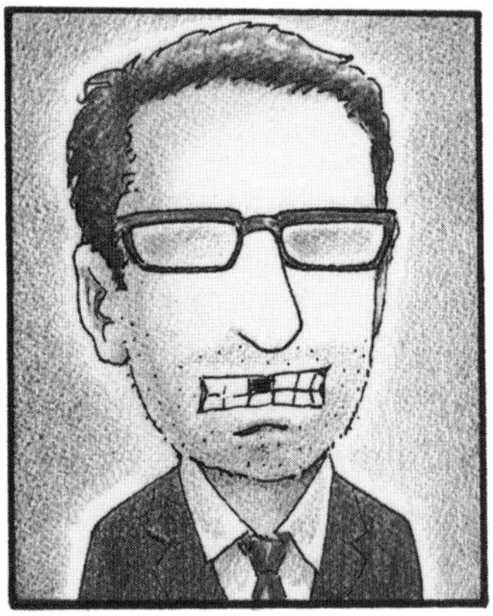

Frequently Asked Questions

- Where do you get your ideas?

I get most of my ideas from all the great dead cartoonists who can no longer sue me for stealing their ideas. Also, my pals say funny stuff and I just draw it.

- Which comes first, the picture or the caption?

Neither, see above.

- How'd you get started?

How did we all "get started"? The sperm fertilizes the egg. . . .

- I admire . . .

I admire my dog, Penny, specifically the way she's able to catch and release squirrels—amazing. Oh, and I also admire a million dollars.

- How do you deal with rejection?

Are you kidding? I'm constantly reflecting. I'm the most self-reflect—what's that? Rejection? Oh, I thought you said reflection—my bad. Does this mean I'm not going to be included in the book?! What, just because I screwed up on one of your stupid questions?! Do you know who the _uck you're dealing with?! How dare you! I know where you live, mother_ucker!!

- What are some things that make you laugh and why?

One thing that really cracks me up is stalking kiss-ass interviewers who think they have the balls to not publish my work because of one misunderstanding. I laugh so freaking hard when I secretly watch them at home with their family, like the serial killer in *Red Dragon* or like Robert De Niro in *Cape Fear* . . . or what about Glenn Close when she cooked the family's fluffy new bunny in the soup pot . . . hilarious!

- I've got a great idea for a cartoon—wanna hear it?

Sure, go ahead, I'm just gonna leaf blow my yard, but you go ahead. I'm listening.

Infrequently Asked Questions

- Have you mooned or *been* mooned more often in your life?

Nope, never mooned or been mooned . . . nor have I streaked since the '80s.

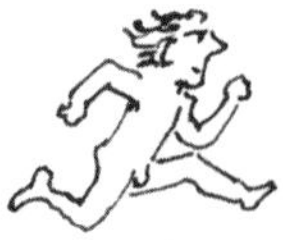

- What would make a terrible pizza topping?

Shredded kitten cartilage.

- What might one expect to find at a really low-budget amusement park?

Dead children.

- What did the shepherd say to the three-legged sheepdog?

Okay, forget corralling the sheep, how proficient are you with PowerPoint?

And Now for a Few More Questions . . .

- What do you hate drawing?

English muffins, tempeh, midwife-toads, cassowaries, the Sistine Chapel, galvanic tractors, and venereal disease.

- Being as accurate as possible, how many desert island cartoons do you think you've come up with and submitted to *The New Yorker*?

Roughly, twenty-seven and two-thirds.

- What's the funniest thing that you witnessed, overheard, or came up with that you couldn't figure out how to use in a cartoon?

I once dreamed that Adolf Hitler and Anne Frank were on The Brady Bunch, except Hitler was Marsha and Anne was Peter and she hit Hitler in the nose with a football and Hitler yelled in German, "Ich vun du shleip von deuth!"

- If you could ask Bob Mankoff, *The New Yorker* cartoon editor, one question, what would it be?

Why don't we make love more than once a week?

Naming Names

- What name might you give to a mild-mannered, slightly overweight dental assistant in one of your cartoons?

Lorthrope.

- Other than Lance, what name would you give to a twenty-eight-year-old metrosexual entertainment lawyer who cycles on weekends?

Wanker.

- What would be a good name for a new, commercially unviable breakfast cereal?

Crack Baby Crunchies.

- Come up with a name for an unpleasant medical procedure.

Testicular Removaloscopy.

- If you used a pen name, what would it be?

Funny Mother_ucker.

Complete the Pie Chart Below

. . . in a way that tells us something about your life or how you think.

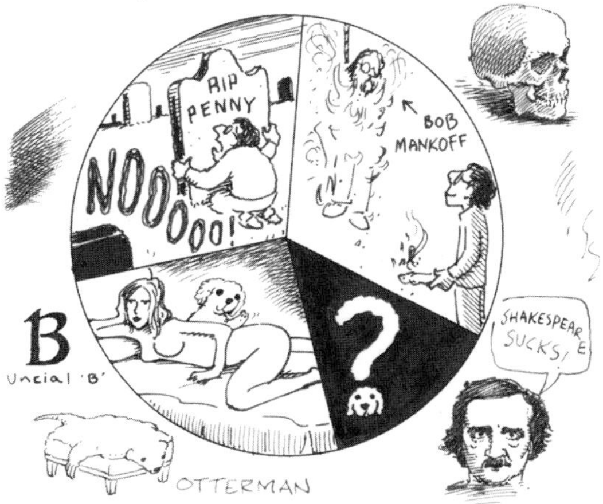
RIP PENNY
NOOOooo!
BOB MANKOFF
SHAKESPEARE SUCKS!
?
B
Uncial 'B'
OTTERMAN

"I'd invite you in, but my crap is all over the place."

"That's it, mister. You just lost your 'free range' status."

"I have an enormous favor to ask you."

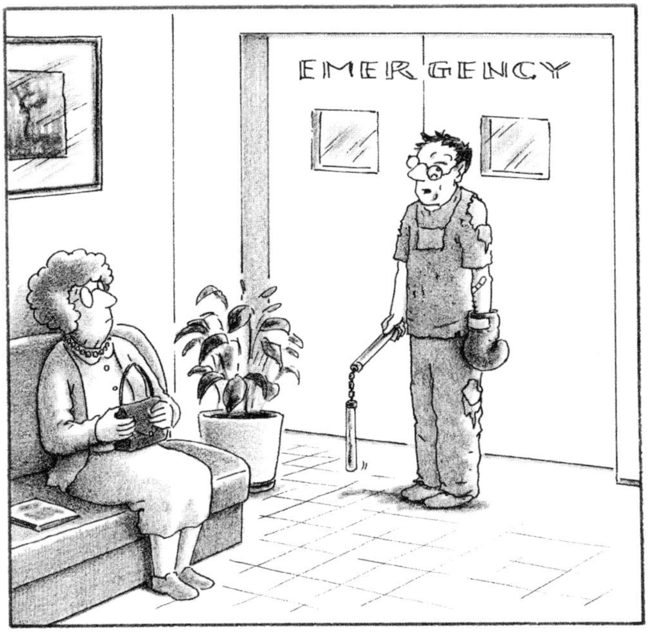
EMERGENCY

"He fought like hell."

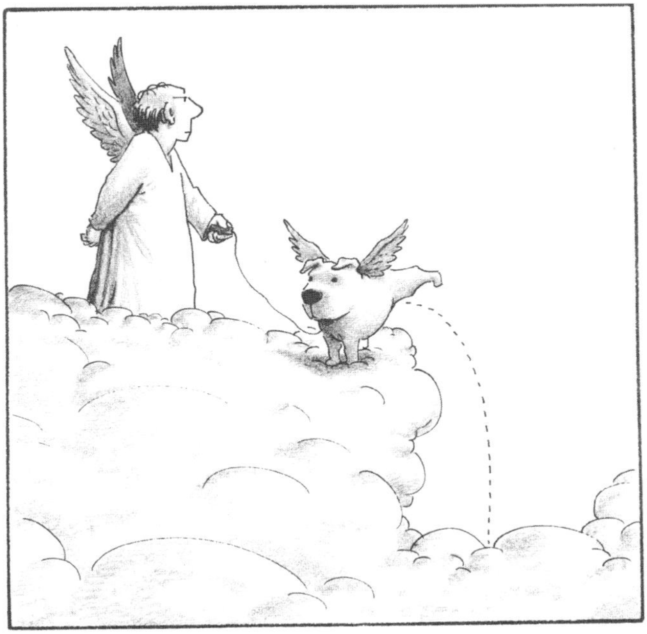

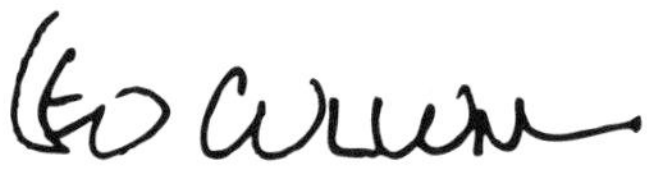

LEO CULLUM

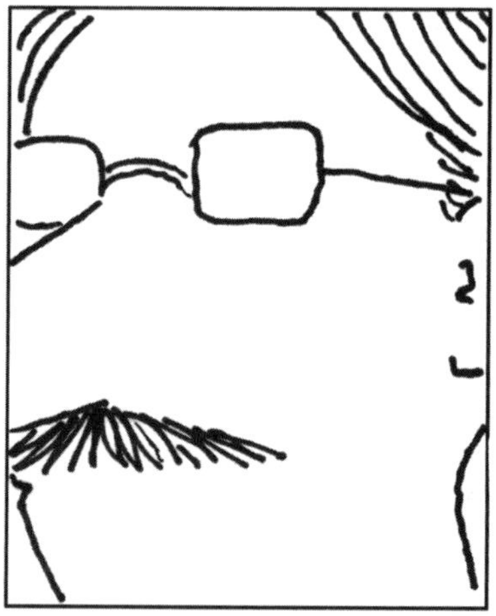

Frequently Asked Questions

- Where do you get your ideas?

  I find them under my pillow when I wake up.

- Which comes first, the picture or the caption?

  The caption, which then smokes a cigarette . . . oh *please!*

- How'd you get started?

  In the child cartoon factories of Korea.

- I admire . . .

  Things from a distance. Usually with binoculars.

- How do you deal with rejection?

  I find someone to publish a book of rejected cartoons. Hey, it's working!

- What are some things that make you laugh and why?

  Being tickled. I guess it's because of sensitive skin or something? Also a good cartoon will occasionally make me laugh out loud and exclaim, "Why, in the name of cosmic justice, didn't *I* think of that!"

- I've got a great idea for a cartoon—wanna hear it?

  Is it in any way hurtful or insensitive?

Draw Something in This Space

. . . that will help us understand your childhood.

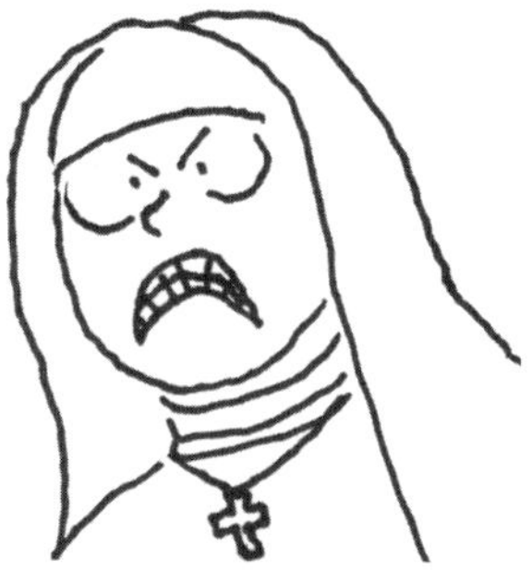

Infrequently Asked Questions

- Have you mooned or *been* mooned more often in your life?

  Been mooned, usually by clergy.

- What would make a terrible pizza topping?

  The leg of a sheepdog.

What might one expect to find at a really low-budget amusement park?

Me, having a fabulous time.

What did the shepherd say to the three-legged sheepdog?

What *could* he say? It was all very sad.

And Now for a Few More Questions . . .

What do you hate drawing?

Most outdoor scenes.

Being as accurate as possible, how many desert island cartoons do you think you've come up with and submitted to *The New Yorker*?

227, and sold every one.

What's the funniest thing that you witnessed, overheard, or came up with that you couldn't figure out how to use in a cartoon?

Sandals with black socks.

If you could ask Bob Mankoff, *The New Yorker* cartoon editor, one question, what would it be?

Bob, may I ask you three questions?

Draw Some Sort of Doodle

. . . using the random lines below as a starting point.

Naming Names

What name might you give to a mild-mannered, slightly overweight dental assistant in one of your cartoons?

Roger.

Other than Lance, what name would you give to a twenty-eight-year-old metrosexual entertainment lawyer who cycles on weekends?

I'd give him my daughter's name.

What would be a good name for a new, commercially unviable breakfast cereal?

Roto Rooties.

Come up with a name for an unpleasant medical procedure.

Cassandra.

If you used a pen name, what would it be?

Sharpie.

Complete the Pie Chart Below

. . . in a way that tells us something about your life or how you think.

"Now I think of Mom whenever it's cold."

"What did Jesus order?"

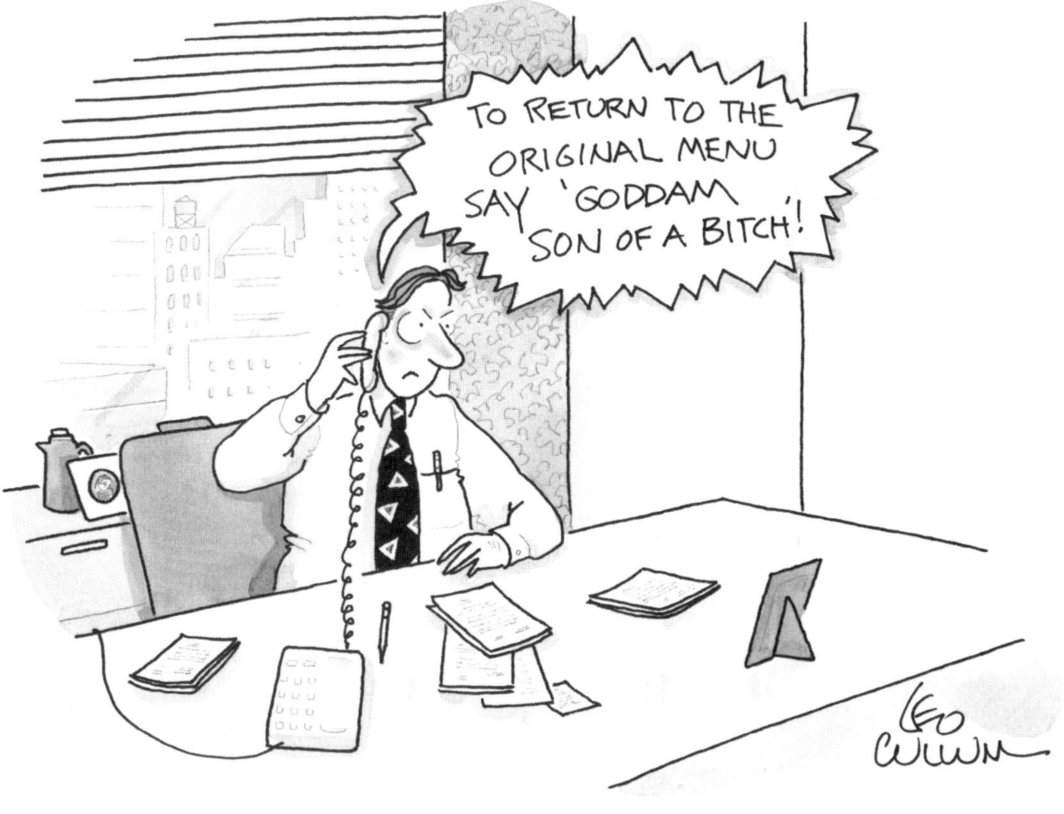
TO RETURN TO THE ORIGINAL MENU SAY 'GODDAM SON OF A BITCH'!
LEO CULLUM

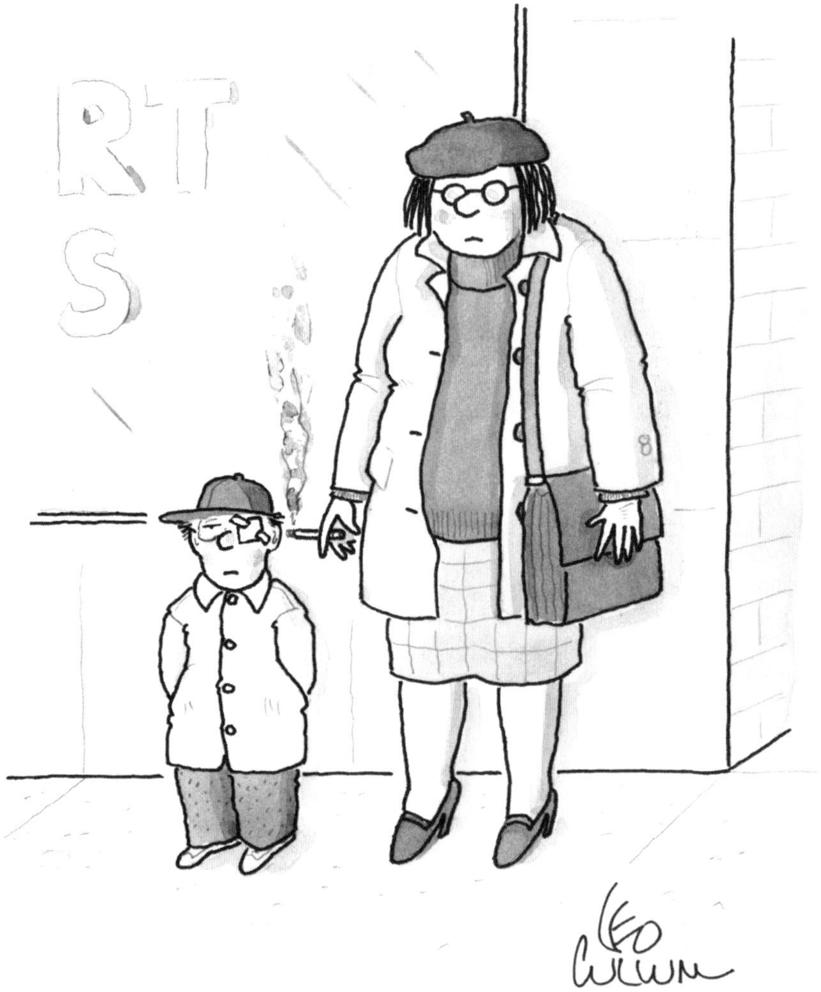
RT
S

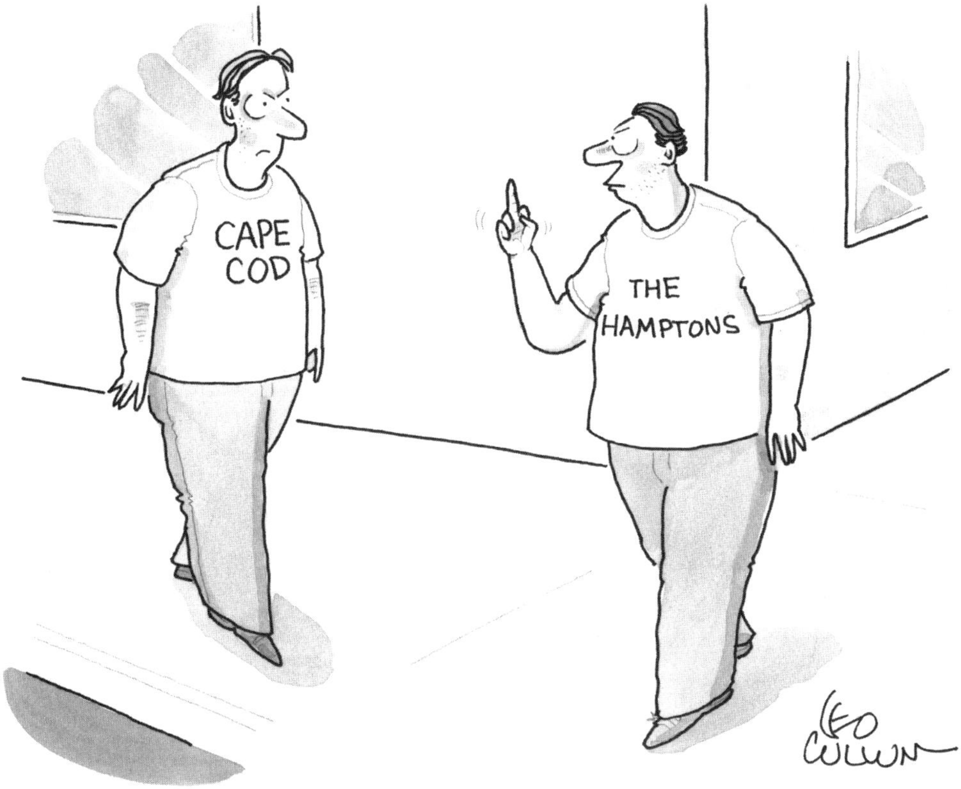
CAPE
COD
THE
HAMPTONS
LEO
CULLUM

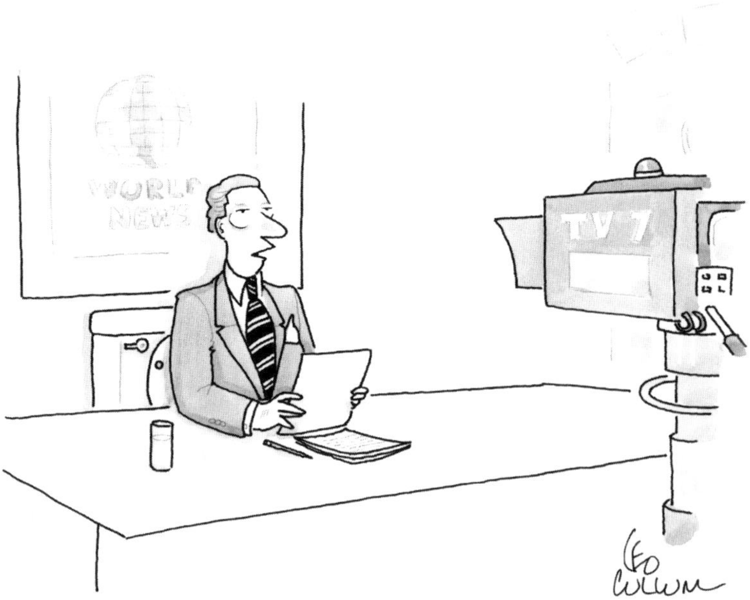

"Good evening, ladies and gentlemen, this is Jack Kruthers on the toilet."

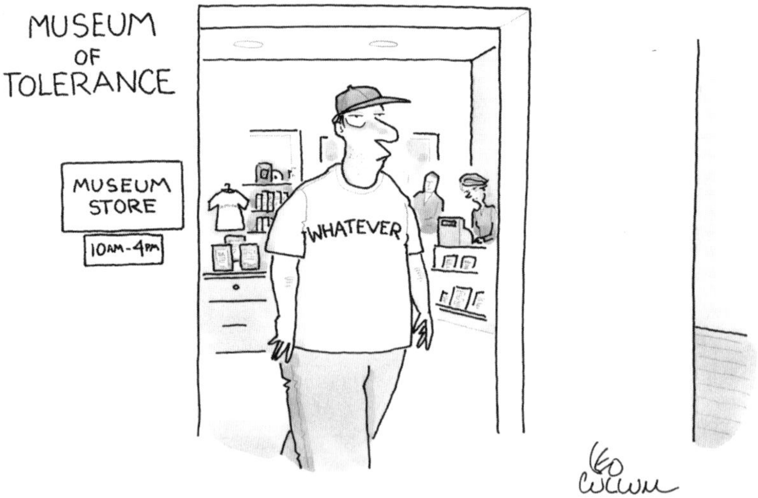
MUSEUM
OF
TOLERANCE
MUSEUM
STORE
10AM-4PM
WHATEVER

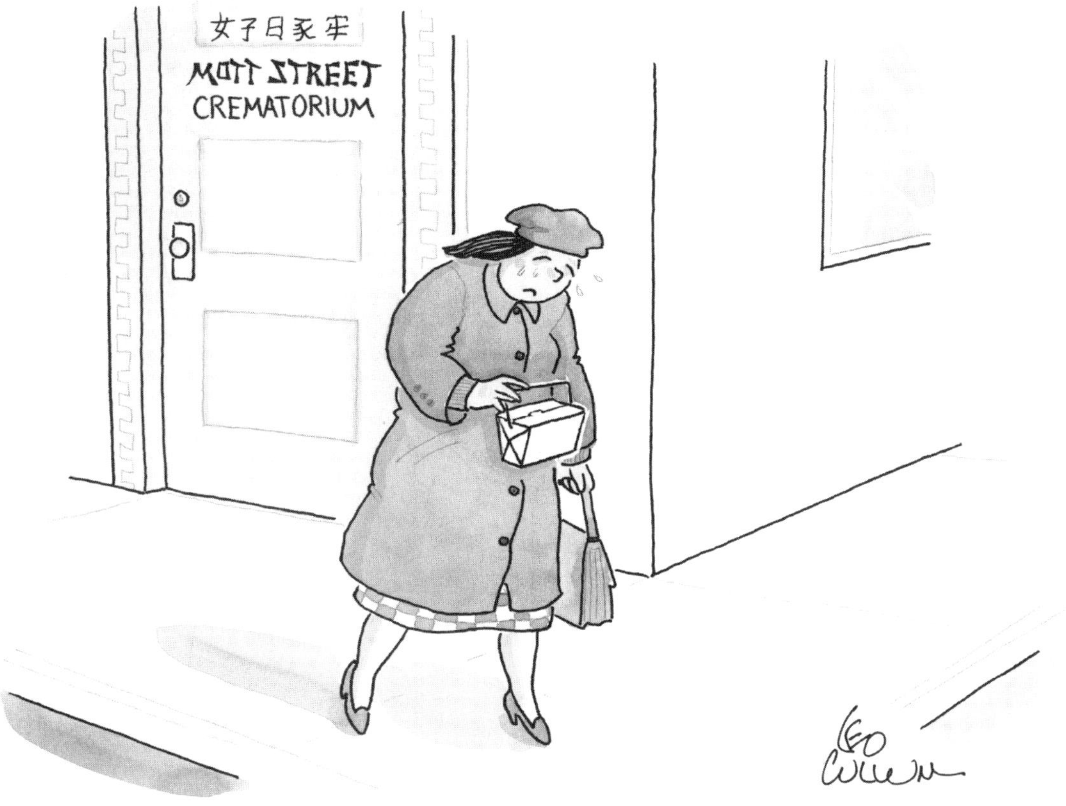
MOTT STREET
CREMATORIUM

"And if we start televising the executions we can also market a hilarious bloopers tape."

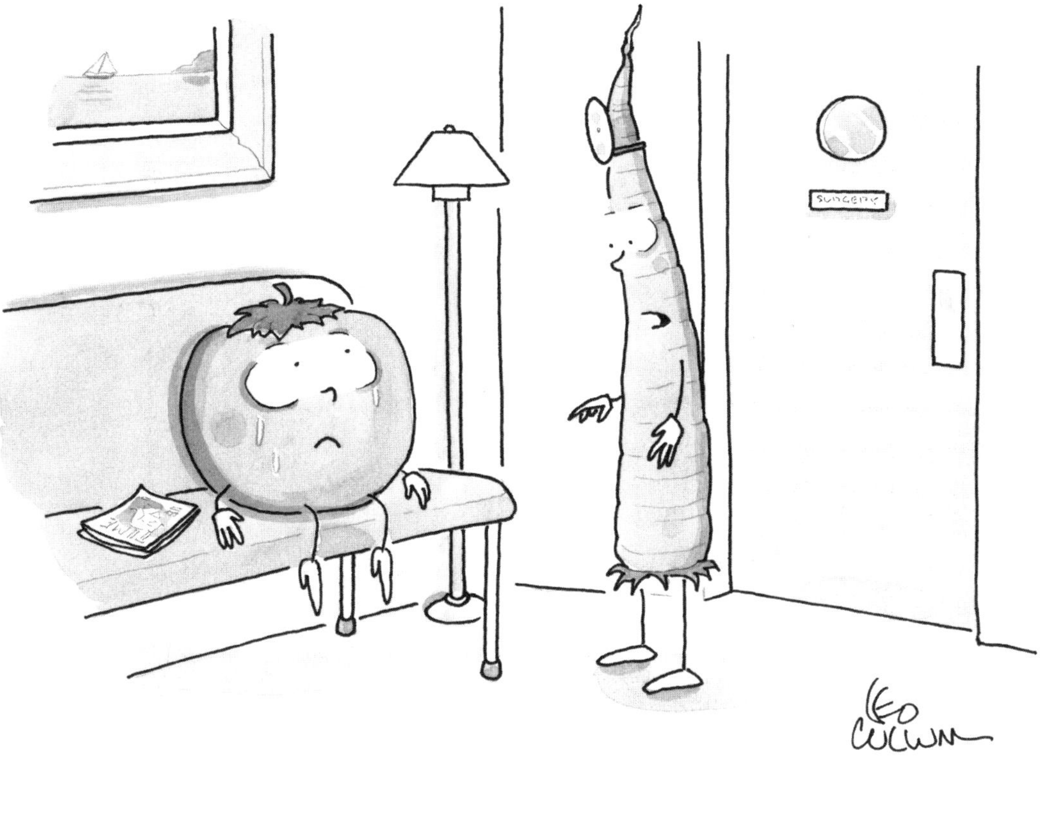
LEO
CULLUM

"He's going to be even more of a vegetable."

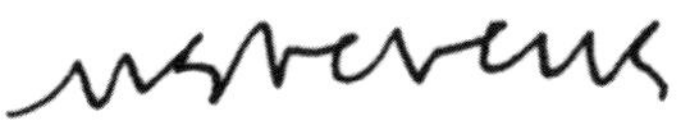

MICK STEVENS

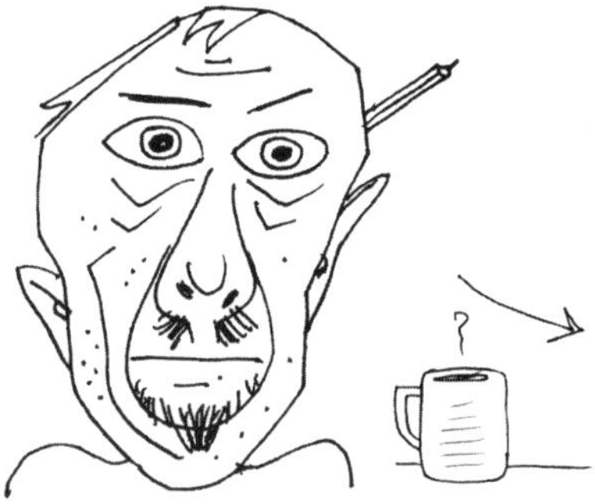

Frequently Asked Questions

- Where do you get your ideas?
  reallyfunnycartoonideas2makeurich.com.

- Which comes first, the picture or the caption?
  The picture. No, the caption. No, the picture. No . . . (I think I smell my circuits overheating.)

- How'd you get started?
  Jumper cables were involved.

- I admire . . .
  John Coltrane, Jimmy Carter, Jennifer Lopez, and Daffy Duck.

- How do you deal with rejection?
  Rant. Rave. Shake my fist at God. Throw the phone across the room.

- What are some things that make you laugh and why?
  The human condition, the State of the Union, presidential politics . . . because it's not manly to cry.

- I've got a great idea for a cartoon—wanna hear it?
  Define "great."

Infrequently Asked Questions

- Have you mooned or *been* mooned more often in your life?
  Define "mooned."

- What would make a terrible pizza topping?
  Spanish moss.

- What might one expect to find at a really low-budget amusement park?
  A child-powered carousel.

- What did the shepherd say to the three-legged sheepdog?
  Where's the other ¼ of the flock?

Draw Something in This Space

. . . that will help us understand your childhood.

And Now for a Few More Questions . . .

- What do you hate drawing?

  Big religious murals. No commissions, please.

- Being as accurate as possible, how many desert island cartoons do you think you've come up with and submitted to *The New Yorker*?

  4,268 as of this week. Hold on, I just got another idea. . . .

- What's the funniest thing that you witnessed, overheard, or came up with that you couldn't figure out how to use in a cartoon?

  A conversation between two trees I overheard during an LSD experience in my youth. (You had to be there.)

- If you could ask Bob Mankoff, *The New Yorker* cartoon editor, one question, what would it be?

  Why was my name on a gravestone in one of your early cartoons? I've been running scared ever since.

Naming Names

- What name might you give to a mild-mannered, slightly overweight dental assistant in one of your cartoons?

  Tubby Molarbuster.

- Other than Lance, what name would you give to a twenty-eight-year-old metrosexual entertainment lawyer who cycles on weekends?

  Spinner Greasely.

- What would be a good name for a new, commercially unviable breakfast cereal?

  Nuts 'n' Bolts.

- Come up with a name for an unpleasant medical procedure.

  Coronary Overpass.

- If you used a pen name, what would it be?

  Max Doubt.

Complete the Pie Chart Below

. . . in a way that tells us something about your life or how you think.

TUESDAY
WEDNESDAY
MONDAY
THURSDAY
FRIDAY
SATURDAY
SUNDAY

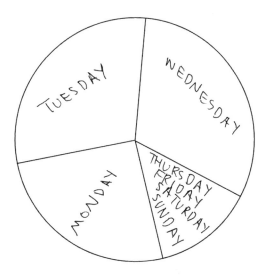

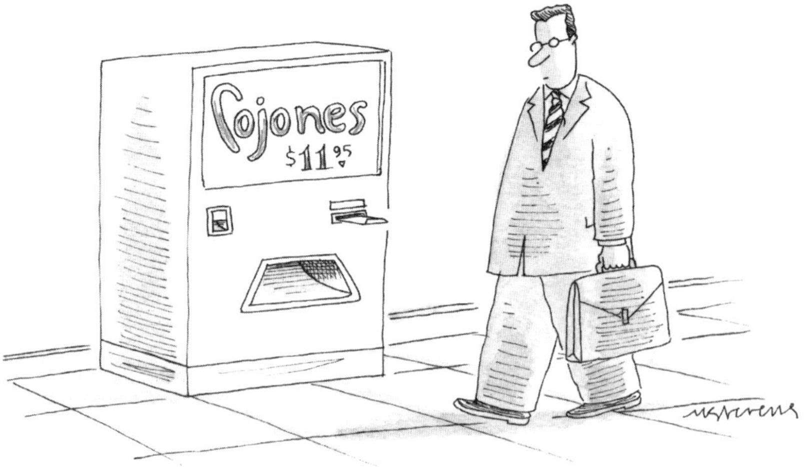
Cojones
$11.95

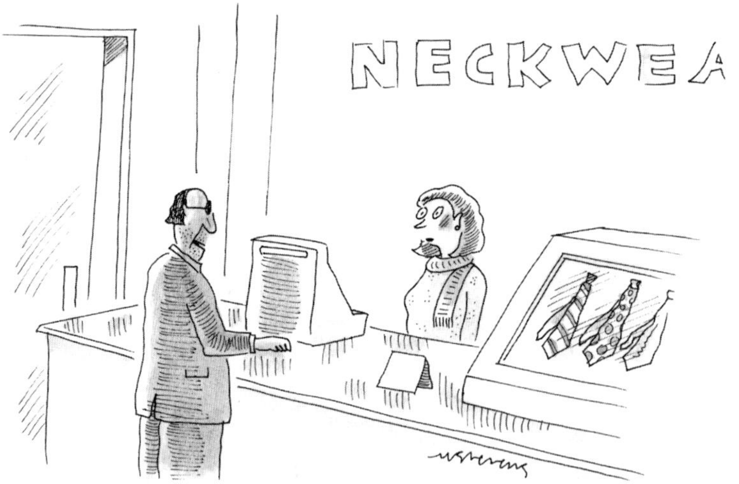
NECKWEA

"I'm looking for a tie that says 'I'm not wearing any underwear.'"

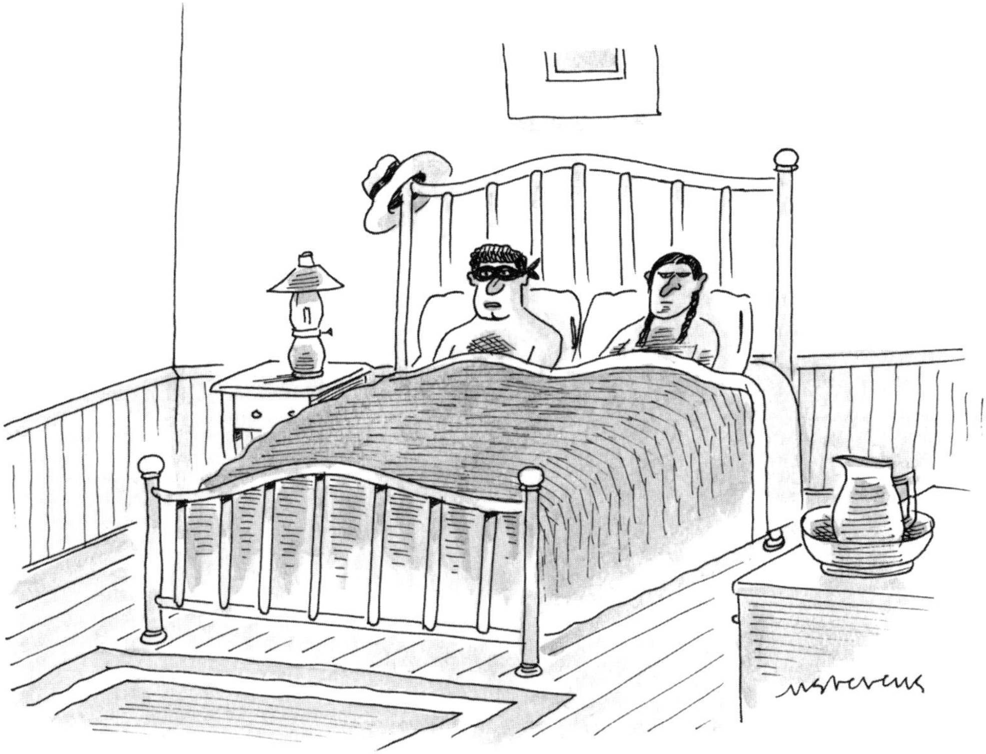
MStevens

"So that's what 'kemosabe' means."

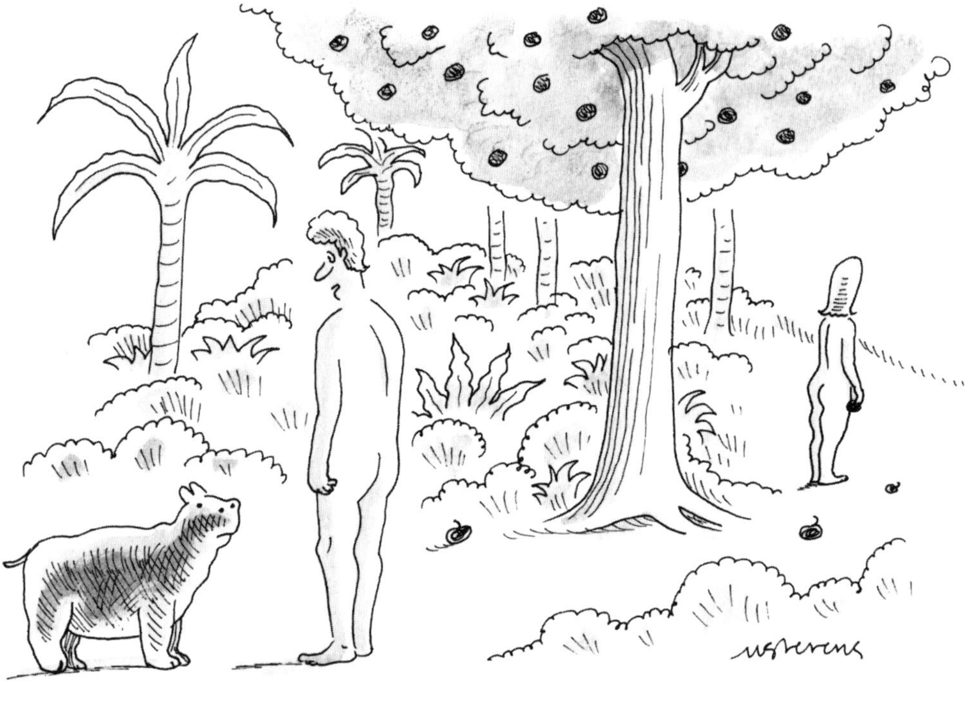
MStevens

"I don't know how to say this, but I've found someone else."

"I'm in for killing a guy for snoring."

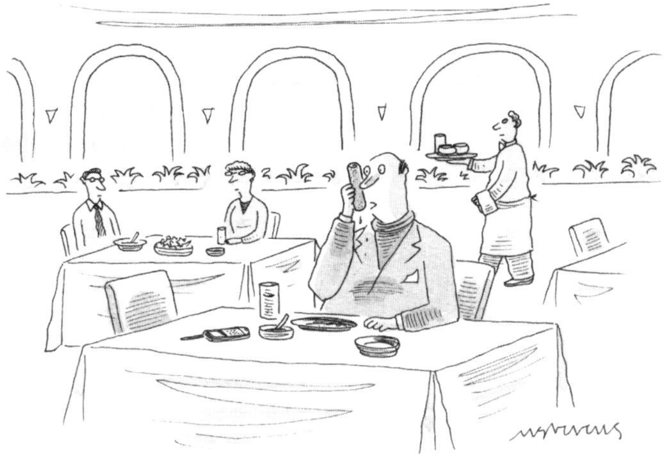
mstevens

"Sorry about the reception, Lou. I grabbed my enchilada by mistake."

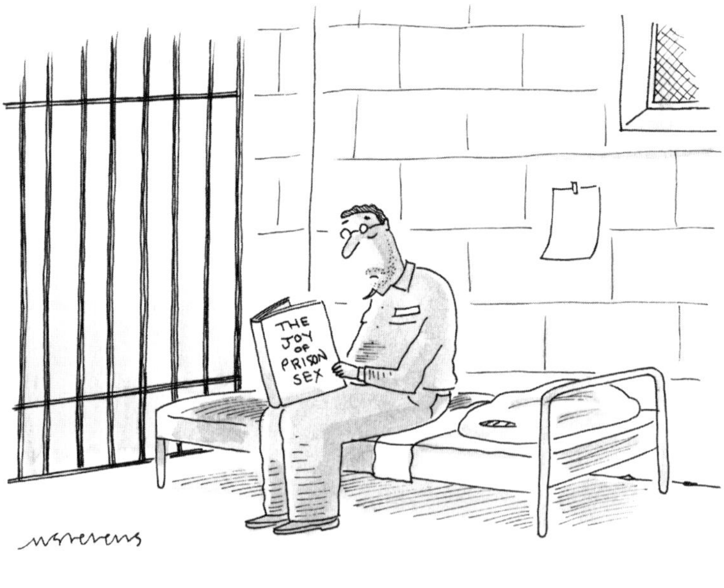
THE JOY OF PRISON SEX
mstevens

"I just can't seem to get the hang of it."

GAHAN WILSON

ON A GOOD DAY

Frequently Asked Questions

■ Where do you get your ideas?

You tell me.

■ Which comes first, the picture or the caption?

They usually crowd in together.

■ How'd you get started?

I noticed I was drawing on walls and tried doing it on paper.

■ I admire . . .

Your nerve in asking these questions.

■ How do you deal with rejection?

I continue.

■ What are some things that make you laugh and why?

Depending on my mood, just about anything. I will admit the laughter is now and then bitter. But usually it's nice. Sometimes downright joyful.

■ I've got a great idea for a cartoon—wanna hear it?

Hey, would you look at the time—I've got to catch a train!

Infrequently Asked Questions

■ Have you mooned or *been* mooned more often in your life?

Neither.

■ What would make a terrible pizza topping?

Yet another pizza.

■ What might one expect to find at a really low-budget amusement park?

Myself killed by a faulty roller coaster.

■ What did the shepherd say to the three-legged sheepdog?

What say we go into another line of work?

Draw Something in This Space

. . . that will help us understand your childhood.

And Now for a Few More Questions . . .

■ What do you hate drawing?

I'm afraid you've mistaken me for somebody else.

■ Being as accurate as possible, how many desert island cartoons do you think you've come up with and submitted to *The New Yorker*?

Something like 250.

■ What's the funniest thing that you witnessed, overheard, or came up with that you couldn't figure out how to use in a cartoon?

So far I've been lucky enough not to run into it.

■ If you could ask Bob Mankoff, *The New Yorker* cartoon editor, one question, what would it be?

What's the meaning of life, Bob?

Draw Some Sort of Doodle

. . . using the random lines below as a starting point.

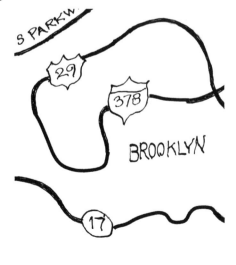

Naming Names

■ What name might you give to a mild-mannered, slightly overweight dental assistant in one of your cartoons?

Lance.

■ Other than Lance, what name would you give to a twenty-eight-year-old metrosexual entertainment lawyer who cycles on weekends?

Fred.

■ What would be a good name for a new, commercially unviable breakfast cereal?

Lance.

■ Come up with a name for an unpleasant medical procedure.

Lance.

■ If you used a pen name, what would it be?

Lance.

Complete the Pie Chart Below

. . . in a way that tells us something about your life or how you think.

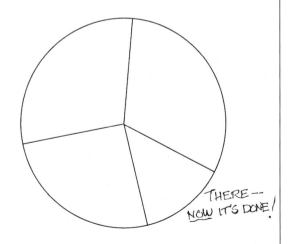

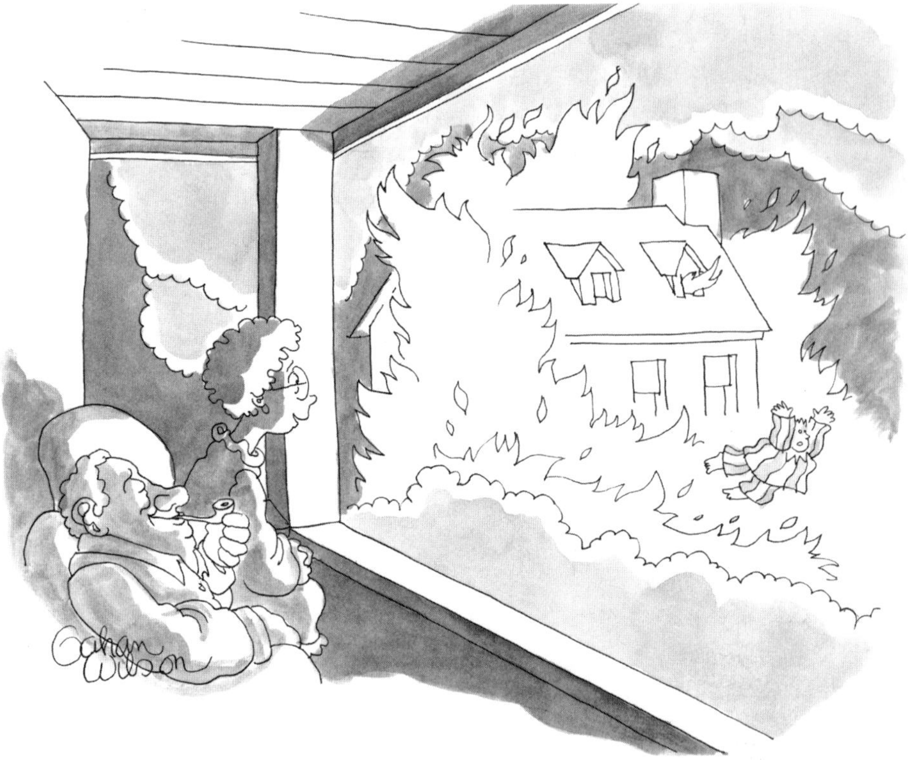
Gahan Wilson

"Well, you certainly were right about the power of prayer, dear!"

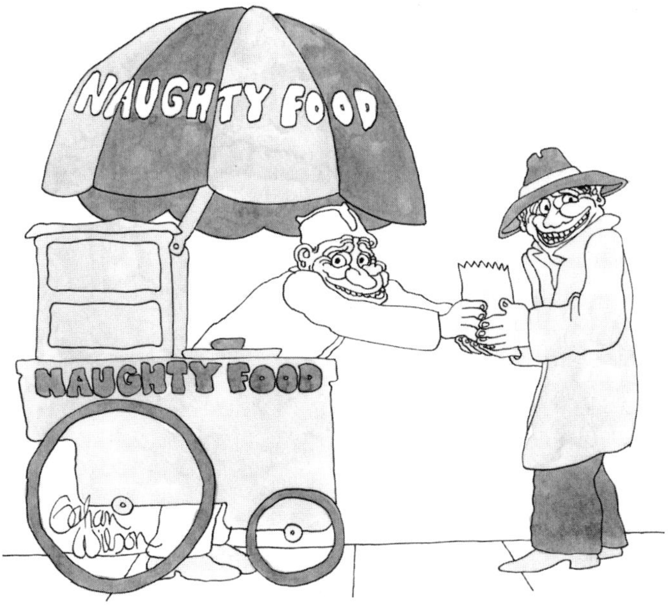
NAUGHTY FOOD
NAUGHTY FOOD
Gahan Wilson

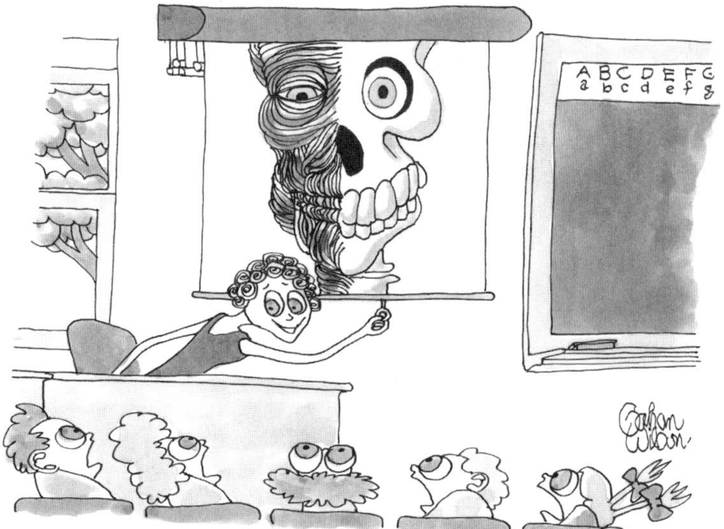
A B C D E F
a b c d e f g
Gahan Wilson

"Sorry—this was supposed to be a map of Peru!"

"*Some like to keep them as souvenirs, some don't.*"

"But if we destroy the planet Earth, they'll stop making these great cheap shoes!"

"I had it stuffed and mounted as a sentimental gesture since it was the one that ate most of Roger."

P.C.VEY

P. C. VEY

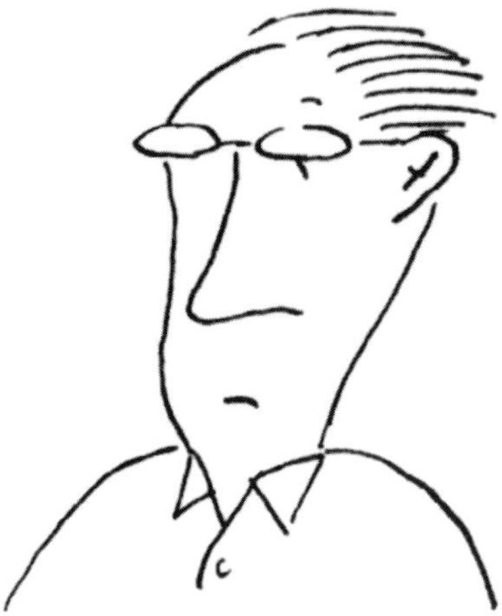

Frequently Asked Questions

- Where do you get your ideas?
  From a box on the shelf.

- Which comes first, the picture or the caption?
  One or the other.

- How'd you get started?
  At the beginning.

- I admire . . .
  The vibrancy of peas and carrots.

- How do you deal with rejection?
  In very colorful ways.

- What are some things that make you laugh and why?
  Long walks on the beach, fine wine, and sunsets. If I don't laugh at them, who will?

- I've got a great idea for a cartoon—wanna hear it?
  Sure.

Infrequently Asked Questions

- Have you mooned or *been* mooned more often in your life?
  I can't remember.

- What would make a terrible pizza topping?
  Cheese.

- What might one expect to find at a really low-budget amusement park?
  "Standing Still, the Ride . . ."

- What did the shepherd say to the three-legged sheepdog?
  Where's your other leg?

Draw Something in This Space

. . . that will help us understand your childhood.

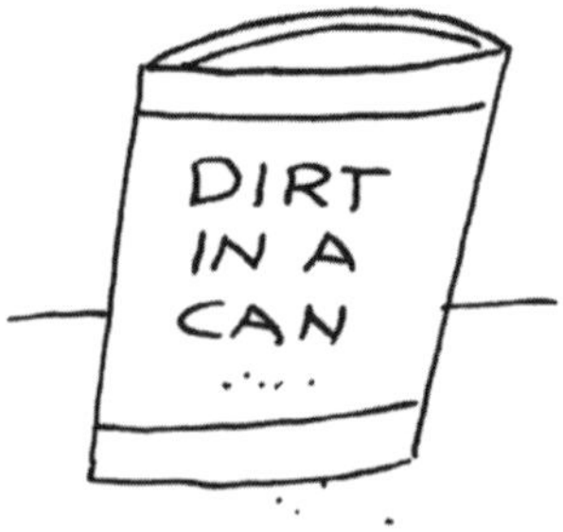
DIRT
IN A
CAN

And Now for a Few More Questions . . .

- What do you hate drawing?

  Steam coming from a freshly slaughtered animal.

- Being as accurate as possible, how many desert island cartoons do you think you've come up with and submitted to *The New Yorker*?

  184.

- What's the funniest thing that you witnessed, overheard, or came up with that you couldn't figure out how to use in a cartoon?

  Naughty pine.

- If you could ask Bob Mankoff, *The New Yorker* cartoon editor, one question, what would it be?

  When is the cartoonists' lounge going to be redecorated?

Naming Names

- What name might you give to a mild-mannered, slightly overweight dental assistant in one of your cartoons?

  Lance.

- Other than Lance, what name would you give to a twenty-eight-year-old metrosexual entertainment lawyer who cycles on weekends?

  Vance.

- What would be a good name for a new, commercially unviable breakfast cereal?

  Steam from a Freshly Slaughtered Animal.

- Come up with a name for an unpleasant medical procedure.

  A doctor extraction.

- If you used a pen name, what would it be?

  P. C. Vey.

Complete the Pie Chart Below

. . . in a way that tells us something about your life or how you think.

STUFF TO DO.
STUFF TO DO.
STUFF TO DO.
STUFF TO DO.

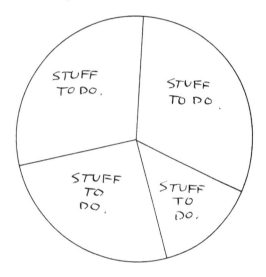

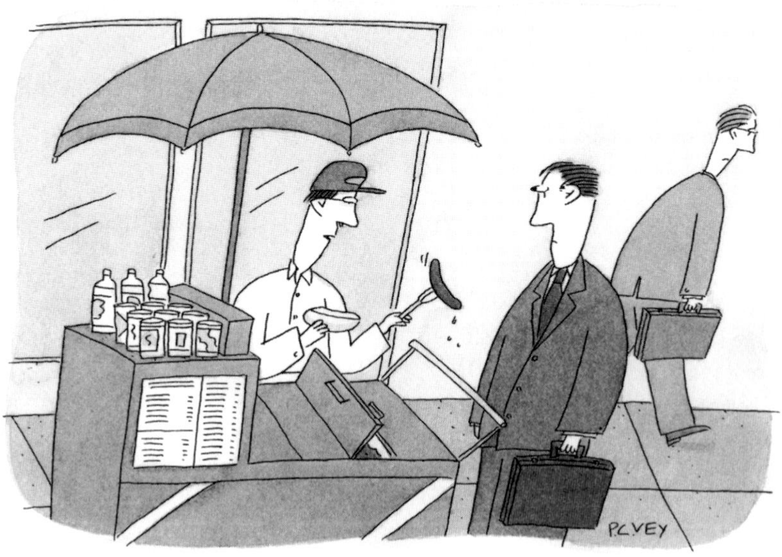
P.C.VEY

"Are you sure you don't want to lick it before I bun it?"

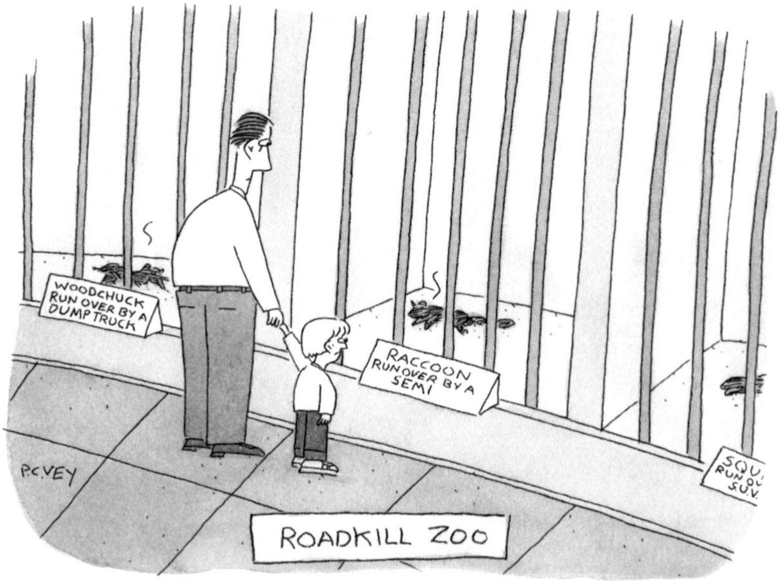
WOODCHUCK RUN OVER BY A DUMP TRUCK
RACCOON RUN OVER BY A SEMI
ROADKILL ZOO
P.C.VEY

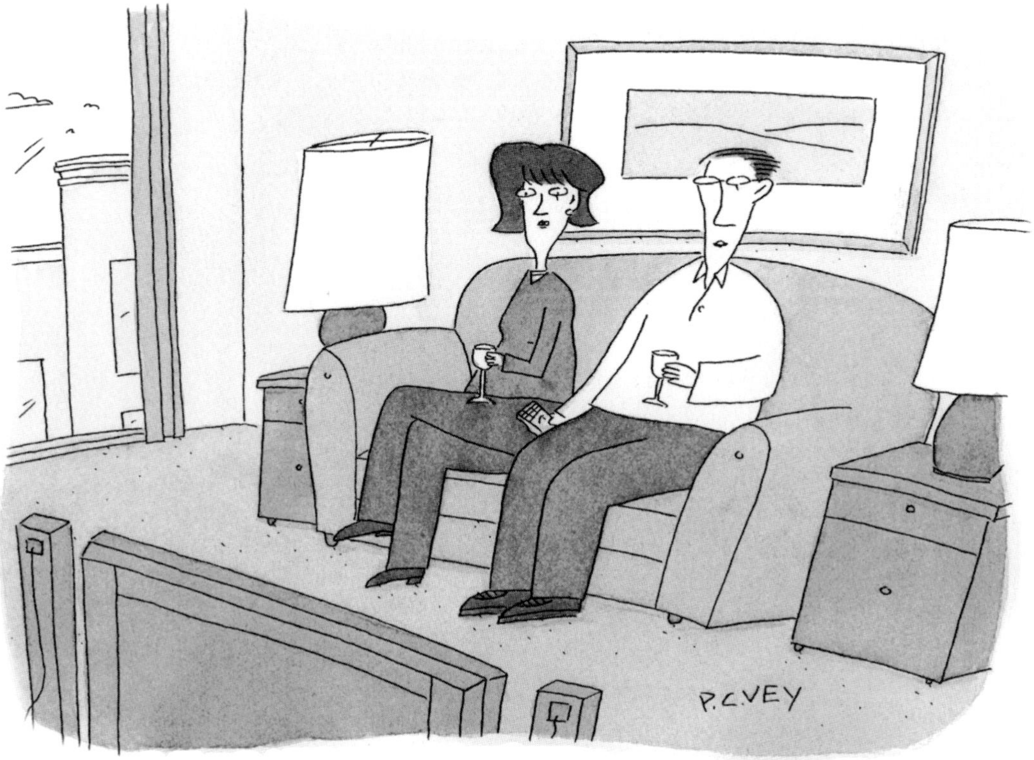
P.C.VEY

"You haven't seen disaster relief till you've seen it in high definition."

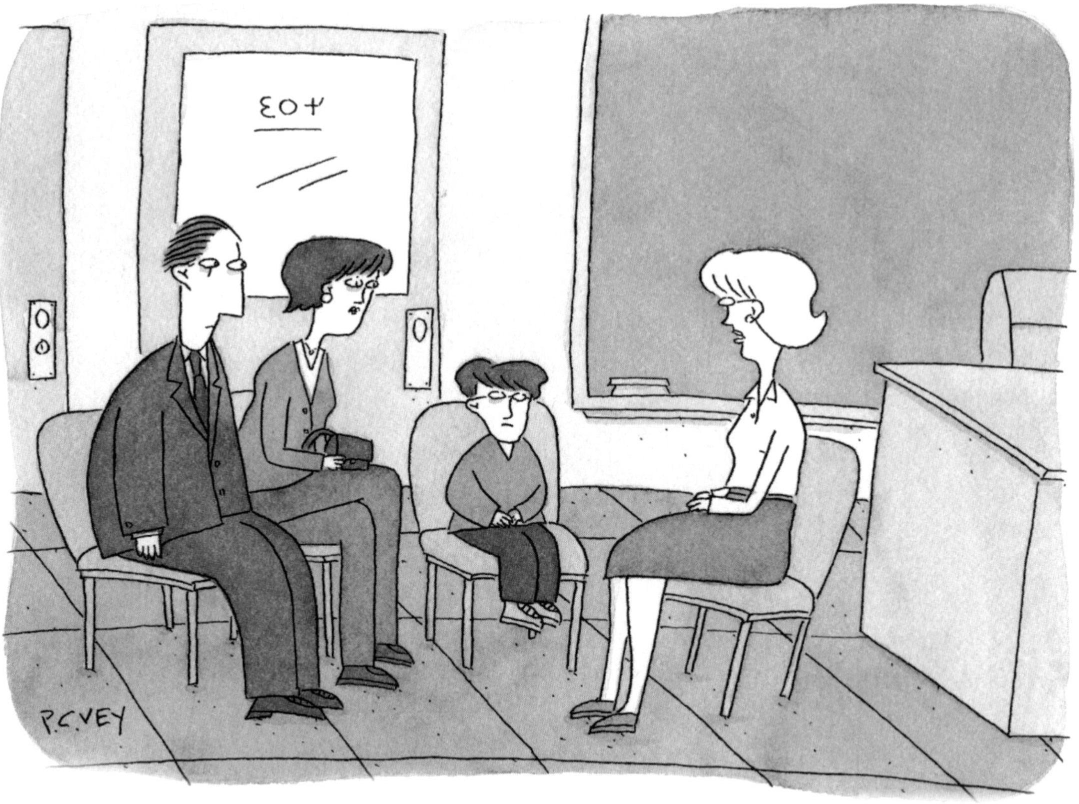
P.C.VEY

"He's at that awkward age when he tells his teachers valuable information about his parents."

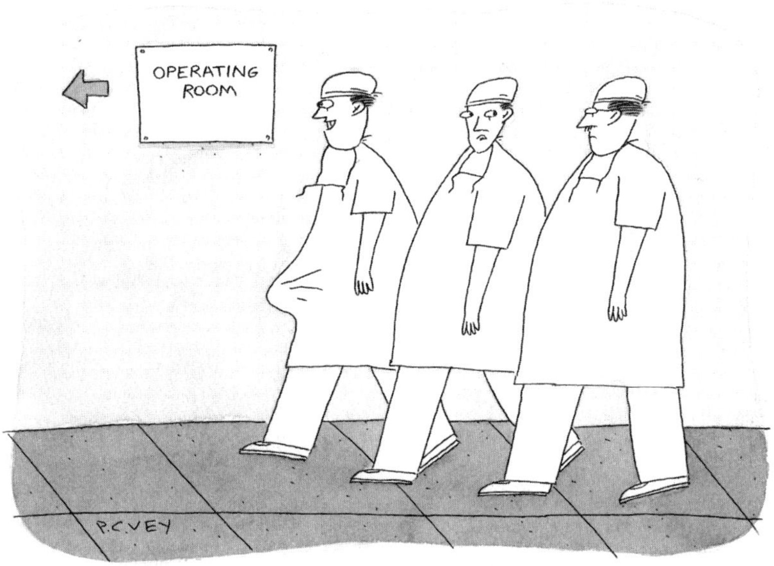
OPERATING ROOM
P.C.VEY

"If you ask me, Roger has the completely wrong attitude about gallbladder surgery."

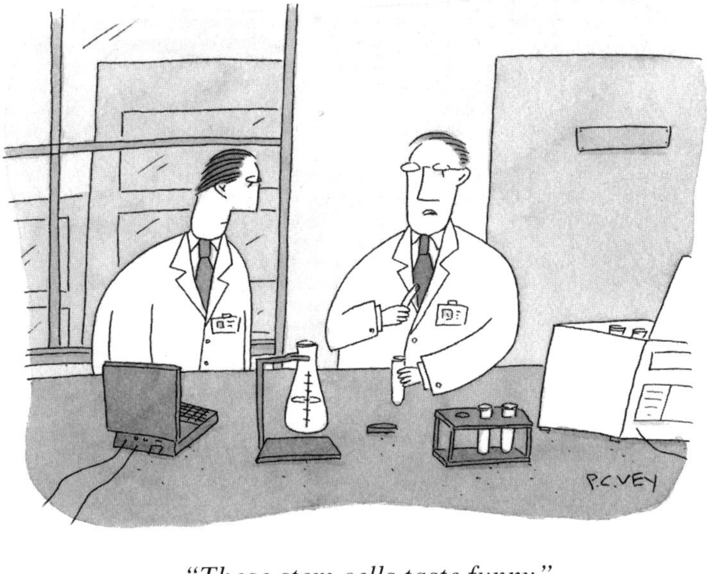
P.C.VEY

"These stem cells taste funny."

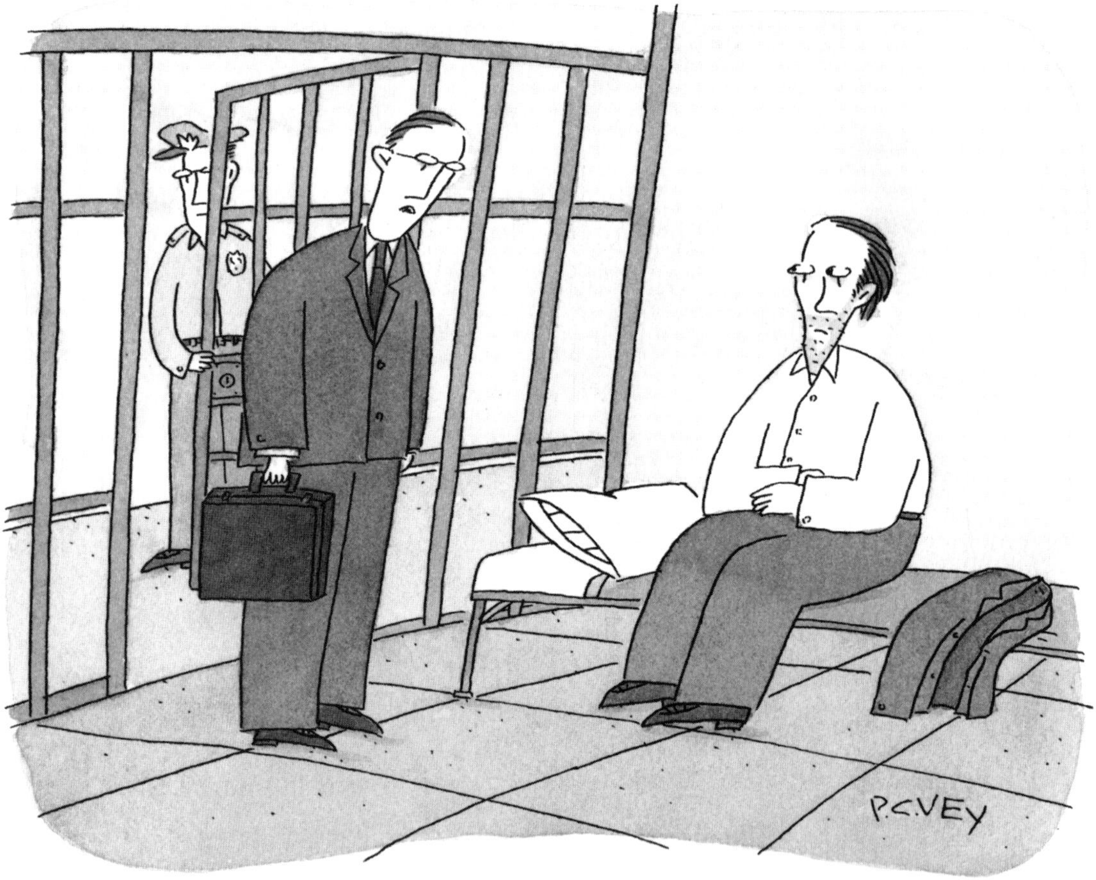
P.C.VEY

"They've agreed to drop the charges, but only if you agree never to stuff the turkey again."

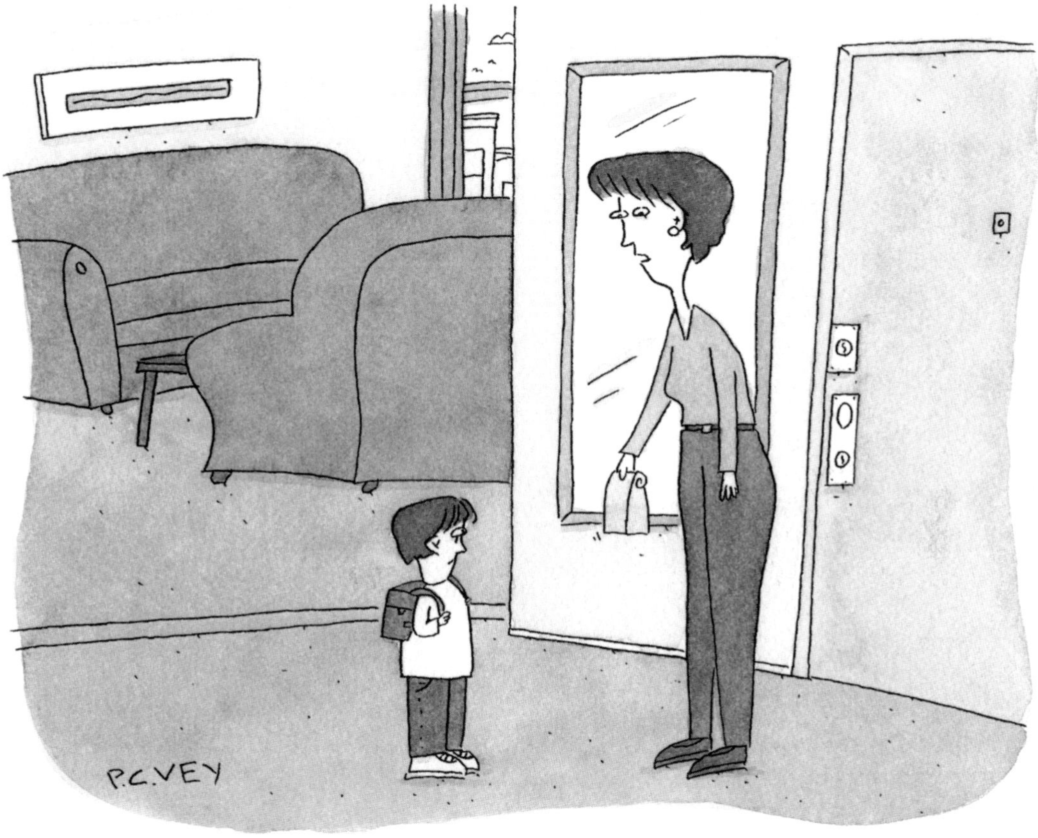
P.C.VEY

"It's something I brought back from the doctor."

PATTERSON

JASON
PATTERSON

Frequently Asked Questions

▪ Where do you get your ideas?

I think of my best ideas when I'm not trying to think of ideas.

▪ Which comes first, the picture or the caption?
Picture.

▪ How'd you get started?

I sold my first cartoon to a local paper for $20, in high school.

▪ I admire . . .

People that like to draw serious grown-up things.

▪ How do you deal with rejection?

I have this little trick where I just think about dinosaurs. I love dinosaurs. Then, I imagine the dinosaurs eating the cartoon editor.

▪ What are some things that make you laugh and why?

People who like to draw serious grown-up things.

▪ I've got a great idea for a cartoon—wanna hear it?

Ok, just keep in mind 9 out of 10 ideas are bad.

Infrequently Asked Questions

▪ Have you mooned or _been_ mooned more often in your life?
Been.

▪ What would make a terrible pizza topping?
Corn.

▪ What might one expect to find at a really low-budget amusement park?
Porn.

▪ What did the shepherd say to the three-legged sheepdog?
How do you do?

And Now for a Few More Questions . . .

▪ What do you hate drawing?
Cars. I can't seem to get them right.

■ Being as accurate as possible, how many desert island cartoons do you think you've come up with and submitted to *The New Yorker*?
20.

■ What's the funniest thing that you witnessed, overheard, or came up with that you couldn't figure out how to use in a cartoon?
Someone farted on the subway really loud, but everyone was completely stoved faced about it. Killed me.

■ If you could ask Bob Mankoff, *The New Yorker* cartoon editor, one question, what would it be?
Where can you get a good sandwich in Midtown?

Draw Some Sort of Doodle

. . . using the random lines below as a starting point.

Naming Names

■ What name might you give to a mild-mannered, slightly overweight dental assistant in one of your cartoons?
Steven.

■ Other than Lance, what name would you give to a twenty-eight-year-old metrosexual entertainment lawyer who cycles on weekends?
Steve.

■ What would be a good name for a new, commercially unviable breakfast cereal?
Bacon Bits.

■ Come up with a name for an unpleasant medical procedure.
Brain transplant.

■ If you used a pen name, what would it be?
Linwood.

Complete the Pie Chart Below

. . . in a way that tells us something about your life or how you think.

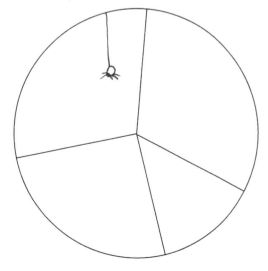

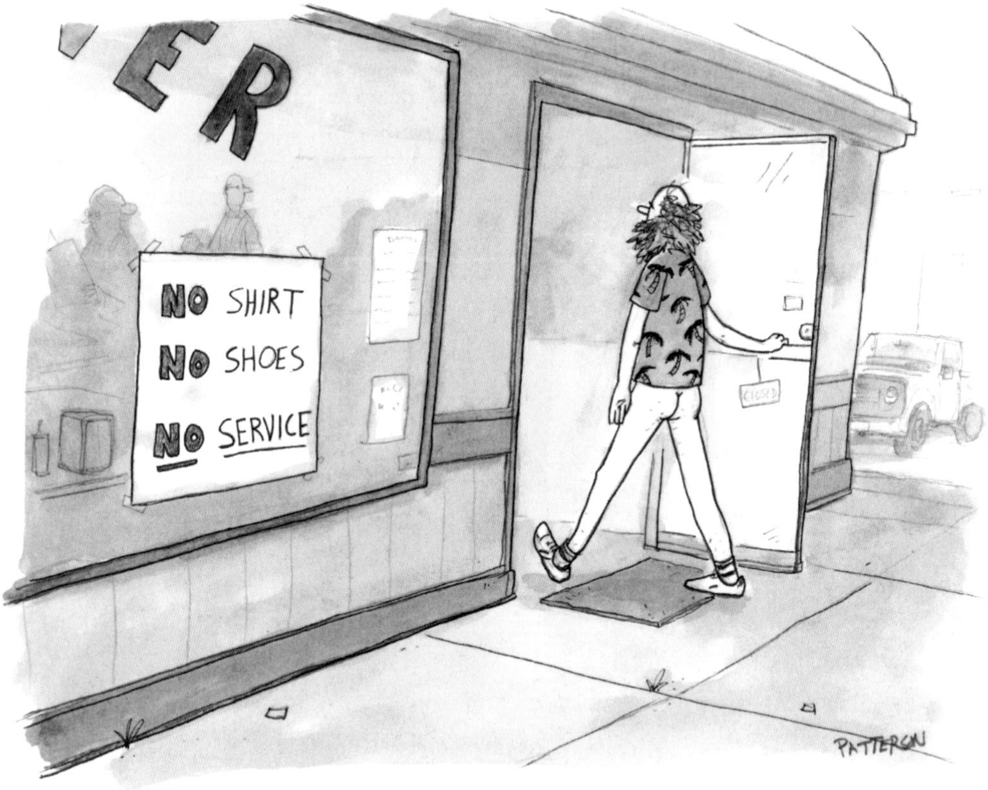
NO SHIRT
NO SHOES
NO SERVICE
CLOSED
PATTERSON

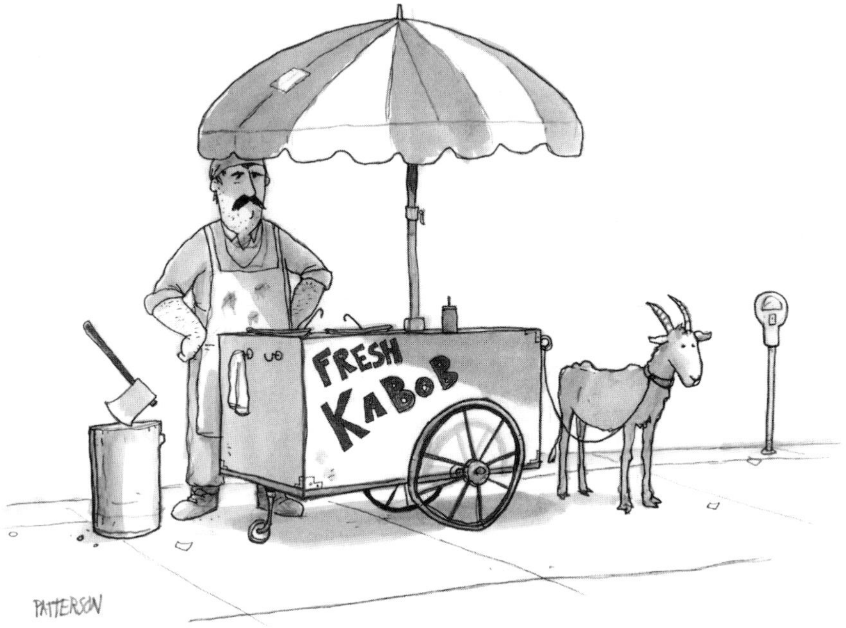
FRESH
KABOB
PATTERSON

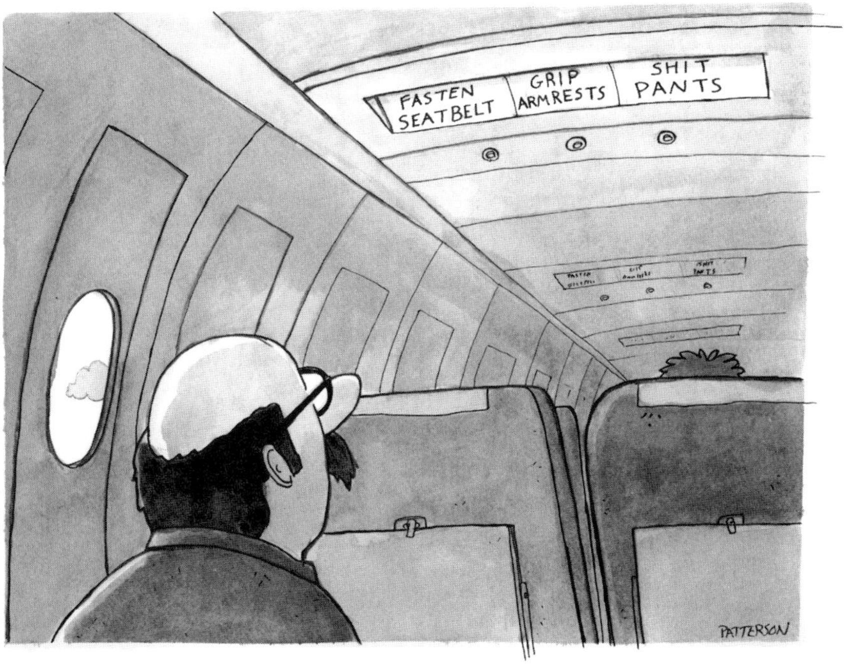
FASTEN SEATBELT
GRIP ARMRESTS
SHIT PANTS
PATTERSON

CAJ

CAROLITA JOHNSON

Frequently Asked Questions

- Where do you get your ideas?

  Not **from the gag-writers who keep e-mailing me with proposals!**

- Which comes first, the picture or the caption?

  70 percent the caption, 29 percent the picture, 1 percent both at the same time.

- How'd you get started?

  Don't get me started.

- I admire . . .

  People who get away with murder (metaphorically speaking, of course).

- How do you deal with rejection?

  Never giving up. Visiting the batting cage at Coney Island and naming all the softballs after the rejector(s). (They know who they are. . . .)

- What are some things that make you laugh and why?

  Men named Dick, birds called "tits," Edgar Allan Poe, very serious people,
  Saint Hildegarde's remedy for leprosy,* my own jokes, and people who think that's wrong. Why? Because they can't help it.

- I've got a great idea for a cartoon—wanna hear it?

  NO!!!

Infrequently Asked Questions

- Have you mooned or _been_ mooned more often in your life?

  I am mooning you right now.

- What would make a terrible pizza topping?

  What doesn't?

- What might one expect to find at a really low-budget amusement park?

  Me—I love low-budget amusement parks!

- What did the shepherd say to the three-legged sheepdog?

  Can you shoot a gun?

Saint Hildegarde's recipe for leprosy control includes a "modicum stercoris gallinarum."

Draw Something in This Space

. . . that will help us understand your childhood.

And I now have four.
I only wanted four!
(9 yrs. old)
Someday I'll have as many flashlights as I want...

And Now for a Few More Questions . . .

- What do you hate drawing?

  Straight lines.

- Being as accurate as possible, how many desert island cartoons do you think you've come up with and submitted to *The New Yorker*?

  15, about a third sold.

- What's the funniest thing that you witnessed, overheard, or came up with that you couldn't figure out how to use in a cartoon?

  President Bush's administration. (So funny I forgot to laugh.)

- If you could ask Bob Mankoff, *The New Yorker* cartoon editor, one question, what would it be?

  Does it hurt you when I stick this pin in this little voodoo doll?

Naming Names

- What name might you give to a mild-mannered, slightly overweight dental assistant in one of your cartoons?

  Matthew.

- Other than Lance, what name would you give to a twenty-eight-year-old metrosexual entertainment lawyer who cycles on weekends?

  Chad, Tad, Brad . . . any "ad" name.

- What would be a good name for a new, commercially unviable breakfast cereal?

  Gassies. Hairy Crunchballs.

- Come up with a name for an unpleasant medical procedure.

  Foreskinoplasty.

- If you used a pen name, what would it be?

  Ms. Pen Name.

Complete the Pie Chart Below

. . . in a way that tells us something about your life or how you think.

1970-1983
NEARLY FATAL BOREDOM
1984-2000
ah-haaa!!
attempt at gainful employment
2000-2002
2002 → present.
"So long, suckers!" + ("the check is in the mail")

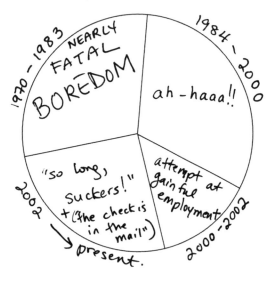

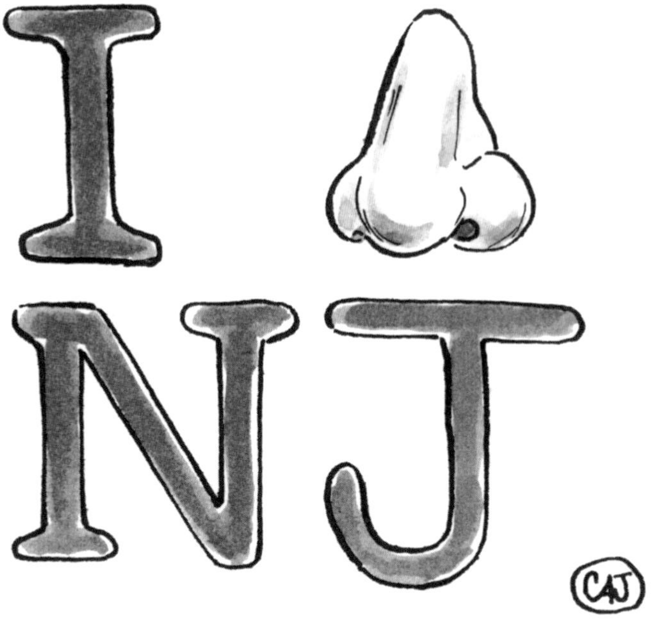
I
NJ
CAJ

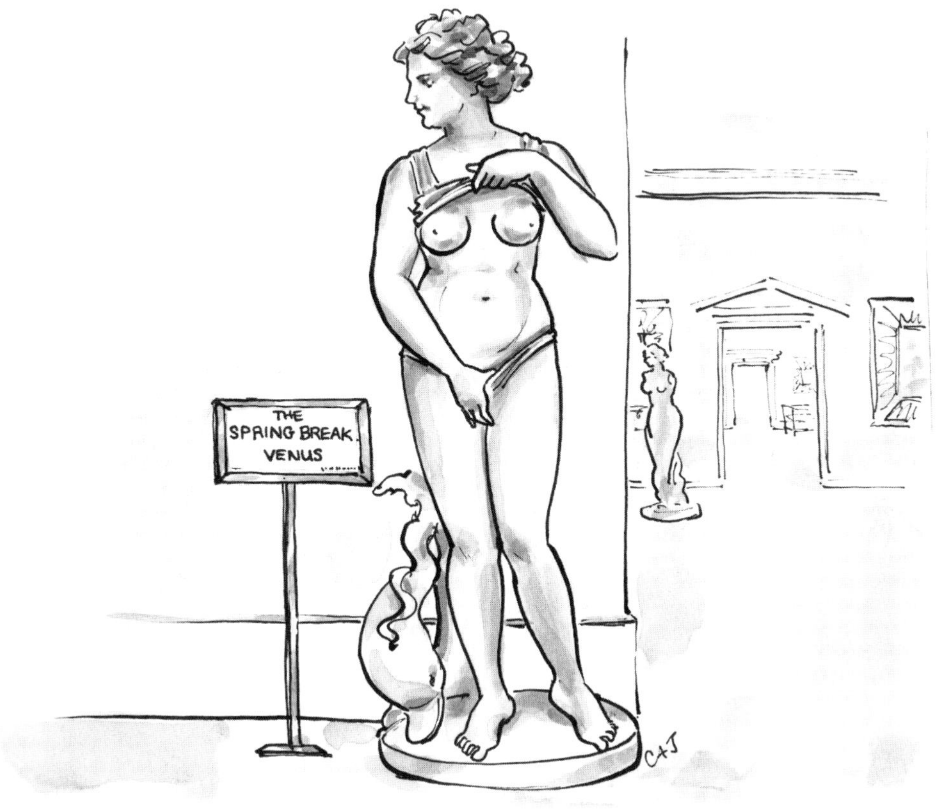
THE
SPRING BREAK
VENUS
CAJ

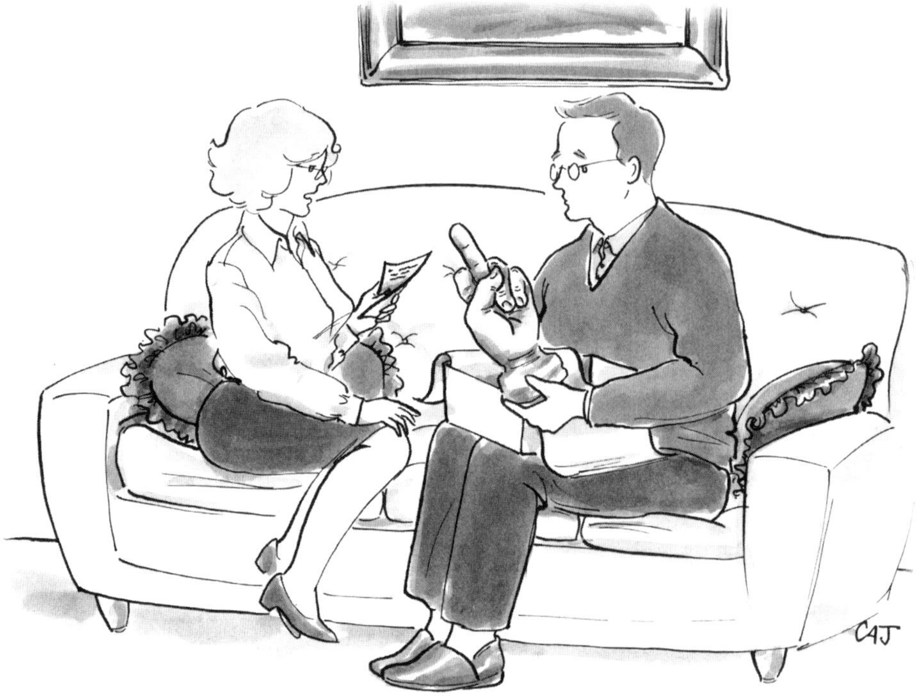
CAJ

"It's from Marcus at sculpture camp."

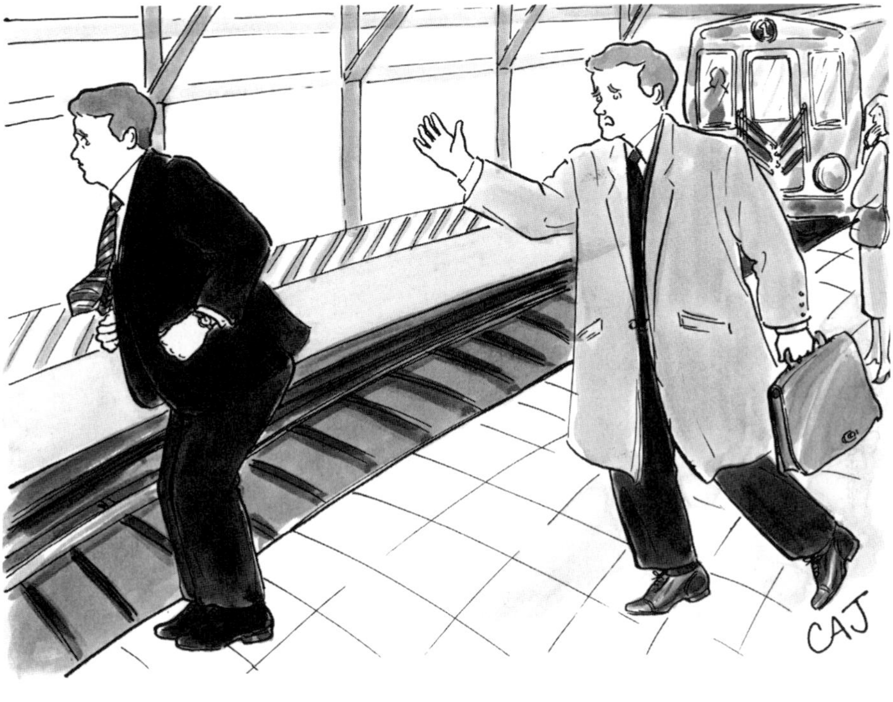
CAJ

"Wait. There's another train right behind this one."

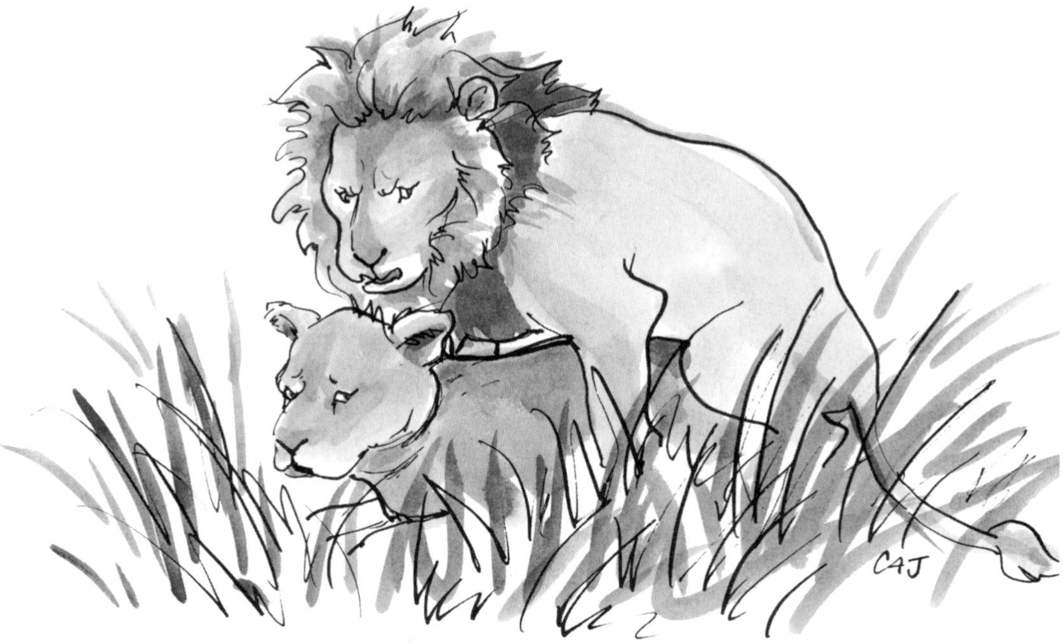
CAJ

"Those pervs from National Geographic are filming us again."

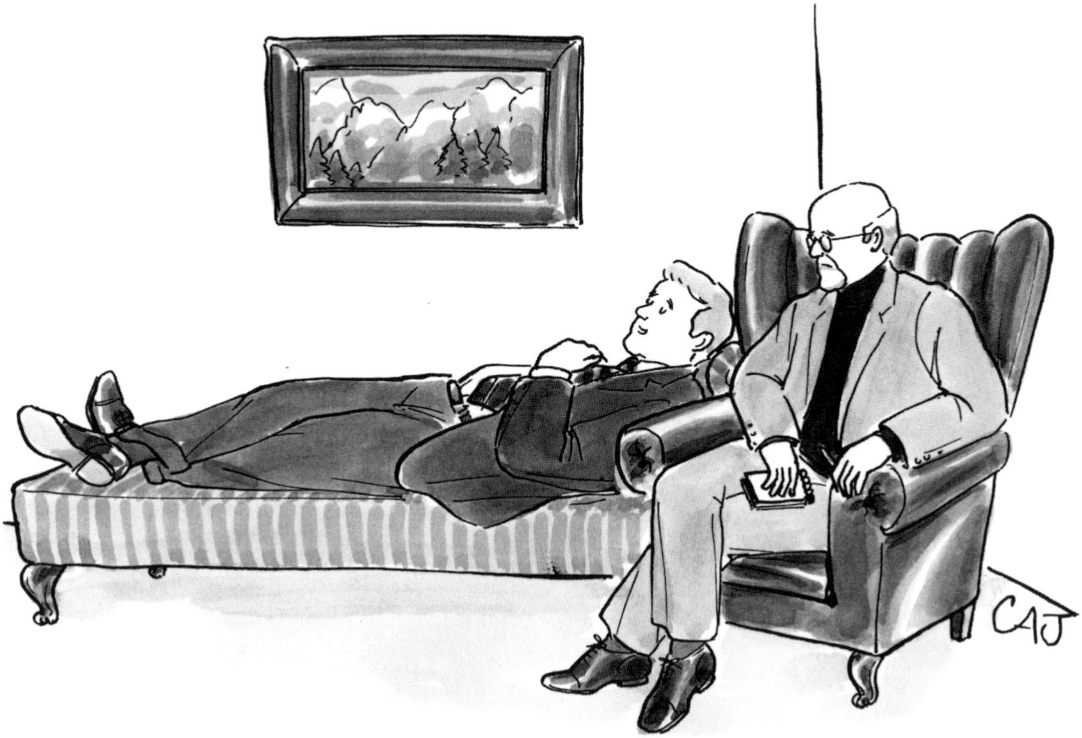
CAJ

"I was bound and beaten for what seemed like hours, and it only cost me a hundred bucks."

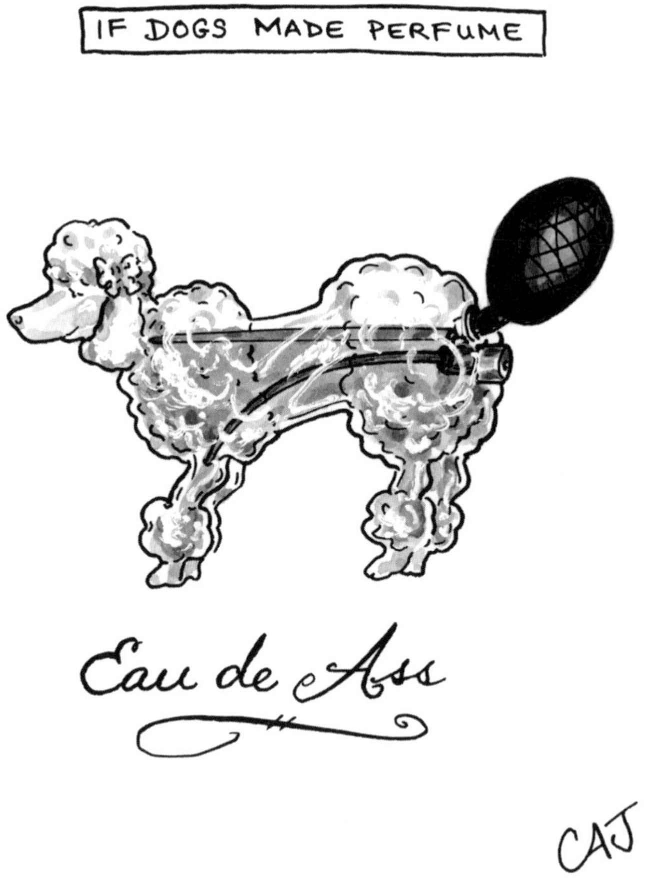
IF DOGS MADE PERFUME
Eau de Ass
CAJ

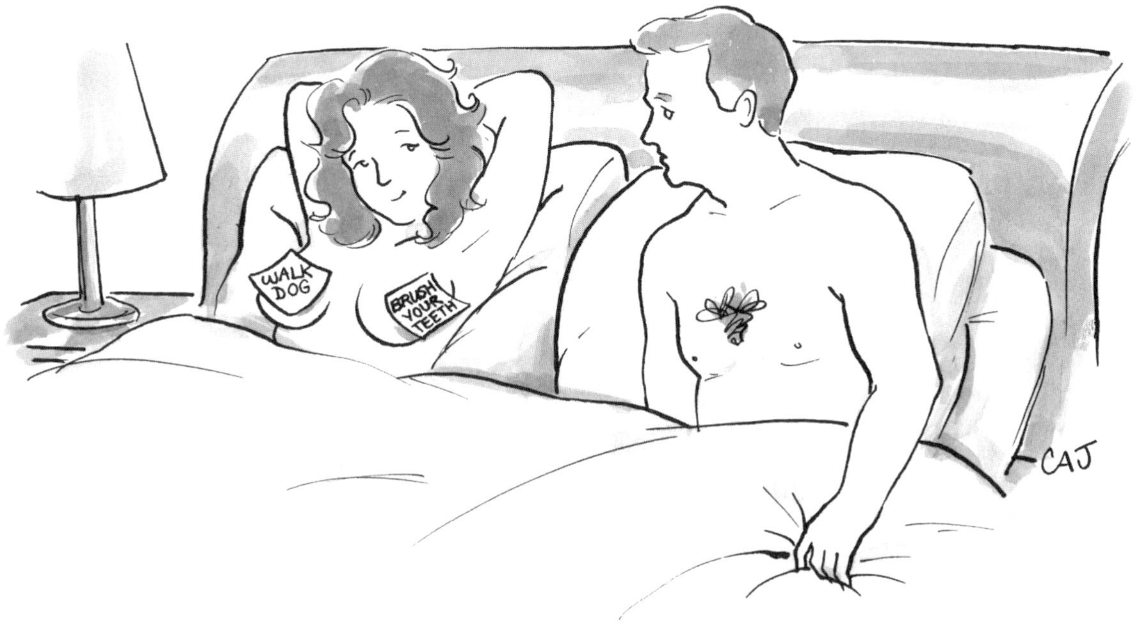
WALK DOG
BRUSH YOUR TEETH
CAJ

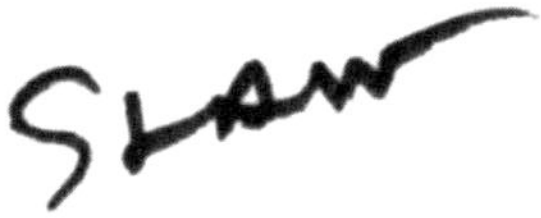

MICHAEL SHAW

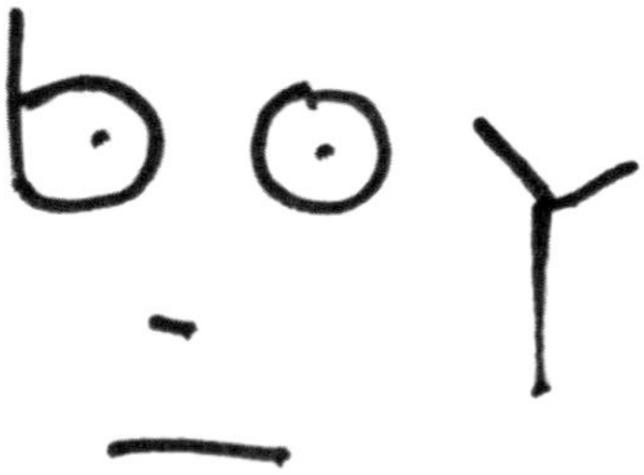
boy

Frequently Asked Questions

- Where do you get your ideas?

  I've never been asked that question.

- Which comes first, the picture or the caption?

  Actually I have been asked that question—but not frequently.

- How'd you get started?

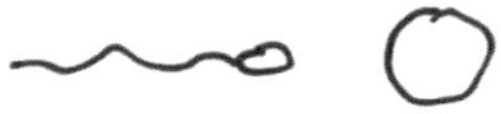

- I admire . . .

  Many, many people—but I would not let them suspect. I do admire my wife for putting up with me. And here's a shout-out to my fellow crusty Missourian, Mr. George Booth! James Thurber remains my favorite dead cartoonist.

- How do you deal with rejection?

  Think reproductively. My rejection rate would send even the most optimistic of souls into despair. But compared to the chances of the average sperm succeeding in its mission, my odds are quite good.

- What are some things that make you laugh and why?

  I laugh at things that aren't meant to be funny. EWTN is hilarious.

  My motto—"Tragedy plus time equals comedy—but who has time anymore?"

  My favorite joke—"What did the sadist do to the masochist? Nothing."

- I've got a great idea for a cartoon—wanna hear it?

  I think you'd have to read it, instead. Two guys walk into a bar . . . the third guy ducked.

Infrequently Asked Questions

- Have you moo[redacted]ed or *been* moo[redacted]ed more often in your life?

  (Lived in Wisconsin.)

- What would make a terrible pizza topping?

  Foil.

- What might one expect to find at a really low-budget amusement park?

  God.

- What did the shepherd say to the three-legged sheepdog?

  Dog.

And Now for a Few More Questions . . .

Sorry, I'm using this space for a cartoon I've submited 127 times and have never sold.

V WL S
W NT D

Draw Something in This Space

. . . that will help us understand your childhood.

NA NA
NA NA
NAA NAA!

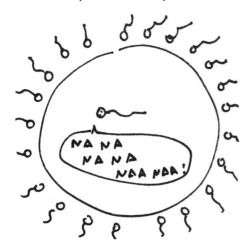

- What's the funniest thing that you witnessed, overheard, or came up with that you couldn't figure out how to use in a cartoon?

"How's the fish?"

- If you could ask Bob Mankoff, *The New Yorker* cartoon editor, one question, what would it be?

  Are you my real father?

Complete the Pie Chart Below

. . . in a way that tells us something about your life or how you think.

PROCRASTINATE
PROCRASTINATE
PROCRASTINATE
PROCRASTINATE
PROCRASTINATE
PROCRASTINATE
PANIC!
PROCRASTINATE
PROCRASTINATE
PROCRASTINATE
PROCRASTINATE
PROCRASTINATE

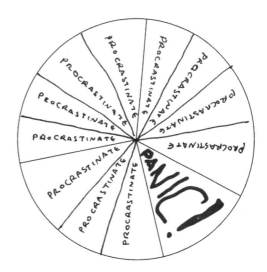

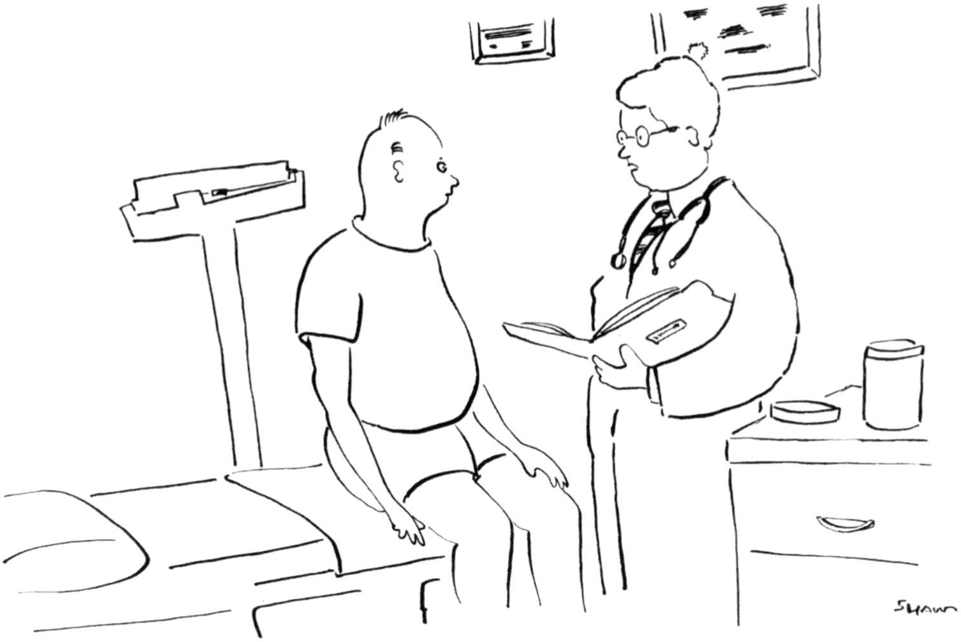
SHAW

"Now, this is going to feel like I'm sticking my finger up your ass."

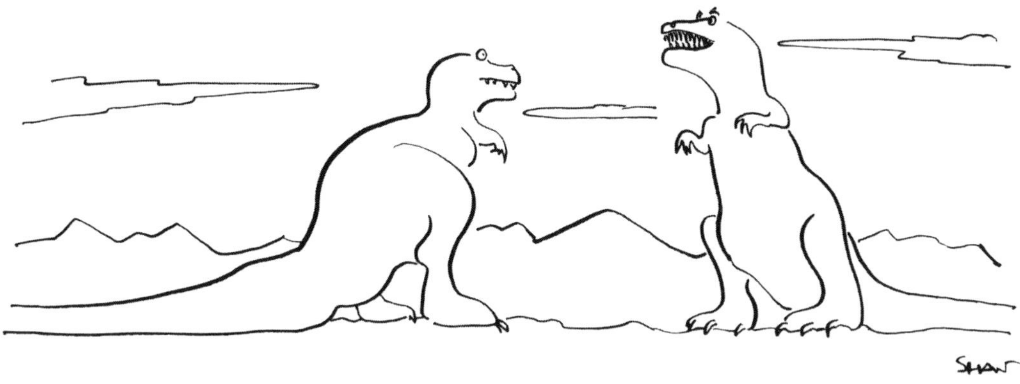
SHAW

"I'd give up being the most fearsome creature on the planet if I could just reach my weenie."

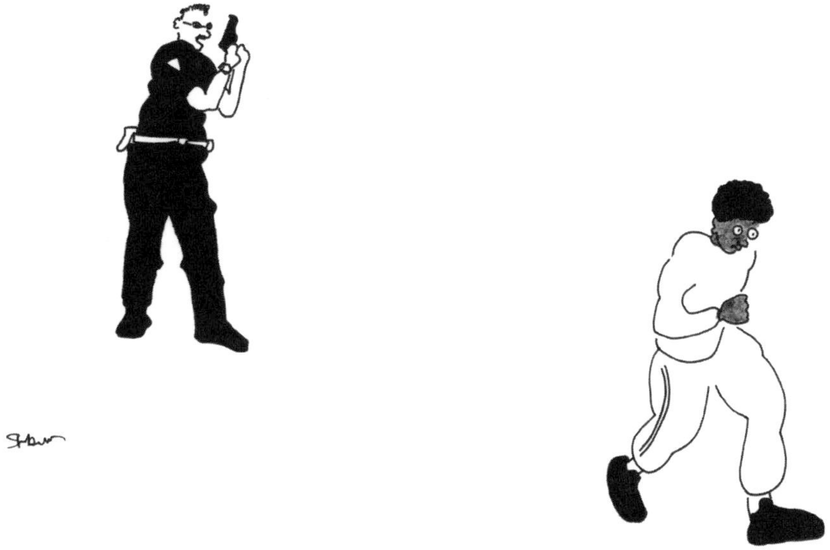
SHAW

"Stop and I'll shoot."

GIVING THE FINGER
GETTING THE FINGER
SHAW

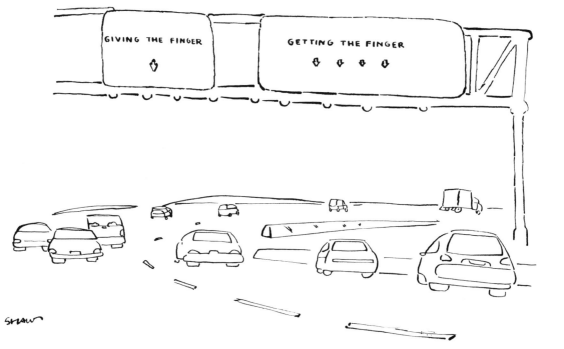

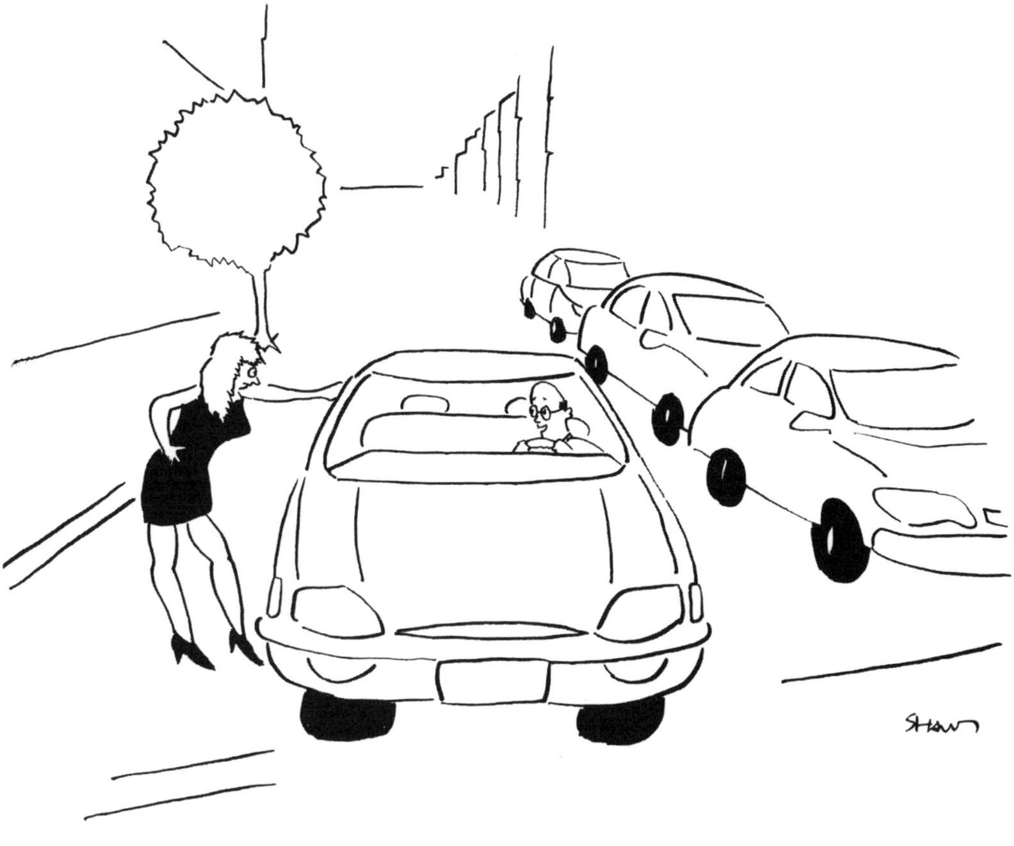
SHAW

"Throw in a prostate exam and you've got a deal!"

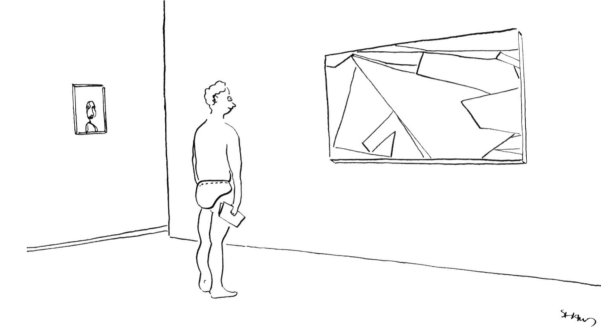

Half-price tighty-whitey day at the MoMA

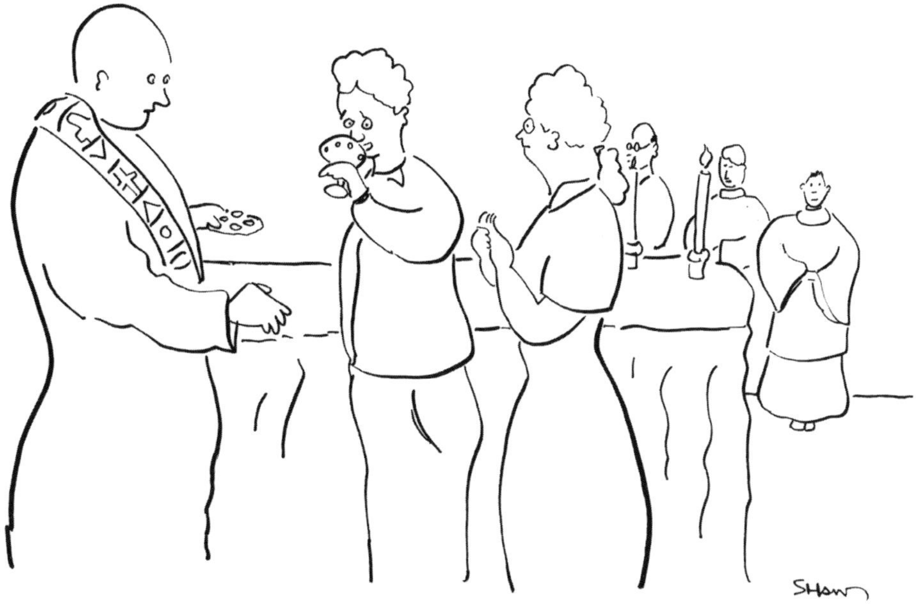
SHAW

"I'm getting earthy overtones of guilt, with just a hint of sexual frustration."

GREGORY

ALEX GREGORY

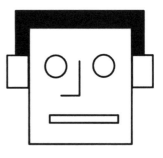

Frequently Asked Questions

- Where do you get your ideas?

  Target.

- Which comes first, the picture or the caption?

  They arrive together arm in arm.

- How'd you get started?

  Dad met Mom at some dance hall in New York.

- I admire . . .

  Nice buttocks, but I try not to be obvious about it. Sunglasses help.

- How do you deal with rejection?

  I remind myself that even though she's really attractive, if my new liver doesn't want to be a part of my life, I'm better off without her.

- What are some things that make you laugh and why?

  I am always amused by nunchucks. I can't recall ever hearing of a single incident where anyone has successfully used nunchucks to either defend himself or to attack someone else, yet they are illegal in three states. They can't be easily concealed, and pose as much of a danger to the wielder as to the target. Presumably, if nunchucks were in any way effective, all soldiers and cops would carry them. And yet every day factories manufacture nunchucks. And every day some teenage boy covers his back and forearms in bruises in his futile quest to master the noble art of nunchuckery.

- I've got a great idea for a cartoon—wanna hear it?

  Just draw it and sign my name. I trust you.

Infrequently Asked Questions

- Have you mooned or *been* mooned more often in your life?

  There's been so much mooning in my life, it's impossible to calculate.

- What would make a terrible pizza topping?

  Gelatin beads filled with children's tears.

- What might one expect to find at a really low-budget amusement park?

  I wouldn't know. The amusement parks I attend are super-classy.

■ What did the shepherd say to the three-legged sheepdog?

Come on, we're both lonely and sick of sheep.

Draw Something in This Space

. . . that will help us understand your childhood.

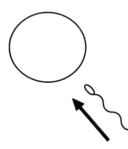

And Now for a Few More Questions . . .

■ What do you hate drawing?

Cars, furniture, shoes, and windows— God, I HATE drawing windows—no idea why.

■ Being as accurate as possible, how many desert island cartoons do you think you've come up with and submitted to *The New Yorker*?

No idea. 10?

■ What's the funniest thing that you witnessed, overheard, or came up with that you couldn't figure out how to use in a cartoon?

The overabundance of fennel in restaurants.

■ If you could ask Bob Mankoff, *The New Yorker* cartoon editor, one question, what would it be?

Why "Bob" and not "Rob"?

Naming Names

■ What name might you give to a mild-mannered, slightly overweight dental assistant in one of your cartoons?

Matt Diffee.

■ Other than Lance, what name would you give to a twenty-eight-year-old metrosexual entertainment lawyer who cycles on weekends?

Matt Diffee.

■ What would be a good name for a new, commercially unviable breakfast cereal?

Curry-O's.

■ Come up with a name for an unpleasant medical procedure.

I defy you to name a *pleasant* medical procedure.

■ If you used a pen name, what would it be?

For all of my criminal activity, I use the alias "Matt Diffee."

Complete the Pie Chart Below

. . . in a way that tells us something about your life or how you think.

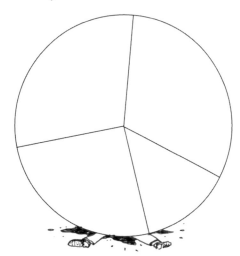

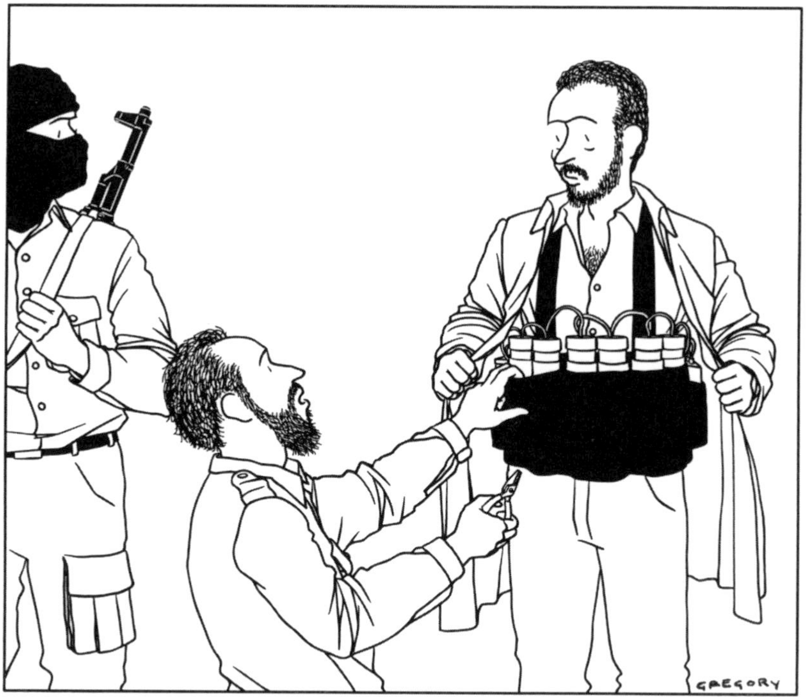
GREGORY

"Too snug?"

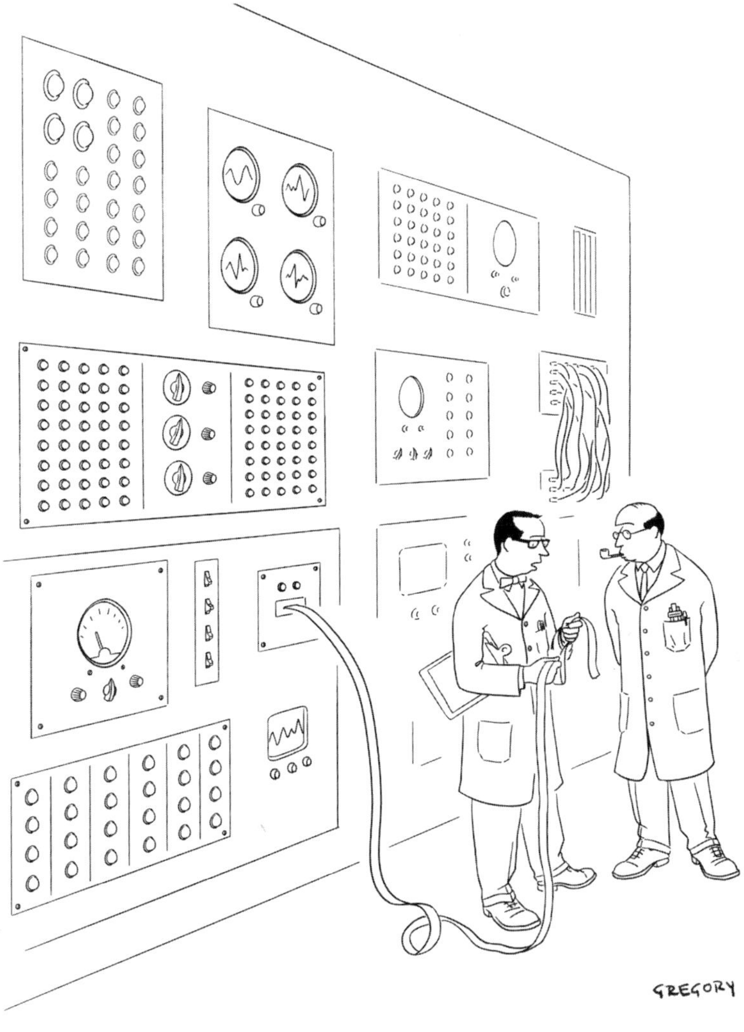
GREGORY

"The results are impressive, but it'll be decades before we can transmit and receive pornography."

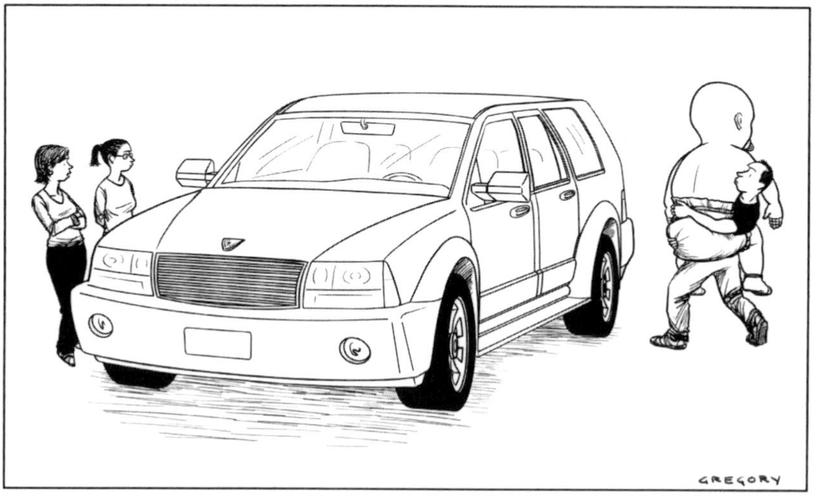
GREGORY

"We were dead set against getting an SUV until we had the baby."

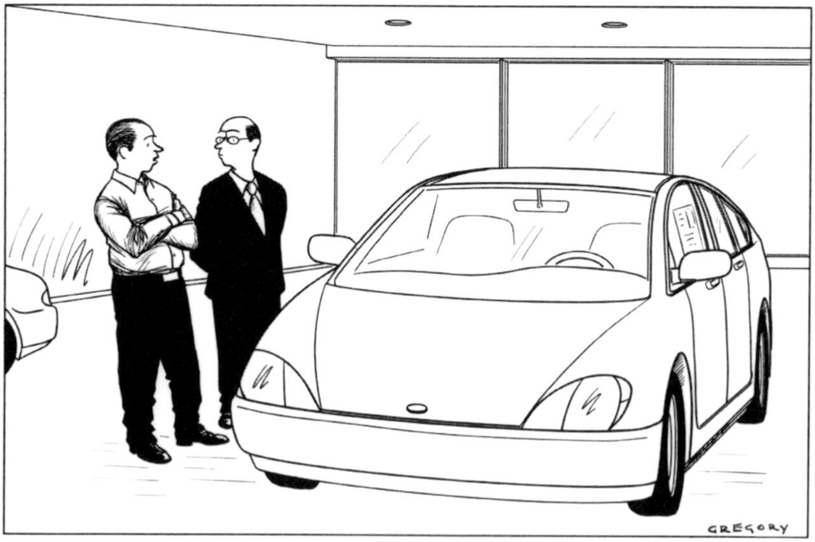
GREGORY

"Will the high mileage and low emissions make my penis seem bigger?"

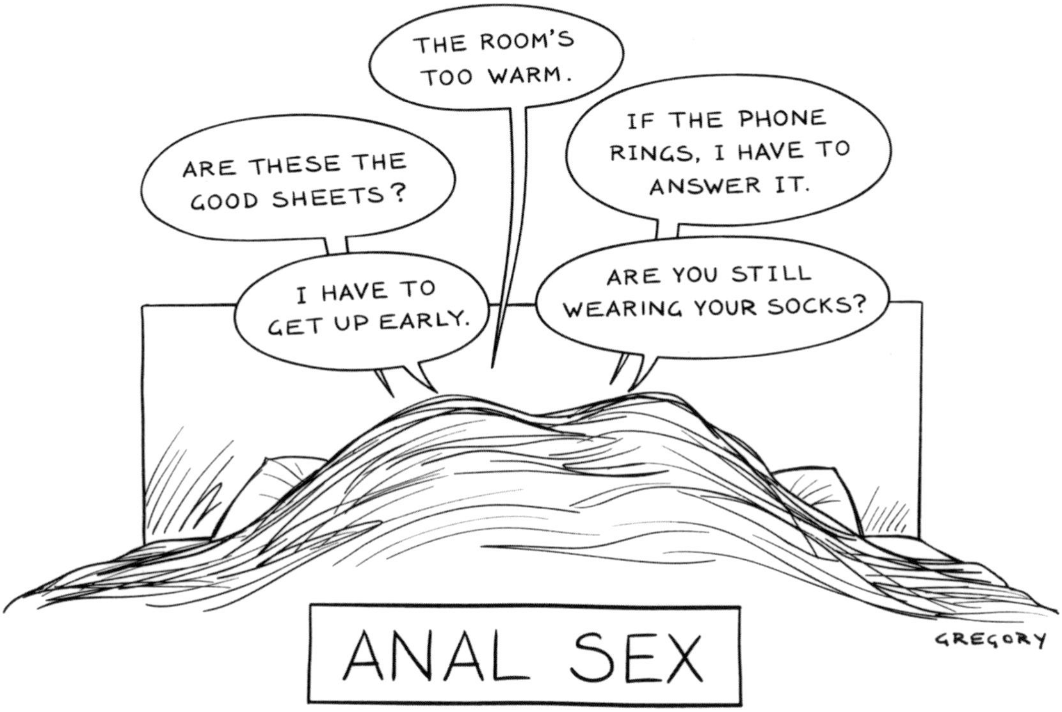
ARE THESE THE GOOD SHEETS?
THE ROOM'S TOO WARM.
IF THE PHONE RINGS, I HAVE TO ANSWER IT.
I HAVE TO GET UP EARLY.
ARE YOU STILL WEARING YOUR SOCKS?
GREGORY

ANAL SEX

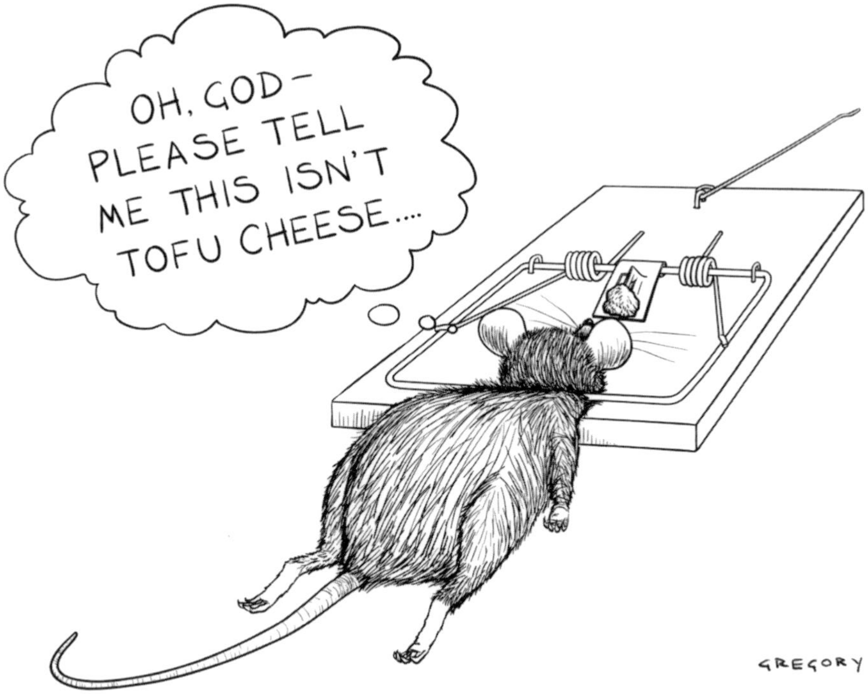
OH, GOD—
PLEASE TELL
ME THIS ISN'T
TOFU CHEESE....
GREGORY

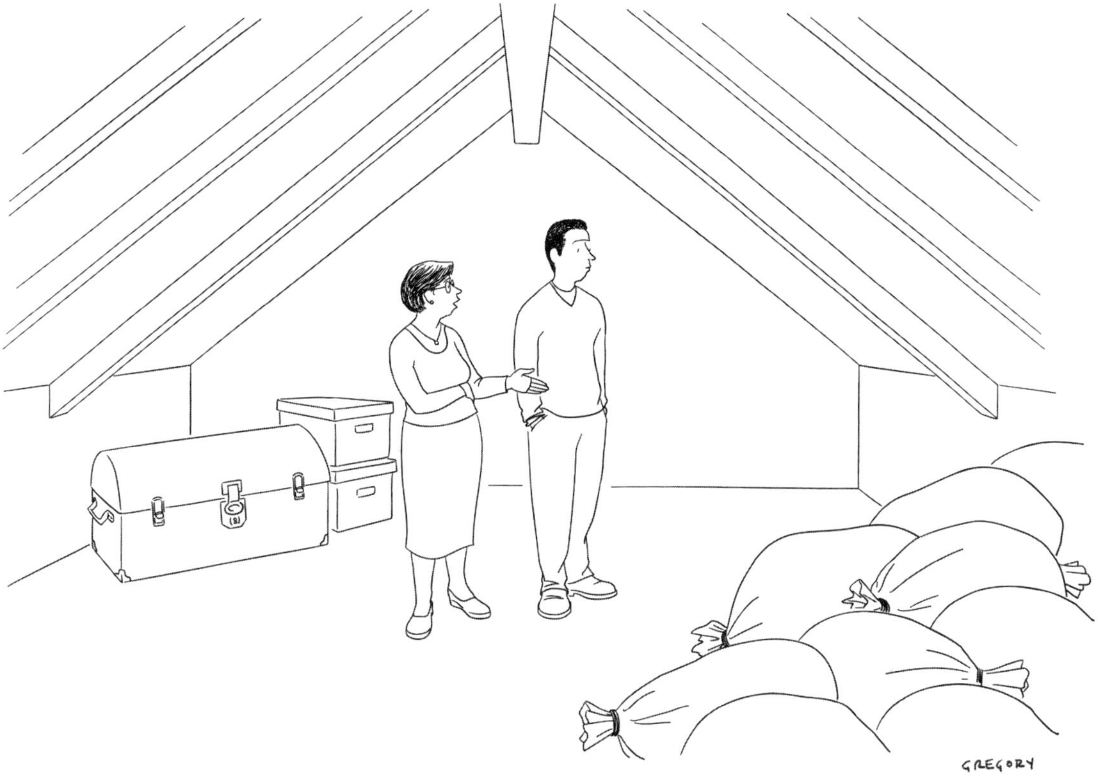
GREGORY

"We saved all your old diapers."

CARGO BRIEFS
GREGORY

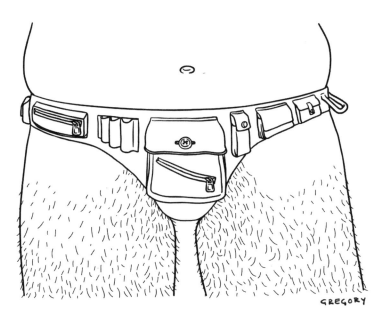

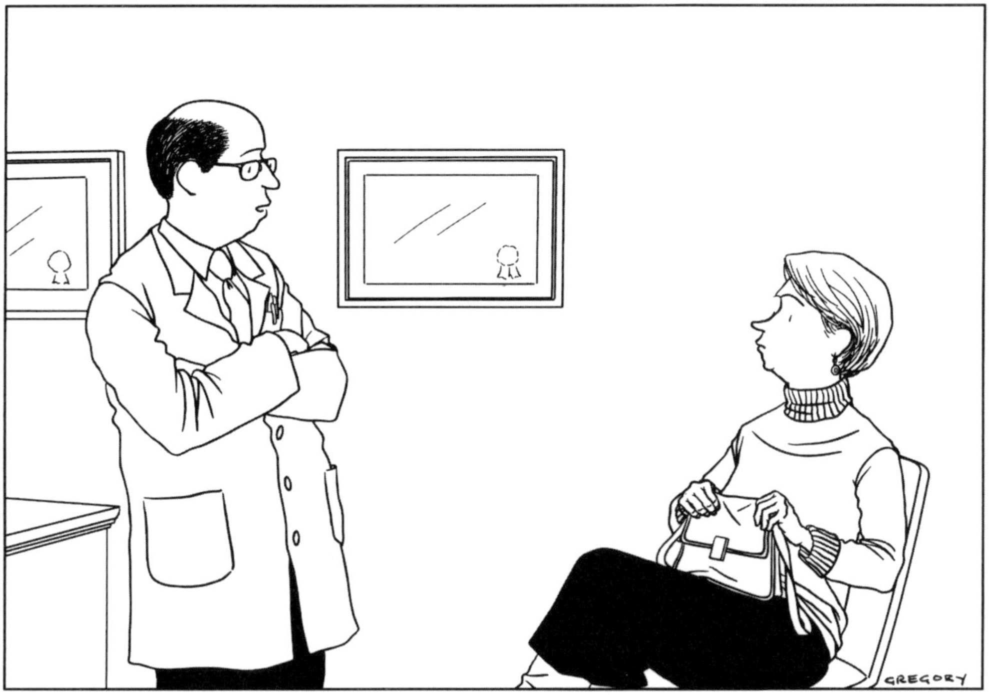
GREGORY

"With the latest advances in cosmetic surgery, I can make a fifty-five-year-old grandmother look like a thirty-five-year-old transsexual."

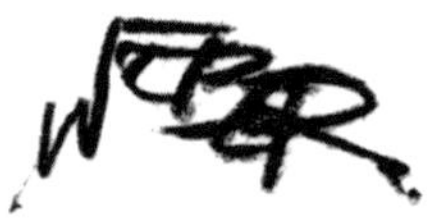

ROBERT WEBER

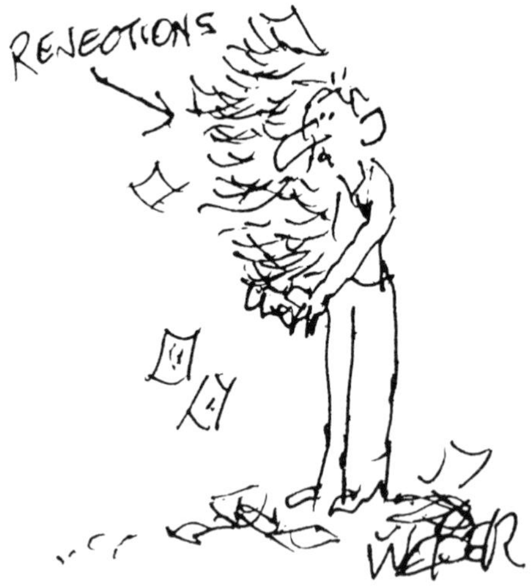
REJECTIONS
WEBER

Frequently Asked Questions

- Where do you get your ideas?
  You think I'd tell you?

- Which comes first, the picture or the caption?
  Both.

- How'd you get started?
  Doing spots for magazines.

- I admire . . .
  All accountants.

- How do you deal with rejection?
  Sink into a deep depression.

- What are some things that make you laugh and why?
  Can't think of anything, actually.

- I've got a great idea for a cartoon—wanna hear it?
  You think I'd tell you?

Infrequently Asked Questions

- Have you mooned or *been* mooned more often in your life?
  Let's not go there.

- What would make a terrible pizza topping?
  That's for you to answer.

- What might one expect to find at a really low-budget amusement park?
  A lot of dashed expectations.

- What did the shepherd say to the three-legged sheepdog?
  Please pass the brandy.

And Now for a Few More Questions . . .

- What do you hate drawing?
  Money from savings account.

- Being as accurate as possible, how many desert island cartoons do you think you've come up with and submitted to *The New Yorker*?
  64,000.

■ What's the funniest thing that you witnessed, overheard, or came up with that you couldn't figure out how to use in a cartoon?

Recovering from bi-lateral knee surgery.

■ If you could ask Bob Mankoff, *The New Yorker* cartoon editor, one question, what would it be?

Bob, are you sure this is something you really want to do?

Draw Some Sort of Doodle

. . . using the random lines below as a starting point.

YOU SAID IT!

Naming Names

■ What name might you give to a mild-mannered, slightly overweight dental assistant in one of your cartoons?

Zandra-Lois.

■ Other than Lance, what name would you give to a twenty-eight-year-old metrosexual entertainment lawyer who cycles on weekends?

Horace Boris.

■ What would be a good name for a new, commercially unviable breakfast cereal?

Organ-Iky.

■ Come up with a name for an unpleasant medical procedure.

Opsy.

■ If you used a pen name, what would it be?

Waterman.

Complete the Pie Chart Below

. . . in a way that tells us something about your life or how you think.

APPLE
LEMON MERENGUE
STRAW-BERRY RUBARB
PIZZA

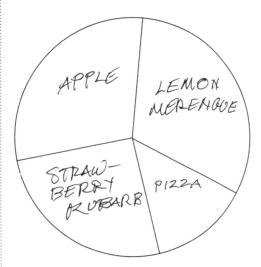

"How many times have I told you to keep your elbows off the table?"

"Wanna see me fake an orgasm?"

"Do you mind if I use your thong as a bookmark?"

P. BYRNES.

PAT BYRNES

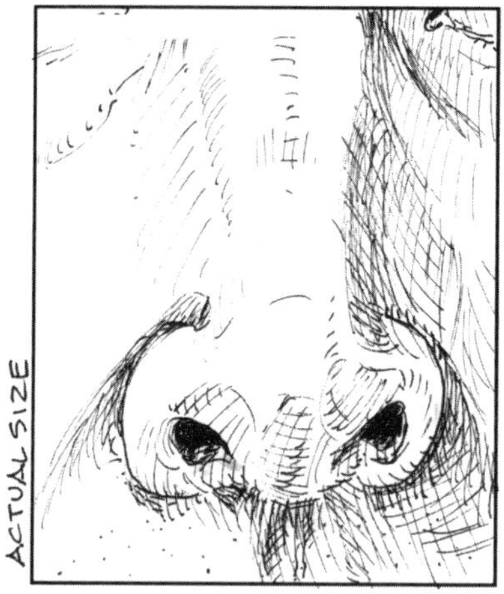
ACTUAL SIZE

Frequently Asked Questions

■ Where do you get your ideas?

Is that what you mean by *frequently* asked questions?

■ Which comes first, the picture or the caption?

Yes.

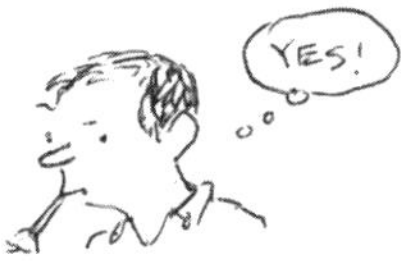
YES!

■ How'd you get started?

The same as everyone else. All kids start out drawing cartoons. Some of us simply don't stop.

■ I admire . . .

My cutie's mommy.

■ How do you deal with rejection?

I've been an ad writer, a comedian, an actor, and I couldn't find a woman to marry me until I was 43. I deal with rejection like you deal with an old friend.

■ What are some things that make you laugh and why?

Corporate jargon, because it doesn't fool me. The Three Stooges' "O Elaine" sketch because it is a magical blend of the high and the low. The way my daughter instantly imitates people's embarrassing noises because she is only 16 months old and can get away with it—and she knows it!

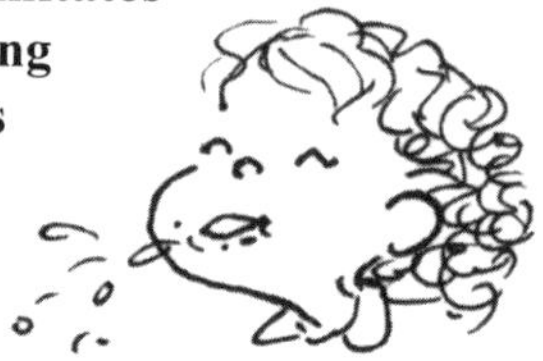

■ I've got a great idea for a cartoon—wanna hear it?

No, I want to *see* it.

Infrequently Asked Questions

■ Have you mooned or *been* mooned more often in your life?

I've successfully repressed those memories, thank you very much.

■ What would make a terrible pizza topping?

Snickers bars, based on how awful they taste deep-fried on a stick.

■ What might one expect to find at a really low-budget amusement park?

The Tunnel of Cousins.

- What did the shepherd say to the three-legged sheepdog?

  Shake.

And Now for a Few More Questions . . .

- What do you hate drawing?

  A blank.

- Being as accurate as possible, how many desert island cartoons do you think you've come up with and submitted to *The New Yorker*?

  Azores < x < Indonesia.

- What's the funniest thing that you witnessed, overheard, or came up with that you couldn't figure out how to use in a cartoon?

BUT YOU REALLY HAD TO BE THERE.

- If you could ask Bob Mankoff, *The New Yorker* cartoon editor, one question, what would it be?

  If a train leaves New York at 9:00 A.M., and another train leaves Albany at 9:30 A.M., and their speeds are, respectively, 50 mph and 42 mph . . .

Naming Names

- What name might you give to a mild-mannered, slightly overweight dental assistant in one of your cartoons?

  Llewelyn.

- Other than Lance, what name would you give to a twenty-eight-year-old metrosexual entertainment lawyer who cycles on weekends?

  Chaz.

- What would be a good name for a new, commercially unviable breakfast cereal?

  Tac-Os. "It's a fiesta in your mouth!"

- Come up with a name for an unpleasant medical procedure.

  Bone Flushing.

- If you used a pen name, what would it be?

  Uni-ball Jetstream.

Complete the Pie Chart Below

. . . in a way that tells us something about your life or how you think.

KEY LIME
APPLE
DUTCH APPLE
LEMON MERINGUE

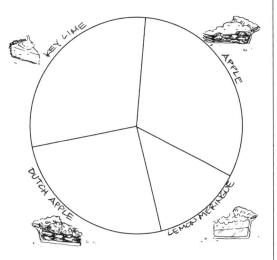

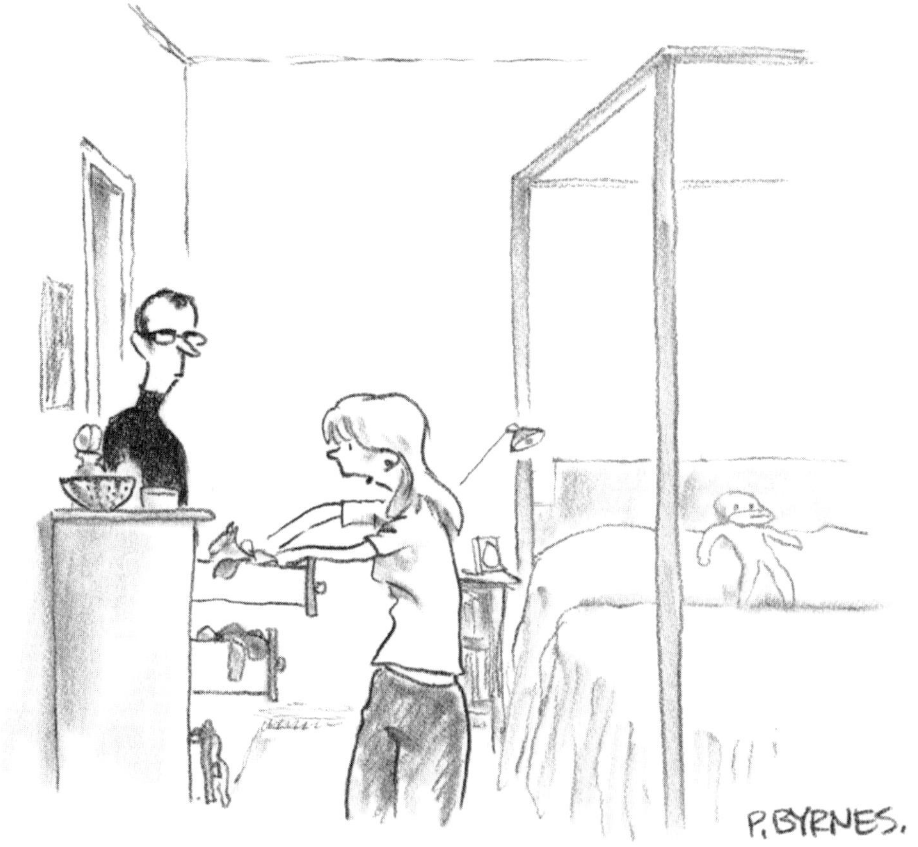
P. BYRNES.

"I've got an important audition today. Have you seen my diaphragm?"

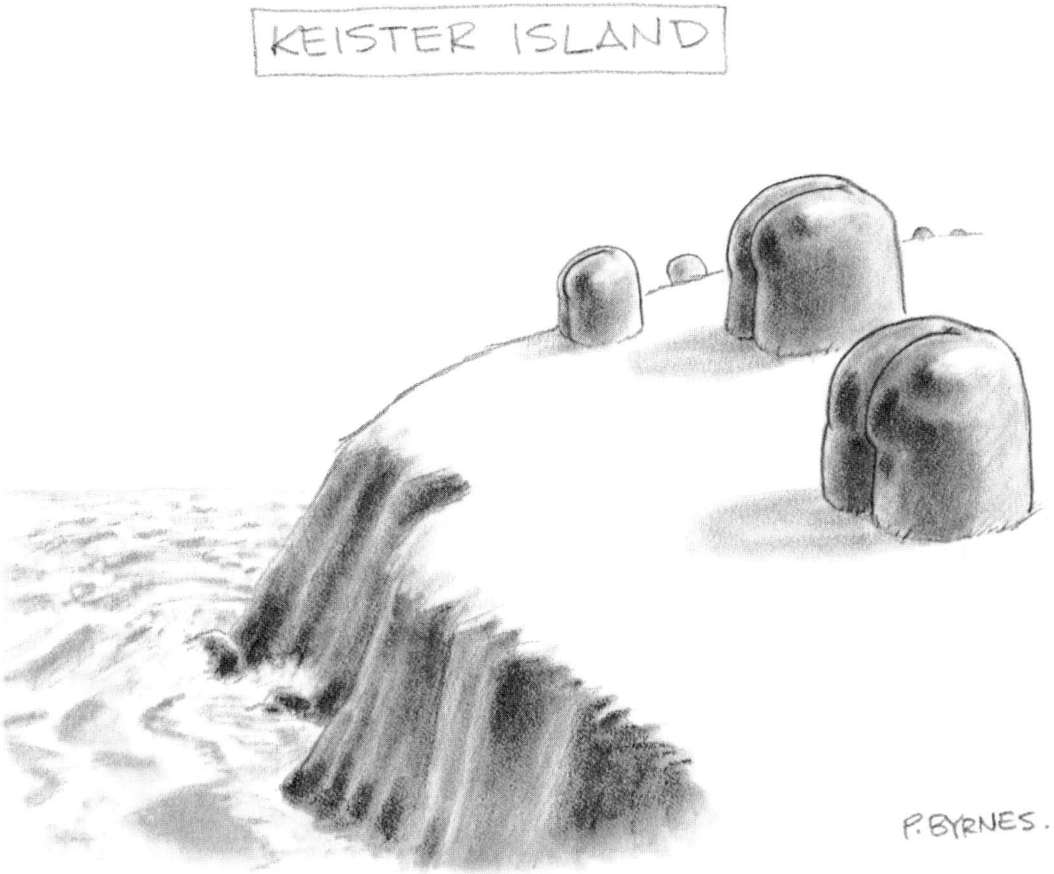
KEISTER ISLAND
P. BYRNES.

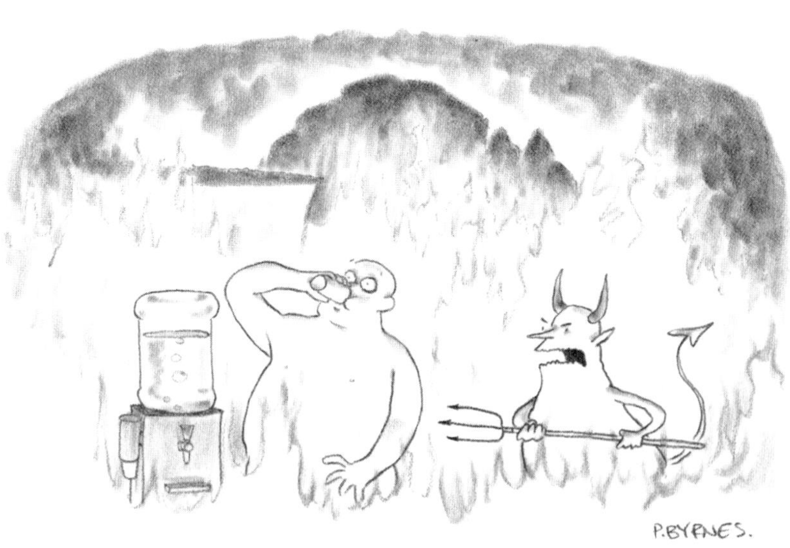
P.BYRNES.

"Hey, get away from the urinal."

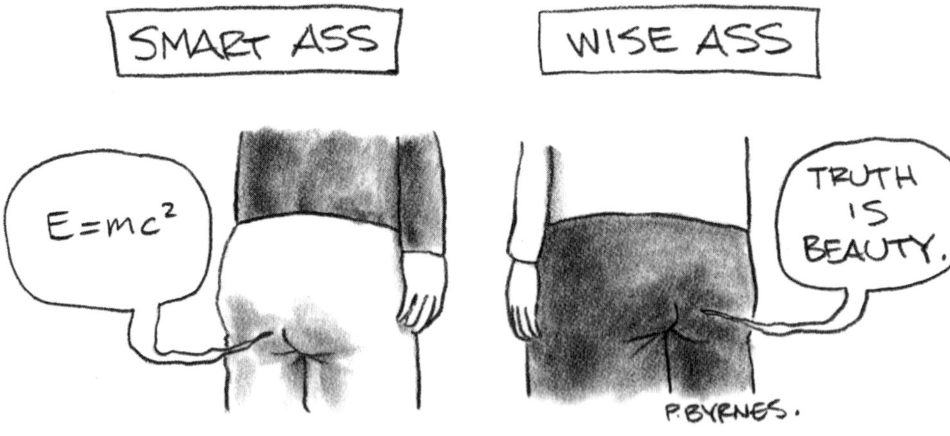
SMART ASS
WISE ASS
E=mc²
TRUTH IS BEAUTY.
P.BYRNES.

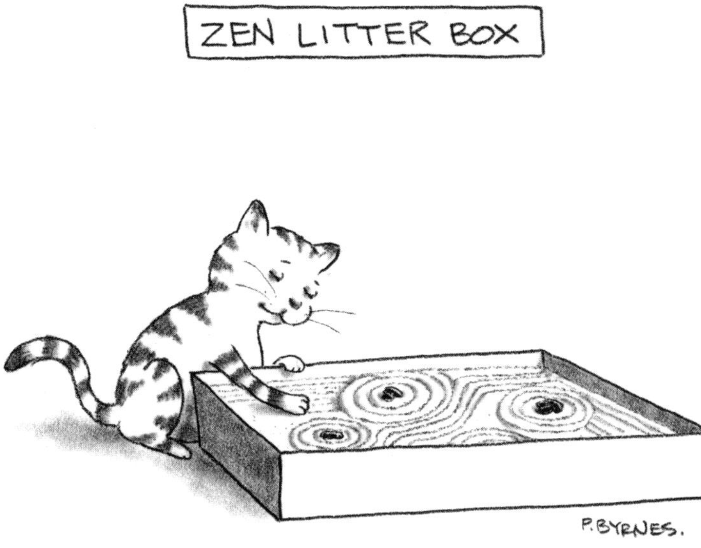
ZEN LITTER BOX
P. BYRNES.

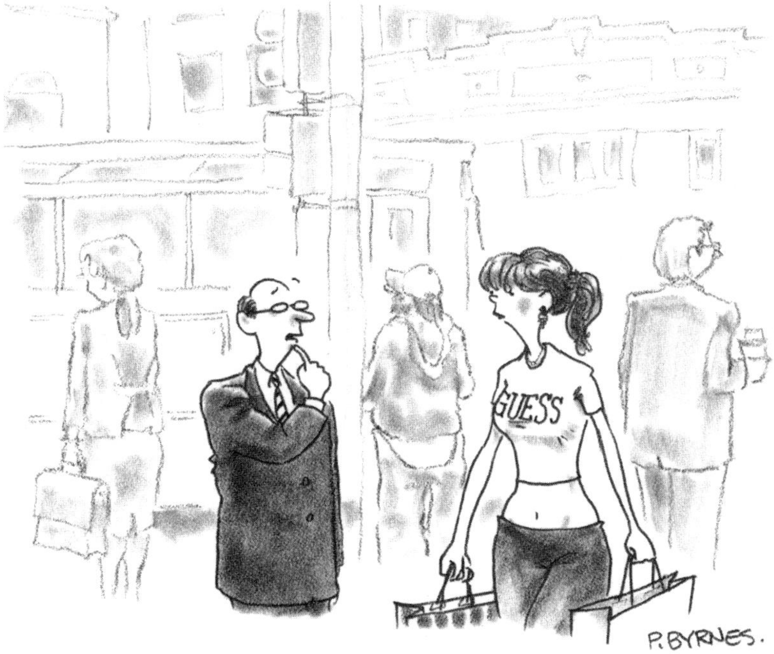
GUESS
P. BYRNES.

"34-C?"

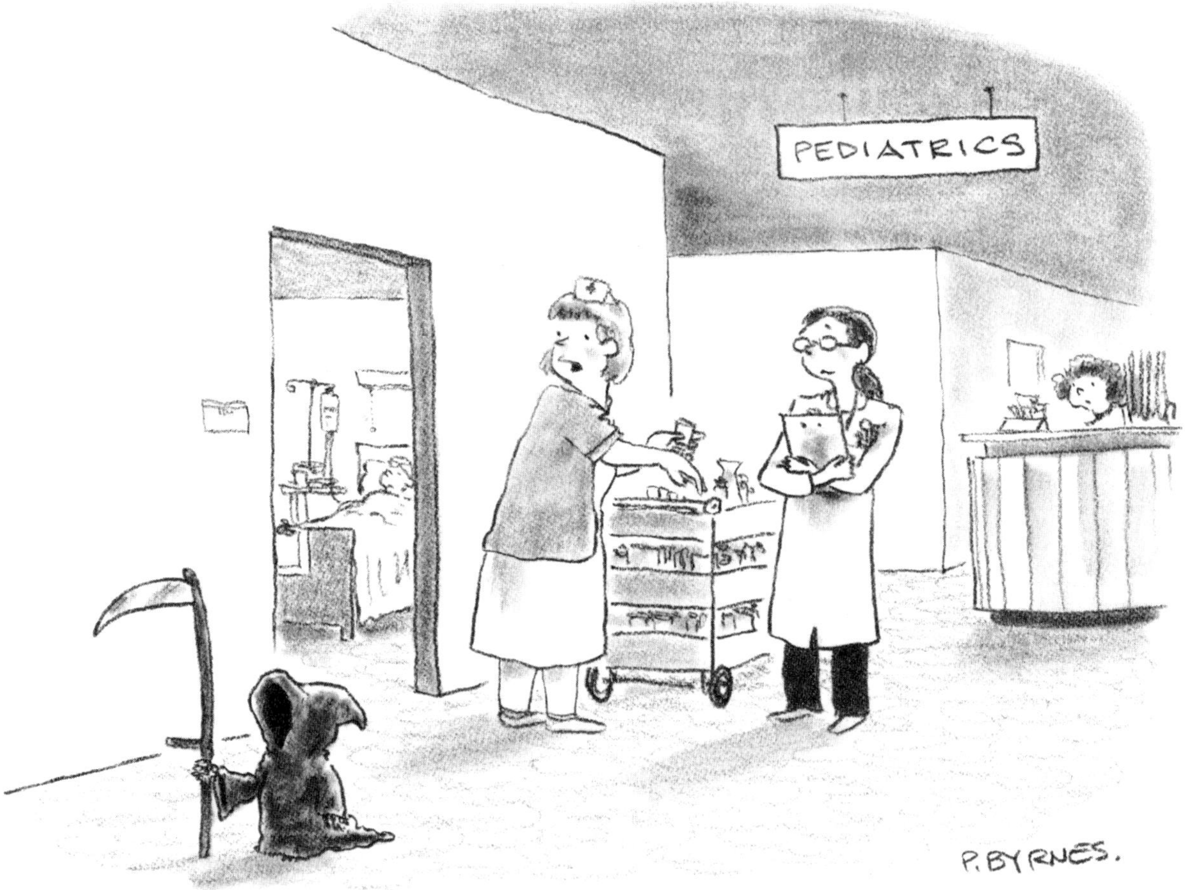
PEDIATRICS
P. BYRNES.

"It would be sad if he wasn't so damned cute."

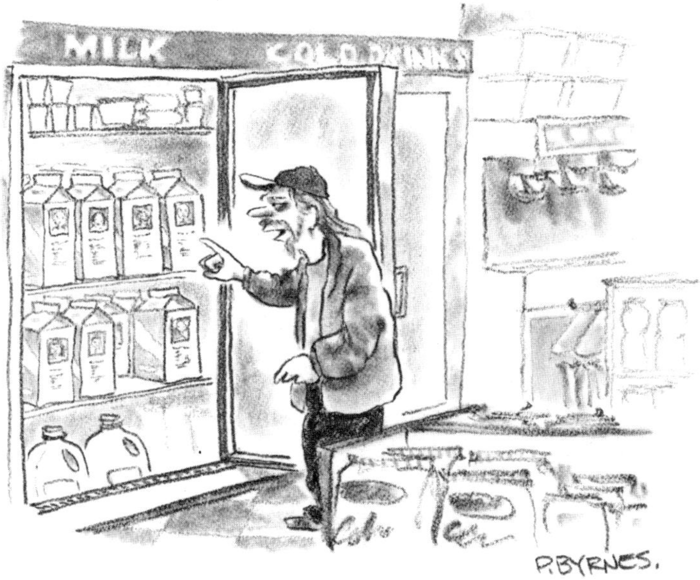
MILK
COLD DRINKS
P. BYRNES.

"Got 'im, got 'im, need 'im, need 'im . . ."

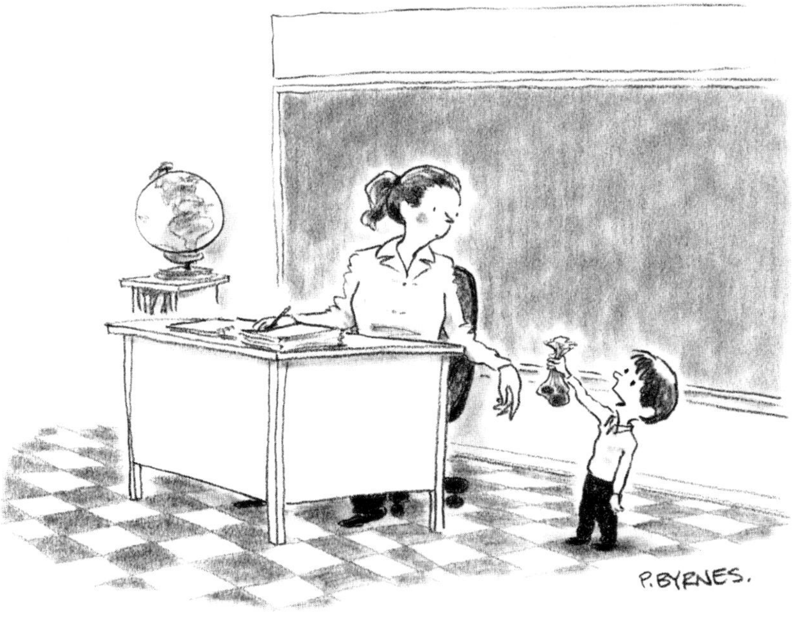
P. BYRNES.

"Remember how I said my dog ate it and you said that was no excuse?"

B. Smaller

BARBARA SMALLER

Frequently Asked Questions

Where do you get your ideas?

I'm guessing, China.

Which comes first, the picture or the caption?

The chicken.

How'd you get started?

I was at a bookstore and I came across a book called, *How to Draw Cartoons*. I didn't actually buy the book, but I did give it a thorough looking over.

I admire . . .

Bob Mankoff, of course . . . oh, and Gandhi.

How do you deal with rejection?

Hey, it just means more cartoons for me.

What are some things that make you laugh and why?

Sex and death, sometimes I think sex is the funniest, and sometimes I think it's the other way around.

I've got a great idea for a cartoon—wanna hear it?

One great idea is of no use, I need at least ten great ideas.

Infrequently Asked Questions

Have you mooned or *been* mooned more often in your life?

I am not now, and have never been a member of the Rev. Sun Myung Moon's church.

What would make a terrible pizza topping?

14.5-gauge baling wire.

What might one expect to find at a really low-budget amusement park?

Sit & Spin.

What did the shepherd say to the three-legged sheepdog?

N/A.

And Now for a Few More Questions . . .

- What do you hate drawing?

  Since I am not now, and never was, a twelve-year-old boy: cars.

- Being as accurate as possible, how many desert island cartoons do you think you've come up with and submitted to *The New Yorker*?

  4.7.

- What's the funniest thing that you witnessed, overheard, or came up with that you couldn't figure out how to use in a cartoon?

  Things that involve cars.

- If you could ask Bob Mankoff, *The New Yorker* cartoon editor, one question, what would it be?

  Why, Bob, why!?

Draw Something in This Space

. . . that will help us understand your childhood.

Naming Names

- What name might you give to a mild-mannered, slightly overweight dental assistant in one of your cartoons?

  Matt.

- Other than Lance, what name would you give to a twenty-eight-year-old metrosexual entertainment lawyer who cycles on weekends?

  Bob.

- What would be a good name for a new, commercially unviable breakfast cereal?

  Sexual Intercourse Flakes.

- Come up with a name for an unpleasant medical procedure.

  What would be the name of a *pleasant* medical procedure?

- If you used a pen name, what would it be?

  B. Larger.

Complete the Pie Chart Below

. . . in a way that tells us something about your life or how you think.

product placement
sleeping
napping
Rhubarb

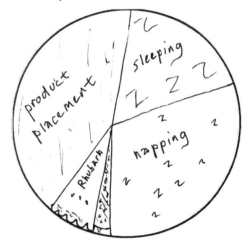

"Does it say 'I'm ovulating'?"

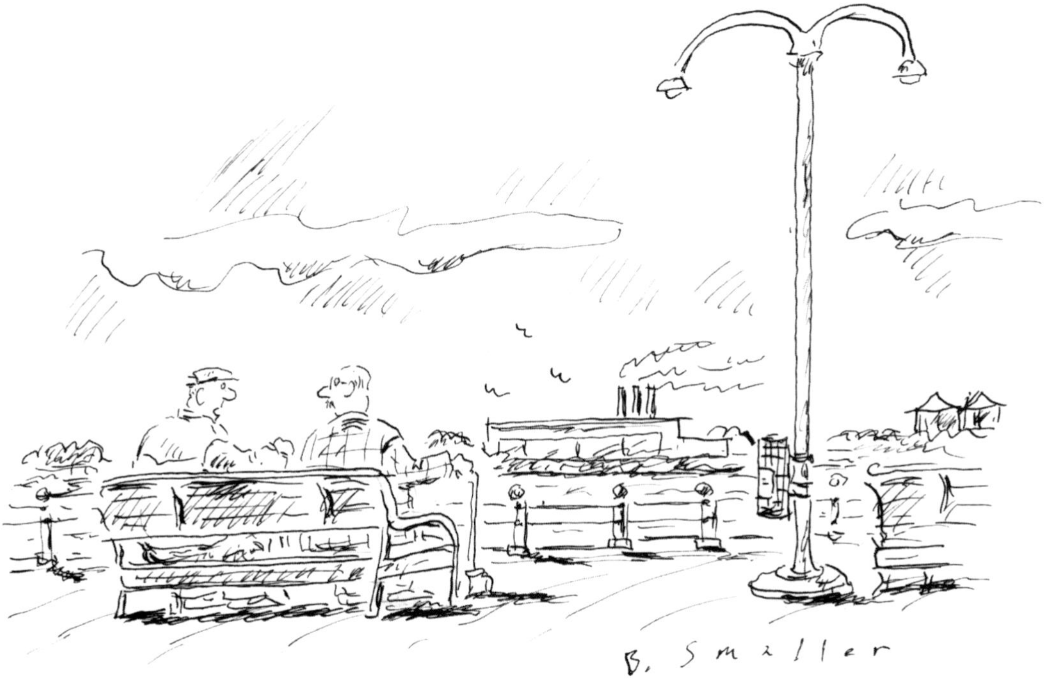
B. Smaller

"I can afford to die or I can afford to be sick, but I can't afford to be sick and then die."

"Here's a lock of your hair, your first tooth, and your placenta."

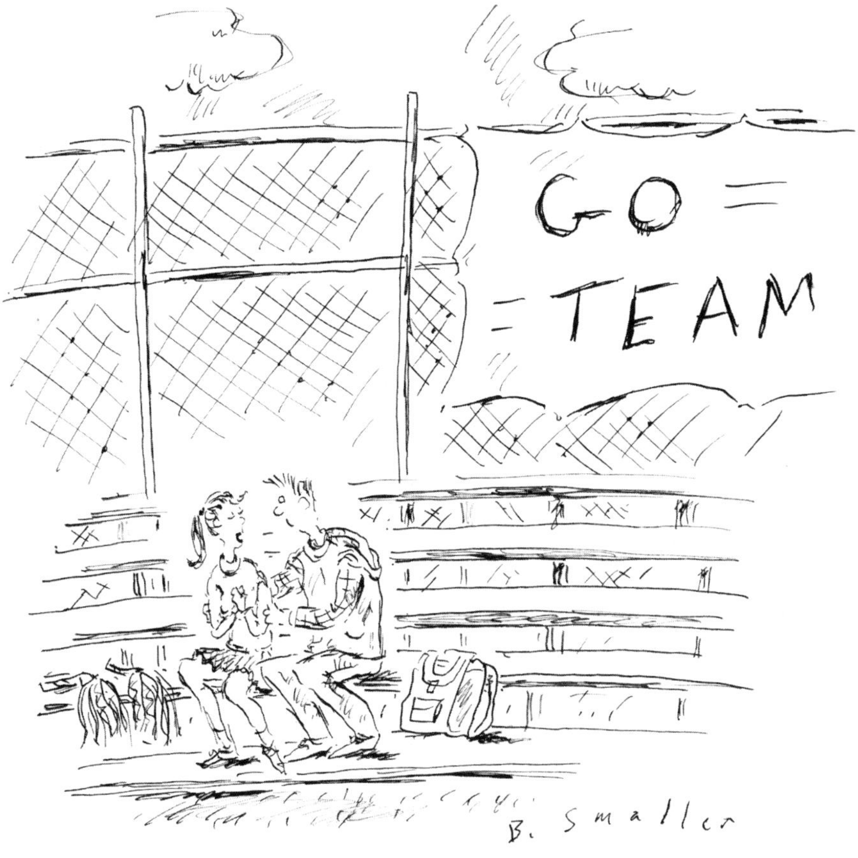
GO
TEAM
B. Smaller

"No, Justin. I'm saving myself for college."

Dd

DREW
DERNAVICH

Frequently Asked Questions

■ Where do you get your ideas?

Behind that tall, shiny-looking thingy with the knob on it, right across from you. No, not that one. The other one.

■ Which comes first, the picture or the caption?
The idea.

■ How'd you get started?
With my first idea.

■ I admire . . .

Anyone whose job it is to make decisions other than whether the word "Wednesday" is funnier than the word "Thursday."

■ How do you deal with rejection?

Denial. I bottle up my anger. Someday I will unleash it on society. I will give you a few days' notice, though.

■ What are some things that make you laugh and why?

I pretty much laugh at everything. When I was nine, my teacher told me I'd probably laugh at a grapefruit. Since then, I have
found grapefruits to be hysterically funny. Humor can, and should, be found in everything in life. If you can't find it, you're an unhealthy person. But being unhealthy is funny, so . . . can you

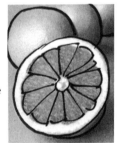

see the vicious (and humorous) cycle?

■ I've got a great idea for a cartoon—wanna hear it?

How about a beer instead?

Infrequently Asked Questions

■ Have you mooned or *been* mooned more often in your life?

After a long day of work, I love to go out and get mooned.

■ What would make a terrible pizza topping?
Nostalgia.

■ What might one expect to find at a really low-budget amusement park?

Matt Diffee, eating circus peanuts.

What did the shepherd say to the three-legged sheepdog?

I've got a great idea for a cartoon—wanna hear it?

And Now for a Few More Questions . . .

What do you hate drawing?

Shrubbery. Feet. Tiny little details.

Being as accurate as possible, how many desert island cartoons do you think you've come up with and submitted to *The New Yorker*?

14.

What's the funniest thing that you witnessed, overheard, or came up with that you couldn't figure out how to use in a cartoon?

There used to be a blind man at my subway stop who would feel for his seat by plunging his stick into everybody's crotch. His aim was painfully accurate. People were terrified. It was great theatre. I could never make it any funnier than it was.

If you could ask Bob Mankoff, *The New Yorker* cartoon editor, one question, what would it be?

Why are you interested in coming to work for me, Mr. Mankoff?

Naming Names

What name might you give to a mild-mannered, slightly overweight dental assistant in one of your cartoons?

Nacho Panza.

Other than Lance, what name would you give to a twenty-eight-year-old metrosexual entertainment lawyer who cycles on weekends?

Chad.

What would be a good name for a new, commercially unviable breakfast cereal?

Individually Wrapped Rice Krispies.

Come up with a name for an unpleasant medical procedure.

Lemon meringue. (The procedure is so painful I couldn't name it for what it really is.)

If you used a pen name, what would it be?

Marcus Chicken-stock.*

Complete the Pie Chart Below

. . . in a way that tells us something about your life or how you think.

---

with apologies to John Hodgman

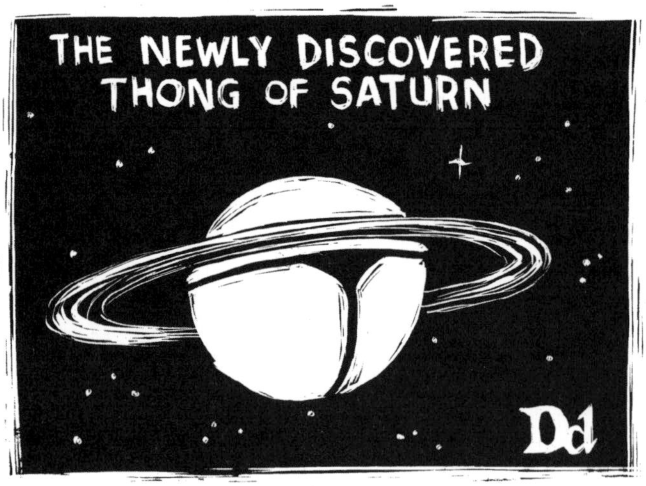
THE NEWLY DISCOVERED
THONG OF SATURN

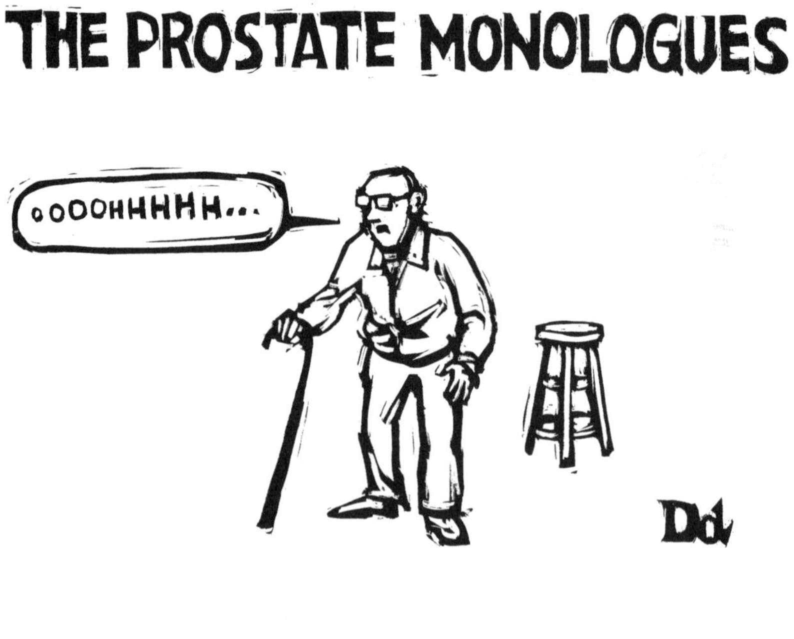
THE PROSTATE MONOLOGUES
OOOOHHHHH...

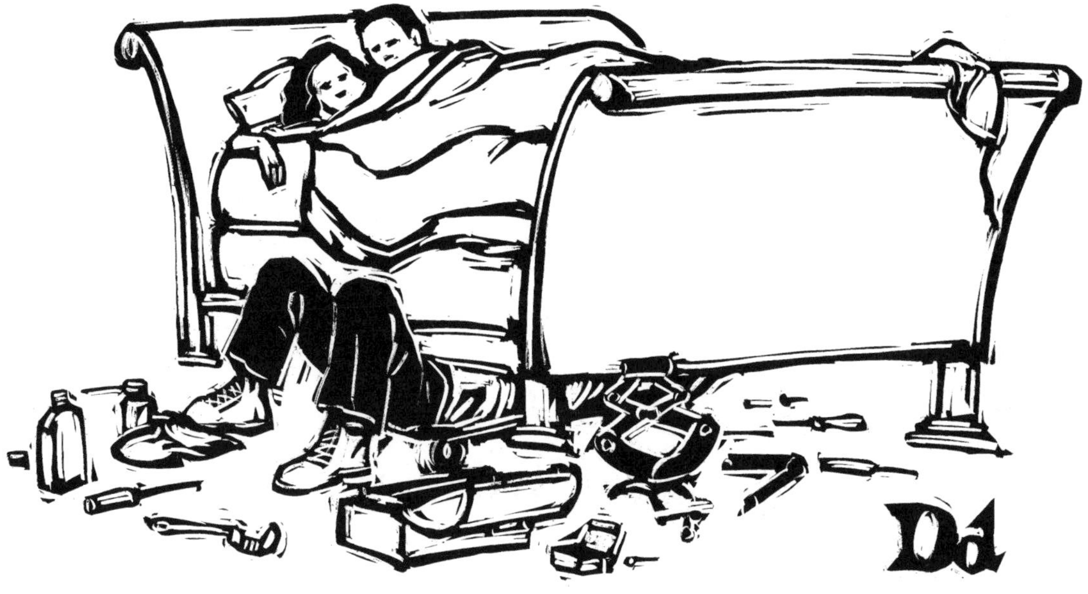
Dd

"Okay, up there, let's give 'er another try."

"Will it be just a cleaning or the full hour of sensual dentistry?"

"*I faked your New Year's resolution.*"

"*We had irreconcilable similarities.*"

*"Give a man an exam and he'll be healthy for a day;
teach a man to examine himself and he'll be healthy for a lifetime."*

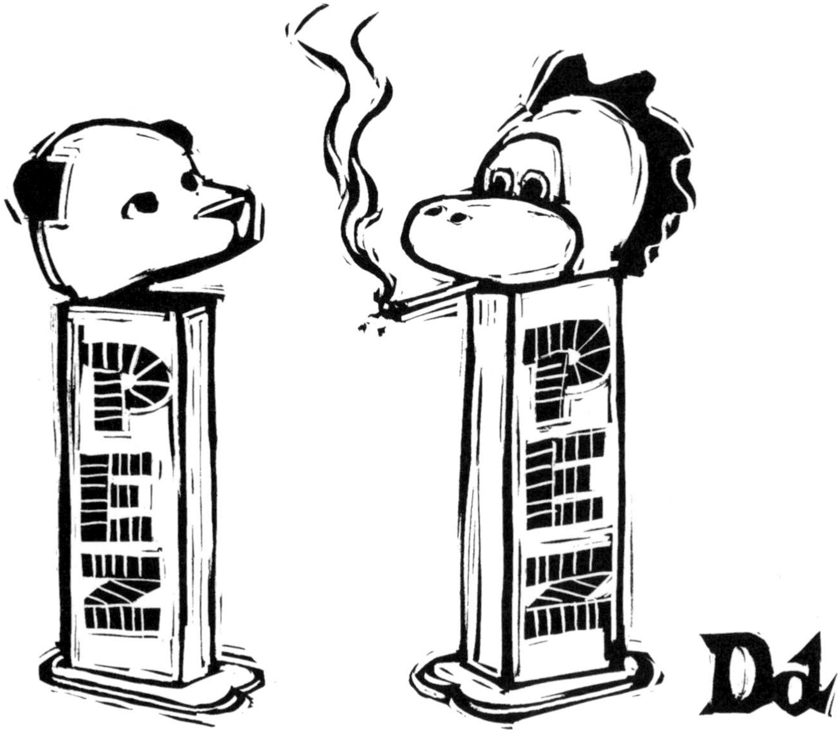
PEZ
PEZ
Dd

"Are you going to dispense candy with that mouth?"

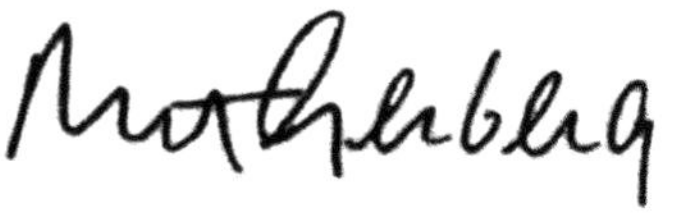

MORT GERBERG

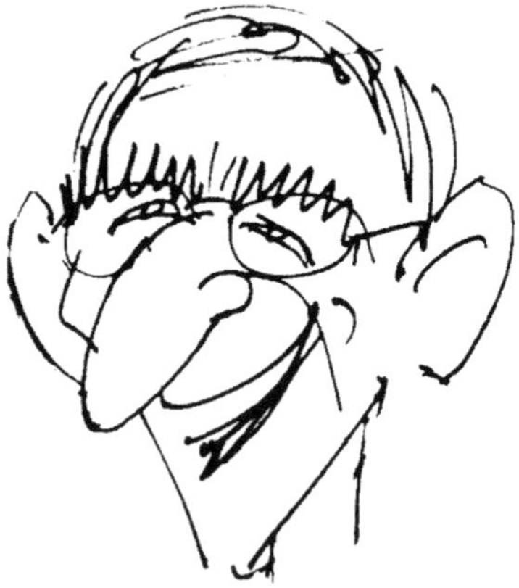

Frequently Asked Questions

- Where do you get your ideas?

I put a tooth under my pillow when I go to sleep and the next morning, when I wake up, there they *are*!

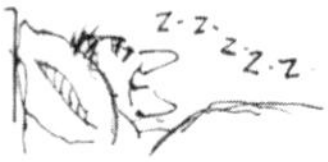

- Which comes first, the picture or the caption?

The one that's more turned on from the foreplay.

- How'd you get started?

Well, the way I understand it, first my father and mother had sex with each other . . .

- I admire . . .

People who get to be 80 so they can ski for free at Alta—and I'm very partial to great bread.

- How do you deal with rejection?

I try to remember that my wife, the career counselor, keeps telling me that I am not my work—but I keep forgetting that.

- What are some things that make you laugh and why?

I can't name them because I never know in advance what they might be—they're "things" I see or hear in any random moment, and because, like most cartoonists, my head is wired weirdly, I simply experience them as "funny."

- I've got a great idea for a cartoon—wanna hear it?

What? What? What did you say? Sorry, but my hearing aid is on the fritz and I can't . . . What? WHAT? You ate a DEER?!?

Infrequently Asked Questions

- Have you mooned or *been* mooned more often in your life?

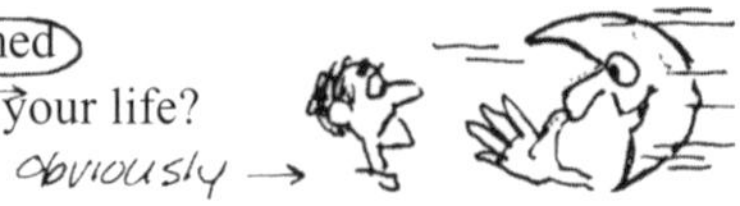
obviously →

- What would make a terrible pizza topping?

A big, fat meditating Buddhist monk.

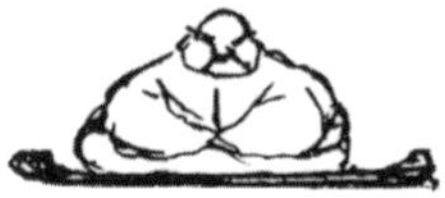

- What might one expect to find at a really low-budget amusement park?

  A flashlight-lit copy of the Gettysburg Address, with a scratchy soundtrack of "The Battle Hymn of the Republic" sung by John Ashcroft.

- What did the shepherd say to the three-legged sheepdog?

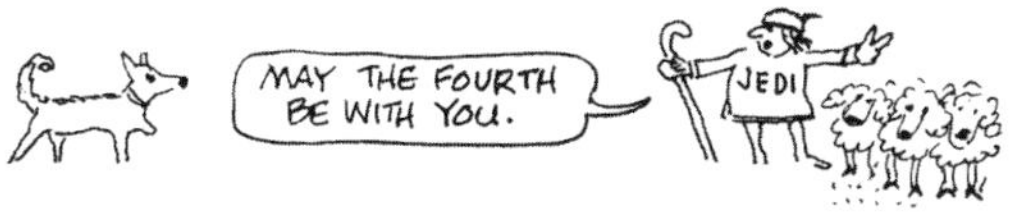
MAY THE FOURTH BE WITH YOU.
JEDI

Draw Something in This Space

. . . that will help us understand your childhood.

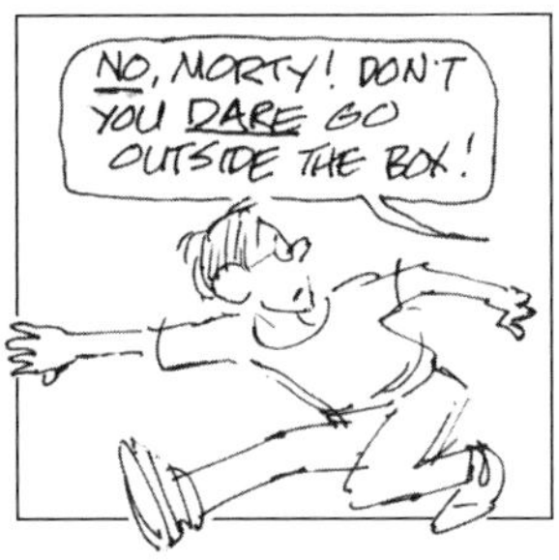
NO, MORTY! DON'T YOU DARE GO OUTSIDE THE BOX!

And Now for a Few More Questions . . .

- What do you hate drawing?

  I hate drawing attention to myself. (Hah! Now there's a laugh!)

- Being as accurate as possible, how many desert island cartoons do you think you've come up with and submitted to *The New Yorker*?

  Only four—because I ran out of little bottles to stuff the drawings in.

- What's the funniest thing that you witnessed, overheard, or came up with that you couldn't figure out how to use in a cartoon?

  George Bush's shipboard "Mission Accomplished" scene. Since it was already 100 percent pure self-satire, it was satire-proof—and I cried because I hadn't thought of the idea myself.

- If you could ask Bob Mankoff, *The New Yorker* cartoon editor, one question, what would it be?

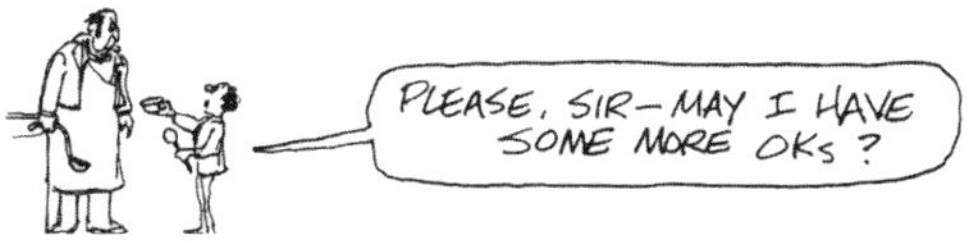
PLEASE, SIR—MAY I HAVE SOME MORE OKs?

Naming Names

- What name might you give to a mild-mannered, slightly overweight dental assistant in one of your cartoons?

  Flossie.

- Other than Lance, what name would you give to a twenty-eight-year-old metrosexual entertainment lawyer who cycles on weekends?

  Geary Wheeler.

- What would be a good name for a new, commercially unviable breakfast cereal?

  Sugar-Soaked Barf-Fart Flakes.

- Come up with a name for an unpleasant medical procedure.

  Upyouroscopy.

- If you used a pen name, what would it be?

  Monsieur Mont Blanc.

Complete the Pie Chart Below

. . . in a way that tells us something about your life or how you think.

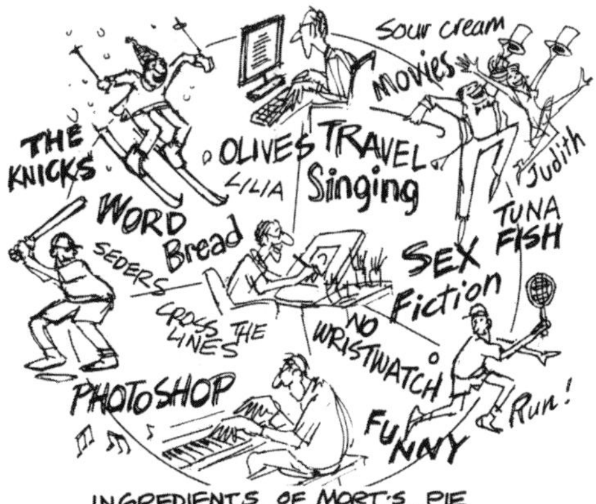
Sour cream
Movies
THE KNICKS
OLIVES
TRAVEL
Judith
LILIA
Singing
WORD
Bread
SEDERS
TUNA FISH
SEX
Fiction
CROSS THE LINES
NO WRISTWATCH
PHOTOSHOP
FUNNY
Run!

INGREDIENTS OF MORT'S PIE
(in no fixed proportion or quantity, which change every day.)

"Take a shower first. You smell like a chimney."

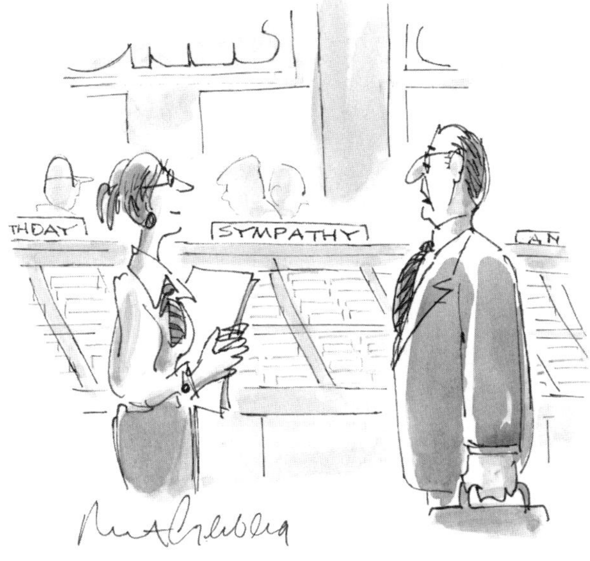
THDAY
SYMPATHY

"I'm looking for a card that says 'Sorry about the herpes.'"

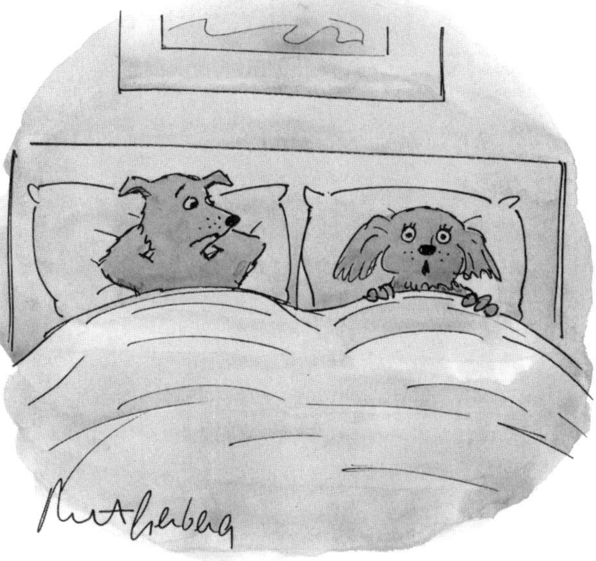

"No, no—it was great. It's just that sometime I'd like to try it missionary style."

"I <u>knew</u> it! You've been sleeping with that Rapunzel bitch!"

"I'm dating the good-looking one."

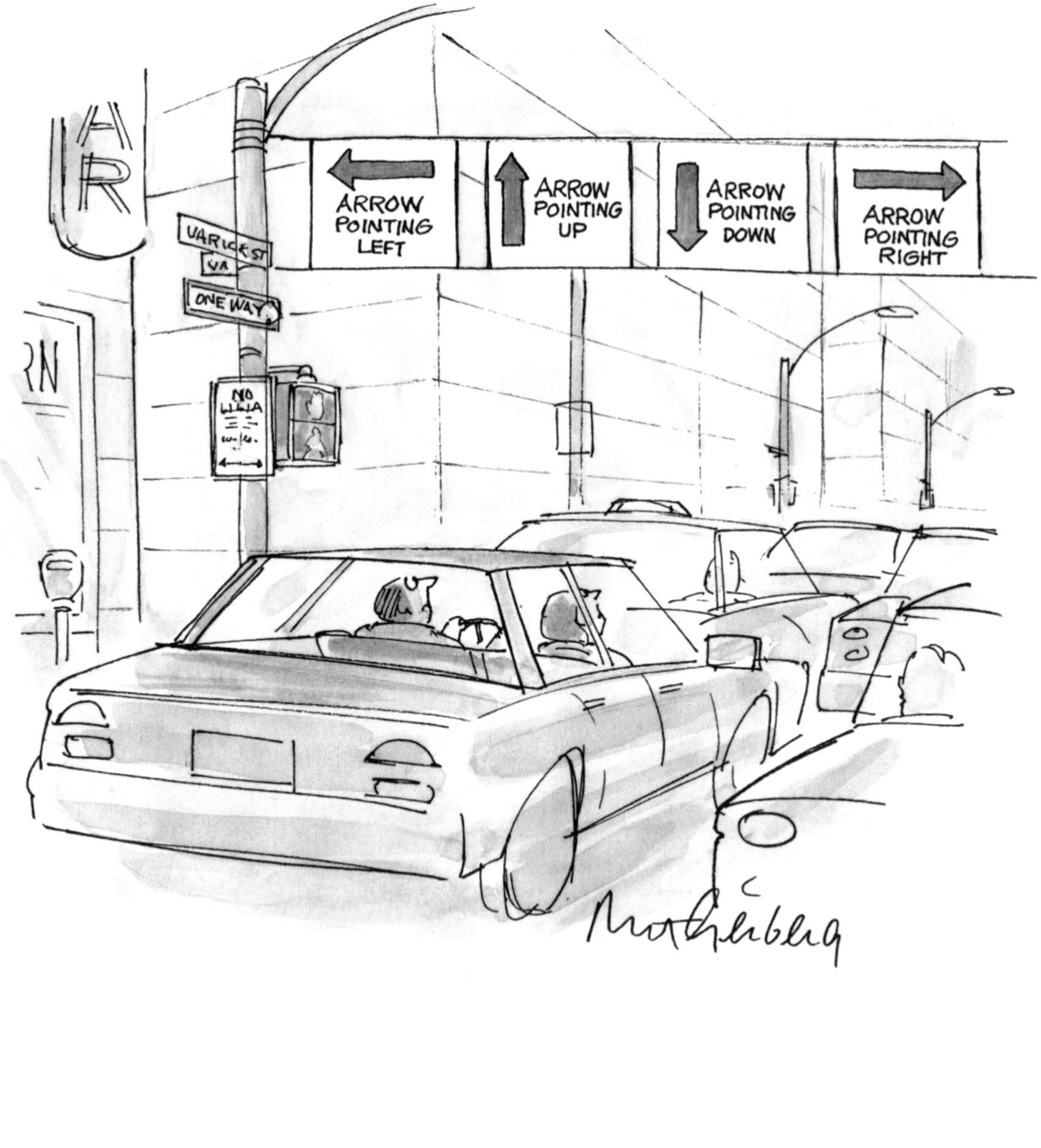
ARROW POINTING LEFT
ARROW POINTING UP
ARROW POINTING DOWN
ARROW POINTING RIGHT
VARICK ST
ONE WAY

"Lately I've had uncontrollable cravings for venison."

SUITS

JULIA SUITS

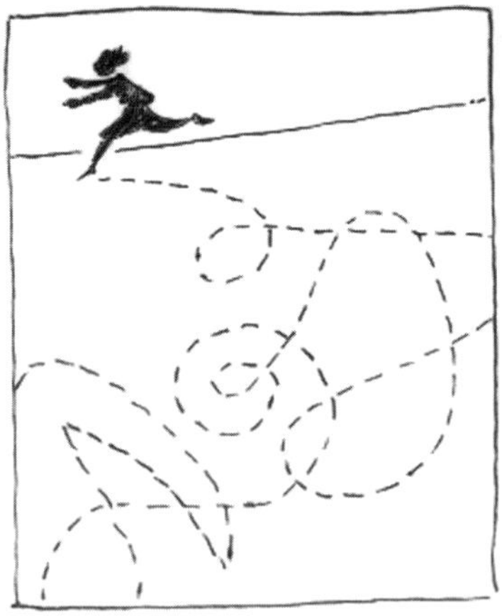

Frequently Asked Questions

- Where do you get your ideas?

  Personal experiences and observations, reading, radio, TV—in that order. Everything is stored in my head; accumulates mercilessly. Best ideas come out of NOWHERE! Fun.

- Which comes first, the picture or the caption?

  The caption, 90 percent.

- How'd you get started?

  One day I decided I wanted to draw cartoons for *The New Yorker.* So, as in tennis—where I had to hit a million balls to achieve a desired skill level—I began the task of drawing a million (actually, several hundred) cartoons.

- I admire . . .

  Mountain goats. They are not afraid of heights and they can cling to just about any surface.

- How do you deal with rejection?

  Ointment.

- What are some things that make you laugh and why?

  What: Genius comedians, guffawing babies. Why: The science or psychology behind it escapes me.

- I've got a great idea for a cartoon—wanna hear it?

  Sure! I need to practice my fake laugh.

Infrequently Asked Questions

- Have you mooned or *been* mooned more often in your life?

  Once. It was not a waxing gibbons . . . more like a gibbon in need of a waxing.

- What would make a terrible pizza topping?

  A manhole cover.

- What might one expect to find at a really low-budget amusement park?

  A higher percentage of safety violations.

- What did the shepherd say to the three-legged sheepdog?

  Nothing. The three-legged dog and the

shepherd lived in different parts of the world: the dog in Canton, Ohio. The shepherd in Béziers, France.

Draw Some Sort of Doodle

. . . using the random lines below as a starting point.

Someone holding a toy car
while smoking a pipe.

And Now for a Few More Questions . . .

- What do you hate drawing?

  Auditoriums or places with a lot of seating and/or crowds of people.

- Being as accurate as possible, how many desert island cartoons do you think you've come up with and submitted to *The New Yorker*?

  25.

- What's the ~~funniest~~ weird, pathetic, horrific thing that you witnessed, overheard, or came up with that you couldn't figure out how to use in a cartoon?

  I once "borrowed" $20 from a corpse.

- If you could ask Bob Mankoff, *The New Yorker* cartoon editor, one question, what would it be?

  Why dots?

Naming Names

- What name might you give to a mild-mannered, slightly overweight dental assistant in one of your cartoons?

  Colleen, Yvonne, Lynette, Latrineesha, Pegotty.

- Other than Lance, what name would you give to a twenty-eight-year-old metrosexual entertainment lawyer who cycles on weekends?

  Travis, Damian, Ethan, Owen.

- What would be a good name for a new, commercially unviable breakfast cereal?

  DingleberriO's or Now Wheatier Wheaties.

- Come up with a name for an unpleasant medical procedure.

  Nipplectomy.

- If you used a pen name, what would it be?

  Beva Lebourveau.

Complete the Pie Chart Below

. . . in a way that tells us something about your life or how you think.

THINGS I CAN SEE RIGHT NOW WHILE SITTING AT MY DESK.
WILD TURKEYS in yard
MY SONS READING THE PAPER
CAST IRON
TAPE DIS PEN SER
COFFEE CUP
circa 1937
NEVER

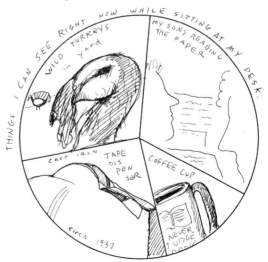

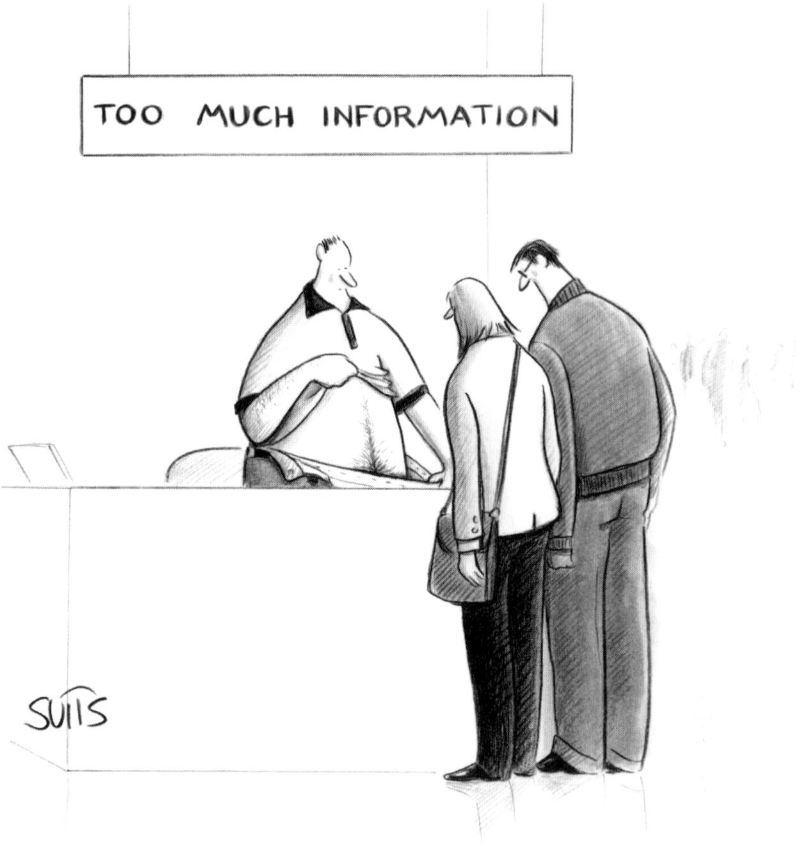
TOO MUCH INFORMATION
SUITS

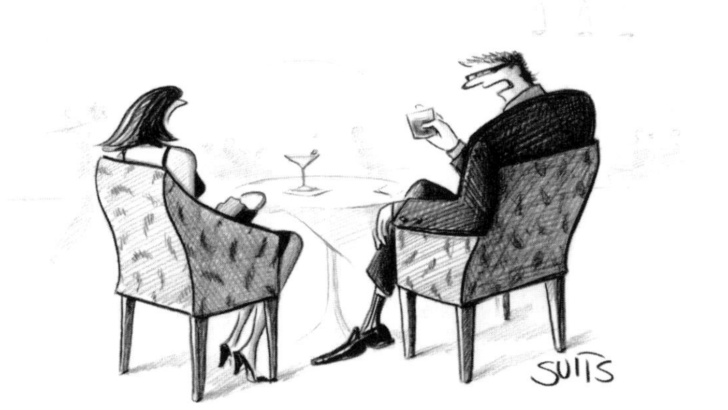
SUITS

"Enough about my penis. What's new with the ol' vagina?"

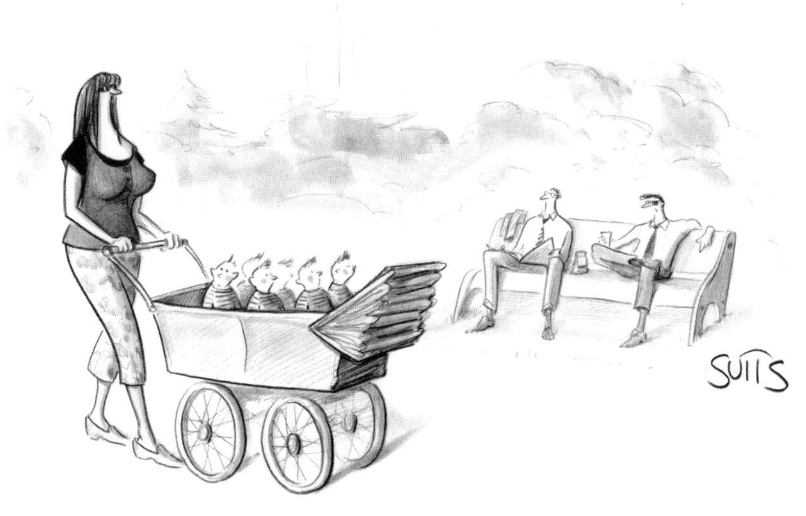
SUITS

"Check those babies out."

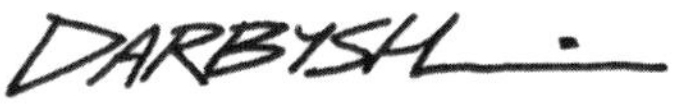

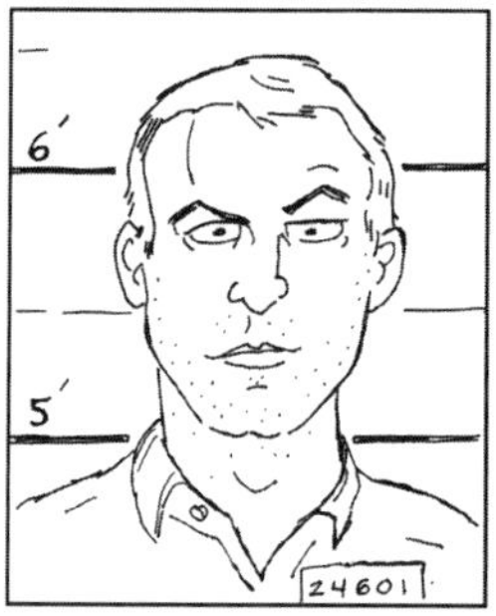
6'
5'
24601

C. COVERT DARBYSHIRE

Frequently Asked Questions

- Where do you get your ideas?

  I rework Drew Dernavich and Matt Diffee's rejects.

- Which comes first, the picture or the caption?

  1) egg
  2) caption
  3) Google images
  4) rubber glove
  5) chicken
  6) picture

- How'd you get started?

  Photos of Mankoff.

- I admire . . .

  The work of Charles Schulz (*Peanuts*), Gary Larson (*The Far Side*), Matt Groening (*Life in Hell*), and the cartoonists at *The New Yorker* who continually crank out great work—like Jack Ziegler.

- How do you deal with rejection?

  First, shock, then denial, followed by anger, confusion, depression, and eventually, through self-medication, acceptance.

- What are some things that make you laugh and why?

  Will Ferrell—funniest man alive, *Seinfeld* reruns, the movie *Rushmore,* any movie by Pixar, *America's Funniest Home Videos,* Conan O'Brien, my kids, other cartoonists.

- I've got a great idea for a cartoon—wanna hear it?

  Hold that thought. . . .

Infrequently Asked Questions

- Have you mooned or *been* mooned more often in your life?

  Been. I used to train baboons in Nairobi.

- What would make a terrible pizza topping?

  Gravy.

- What might one expect to find at a really low-budget amusement park?

  People being mauled by lions.

- What did the shepherd say to the three-legged sheepdog?

  How was the amusement park?

Draw Something in This Space

. . . that will help us understand your childhood.

GAS

And Now for a Few More Questions . . .

- What do you hate drawing?

  Fudge (with nuts).

- Being as accurate as possible, how many desert island cartoons do you think you've come up with and submitted to *The New Yorker*?

  36.37, if you count this one.

- What's the funniest thing that you witnessed, overheard, or came up with that you couldn't figure out how to use in a cartoon?

  A car dealership where each car, in addition to a spare tire, comes with a German midget mechanic in a case—in the back, next to the tire.

- If you could ask Bob Mankoff, *The New Yorker* cartoon editor, one question, what would it be?

  Could you please stop hitting on my wife?

Naming Names

- What name might you give to a mild-mannered, slightly overweight dental assistant in one of your cartoons?

  Wendall.

- Other than Lance, what name would you give to a twenty-eight-year-old metrosexual entertainment lawyer who cycles on weekends?

  Dexter.

- What would be a good name for a new, commercially unviable breakfast cereal?

  Bowel Movers.

- Come up with a name for an unpleasant medical procedure.

  Johnsonectomy.

- If you used a pen name, what would it be?

  Dexter Wendallston.

Complete the Pie Chart Below

. . . in a way that tells us something about your life or how you think.

REASONS WHY I SHOULD HAVE AN IPOD BUT DON'T.
NUMBER OF PEOPLE STARVING IN AFRICA WITH NO IPOD.
NUMBER OF SONGS I'D TOTALLY PUT ON MY IPOD IF I WERE GOING TO AFRICA.
BONO.

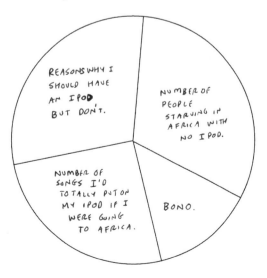

"Sure, it was a sweet gig, but I'm a carnivore for Pete's sake."

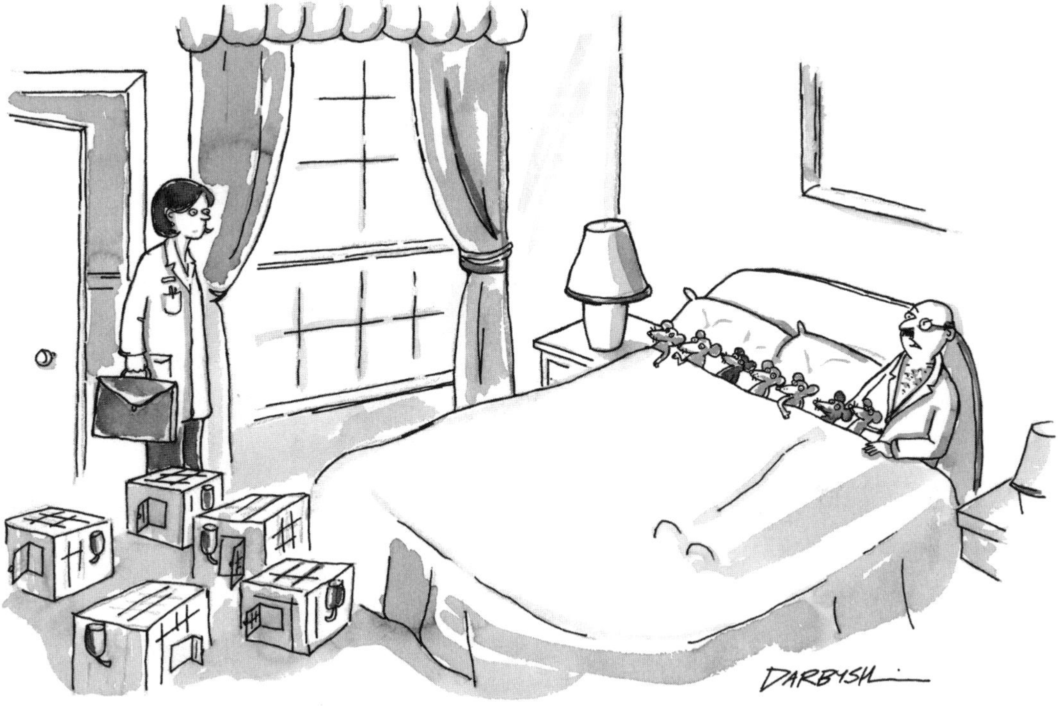
DARBYSH

"Yes, it's exactly what it looks like, and no, I don't know where this leaves us and our research."

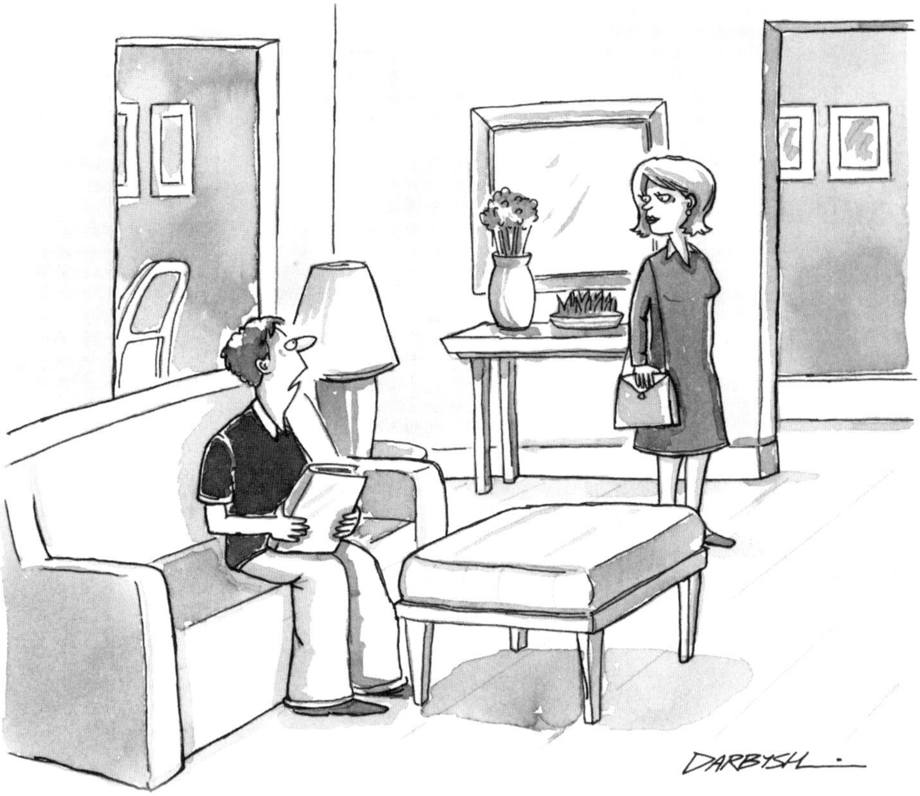
DARBYSH

"I was just flippin' through your yearbook and couldn't help noticing that you used to be a dude."

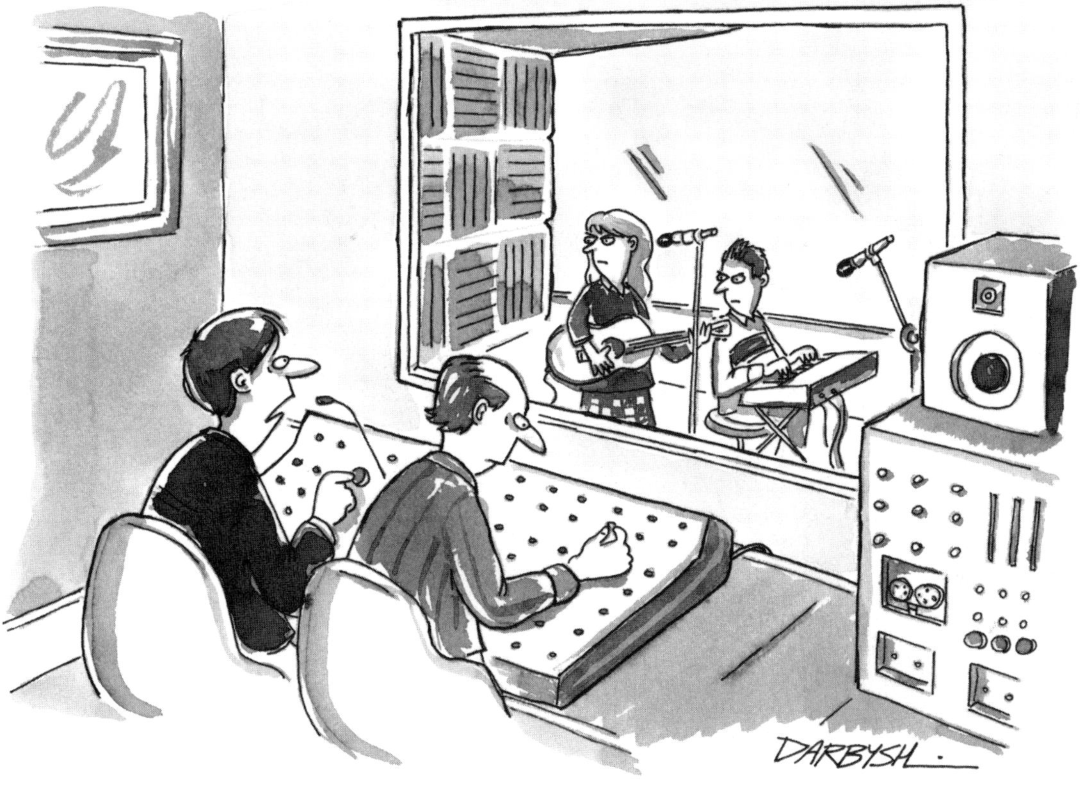
DARBYSH.

"That was nice—but this time with a little more of that Canadian angst."

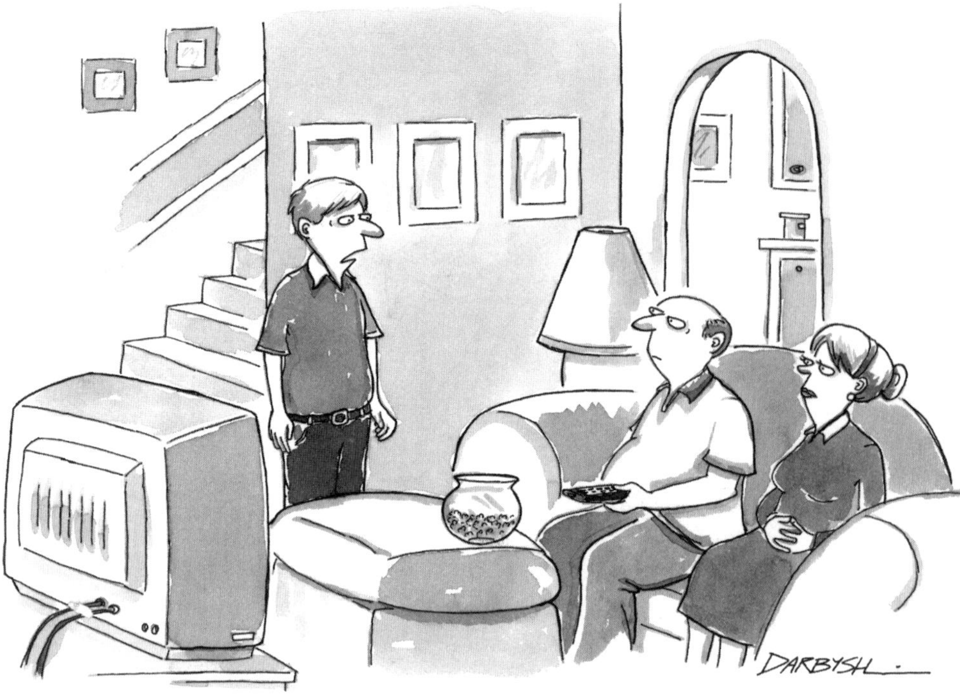
DARBYSH

"Mom, Dad, as you both know, I collect vintage dolls and listen to Cher regularly and without irony. I work as a perfume consultant at Bloomingdale's and am currently working on getting a degree in massage therapy. I own four glitter wigs, I use the word 'fabulous' way too much, and I, of course, love a cabaret. I also have a tattoo on the inside of my left ankle that says 'Ronald Forever,' who happens to be my quote unquote roommate going on five and a half years. . . . Oh, and I'm currently wearing stilettos. Stop me if you know where I'm going with this. . . ."

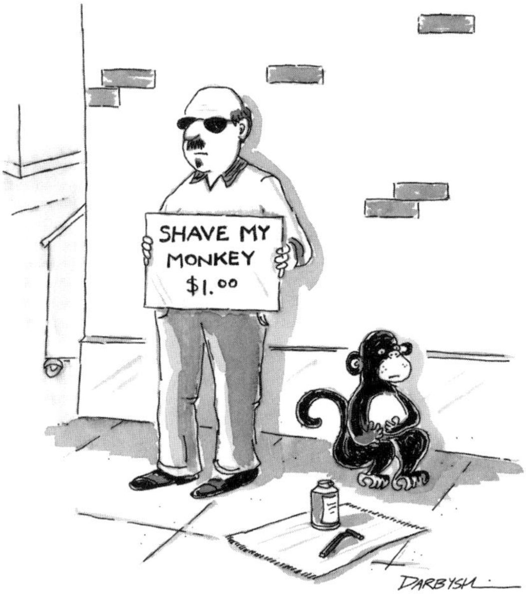
SHAVE MY
MONKEY
$1.00
DARBYSH

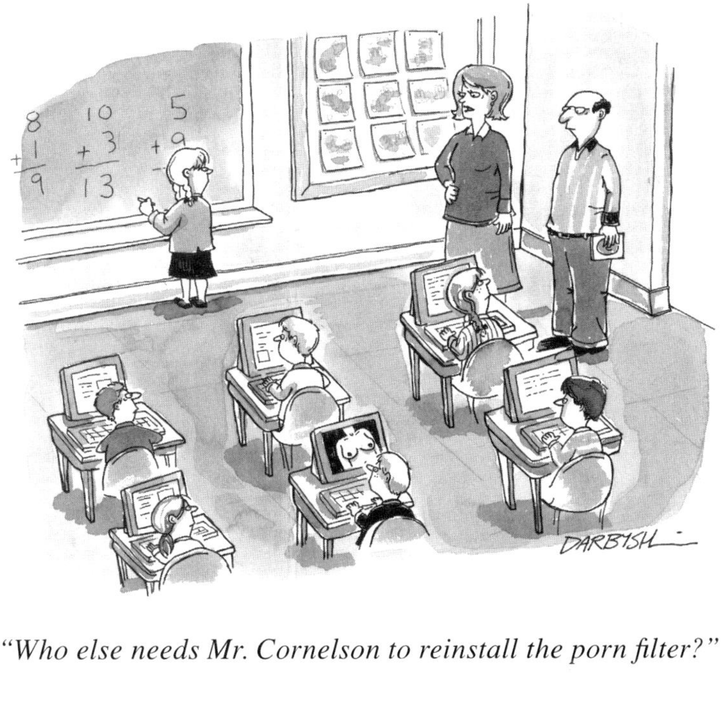
8
+1
9
10
+3
13
5
+9
DARBYSH

"Who else needs Mr. Cornelson to reinstall the porn filter?"

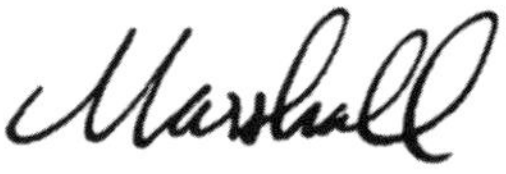
Marshall

MARSHALL HOPKINS

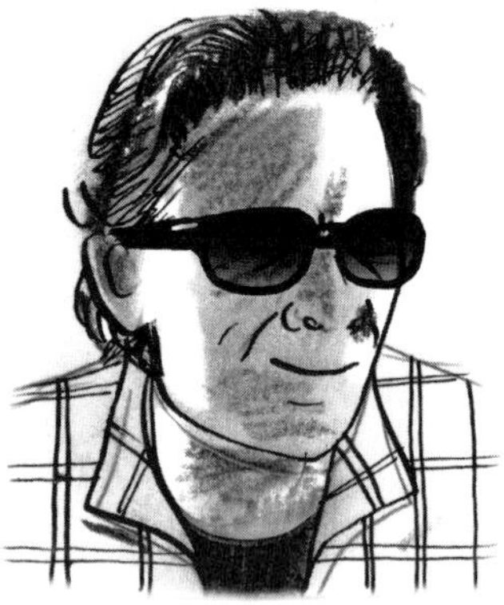

Frequently Asked Questions

- Where do you get your ideas?
  50 percent Dead Cartoonists.
  50 percent Thin Air.

- Which comes first, the picture or the caption?
  The picture usually comes first, and then I attach the caption with glue and a large mallet.

- How'd you get started?
  Coffee.

- I admire . . .
  Stanley Tucci.

- How do you deal with rejection?
  I buy another self-help audiobook.

- What are some things that make you laugh and why?
  A good fake accent, because they're like magic. That person shouldn't sound like that, but somehow they do.

- I've got a great idea for a cartoon—wanna hear it?
  Absolutely, just sign right here.

Infrequently Asked Questions

- Have you mooned or *been* mooned more often in your life?
  Been mooned, I guess.

- What would make a terrible pizza topping?
  Liquid helium.

- What might one expect to find at a really low-budget amusement park?
  Tetanus.

- What did the shepherd say to the three-legged sheepdog?
  Let us know what happens on *General Hospital.*

And Now for a Few More Questions . . .

- What do you hate drawing?
  That Calvin peeing from *Calvin & Hobbes.*

- Being as accurate as possible, how many desert island cartoons do you think you've come up with and submitted to *The New Yorker*?
  Around 20 to 25.

- What's the funniest thing that you witnessed, overheard, or came up with that you couldn't figure out how to use in a cartoon?

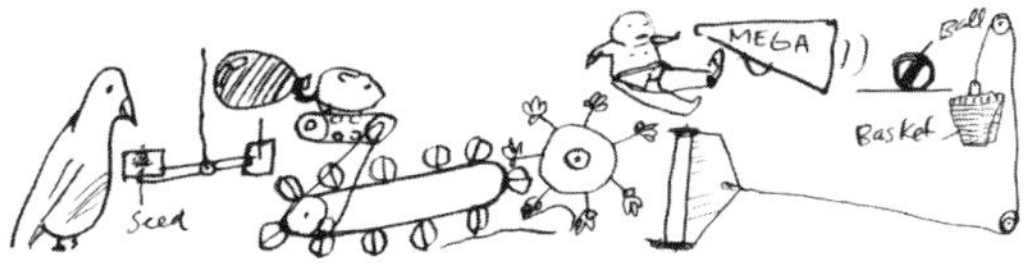
MEGA
Basket
Seed

- If you could ask Bob Mankoff, *The New Yorker* cartoon editor, one question, what would it be?

  Is "never" good for you?

Draw Some Sort of Doodle

... using the random lines below as a starting point.

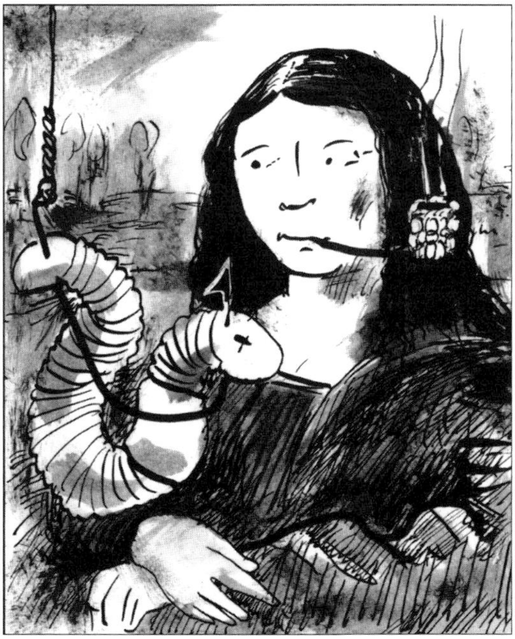

Naming Names

- What name might you give to a mild-mannered, slightly overweight dental assistant in one of your cartoons?

  Hopkins.

- Other than Lance, what name would you give to a twenty-eight-year-old metrosexual entertainment lawyer who cycles on weekends?

  Hillary Clinton.

- What would be a good name for a new, commercially unviable breakfast cereal?

  Coco Meth.

- Come up with a name for an unpleasant medical procedure.

  Buttectomy.

- If you used a pen name, what would it be?

  George Booth.

Complete the Pie Chart Below

... in a way that tells us something about your life or how you think.

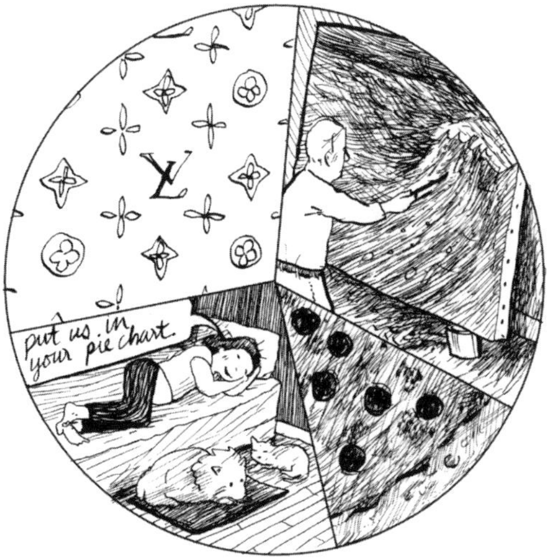
put us in your pie chart.

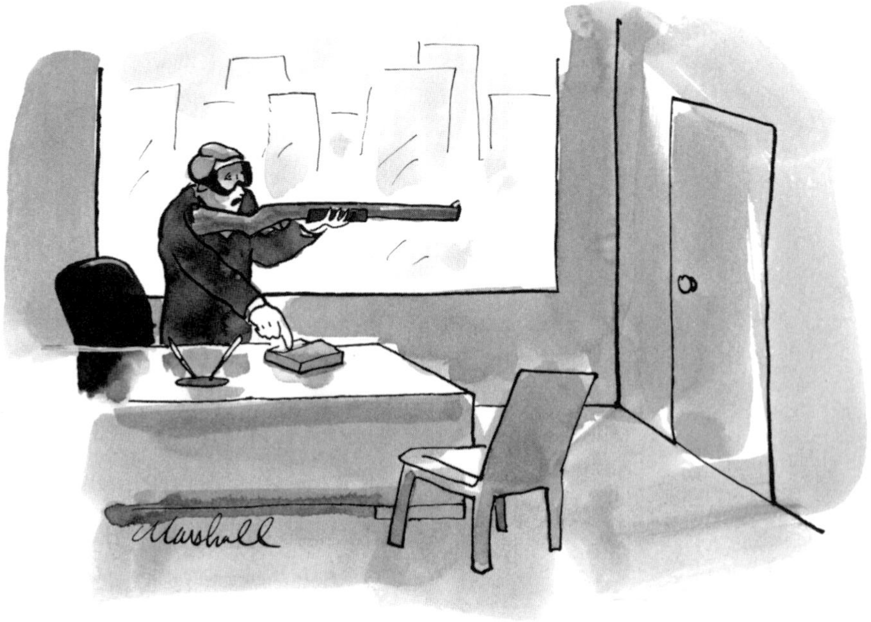
Marshall

"Pull."

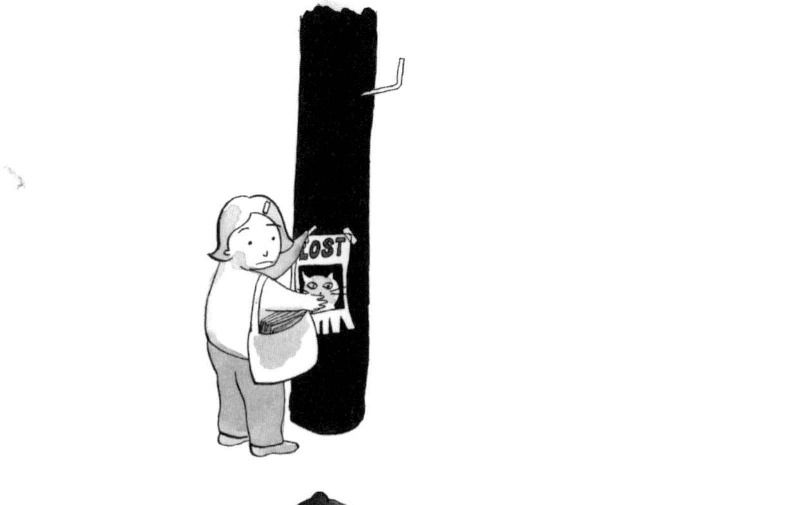
LOST
Marshall

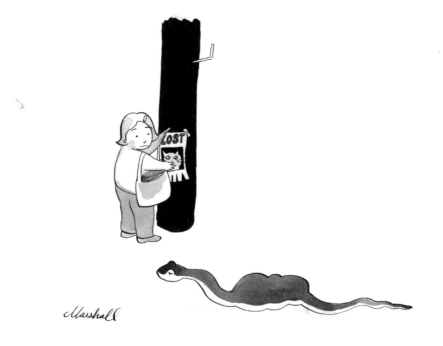

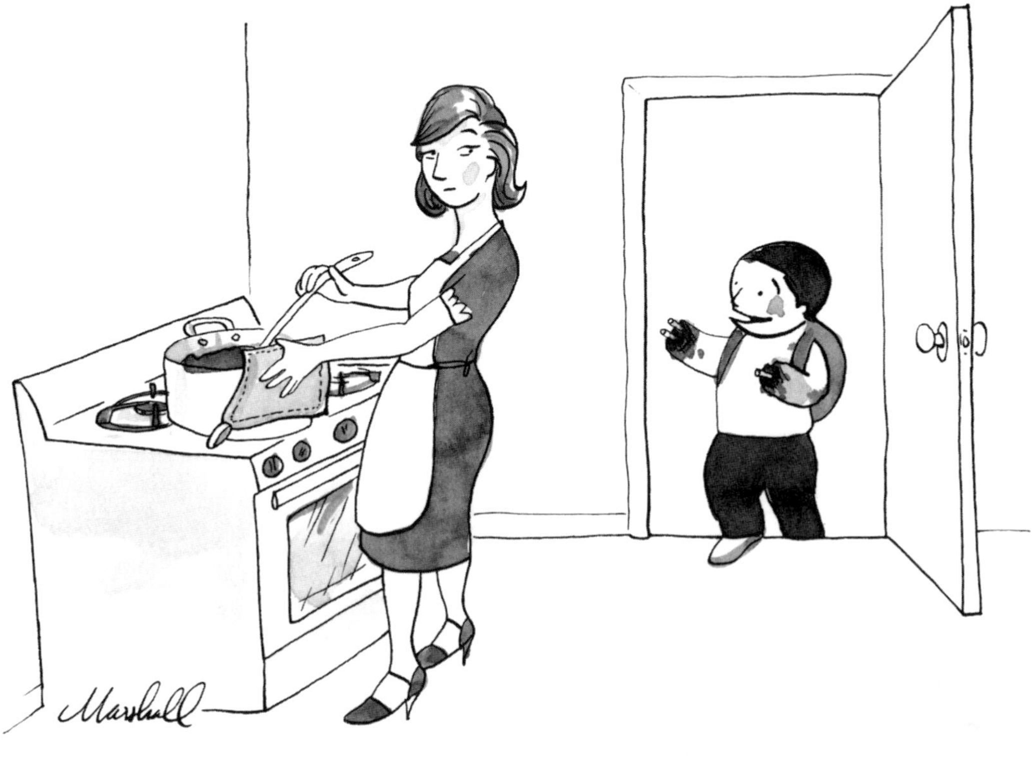
Marshall

"Look, Ma."

John O'Brien

JOHN
O'BRIEN

Frequently Asked Questions

■ Where do you get your ideas?

■ Which comes first, the picture or the caption?

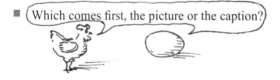

■ How'd you get started?

■ I admire . . .

Pranksters, wiseguys, and cheapshot artists.

■ How do you deal with rejection?

I put my ATM card back in the slot with the black stripe facing down and to the right . . . then I repeat the process.

■ What are some things that make you laugh and why?

**The absurd, vaudeville skits, the sophomoric, other peoples' misfortunes.
Why? Come on!**

■ I've got a great idea for a cartoon—wanna hear it?

Infrequently Asked Questions

■ Have you mooned or *been* mooned more

often in your life?

■ What would make a terrible pizza topping?

The unwashed hands of a restaurant employee returning from the restroom?

■ What might one expect to find at a really low-budget amusement park?

Dangling keys.

■ What did the shepherd say to the three-legged sheepdog?

HERE, PIANO!

And Now for a Few More Questions . . .

■ What do you hate drawing?

If I knew I'd have to shoot myself.

■ Being as accurate as possible, how many desert island cartoons do you think you've come up with and submitted to *The New Yorker*?

Many, but I'm not sure if the bottles washed up in Manhattan yet.

■ What's the funniest thing that you witnessed, overheard, or came up with that you couldn't figure out how to use in a cartoon?

HMMM! LET ME THINK OUT LOUD
Oooo

■ If you could ask Bob Mankoff, *The New Yorker* cartoon editor, one question, what would it be?

What was wrong with that idea, eleventh from the bottom of that batch I sent on February 15, 2002?

Naming Names

■ What name might you give to a mild-mannered, slightly overweight dental assistant in one of your cartoons?

Hugh Brushmore, Perry Donis, Ginger Vitus, Kay Nines, E. Namel, X. Traction, N. Cisors, D. Kaye . . . ok, ok, I'll stop.

■ Other than Lance, what name would you give to a twenty-eight-year-old metrosexual entertainment lawyer who cycles on weekends?

Any name I feel like calling him, and he'll thank me for it while I'm dating his girlfriend.

■ What would be a good name for a new, commercially unviable breakfast cereal?

CAVITY CHEX

■ Come up with a name for an unpleasant medical procedure.

The-doctor-has-to-catch-a-flight-to-Miami-so-we're-rescheduling-you-for-next-Monday-sorry-about-the-seven-hour-wait-ectomy.

■ If you used a pen name, what would it be?

I'm still waiting for the test results but if it's a boy I'll call it Bic and if it's a girl I'll probably call it Koh-i-noor.

Complete the Pie Chart Below

. . . in a way that tells us something about your life or how you think.

VIEW THIS WAY

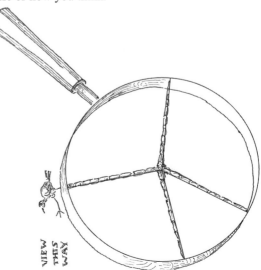

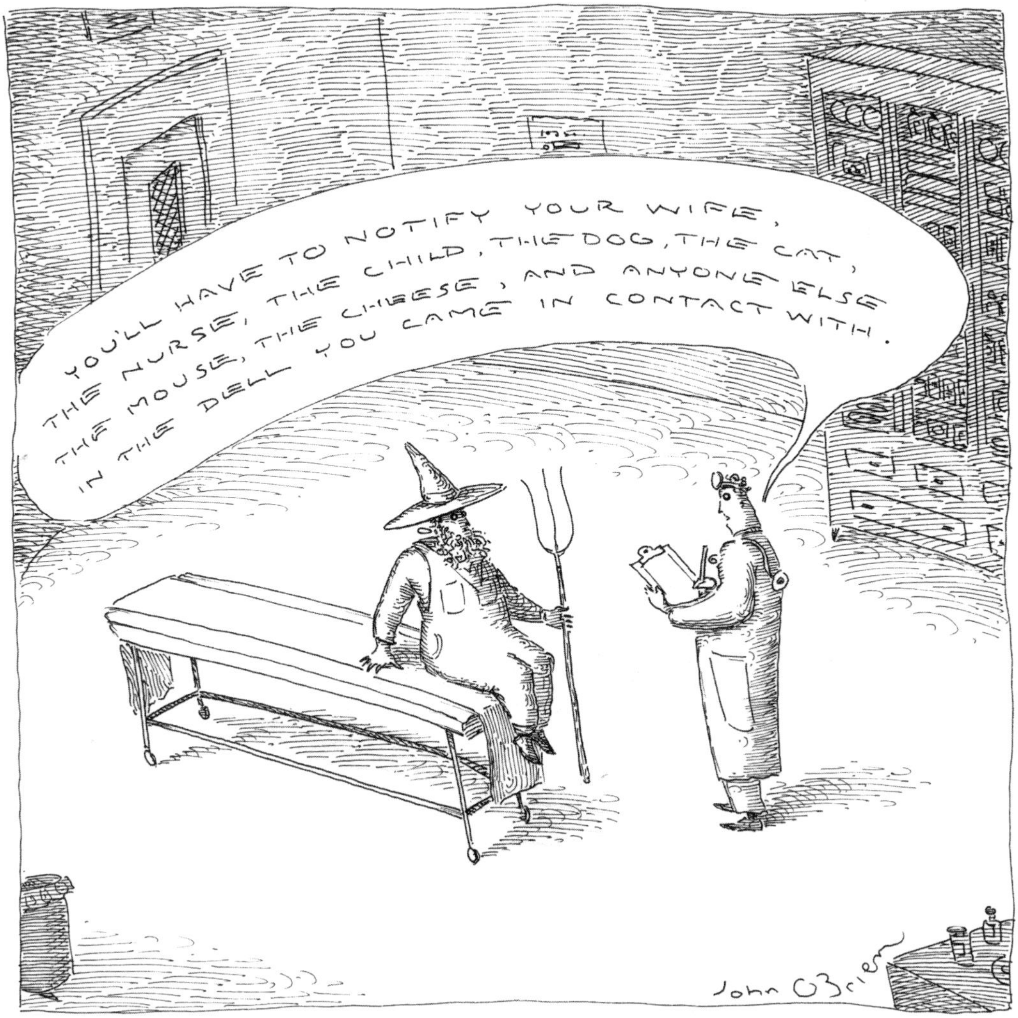
YOU'LL HAVE TO NOTIFY YOUR WIFE, THE NURSE, THE CHILD, THE DOG, THE CAT, THE MOUSE, THE CHEESE, AND ANYONE ELSE IN THE DELL YOU CAME IN CONTACT WITH.
John O'Brien

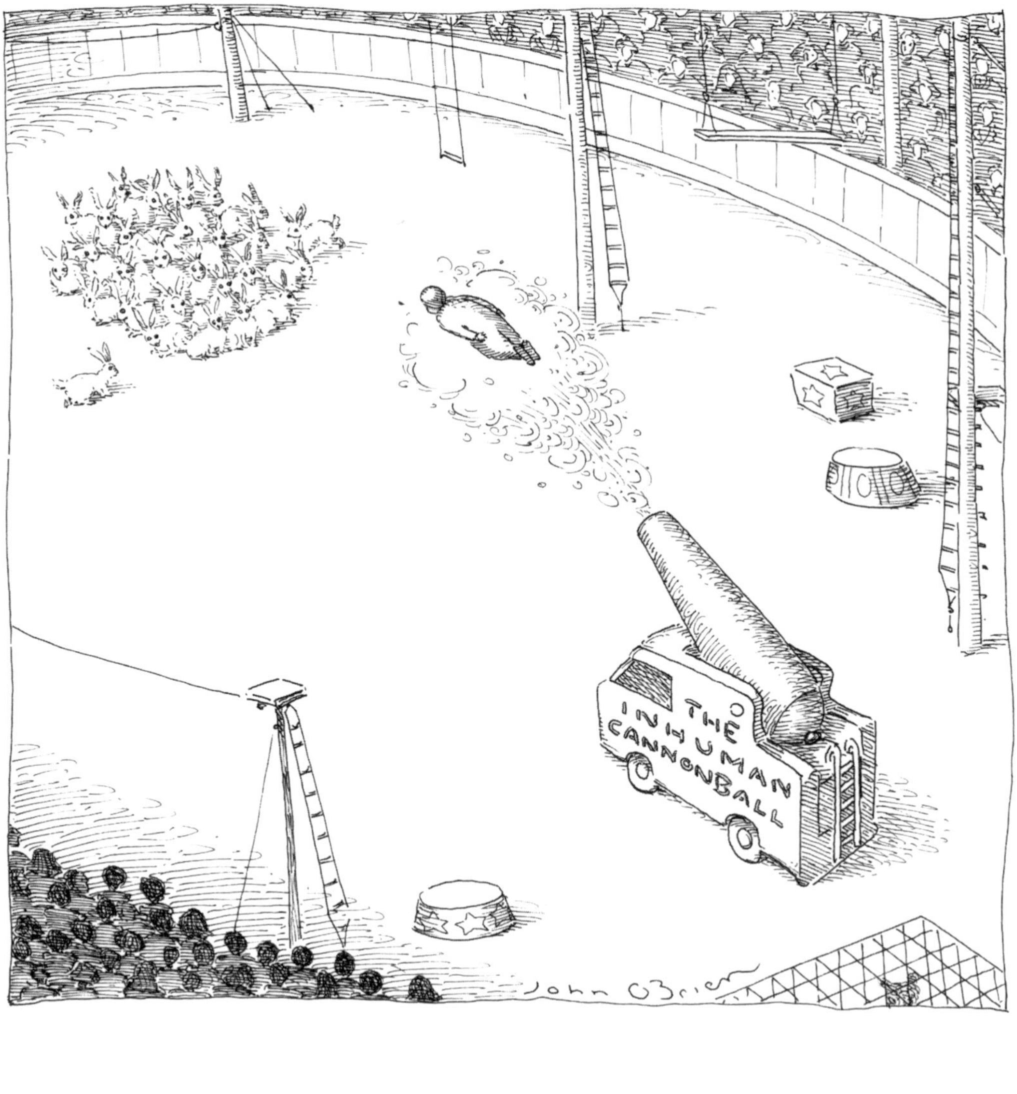
THE
INHUMAN
CANNONBALL
John O'Brien

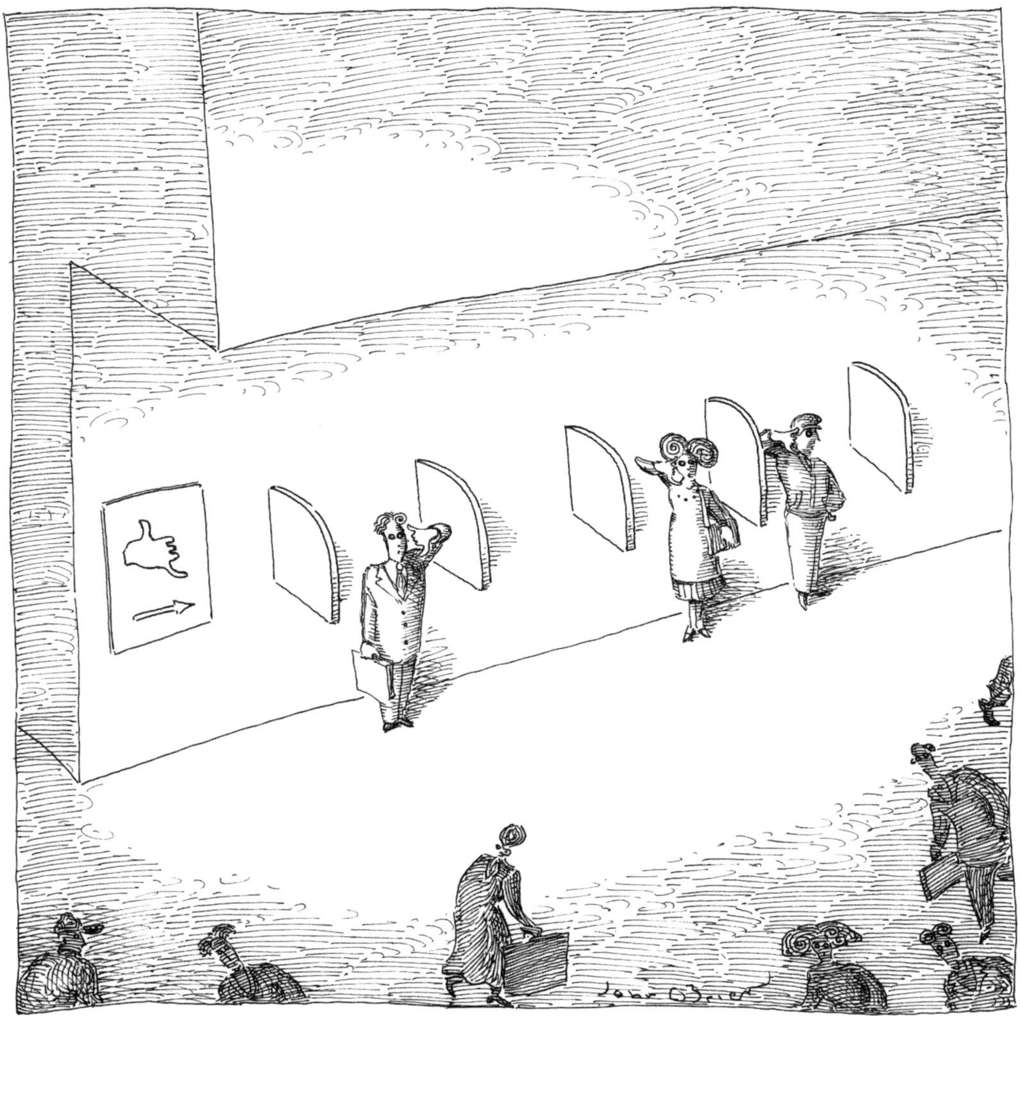
John O'Brien

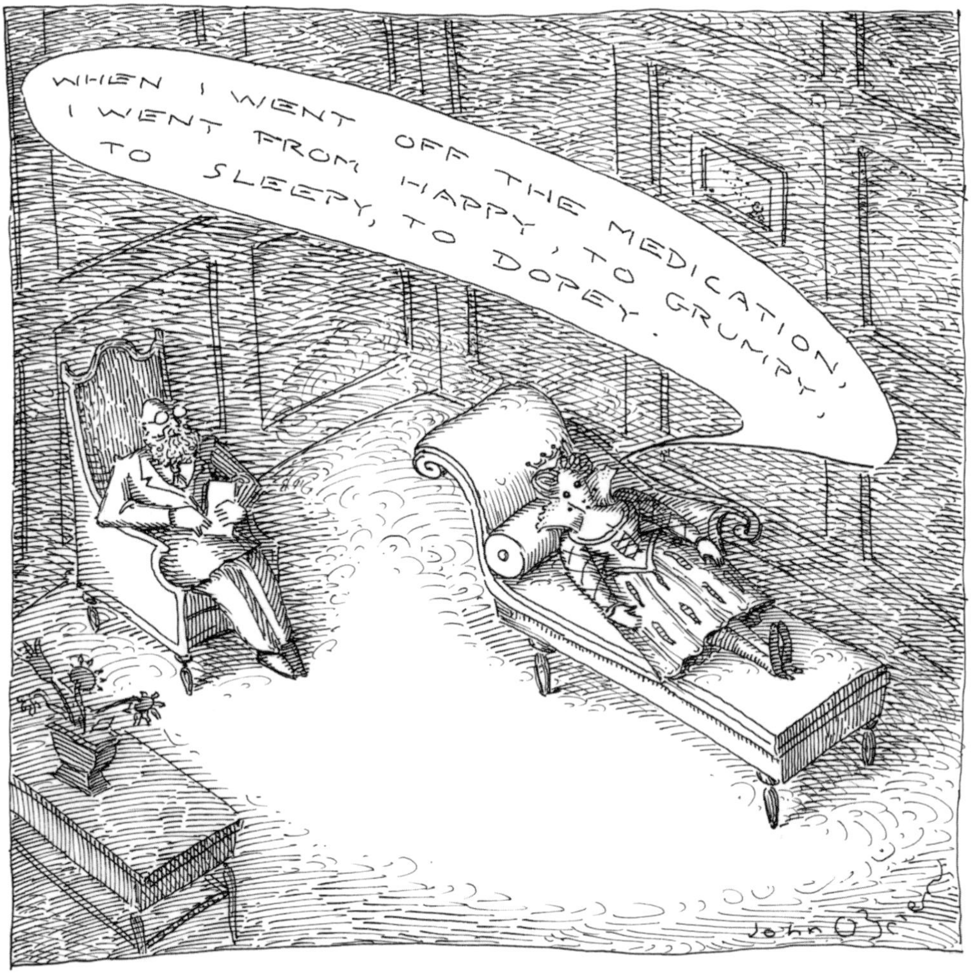
WHEN I WENT OFF THE MEDICATION, I WENT FROM HAPPY, TO GRUMPY, TO SLEEPY, TO DOPEY.
John O'Brien

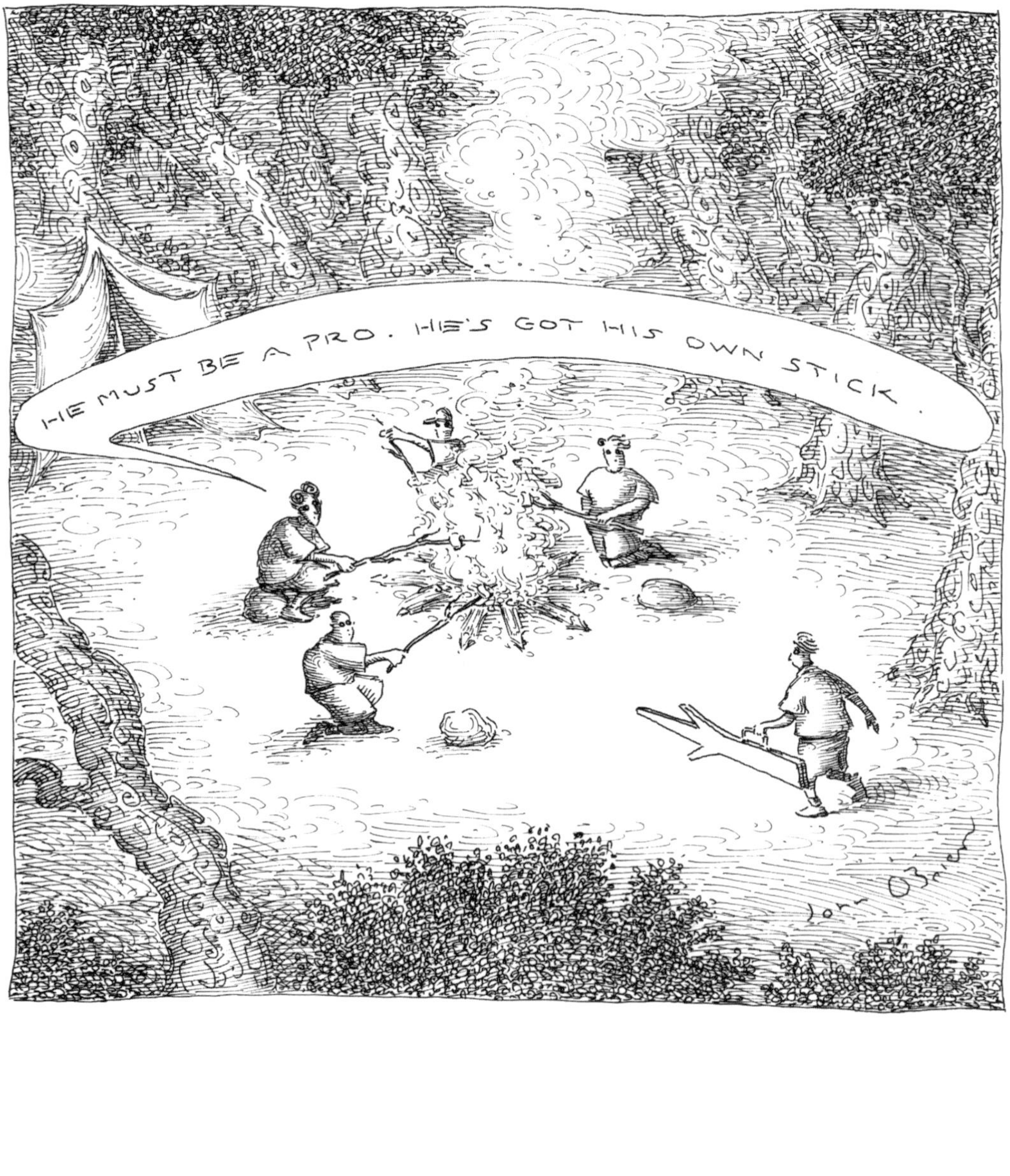
HE MUST BE A PRO. HE'S GOT HIS OWN STICK.

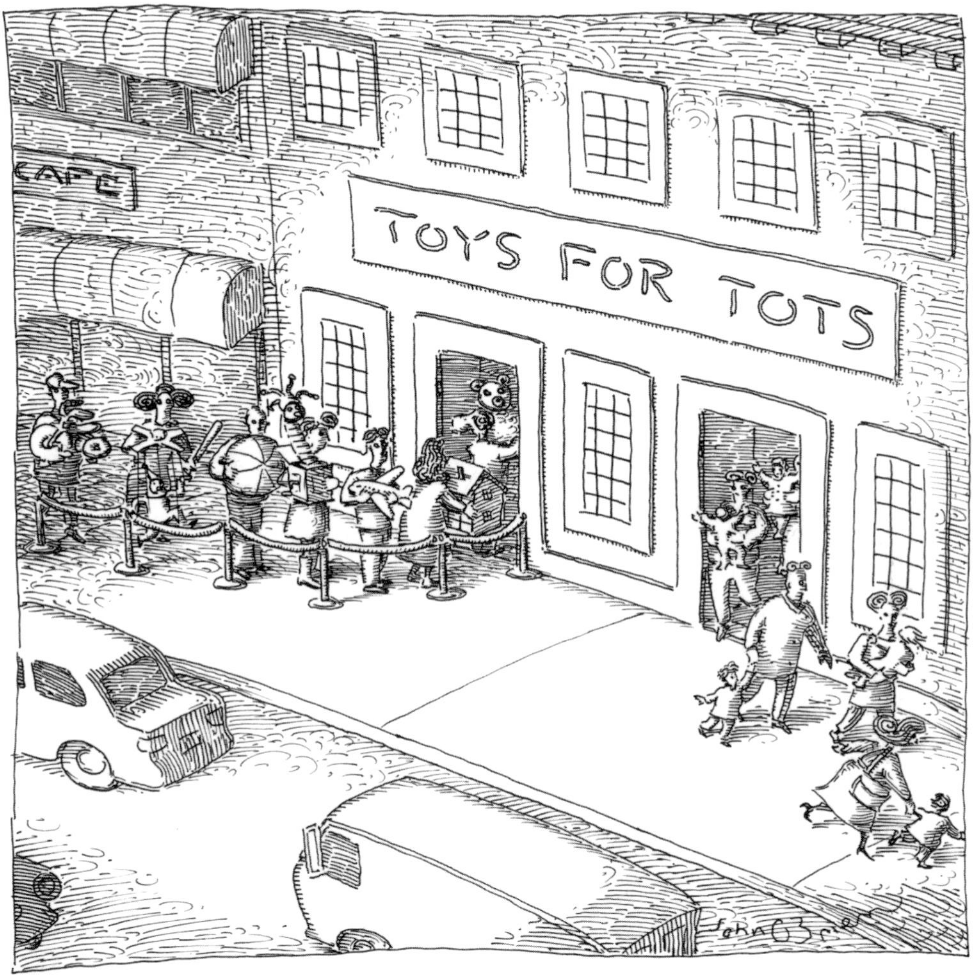
CAFE
TOYS FOR TOTS

Kanin

ZACHARY KANIN

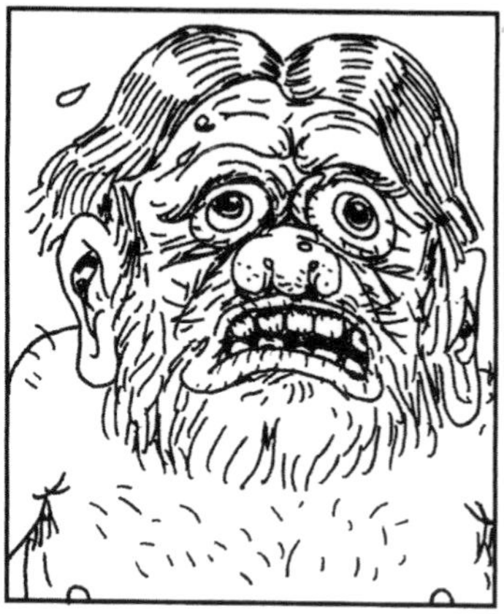

Frequently Asked Questions

- Where do you get your ideas?

  A friend of a friend.

- Which comes first, the picture or the caption?

  He gives me them in code, sometimes with no pictures.

- How'd you get started?

  Technical high school for cartooning.

- I admire . . .

  Charles Burns, Little Walter, Alice Neel, Chris Onstad, Max Beckmann, Aretha Franklin, my parents, Batman.

- How do you deal with rejection?

  The same as anyone else—I dust off my pants, pat down my hair, get back up on that horse and tell it we're gonna be married whether he likes it or not and there's not a damned army in the world that can keep us apart.

- What are some things that make you laugh and why?

  Worms. They have no shame!

- I've got a great idea for a cartoon—wanna hear it?

  Is it in code?

Infrequently Asked Questions

- Have you mooned or *been* mooned more often in your life?

  Is it mooning if you never wear pants?

- What would make a terrible pizza topping?

  Anything except cheese or tomato.

- What might one expect to find at a really low-budget amusement park?

  A ride where a guy pushes old people out of wheelchairs into mud.

- What did the shepherd say to the three-legged sheepdog?

  Follow your dreams.

And Now for a Few More Questions . . .

- ~~What~~ Why do you hate drawing?

  I don't. Look.

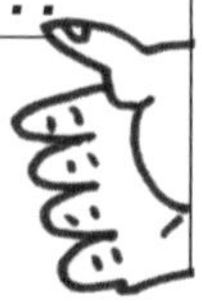

■ Being as accurate as possible, how many desert island cartoons do you think you've come up with and submitted to *The New Yorker?* [*Nobel Prize Committee?*]
5,000.

■ What's the funniest thing that you witnessed, overheard, or came up with that you couldn't figure out how to use in a cartoon?
There is a YouTube clip of Frasier falling off a stage that I'm really in love with.

■ If you could ask Bob Mankoff, *The New Yorker* cartoon editor, one question, what would it be?
Where do you get your ideas?

Draw Some Sort of Doodle

. . . using the random lines below as a starting point.

Naming Names

■ What name might you give to a mild-mannered, slightly overweight dental assistant in one of your cartoons?
Robert Throngman.

■ Other than Lance, what name would you give to a twenty-eight-year-old metrosexual entertainment lawyer who cycles on weekends?
Elliot Crogan-Josh.

■ What would be a good name for a new, commercially unviable breakfast cereal?
Assholes.

■ Come up with a name for an unpleasant medical procedure.
"Feeling-up"-expulsion.

■ If you used a pen name, what would it be?
Wart Manhog.

Complete The Pie Chart Below

. . . in a way that tells us something about your life or how you think.

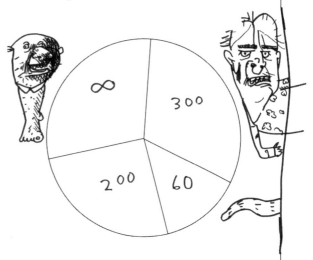

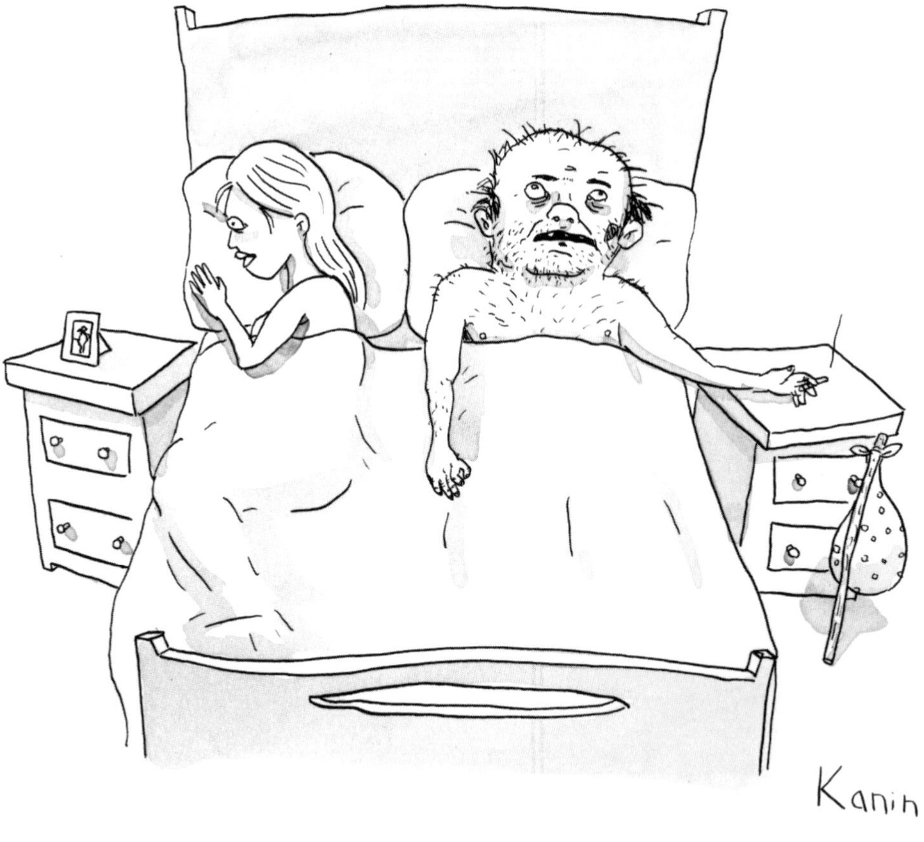
Kanin

"I really would've just settled for some spare change."

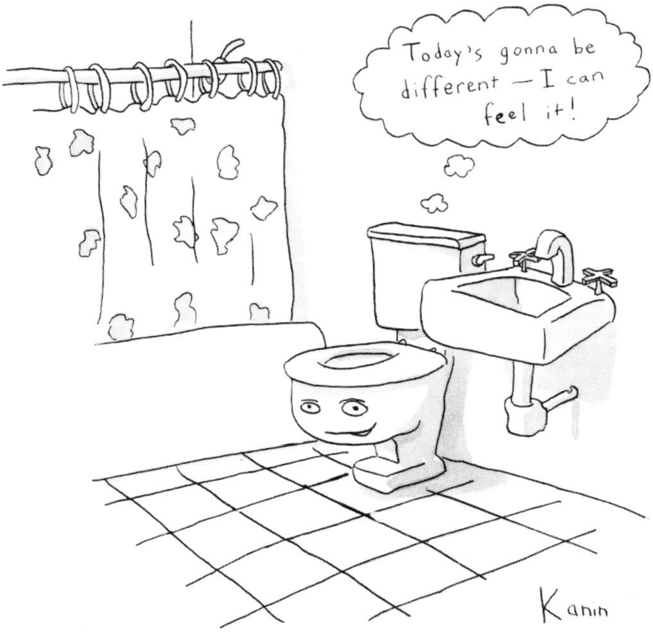
Today's gonna be different — I can feel it!
Kanin

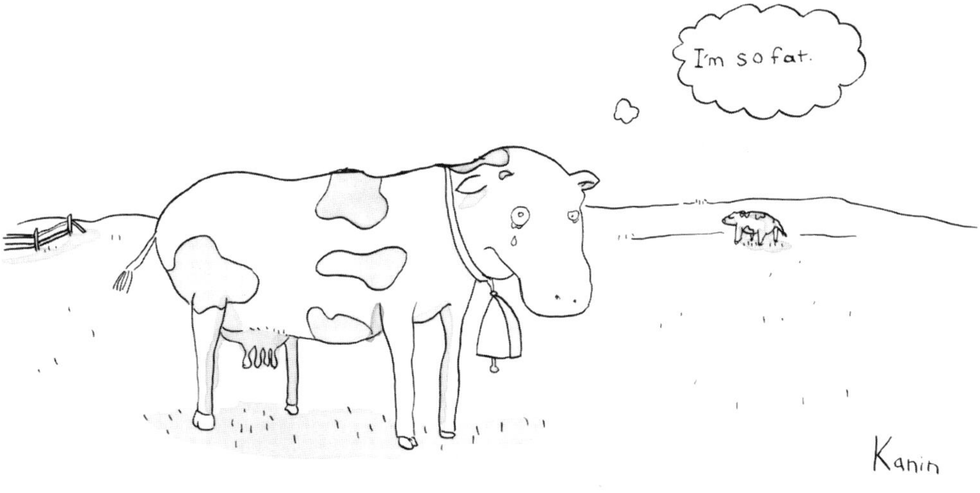
I'm so fat.
Kanin

SAD COW DISEASE

Shanahan

DANNY SHANAHAN

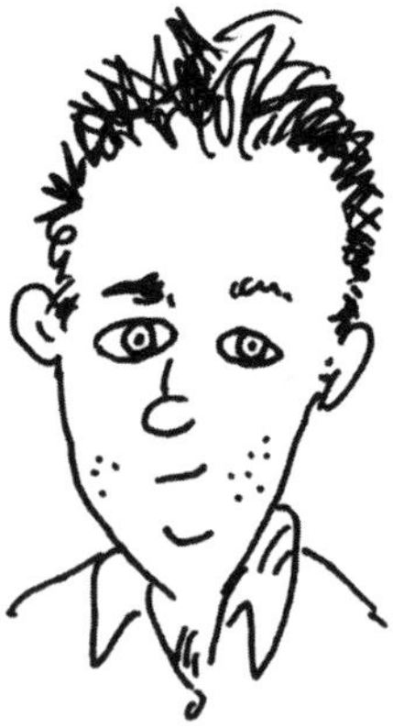

Frequently Asked Questions

- Where do you get your ideas?

  From Thomas Edison's slush pile.

- Which comes first, the picture or the caption?

  The caption.

- How'd you get started?

  Coffee and crystal.

- I admire . . .

  The way you hold your knife, they way we danced 'til three, the way you changed my life, and "the man" can't take that away from me.

- How do you deal with rejection?

  With my innate, overbearing stubbornness. I just keep banging my head against the wall until something happens.

- What are some things that make you laugh and why?

  People, and the things people do and say (and don't do, and don't say). That includes children and babies. They're all just inherently funny, whether they realize it or not. And questionnaires are freaking *hilarious*.

- I've got a great idea for a cartoon—wanna hear it?

  Thanks, heard it.

Infrequently Asked Questions

- Have you mooned or *been* mooned more often in your life?

  Been mooned.

- What would make a terrible pizza topping?

  Cookie dough.

- What might one expect to find at a really low-budget amusement park?

  Ride the Spatula.

- What did the shepherd say to the three-legged sheepdog?

  And my father's Rolex?

And Now for a Few More Questions . . .

- What do you hate drawing?

  Orchestras; the Vatican; love, in all its myriad guises.

- Being as accurate as possible, how many desert island cartoons do you think you've come up with and submitted to *The New Yorker*?

  At least three dozen.

- What's the funniest thing that you witnessed, overheard, or came up with that you couldn't figure out how to use in a cartoon?

  Wow, wouldn't that be something? If that ever happened? Wow. Wow. Wow. Wow.

- If you could ask Bob Mankoff, *The New Yorker* cartoon editor, one question, what would it be?

  Is it I, Lord?

Draw Some Sort of Doodle

. . . using the random lines below as a starting point.

operators are standing by

Naming Names

- What name might you give to a mild-mannered, slightly overweight dental assistant in one of your cartoons?

  Jack Plaque.

- Other than Lance, what name would you give to a twenty-eight-year-old metrosexual entertainment lawyer who cycles on weekends?

  Flash.

- What would be a good name for a new, commercially unviable breakfast cereal?

  Placent-Os.

- Come up with a name for an unpleasant medical procedure.

  Aortic Martinizing.

- If you used a pen name, what would it be?

  Penny.

Complete the Pie Chart Below

. . . in a way that tells us something about your life or how you think.

Orthopedics
Charismatics
Parenthetics
The Tick Tock Man

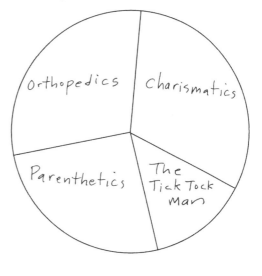

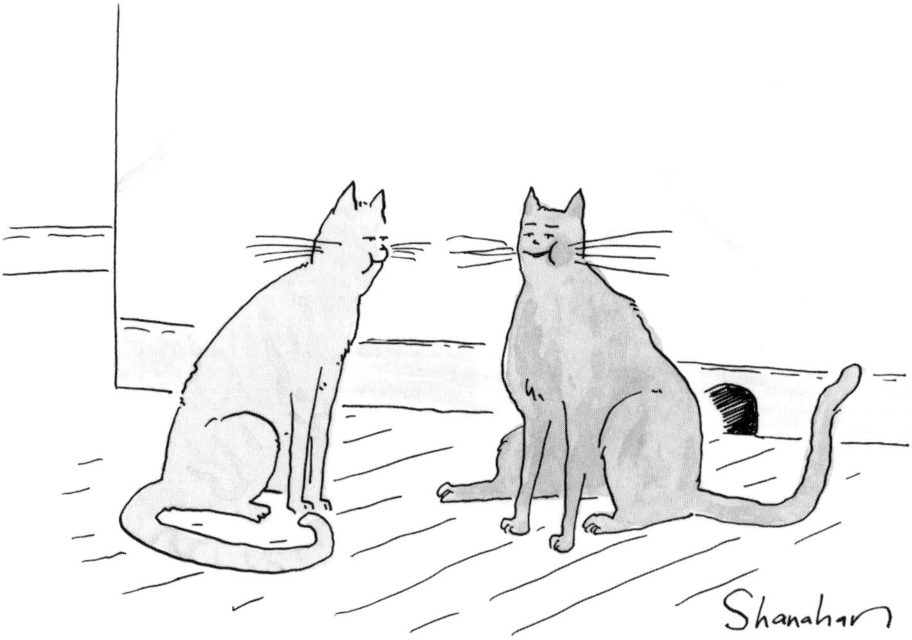
Shanahan

"Mmmm . . . I got a cheese-filled one."

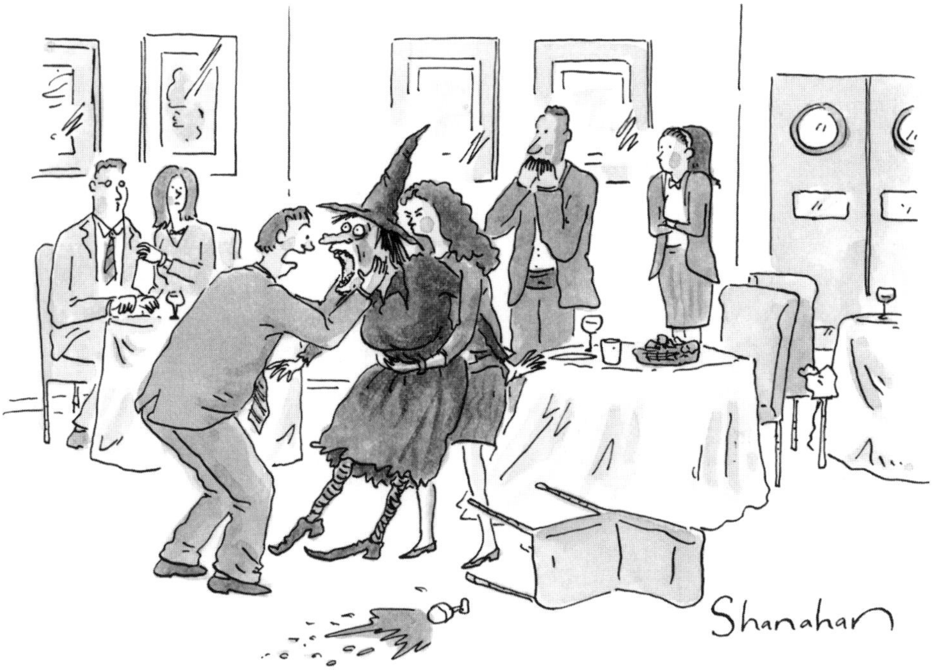
Shanahan

"Keep pushing—I can see the baby's head!"

"You have the most adorable lesions in your lungs."

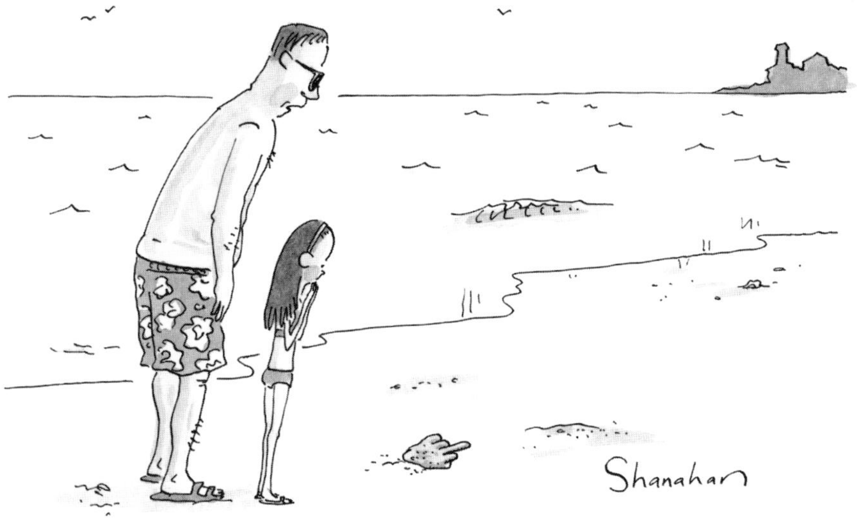
Shanahan

"Well, sweetheart, it's Mr. Sea Star's only defense mechanism."

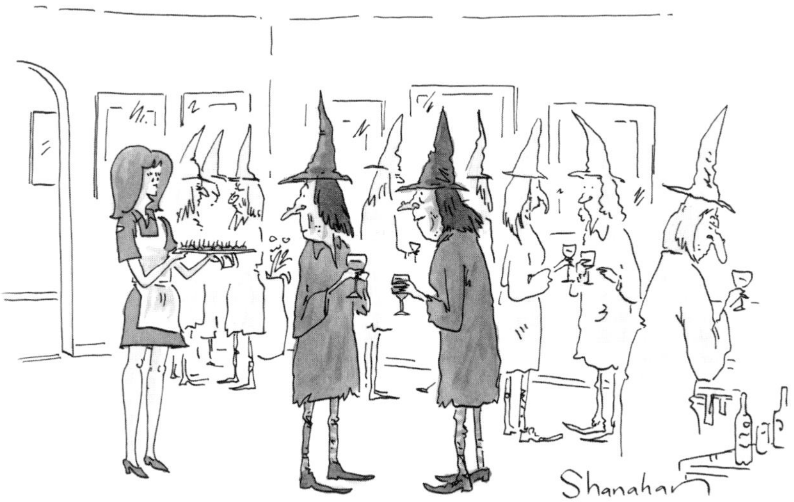
Shanahan

"Fetus?"

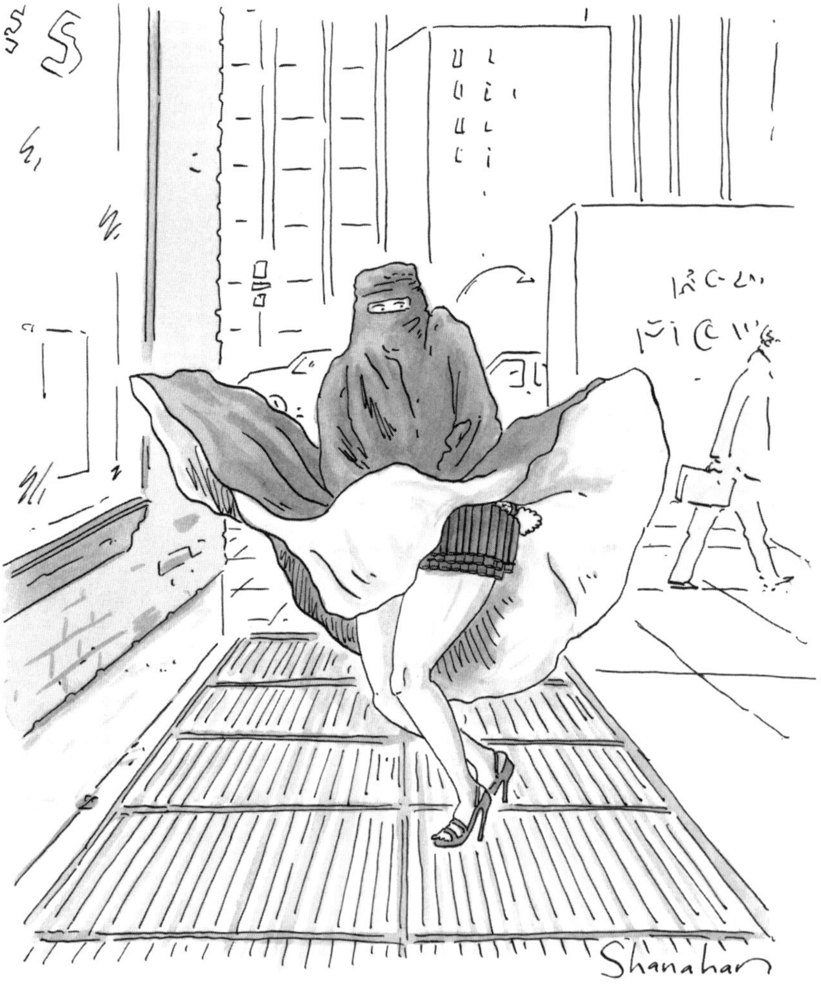
Shanahan

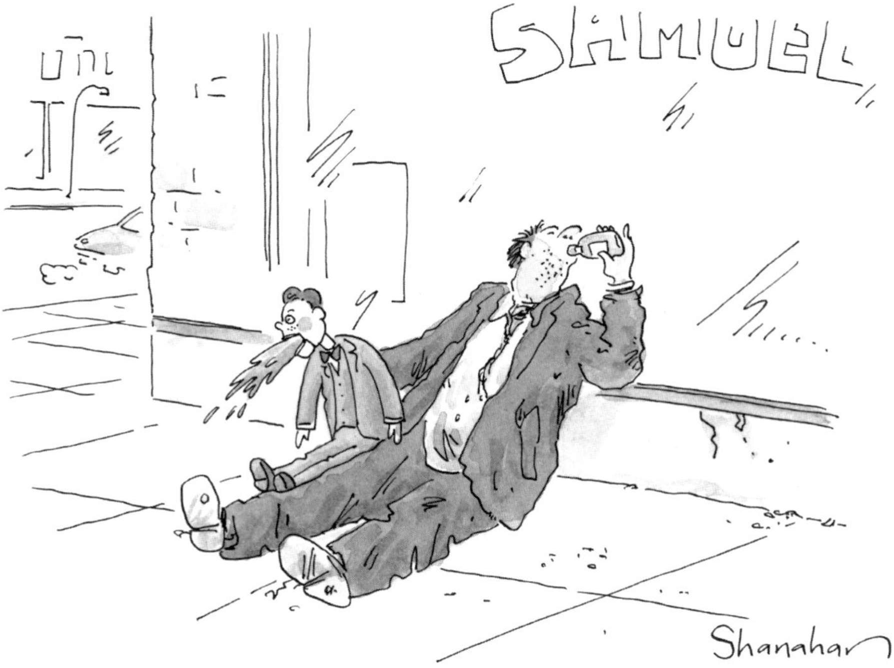
SAMUEL
Shanahan

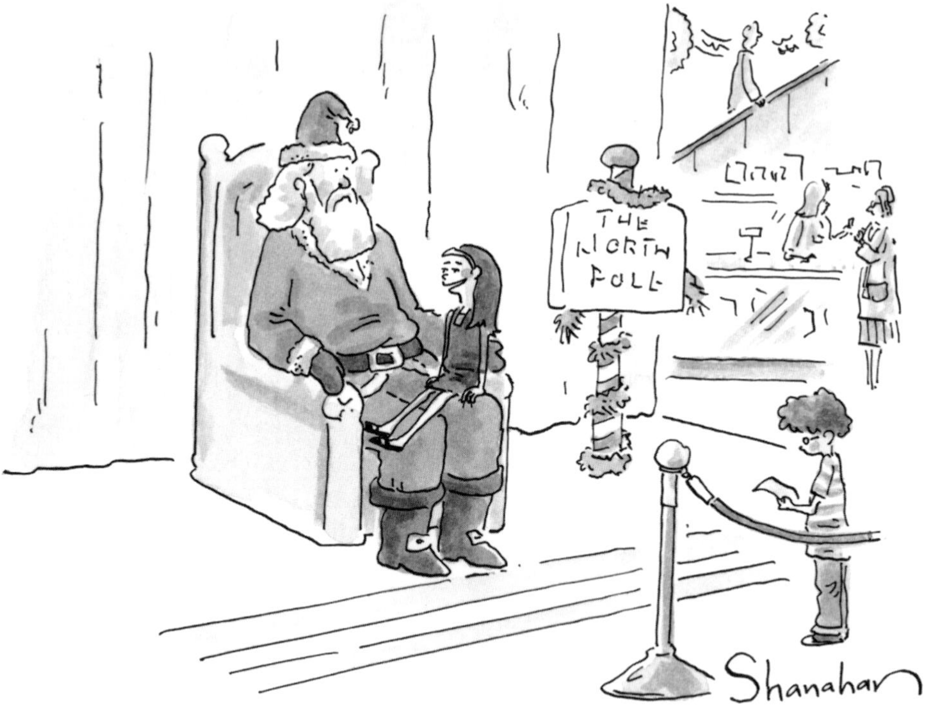
THE
NORTH
POLE
Shanahan

"Your thighs are like iron."

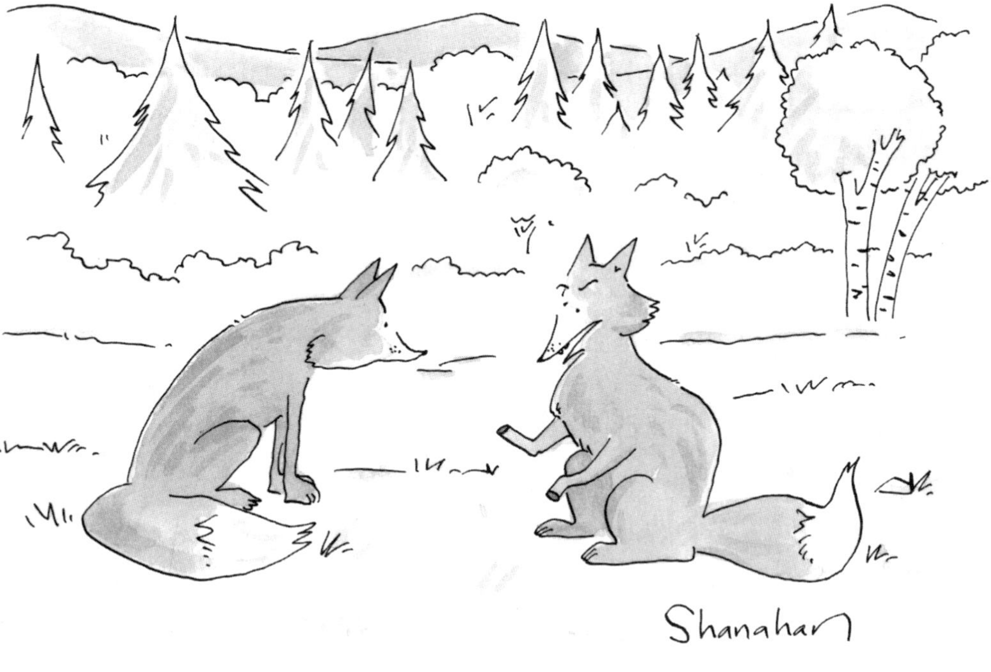
Shanahan

"I chewed the left one out of a trap; this one was pure nervous energy."

J. B. HANDELSMAN

Frequently Asked Questions

■ Where do you get your ideas?

I steal them, accidentally, of course.

■ Which comes first, the picture or the caption?

The idea comes all at once.

■ How'd you get started?

Like Abou Ben Adhem, I awoke from a deep dream of peace.

■ On a scale of 1 to 10 (1 being not very much at all and 10 being quite a bit), how much do you enjoy bowling?

4.

■ How often do you curse?

10.

■ How close have you ever come to getting a tattoo?

1.

■ I've got a great idea for a cartoon—wanna hear it?

Please spare me.

Infrequently Asked Questions

■ Have you mooned or *been* mooned more often in your life?

Question not understood.

■ What would make a terrible pizza topping?

Editors' brains, if any.

■ What might one expect to find at a really low-budget amusement park?

Nothing.

■ What did the shepherd say to the three-legged sheepdog?

You have my profoundest sympathy.

And Now for a Few More Questions . . .

■ What do you hate drawing?

I don't hate drawing anything.

■ Being as accurate as possible, how many desert island cartoons do you think you've come up with and submitted to *The New Yorker*?

Four.

- What's the funniest thing that you witnessed, overheard, or came up with that you couldn't figure out how to use in a cartoon?

  Can't remember.

- If you could ask Bob Mankoff, *The New Yorker* cartoon editor, one question, what would it be?

  Why is *The New Yorker* prejudiced against me and/or my work?

Draw Some Sort of Doodle

. . . using the random lines below as a starting point.

THESE
ARE SPERM CELLS AND
I WOULDN'T DARE
INTERFERE WITH THEM.

Naming Names

- What name might you give to a mild-mannered, slightly overweight dental assistant in one of your cartoons?

  Handelsman.

- Other than Lance, what name would you give to a twenty-eight-year-old metrosexual entertainment lawyer who cycles on weekends?

  James.

- What would be a good name for a commercially unviable cereal?

  Stupid flakes.

- Come up with a name for an unpleasant medical procedure.

  Brain removal, followed by appointment as editor.

- If you used a pen name, what would it be?

  Jughead.

Complete the Pie Chart Below

. . . in a way that tells us something about your life or how you think.

?
?
?

Mr. Waldvogel has a junior moment.

"The name's Moby Richard. Who's he callin' Dick?"

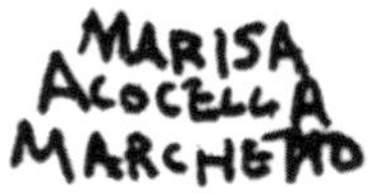
MARISA
ACOCELLA
MARCHETTO

MARISA ACOCELLA MARCHETTO

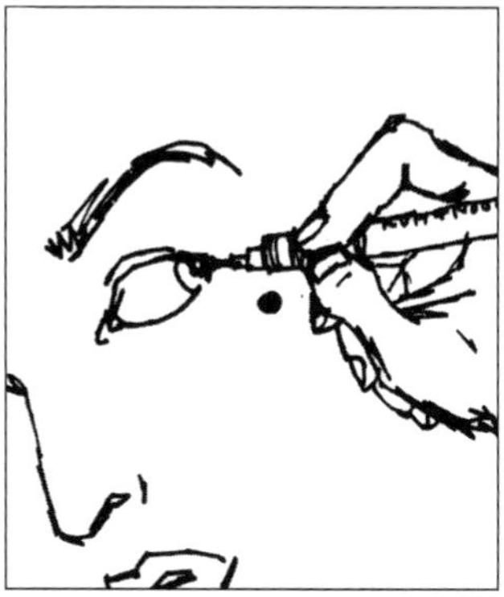

Frequently Asked Questions

- Where do you get your ideas?
  If I knew, I'd have more. Just kidding. From life.

- Which comes first, the picture or the caption?
  The egg.

- How'd you get started?
  See above.

- I admire . . .
  Anyone who makes me laugh.

- How do you deal with rejection?
  Rejection is crack.

- What are some things that make you laugh and why?
  Trauma and embarassment make me laugh—because after you get over the initial feeling of mortification, it's always the best material.

- I've got a great idea for a cartoon—wanna hear it?
  Please, then you'll ask me to draw it. Nope. No way.

Infrequently Asked Questions

- Have you mooned or *been* mooned more often in your life?
  I prefer the sun.

- What would make a terrible pizza topping?
  A top hat.

- What might one expect to find at a really low-budget amusement park?
  No one having any fun.

- What did the shepherd say to the three-legged sheepdog?
  "Herd any good jokes?"
  I can't believe I wrote that.

Draw Something in This Space

. . . that will help us understand your childhood.

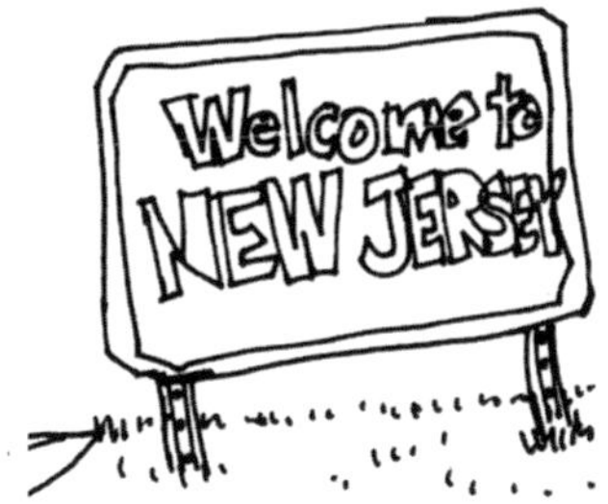
Welcome to
NEW JERSEY

And Now for a Few More Questions . . .

- What do you hate drawing?

  Babies.

- Being as accurate as possible, how many desert island cartoons do you think you've come up with and submitted to *The New Yorker*?

  Actually, none.

- What's the funniest thing that you witnessed, overheard, or came up with that you couldn't figure out how to use in a cartoon?

  If I told you, then I'd be giving you material.

- If you could ask Bob Mankoff, *The New Yorker* cartoon editor, one question, what would it be?

  Why are YOU always published?

Naming Names

- What name might you give to a mild-mannered, slightly overweight dental assistant in one of your cartoons?

  Esther.

- Other than Lance, what name would you give to a twenty-eight-year-old metrosexual entertainment lawyer who cycles on weekends?

  Jonathan.

- What would be a good name for a new, commercially unviable breakfast cereal?

  Cereal Killer.

- Come up with a name for an unpleasant medical procedure.

  What medical procedure is pleasant?

- If you used a pen name, what would it be?

  Rapidograph.

Complete the Pie Chart Below

. . . in a way that tells us something about your life or how you think.

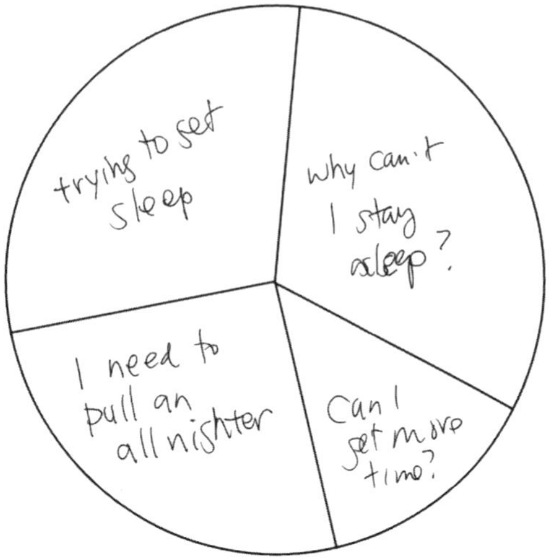
trying to get sleep
why can't I stay asleep?
I need to pull an allnighter
Can I get more time?

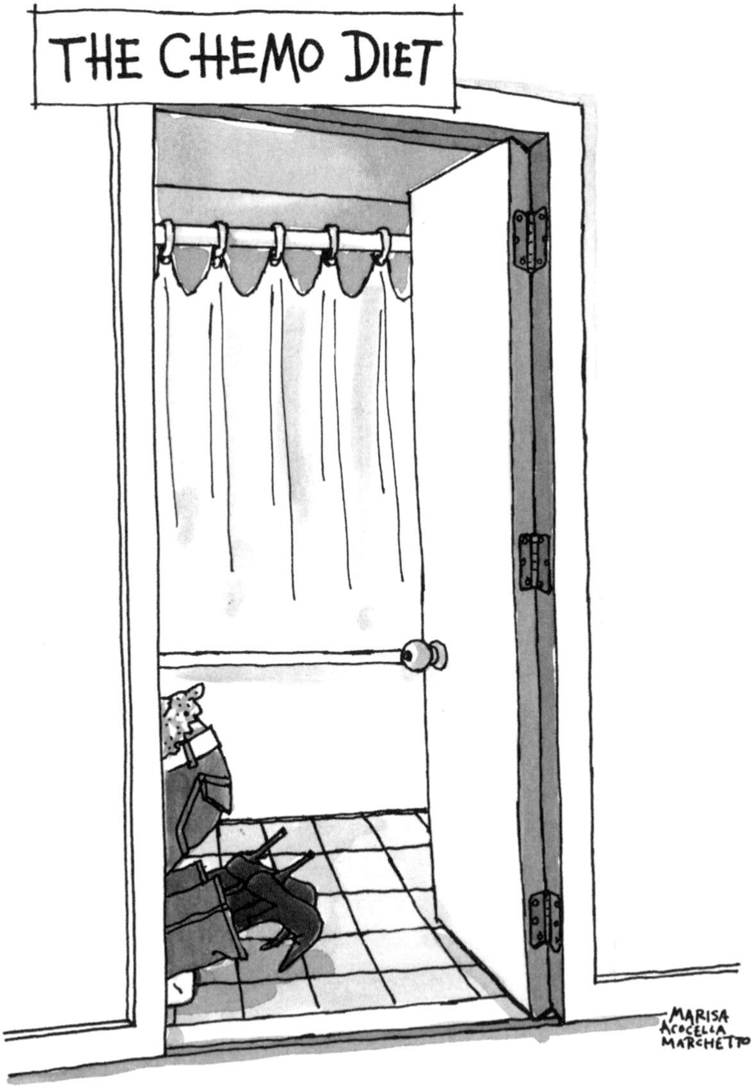
THE CHEMO DIET
MARISA ACOCELLA MARCHETTO

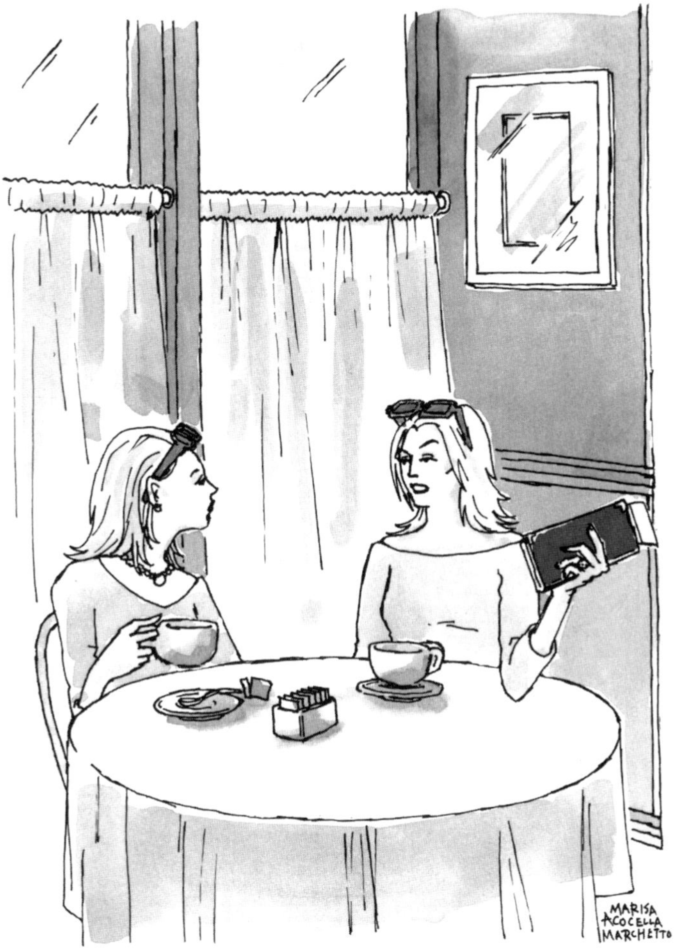
MARISA
ACOCELLA
MARCHETTO

"Your husband got the last one. This one's on mine."

JESUS CHRISTO
INRI
MARISA
ACOCELLA
MARCHETTO

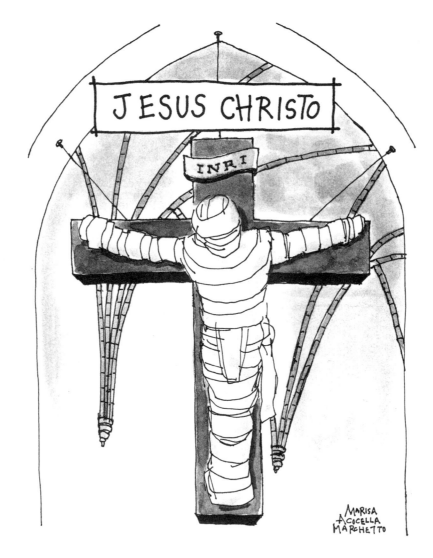

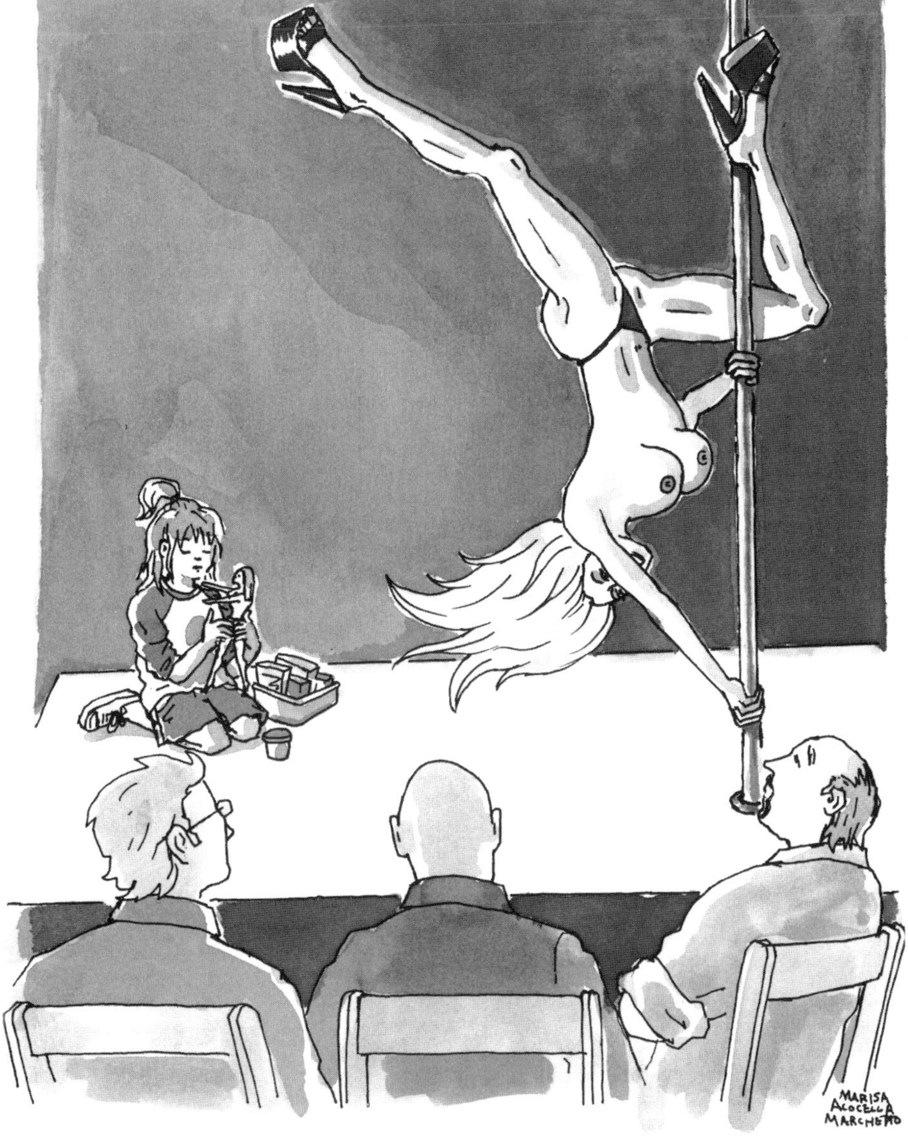
MARISA ACOCELLA MARCHETTO

"It's 'Take Your Daughter to Work Day.'"

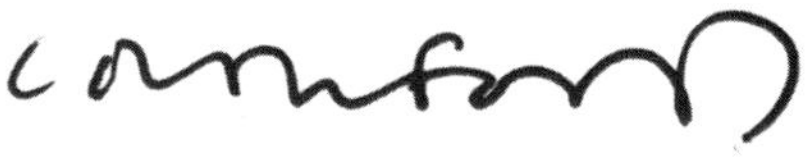

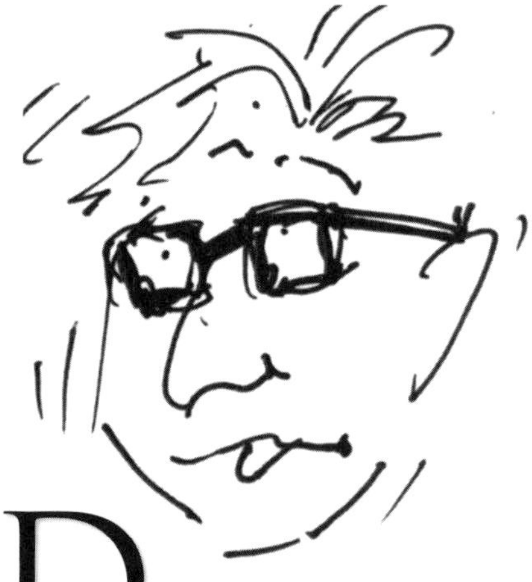

MICHAEL CRAWFORD

Frequently Asked Questions

- Where do you get your ideas?
  My best friend's girl.

- Which comes first, the picture or the caption?
  You Americans!

- How'd you get started?
  In the spring the larvae hatch and the cycle begins again.

- I admire . . .
  People who mind their own beeswax.

- How do you deal with rejection?
  I just keep pinching myself!

- What are some things that make you laugh and why?
  Taken a walk down 8th Avenue lately?

- I've got a great idea for a cartoon—wanna hear it?
  Maybe we can touch base in hell.

Infrequently Asked Questions

- Have you mooned or *been* mooned more often in your life?
  You late-rising professionals!

- What would make a terrible pizza topping?
  A Lincoln full of Mexicans.

- What might one expect to find at a really low-budget amusement park?
  Rabid Beaver Petting Zoo.

- What did the shepherd say to the three-legged sheepdog?
  You want my number?

And Now for a Few More Questions . . .

- What do you hate drawing?
  My best friend's girl.

- Being as accurate as possible, how many desert island cartoons do you think you've come up with and submitted to *The New Yorker*?
  ~~Three.~~ Zero.

What's the funniest thing that you witnessed, overheard, or came up with that you couldn't figure out how to use in a cartoon?

Jesus in the "12 Apostles or Less" line at Fairway.

If you could ask Bob Mankoff, *The New Yorker* cartoon editor, one question, what would it be?

Could you supersize that for me, Sonny?

Draw Something in This Space

. . . that will help us understand your childhood.

Naming Names

What name might you give to a mild-mannered, slightly overweight dental assistant in one of your cartoons?

Nursey Nurse.

Other than Lance, what name would you give to a twenty-eight-year-old metrosexual entertainment lawyer who cycles on weekends?

Whoa! You've got a lot of anger.

What would be a good name for a new, commercially unviable breakfast cereal?

Barf Loops.

Come up with a name for an unpleasant medical procedure.

A peckerectomy.

If you used a pen name, what would it be?

Uniball Gel Impact.

Complete the Pie Chart Below

. . . in a way that tells us something about your life or how you think.

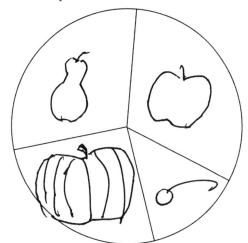

"Going to be long over there, Mr. Happy? I need to get my casserole in."

"Give me a hint. I'm sleeping with a lot of lobbyists."

"Wanna swap?"

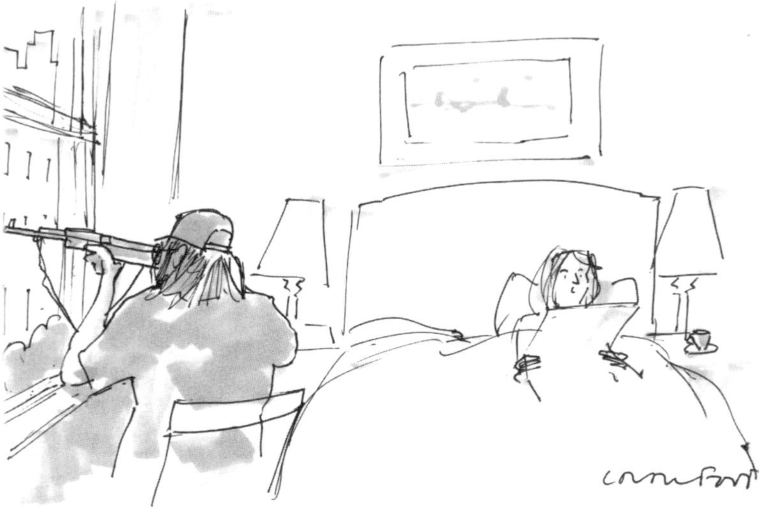
crawford

"I thought you liked hip-hop."

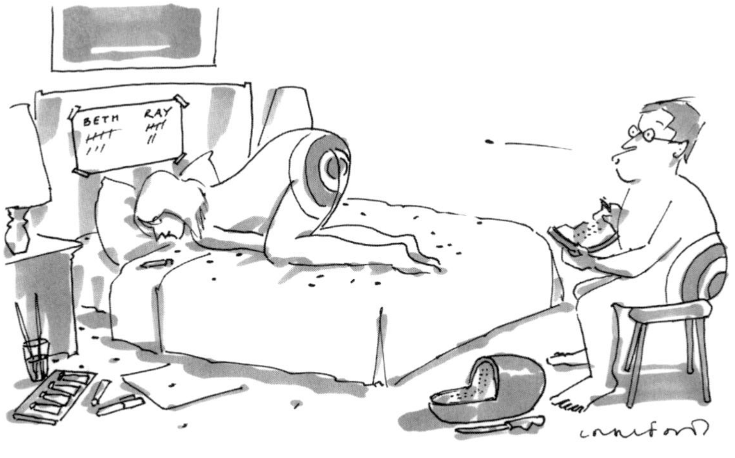
BETH
RAY
crawford

LET THE SUMMER GAMES BEGIN!

Haefeli

WILLIAM
HAEFELI

circa 1990
(Based on self-portrait
that ran in <u>Punch</u>)

Frequently Asked Questions

■ Where do you get your ideas?

Rummaging around in my brain.

■ Which comes first, the picture or the caption?

Caption.

■ How'd you get started?

With great enthusiasm!

■ I admire . . .

The cartoonists Charles Saxon, for the lushness of his drawings and the keenness of his observations, and Gluyas Williams, for how well he captured his times and the precision of his drawing (I can't catch him cheating). For diplomacy I'm not mentioning living cartoonists.

■ How do you deal with rejection?

No cartoon is ever definitively rejected. There's always a chance to resubmit it at a later date or sell it elsewhere. However some cartoons and their topics have a certain shelf life and it is always sad when they don't get sold by their "sell-by" date.

■ What are some things that make you laugh and why?

TV SHOWS: *NewsRadio:* **The funny comes from so many directions: character comedy, verbal humor, slapstick, obscure cultural references. It can be subtle, broad, off-the-wall.** *The Mary Tyler Moore Show:* **Mary is so nice.** *Fawlty Towers:* **Basil is so awful.**

MOVIES: Harold Lloyd and his wonderful 1920s American energy. I love when attractive and sophisticated people are nonchalantly goofy. e.g., Cary Grant in most of his comedies; e.g., Capucine in the original *Pink Panther* **when she hits her head on the bar or falls into the closet.**

BOOKS: I can't say because my taste in humorous writing keeps changing. What I found funny 20 years ago seems tedious now.

■ I've got a great idea for a cartoon—wanna hear it?

No.

Infrequently Asked Questions

■ Have you mooned or *been* mooned more often in your life?

Equal.

■ What would make a terrible pizza topping?

Shoelaces.

■ What might one expect to find at a really low-budget amusement park?

Pizza with shoelaces.

■ What did the shepherd say to the three-legged sheepdog?

Here, eat my pizza with shoelaces.

Draw Something in This Space

. . . that will help us understand your childhood.

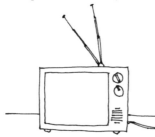

And Now for A Few More Questions . . .

■ What do you hate drawing?

Concentric circles.

■ Being as accurate as possible, how many desert island cartoons do you think you've come up with and submitted to *The New Yorker*?

12.

■ What's the funniest thing that you witnessed, overheard, or came up with that you couldn't figure out how to use in a cartoon?

Don't you mean one that I couldn't figure out how to use in a cartoon yet?

■ If you could ask Bob Mankoff, *The New Yorker* cartoon editor, one question, what would it be?

Where are you taking me to lunch?

Naming Names

■ What name might you give to a mild-mannered, slightly overweight dental assistant in one of your cartoons?

Flossie. (Wouldn't everyone?)

■ Other than Lance, what name would you give to a twenty-eight-year-old metrosexual entertainment lawyer who cycles on weekends?

H.B. (For "handlebar" cuz he cycles and/or "handle bar" cuz he's a lawyer.)

■ What would be a good name for a new, commercially unviable breakfast cereal?

Ugh-ums!

■ Come up with a name for an unpleasant medical procedure.

Hatchet job.

■ If you used a pen name, what would it be?

Penn Tell.

Complete the Pie Chart Below

. . . in a way that tells us something about your life or how you think.

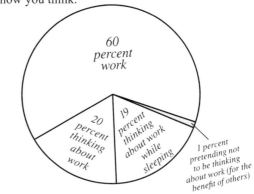

*"Mommy wants you to have everything she had when
she was growing up—starting with divorced parents."*

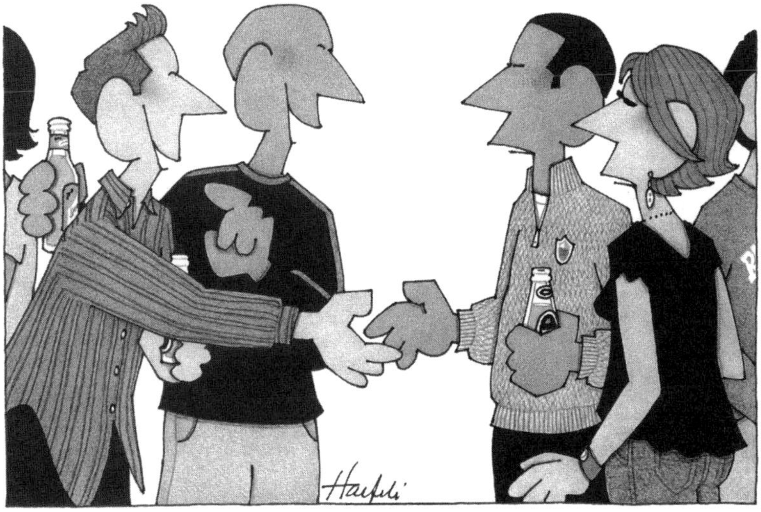
Haefeli

"This is Jerry. His family used to own my family."

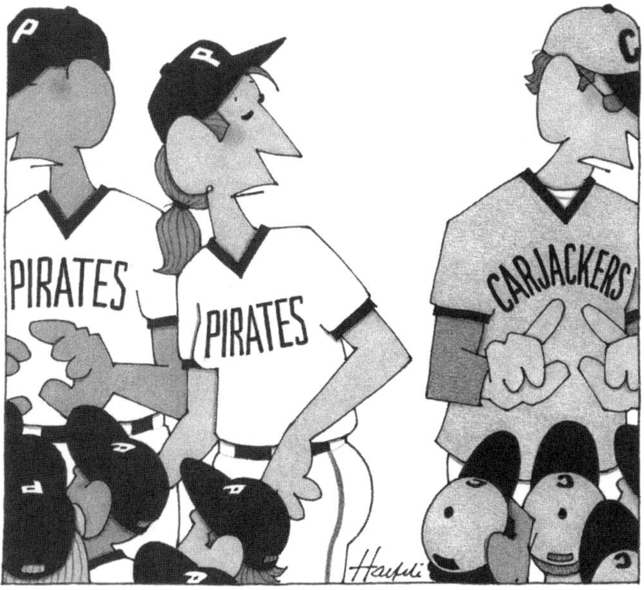
PIRATES
PIRATES
CARJACKERS
Haefeli

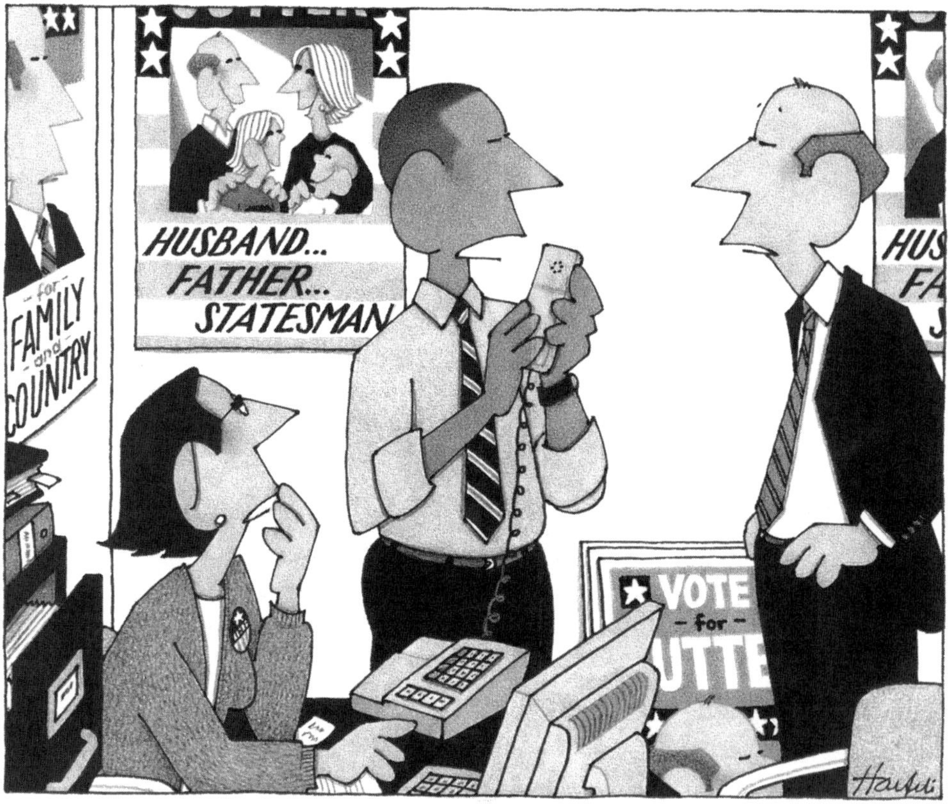
for
FAMILY
and
COUNTRY
HUSBAND...
FATHER...
STATESMAN
VOTE
for
Haefeli

"He claims he has you on video—how can I put this?—'courting the gay vote.'"

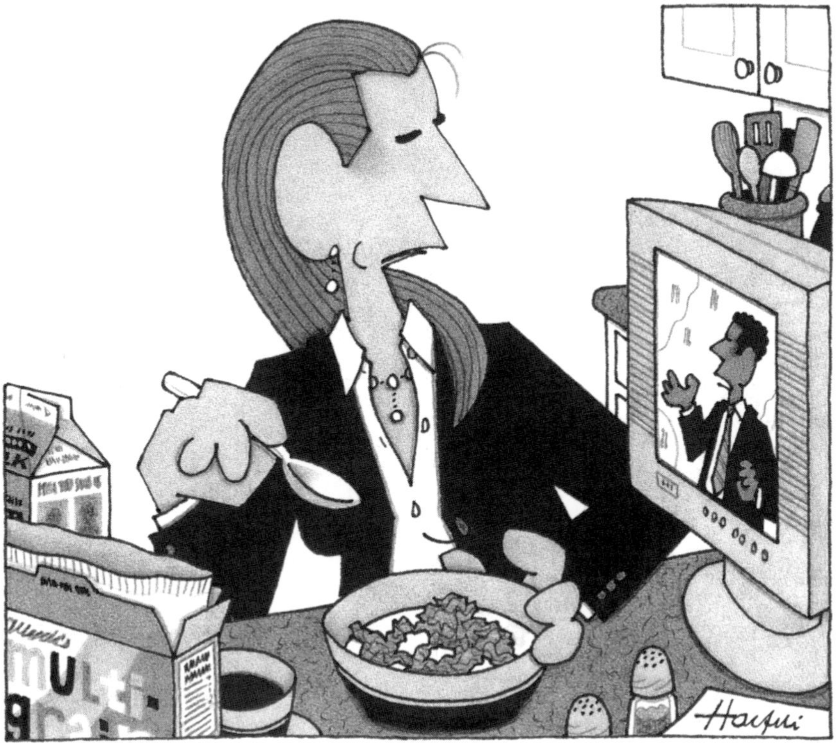
Haefeli

"For those of you headed to the office, today will be 68 degrees and fluorescent."

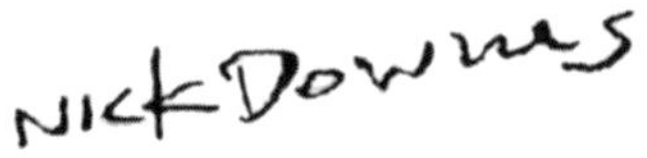

NICK DOWNES

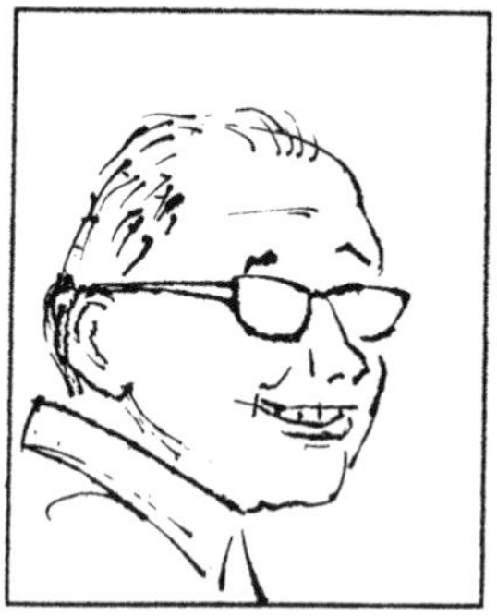

Frequently Asked Questions

- Where do you get your ideas?
  Out of extremely thin, anorexic, really, air.

- Which comes first, the picture or the caption?
  The caption—absolutely no staying power.

- How'd you get started?
  As a twinkle in my dad's rather myopic eye, I guess.

- I admire . . .
  From afar.

- How do you deal with rejection?
  Stunned disbelief.

- What are some things that make you laugh and why?
  Things that are funny precisely because they aren't supposed to be at all.

- I've got a great idea for a cartoon—wanna hear it?
  Save it for when I'm a desperate, dried-up hack. Okay, let's hear it.

Infrequently Asked Questions

- Have you mooned or *been* mooned more often in your life?
  I was slightly mooned, once. Sort of a crescent mooning.

- What would make a terrible pizza topping?
  Blood, sweat, and tears.

- What might one expect to find at a really low-budget amusement park?
  A Pitch 'n' Putt 'n' Pass Out.

- What did the shepherd say to the three-legged sheepdog?
  We'll always have Paris What'sername.

And Now for a Few More Questions . . .

- What, do you hate drawing?
  Sometimes, yes.

- Being as accurate as possible, how many desert island cartoons do you think you've come up with and submitted to *The New Yorker*?
  104.

What's the funniest thing that you witnessed, overheard, or came up with that you couldn't figure out how to use in a cartoon?

Tail end of a conversation among group of men I walked by in Brooklyn, ". . . it was a closed casket—what does that tell me?"

If you could ask Bob Mankoff, *The New Yorker* cartoon editor, one question, what would it be?

Who will be wearing what on Oscar night?

Draw Some Sort of Doodle

. . . using the random lines below as a starting point.

Naming Names

What name might you give to a mild-mannered, slightly overweight dental assistant in one of your cartoons?

Rence 'n' Spitt.

Other than Lance, what name would you give to a twenty-eight-year-old metrosexual entertainment lawyer who cycles on weekends?

Sue.

What would be a good name for a new, commercially unviable breakfast cereal?

Luckless Charms.

Come up with a name for an unpleasant medical procedure.

Tag Team Neurosurgery.

If you used a pen name, what would it be?

Phineas T. Farquar.

Complete the Pie Chart Below

. . . in a way that tells us something about your life or how you think.

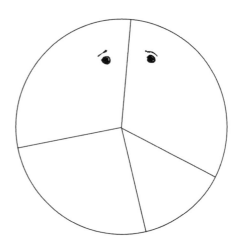

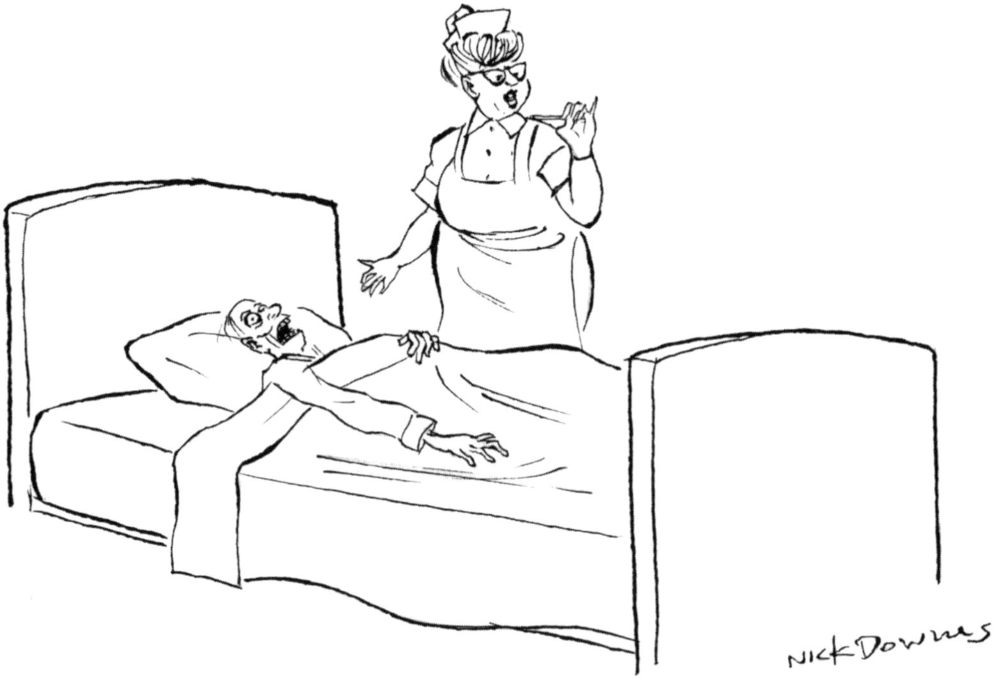
NICK DOWNES

"Oh my, your fever's way down."

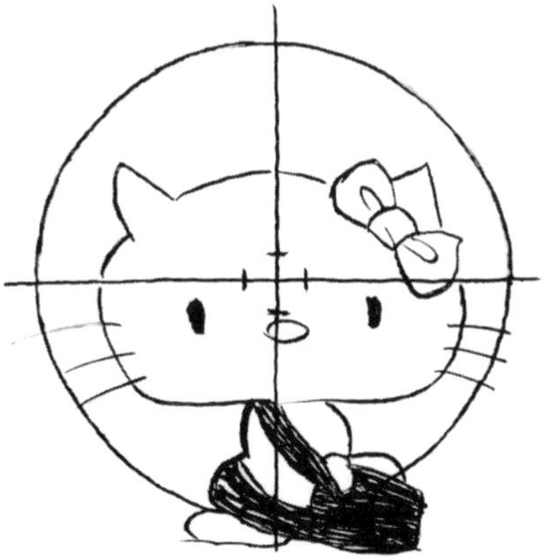

Good-bye Kitty

NDownes

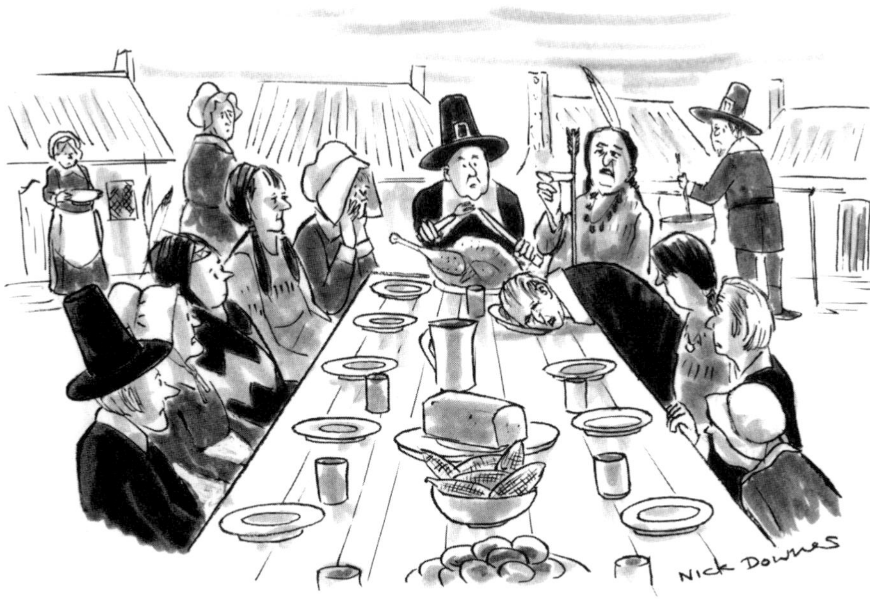
NICK DOWNES

"Running Deer sends his regrets."

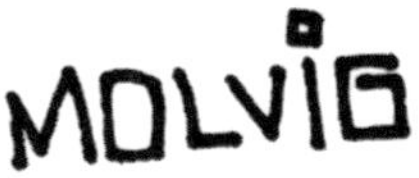

MOLVIG

ARIEL MOLVIG

Frequently Asked Questions

■ Where do you get your ideas?

It's unsightly, but the doctors think stem cells may help.

■ Which comes first, the picture or the caption?

THE CAPTION GOES DOWN WITH THE

■ How'd you get started?

CLEVER LITTLE HANDS
\+ SOCIAL PARIAH
—————————————
CARTOONIST

■ I admire . . .

Clear vision in dark times.

■ How do you deal with rejection?

A pillow is a great way to hide an rejection.

■ What are some things that make you laugh and why?

A kick to someone else's gonads. Laughter is an instinctual reflex of relief that one's own gonads are unscathed. Anything funny is a metaphorical gonad assault.

■ I've got a great idea for a cartoon—wanna hear it?

No. Stop showing off.

Infrequently Asked Questions

■ Have you mooned or *been* mooned more often in your life?

I've practiced A LOT in the mirror, but I figure that's a wash.

■ What would make a terrible pizza topping?

Another Bush presidency.

■ What might one expect to find at a really low-budget amusement park?

"F Train: The Ride."

- What did the shepherd say to the three-legged sheepdog?

  Thanks for dinner. That was delish.

Draw Some Sort of Doodle

. . . using the random lines below as a starting point.

And Now for a Few More Questions . . .

- What do you hate drawing?

  Speaking as a cartoonist—horses. Speaking as a horse—carriages.

- Being as accurate as possible, how many desert island cartoons do you think you've come up with and submitted to *The New Yorker*?

  2 lbs. 7.5 oz.

- What's the funniest thing that you witnessed, overheard, or came up with that you couldn't figure out how to use in a cartoon?

  That's a hard one, humor is so subtle and subjective . . . probably King Kong coating Manhattan with huge monkey feces.

- If you could ask Bob Mankoff, *The New Yorker* cartoon editor, one question, what would it be?

WHY DON'T YOU WUV ME?

Naming Names

- What name might you give to a mild-mannered, slightly overweight dental assistant in one of your cartoons?

  Candy.

- Other than Lance, what name would you give to a twenty-eight-year-old metrosexual entertainment lawyer who cycles on weekends?

  Houston, Austin, but not Corpus Christi.

- What would be a good name for a new, commercially unviable breakfast cereal?

crack-ho's

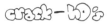

- Come up with a name for an unpleasant medical procedure.

  Eugenbertholdfriedrichbrechtomy.

- If you used a pen name, what would it be?

  Bic.

Complete the Pie Chart Below

. . . in a way that tells us something about your life or how you think.

PIE

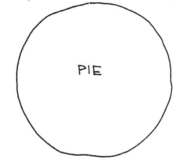

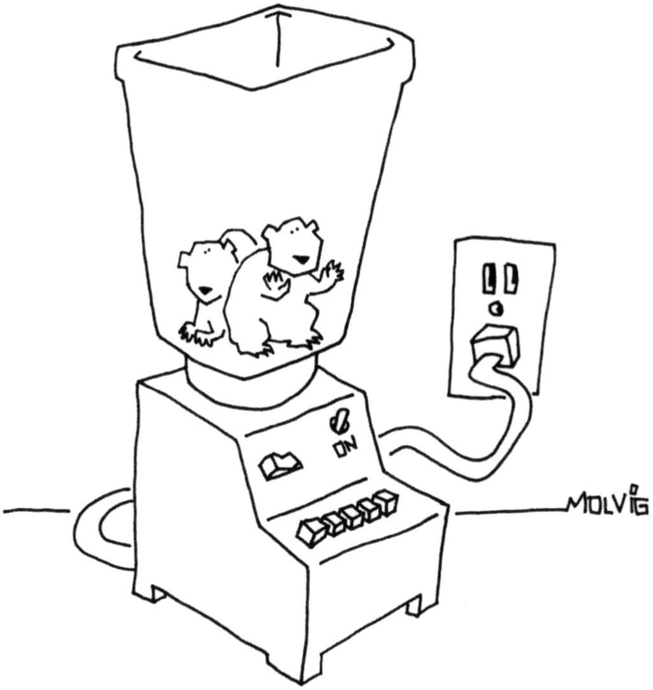
ON
MOLVIG

IF LIFE GIVES YOU LEMMINGS...

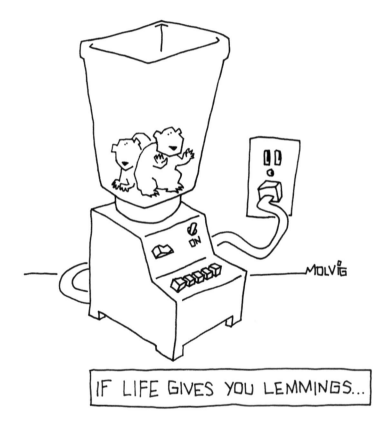

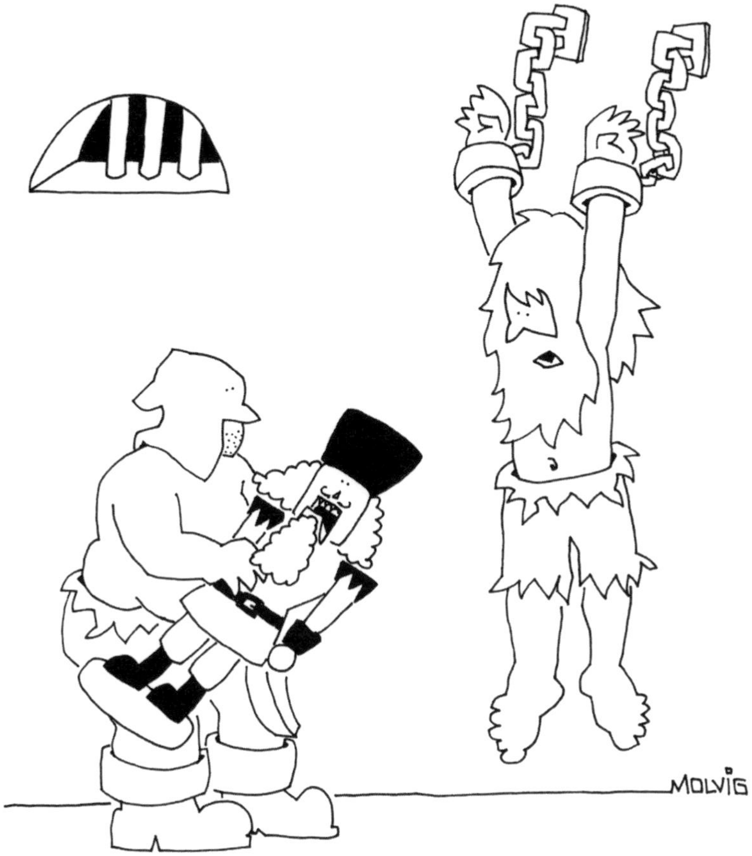
MOLVIG

"I'll talk."

FIRST CLASS
BUSINESS
COACH
BITCH
MOLVIG

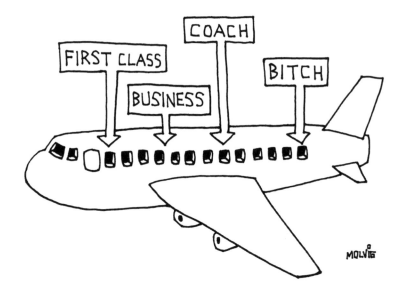

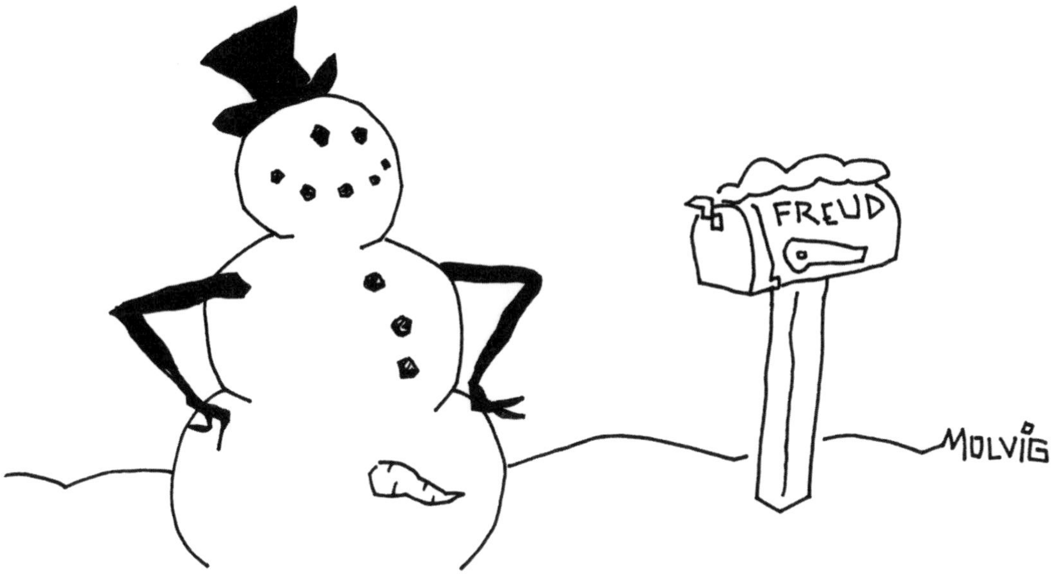
FREUD
MOLVIG

I LOOK STUPID IN HATS.
MOLVIG

AN OPTIMIST, A PESSIMIST & AN OPTOMETRIST
THE GLASS IS HALF FULL!
THE GLASS IS HALF EMPTY.
UH, GUYS...
MOLVIG

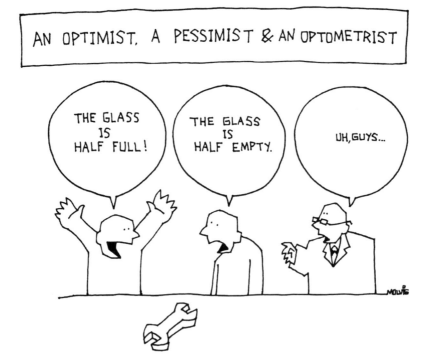

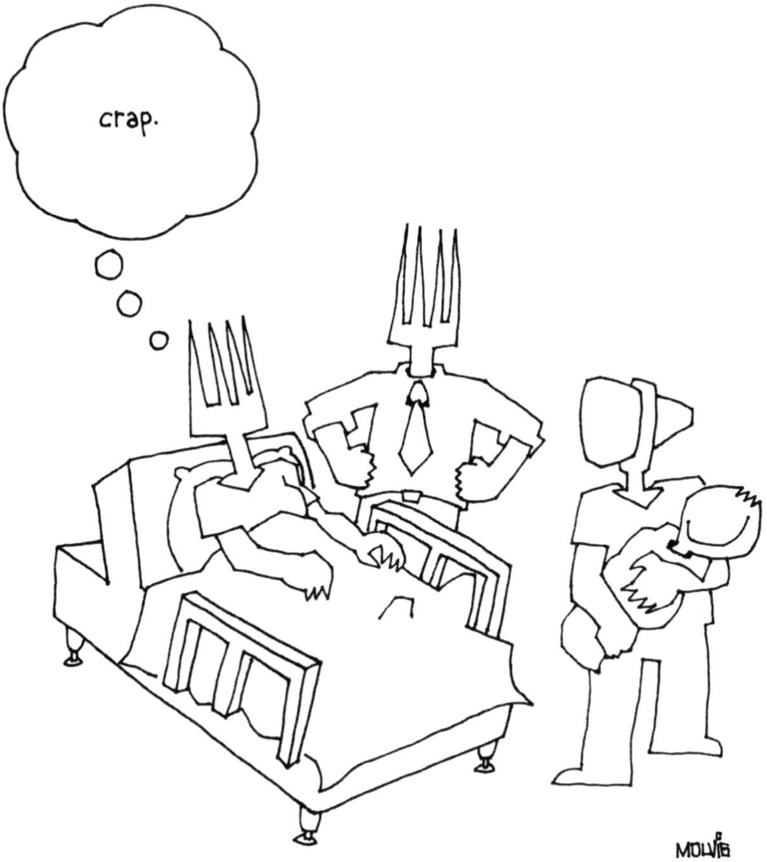
crap.
MOLVIG

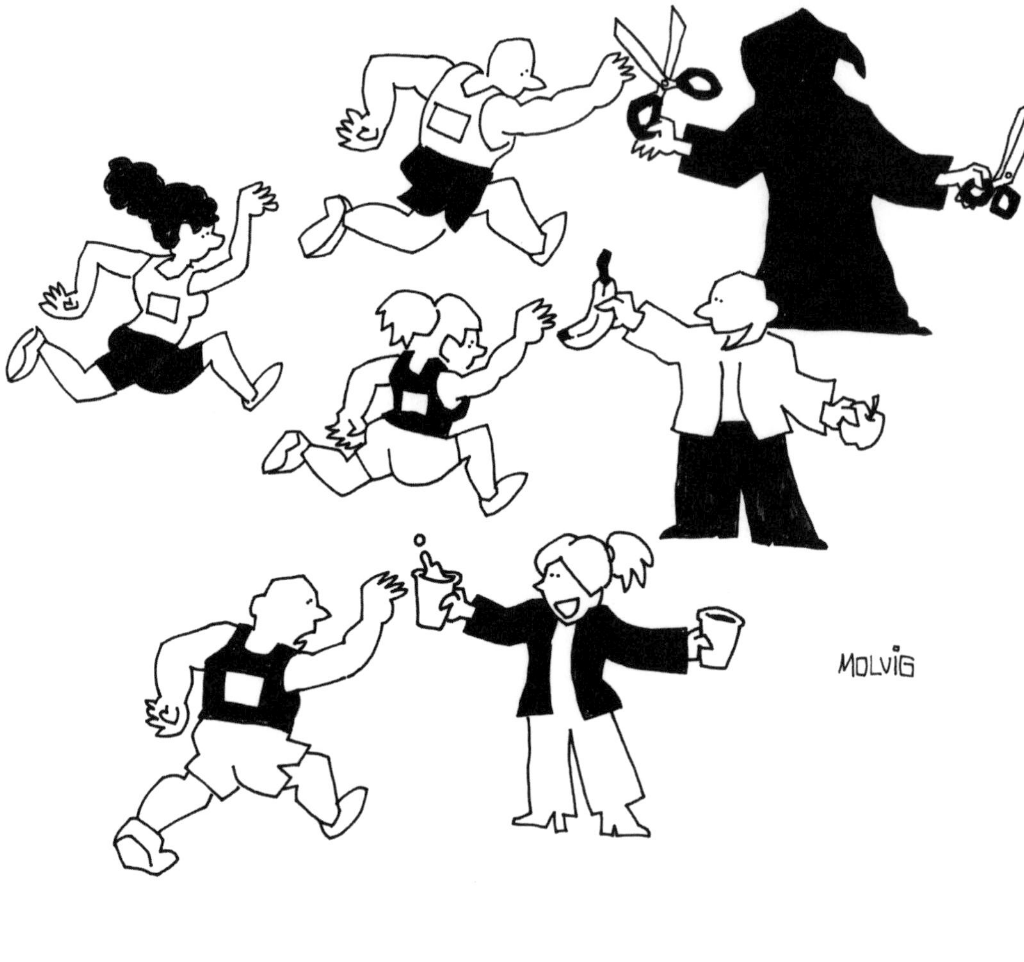
MOLVIG

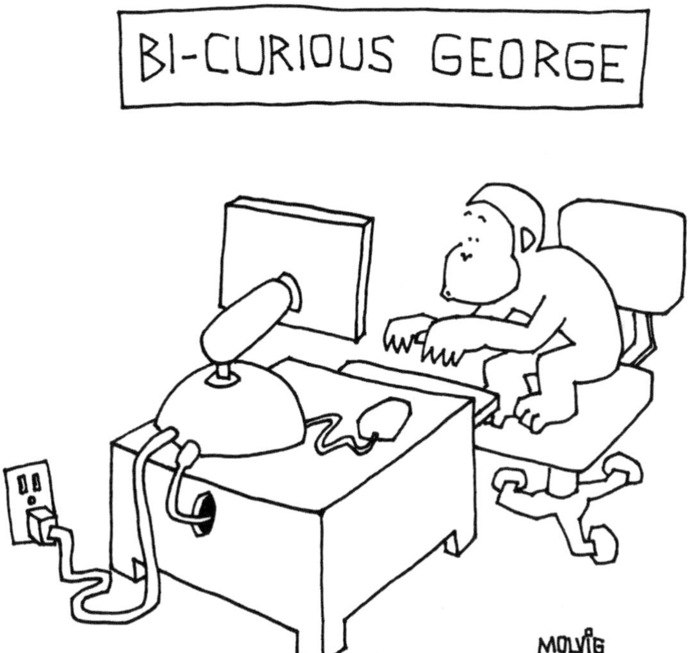
BI-CURIOUS GEORGE
MOLVIG

Levin

ARNIE LEVIN

Frequently Asked Questions

■ Where do you get your ideas?

I don't *get* ideas, *they* come to me.

■ Which comes first, the picture or the caption?

The one who phoned ahead.

■ How'd you get started?

When I was in my mid-twenties I had an auto accident in which I broke my hip and dislocated both of my shoulders. My mom had a copy of *Writer's Digest* in which there was a "how-to" for sending batches of cartoons to magazines.

■ I admire . . .

Lee Lorenz and Victoria Roberts who are back . . . on their own terms . . .

■ How do you deal with rejection?

Denial—wonder—rebuttal—Composure . . .

■ What are some things that make you laugh and why?

Someone carving a pumpkin (a sadistic laugh). An e-mail from a lawyer in Hong Kong, asking me to join in on a scheme for millions of dollars . . . (just makes me happy). *Curb Your Enthusiasm* (out loud). A White House press conference . . . (anticipated joy). Overhearing dialogue of a policeman giving directions to someone. Putting my underwear on backwards, unintentional guffaw.

■ I've got a great idea for a cartoon—wanna hear it?

EH?

Infrequently Asked Questions

■ Have you mooned or *been* mooned more often in your life?

I was once half mooned.

■ What would make a terrible pizza topping?

Terrible ingredients.

■ What might one expect to find at a really low-budget amusement park?

Ambulances.

■ What did the shepherd say to the three-legged sheepdog?

Let's see the pirouette again.

Draw Something in This Space

. . . that will help us understand your childhood.

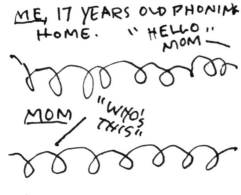

And Now for a Few More Questions . . .

■ What do you hate drawing?

Bowling pins. I have never been able to freehand one I liked. Even the ones I tried to do mechanically . . . Also horses' legs . . .

■ Being as accurate as possible, how many desert island cartoons do you think you've come up with and submitted to *The New Yorker*?

Two . . . sold them both.

■ What's the funniest thing that you witnessed, overheard, or came up with that you couldn't figure out how to use in a cartoon?

**More perplexing than funny . . .
The electric warning signs on the highways that read:
IT'S THE LAW!
MOVE OVER FOR STOPPED
EMERGENCY VEHICLES.**

■ If you could ask Bob Mankoff, *The New Yorker* cartoon editor, one question, what would it be?

Bob, in no more than 5,000 words . . . ?

Naming Names

■ What name might you give to a mild-mannered, slightly overweight dental assistant in one of your cartoons?

Dwane.

■ Other than Lance, what name would you give to a twenty-eight-year-old metrosexual entertainment lawyer who cycles on weekends?

Cash.

■ What would be a good name for a new, commercially unviable breakfast cereal?

Algae.

■ Come up with a name for an unpleasant medical procedure.

Co-payment.

■ If you used a pen name, what would it be?

Speedball.

Complete the Pie Chart Below

. . . in a way that tells us something about your life or how you think.

"Perhaps I'm not hearing you right, stranger. Did you just call me 'cupcake'?"

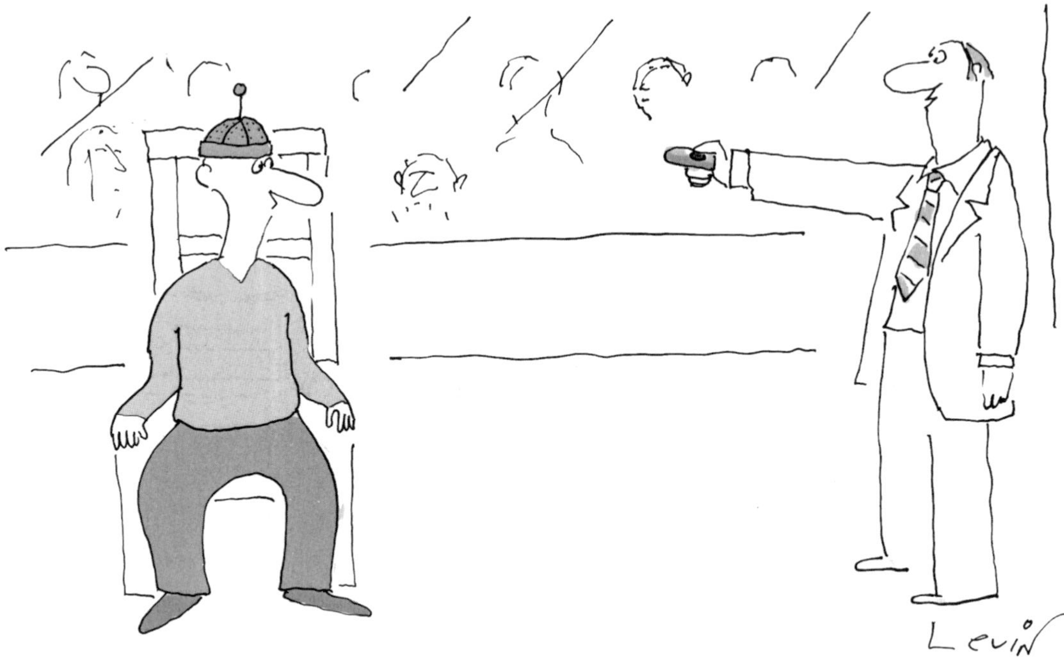
Levin

"My wife! My best tie!"

WARP

KIM
WARP

Frequently Asked Questions

■ Where do you get your ideas?

Brooding, obsessing, daydreaming.

■ Which comes first, the picture or the caption?

The embryonic idea comes at once—then evolves.

■ How'd you get started?

We had drawing time every day.

■ I admire . . .

Other cartoonists' pens.

■ How do you deal with rejection?

I don't think about it. I just draw more.

■ What are some things that make you laugh and why?

I laugh at everything—it's a problem.

■ I've got a great idea for a cartoon—wanna hear it?

No, but Diffee does!

Infrequently Asked Questions

■ Have you mooned or *been* mooned more often in your life?

The pets moon me every day.

■ What would make a terrible pizza topping?

Cat food—right, Mom?

■ What might one expect to find at a really low-budget amusement park?

Teeny Tiny Roller Coasters.

■ What did the shepherd say to the three-legged sheepdog?

I just hope it was empathetic and not some dumb joke.

And Now for a Few More Questions . . .

■ What do you hate drawing?

Nothing.

■ Being as accurate as possible, how many desert island cartoons do you think you've come up with and submitted to *The New Yorker*?

12.5.

■ What's the funniest thing that you witnessed, overheard, or came up with that you couldn't figure out how to use in a cartoon?

Nice try, Diffee!

■ If you could ask Bob Mankoff, *The New Yorker* cartoon editor, one question, what would it be?

Have you ever laughed out loud at one of my cartoons? Smiled to yourself? Never mind.

Draw Something in This Space

. . . that will help us understand your childhood.

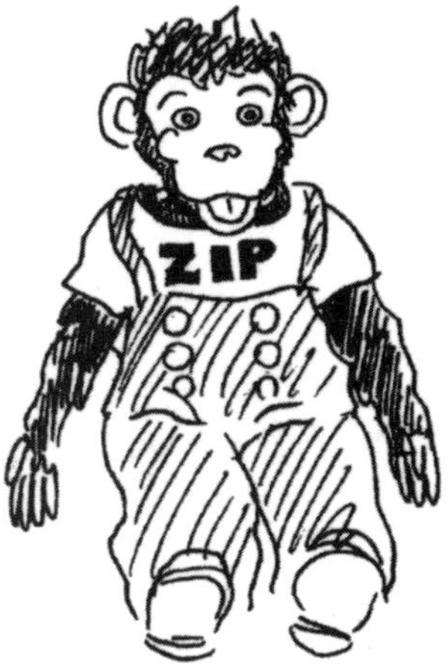
ZIP

Naming Names

■ What name might you give to a mild-mannered, slightly overweight dental assistant in one of your cartoons?

Amy.

■ Other than Lance, what name would you give to a twenty-eight-year-old metrosexual entertainment lawyer who cycles on weekends?

Josh.

■ What would be a good name for a new, commercially unviable breakfast cereal?

Chunks.

■ Come up with a name for an unpleasant medical procedure.

Nosectomy.

■ If you used a pen name, what would it be?

Warp—but it's not.

Complete the Pie Chart Below

. . . in a way that tells us something about your life or how you think.

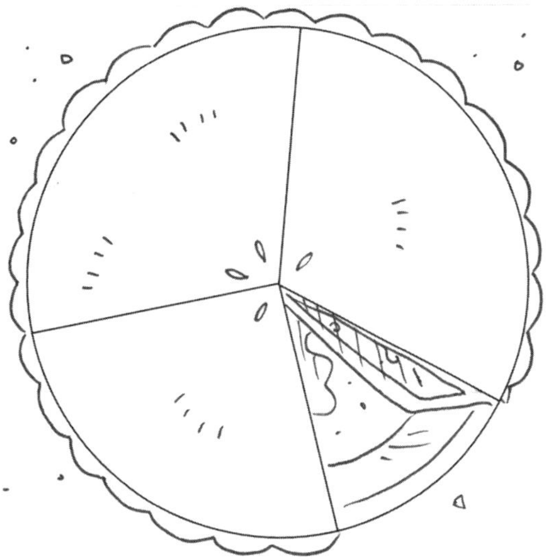

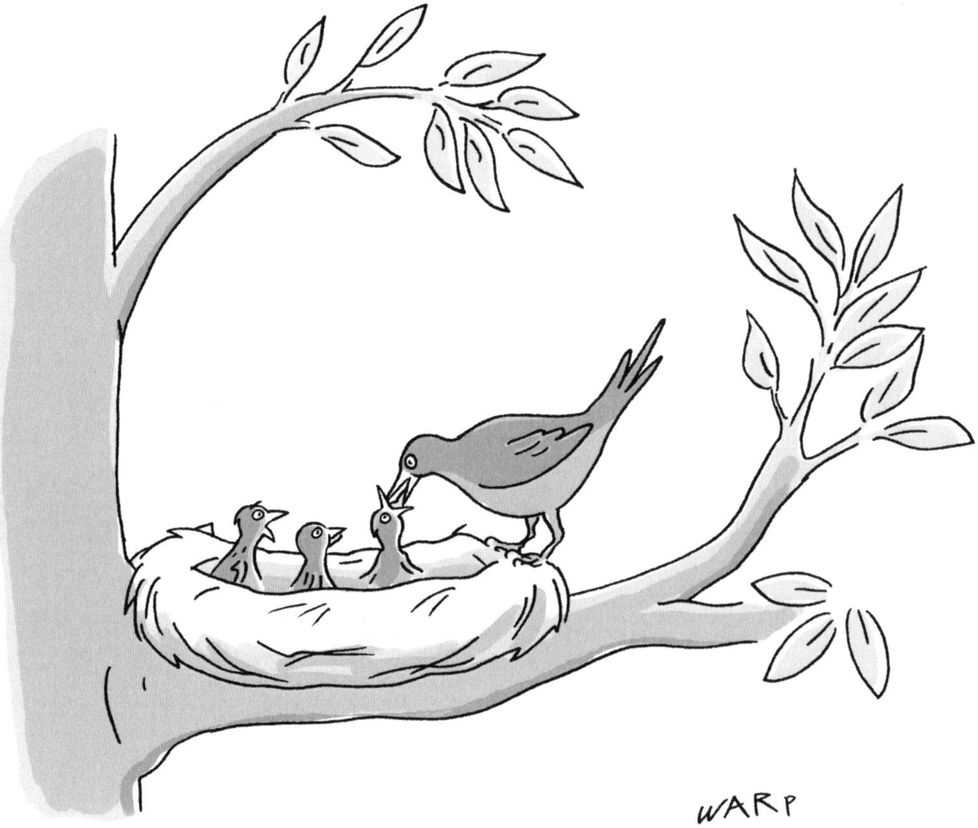
WARP

"Smoothies again?"

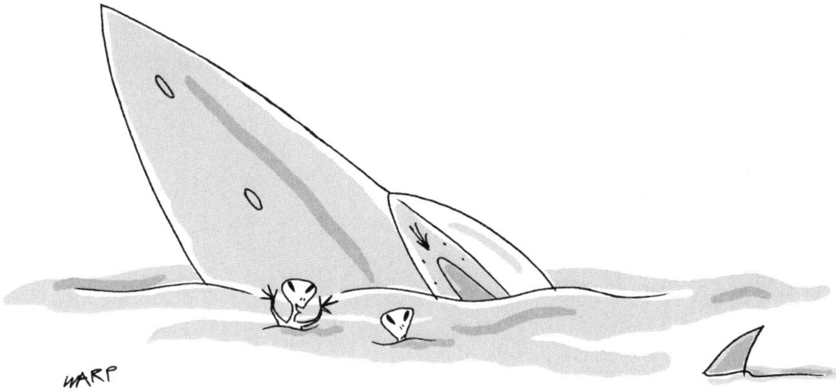
WARP

"We're saved! We're saved!"

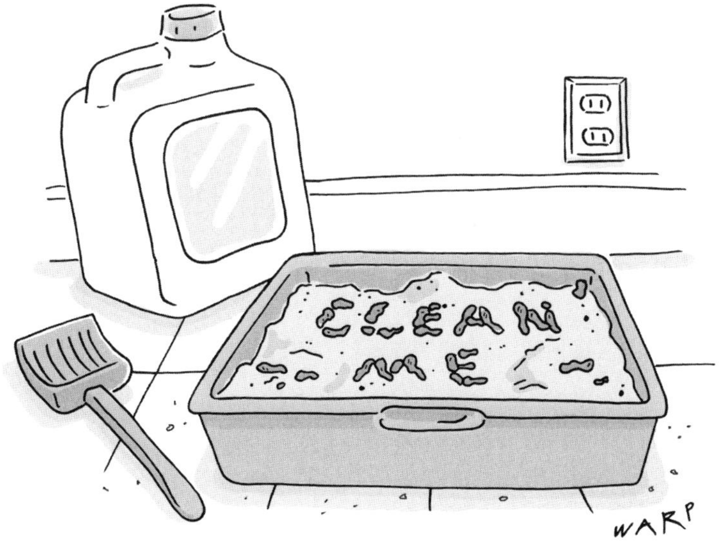
CLEAN
ME
WARP

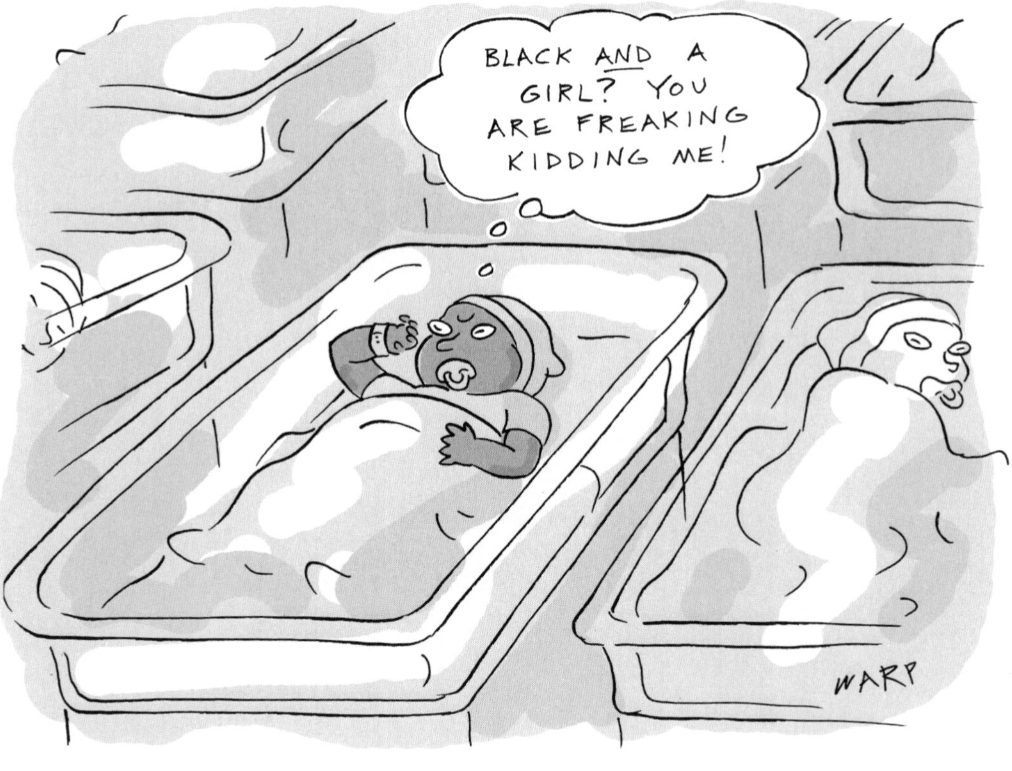
BLACK AND A GIRL? YOU ARE FREAKING KIDDING ME!
WARP

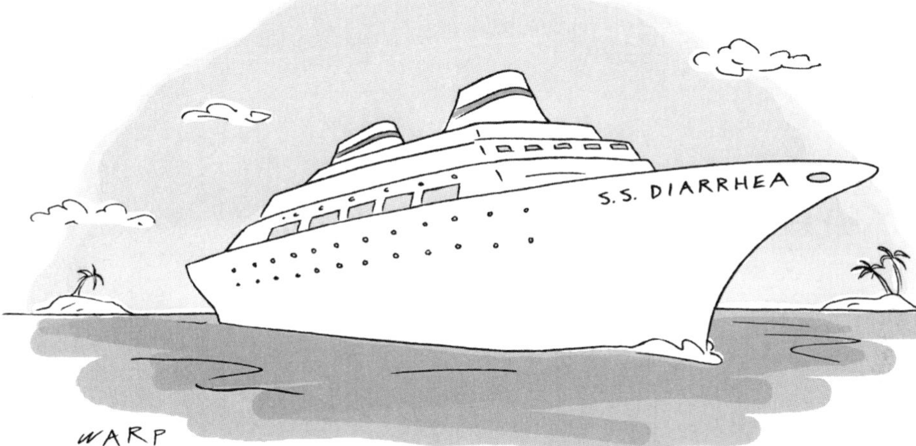
S.S. DIARRHEA
WARP

Corvette With Spoiler

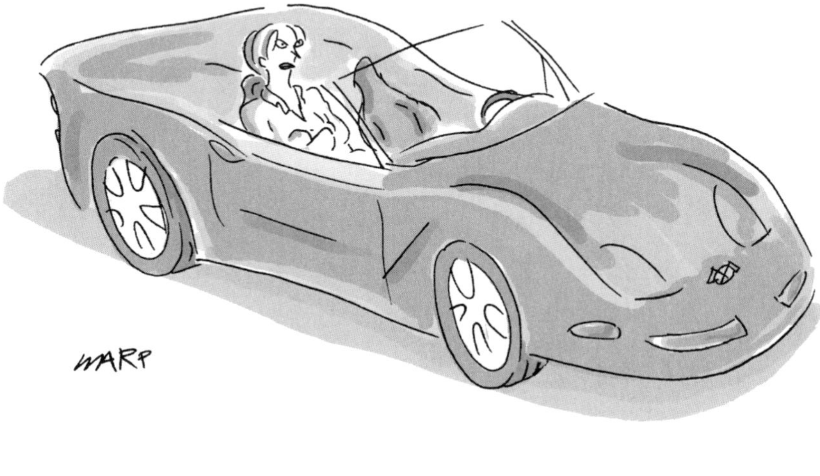
WARP

"Who even knew they made dog thongs?"

WHO KNOWS WHAT MONTH
OLD MAN JOURNAL
OLD MAN JOURNAL
What the Hell is everyone mumbling about?
WWII
WWII revisited
More WWII
Same stories as last month
Reader Gripes
ISSUE 2,486,501
WARP

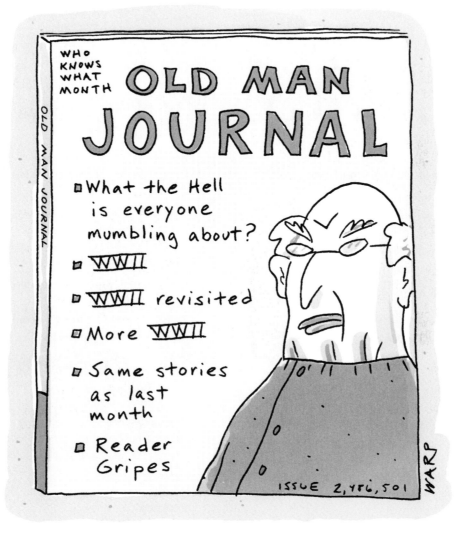

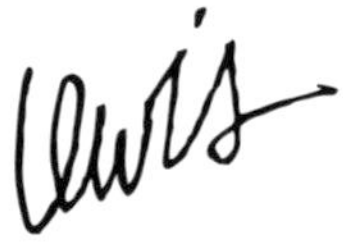

ERIC LEWIS

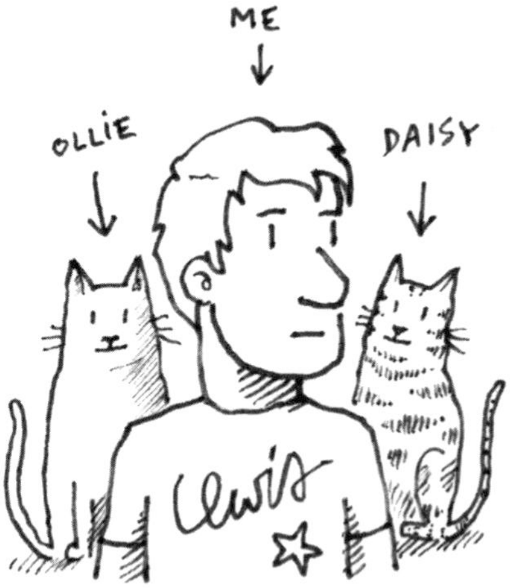
ME
OLLIE
DAISY

Frequently Asked Questions

■ Where do you get your ideas?
At a place off Route 6 called "Idea Barn."

■ Which comes first, the picture or the caption?
It's best when they come at the same time. What!?

■ How'd you get started?
I blew Bob at a party.

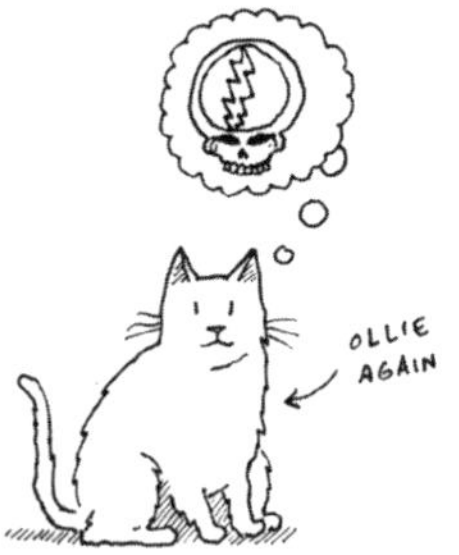
OLLIE AGAIN

■ I admire . . .
. . . Jerry Garcia, George Herriman (creator of *Krazy Kat*).

■ How do you deal with rejection?
Crying, breaking windows, and then, a long, hot bubble bath.

■ What are some things that make you laugh and why?
My cats—Oliver and Daisy. Because they're never phony or contrived, and yet they do goofy things. For example, Daisy nurses on my earlobes.

■ I've got a great idea for a cartoon—wanna hear it?
NO!!! Okay, yes, mom, tell me. . . .

Infrequently Asked Questions

■ Have you mooned or *been* mooned more often in your life?
I wish I could say, but I've completely repressed those memories.

■ What would make a terrible pizza topping?
Fried dark matter.

■ What might one expect to find at a really low-budget amusement park?
A View-Master reel library.

■ What did the shepherd say to the three-legged sheepdog?
I got nothin'.

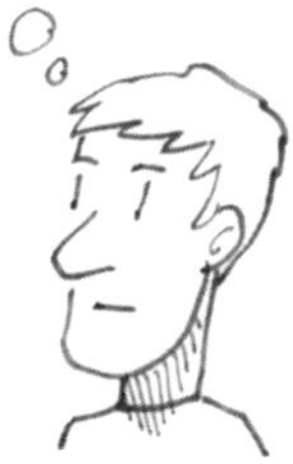

Draw Something in This Space

. . . that will help us understand your childhood.

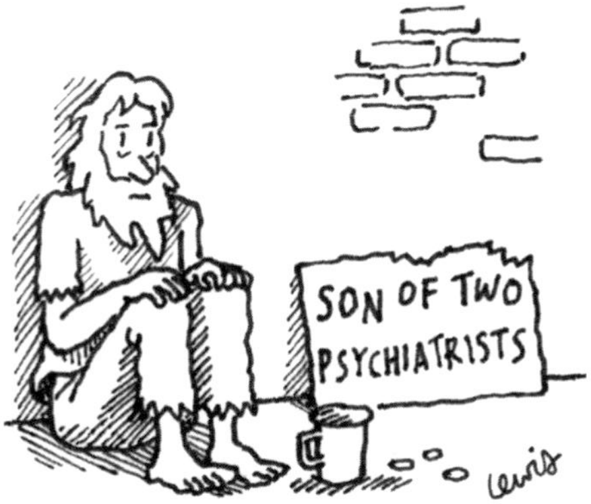
SON OF TWO
PSYCHIATRISTS

And Now for a Few More Questions . . .

- What do you hate drawing?

  Perspective. I don't even believe in perspective, actually. It's just a theory!

- Being as accurate as possible, how many desert island cartoons do you think you've come up with and submitted to *The New Yorker*?

  Maybe fifty. Sold two!

- What's the funniest thing that you witnessed, overheard, or came up with that you couldn't figure out how to use in a cartoon?

  I'm convinced that Dick Cheney has some kind of emergency escape pod that could bring him safely to the moon in a time of crisis.

- If you could ask Bob Mankoff, *The New Yorker* cartoon editor, one question, what would it be?

  Do you still love me?

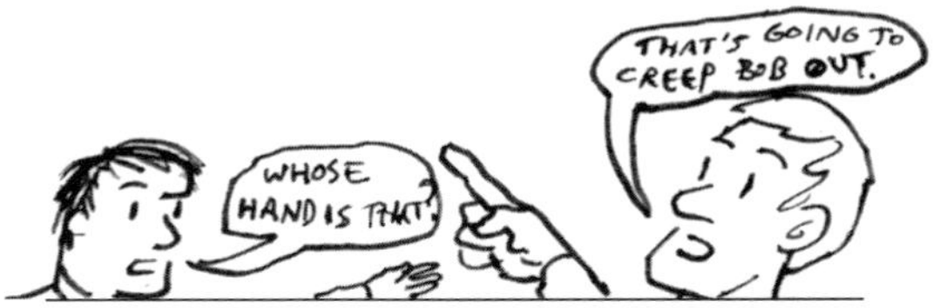
WHOSE HAND IS THAT?
THAT'S GOING TO CREEP BOB OUT.

Naming Names

- What name might you give to a mild-mannered, slightly overweight dental assistant in one of your cartoons?

  Matt Diffee.

- Other than Lance, what name would you give to a twenty-eight-year-old metrosexual entertainment lawyer who cycles on weekends?

  Matthew Diffee.

- What would be a good name for a new, commercially unviable breakfast cereal?

  Whore Flakes. Money Shot Clusters?

- Come up with a name for an unpleasant medical procedure.

  Laser Urethrabrasion.

- If you used a pen name, what would it be?

  Dr. Sanford Sharpie.

Complete the Pie Chart Below

. . . in a way that tells us something about your life or how you think.

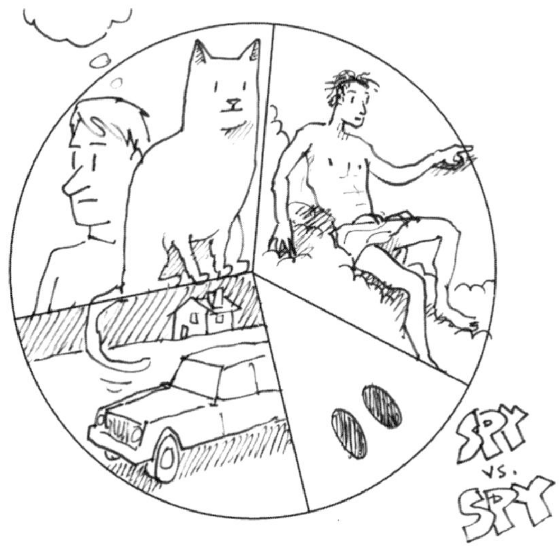
SPY
VS.
SPY

"If I ever start showing signs of Stockholm syndrome, kill me."

MOMS GONE WILD

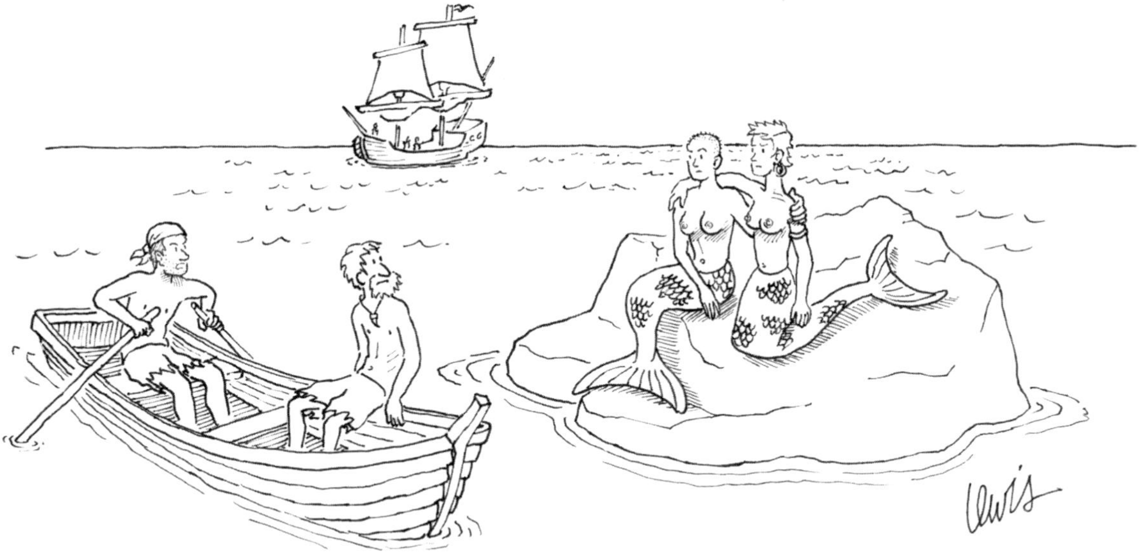
lewis

"Arrg. Just our luck!"

"Hold that thought. I have to go take a number five."

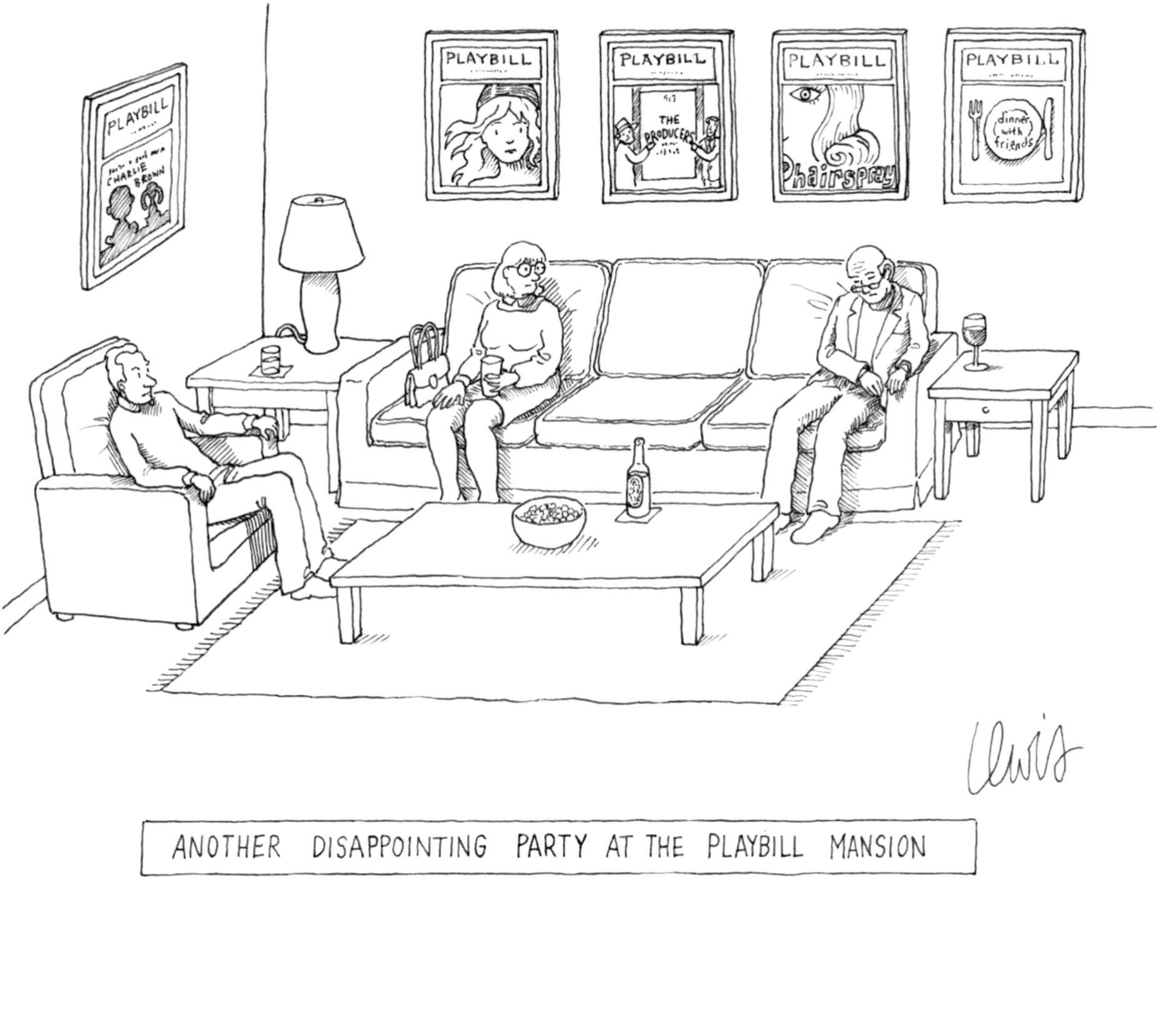
PLAYBILL
CHARLIE BROWN
PLAYBILL
PLAYBILL
THE PRODUCERS
PLAYBILL
hairspray
PLAYBILL
dinner with friends
Lewis

ANOTHER DISAPPOINTING PARTY AT THE PLAYBILL MANSION

WOMEN'S SYNCHRONIZED PEEING

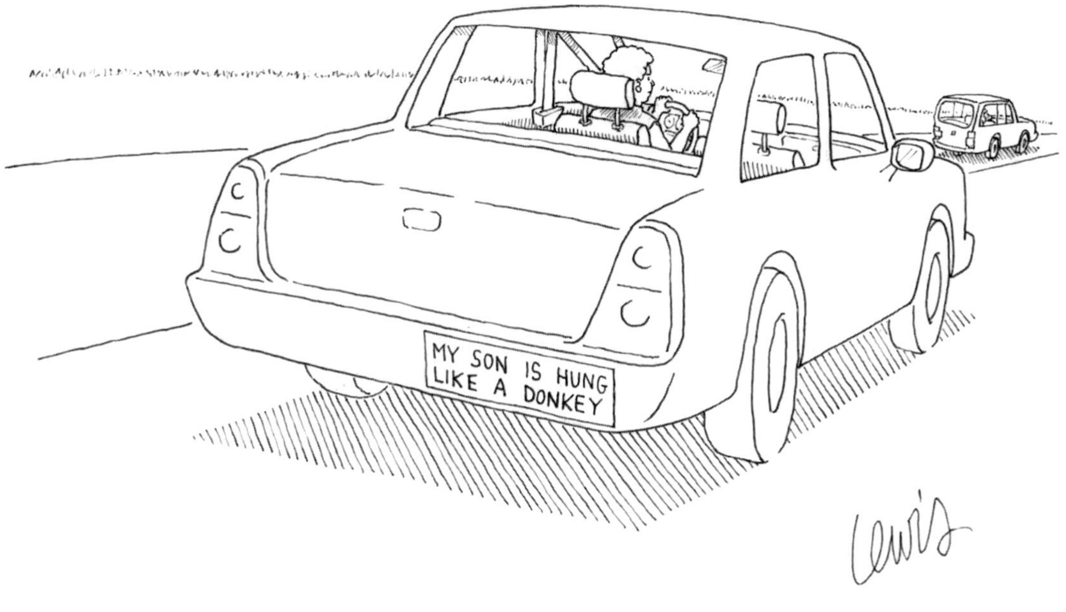
MY SON IS HUNG
LIKE A DONKEY
Lewis

S. Harris

SIDNEY HARRIS

Frequently Asked Questions

■ Where do you get your ideas?

Mostly, while sitting—rarely standing.

■ Which comes first, the ~~picture or the caption?~~
VAGUE IDEA, THEN THE CAPTION.

■ How'd you get started?

I had nothing else to do.

■ I admire . . .

Zero Mostel, Mae West, Gene Tierney, George Gershwin, Jimmy Durante, Woody Allen, Lena Horne, Mel Brooks, Michael Jordan, Clara Bow, Rita Hayworth (Margarita Cansino), Carl Sagan, Arlo Guthrie, Mike Tyson, Lauren Bacall, Sandy Koufax, and those two dynamite ladies, Marisa Tomei and Rosie Perez. I could probably think of some people who weren't born in Brooklyn who could also be mentioned here, but these will do.

■ How do you deal with rejection?

A freelance cartoonist obviously has a short attention span, or he'd be writing something longer than single sentences, **so, fortunately, I forget the rejections very soon.**

■ What are some things that make you laugh and why?

Sid Caesar always makes me laugh— although it's often more than just laughter; others do only occasionally.

■ I've got a great idea for a cartoon—wanna hear it?

NO!!

Infrequently Asked Questions

■ Have you mooned or _been_ mooned more often in your life?

No.

■ What would make a terrible pizza topping?

Cheese and tomato sauce.

■ What might one expect to find at a really low-budget amusement park?

One bumper car.

- What did the shepherd say to the three-legged sheepdog?

  Here, tripod!

And Now for a Few More Questions . . .

- What do you hate drawing?

  Shoes. Socks are easier.

- Being as accurate as possible, how many desert island cartoons do you think you've come up with and submitted to *The New Yorker*?

  Two.

- What's the funniest thing that you witnessed, overheard, or came up with that you couldn't figure out how to use in a cartoon?

  Never saw anything funny.

- If you could ask Bob Mankoff, *The New Yorker* cartoon editor, one question, what would it be?

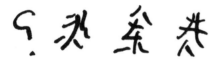

Draw Some Sort of Doodle

. . . using the random lines below as a starting point.

Naming Names

- What name might you give to a mild-mannered, slightly overweight dental assistant in one of your cartoons?

  Fritzi.

- Other than Lance, what name would you give to a twenty-eight-year-old metrosexual entertainment lawyer who cycles on weekends?

  Fritz.

- What would be a good name for a new, commercially unviable breakfast cereal?

  Ritz.

- Come up with a name for an unpleasant medical procedure.

  Itz.

- If you used a pen name, what would it be?

  If it was the state pen: 376148902.

Complete the Pie Chart Below

. . . in a way that tells us something about your life or how you think.

Thomas Pynchon
Rembrandt
Art Tatum
Lemon Meringue

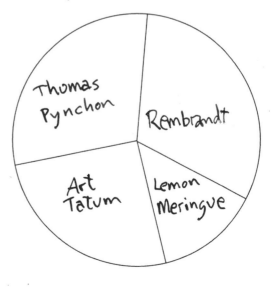

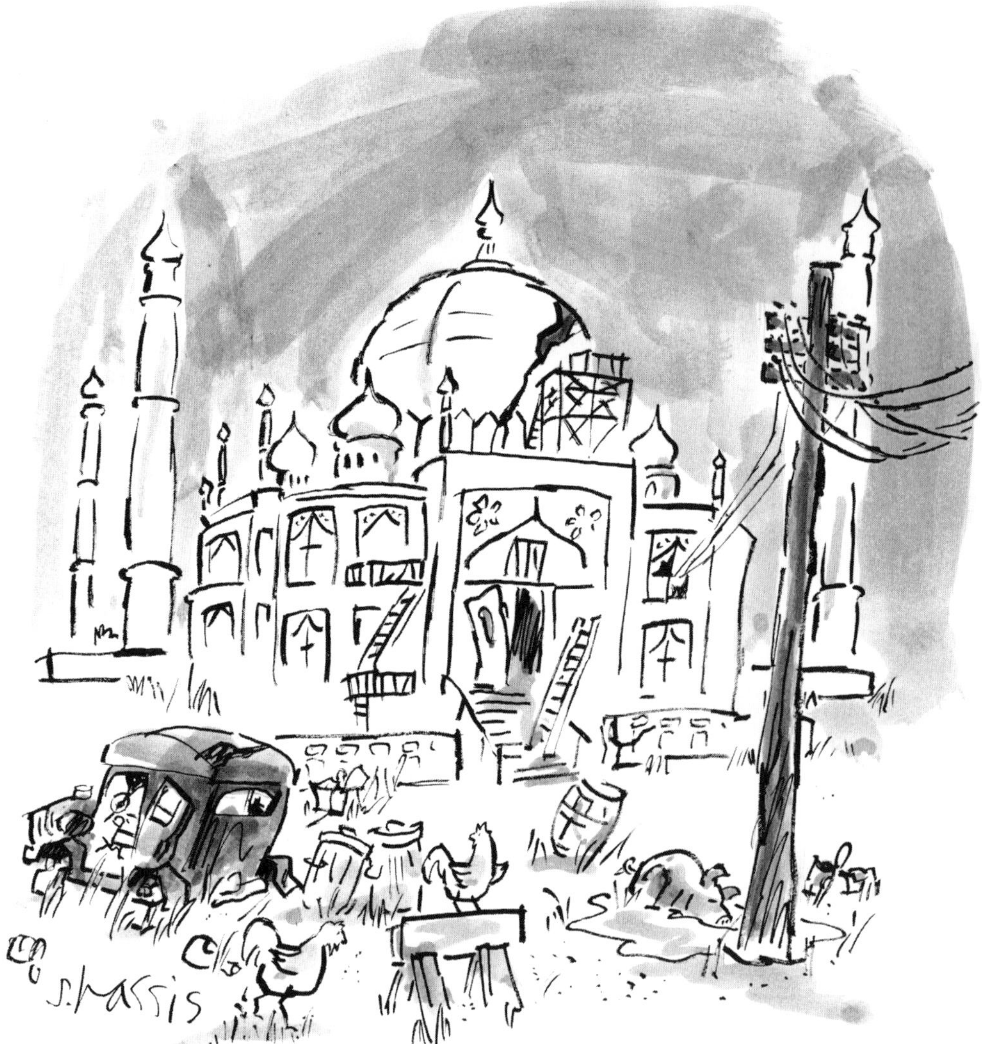
S. Gross

THE BACK OF THE TAJ MAHAL

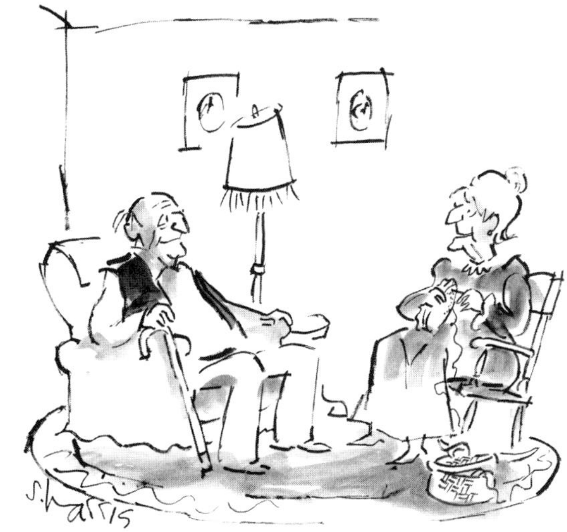
S. Harris

"Now that the kids and grandkids are grown I can get back to doing more erotic embroidery."

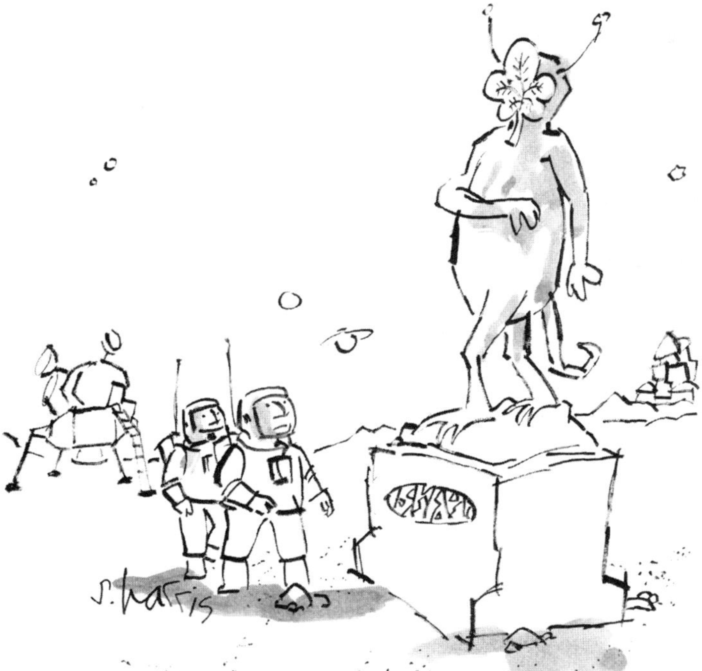
S. Harris

J. C. DUFFY

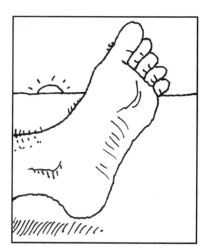

Frequently Asked Questions

■ Where do you get your ideas?

The Idea Place.

■ Which comes first, the picture or the caption?

Usually, the caption, sometimes the picture.

■ How'd you get started?

Hey, when it comes to how I got started, don't get me started!

■ I admire . . .

The dimples behind a woman's knees, and Gandhi.

■ How do you deal with rejection?

Alcohol and meaningless sex.

■ What are some things that make you laugh and why?

A man slipping on a banana peel . . . a moron throwing a clock out the window in order to see time fly . . . a chicken (funny already!) crossing the road, but only when it's "to get to the other side" . . . obviously, I'm easily amused.

■ I've got a great idea for a cartoon—wanna hear it?

I used to say no; now I say yes, but the ideas usually suck.

Infrequently Asked Questions

■ Have you mooned or *been* mooned more often in your life?

It's a tie: mooner, never. Moonee, never.

■ What would make a terrible pizza topping?

A human head.

■ What might one expect to find at a really low-budget amusement park?

50 percent polyester cotton candy.

■ What did the shepherd say to the three-legged sheepdog?

Come here often?

Draw Something in This Space

. . . that will help us understand your childhood.

WILL YOU BE MY FRIEND?

And Now for a Few More Questions . . .

- What do you hate drawing?
  Crowds, bicycles, iron lung machines.

- Being as accurate as possible, how many desert island cartoons do you think you've come up with and submitted to *The New Yorker*?
  Maybe thirty or so.

- What's the funniest thing that you witnessed, overheard, or came up with that you couldn't figure out how to use in a cartoon?
  Whatever it is, I'm saving it for use in a noncartoon.

- If you could ask Bob Mankoff, *The New Yorker* cartoon editor, one question, what would it be?
  Was it something I said?

Naming Names

- What name might you give to a mild-mannered, slightly overweight dental assistant in one of your cartoons?
  Prunella.

- Other than Lance, what name would you give to a twenty-eight-year-old metrosexual entertainment lawyer who cycles on weekends?
  Vance.

- What would be a good name for a new, commercially unviable breakfast cereal?
  Mouse Clusters.

- Come up with a name for an unpleasant medical procedure.
  Surgery.

- If you used a pen name, what would it be?
  Chad Manwaring.

Complete the Pie Chart Below

. . . in a way that tells us something about your life or how you think.

ME.
ME.
ME.
WORLD PEACE.

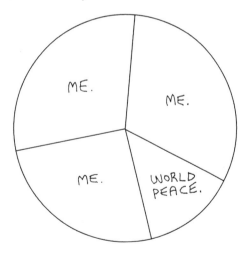

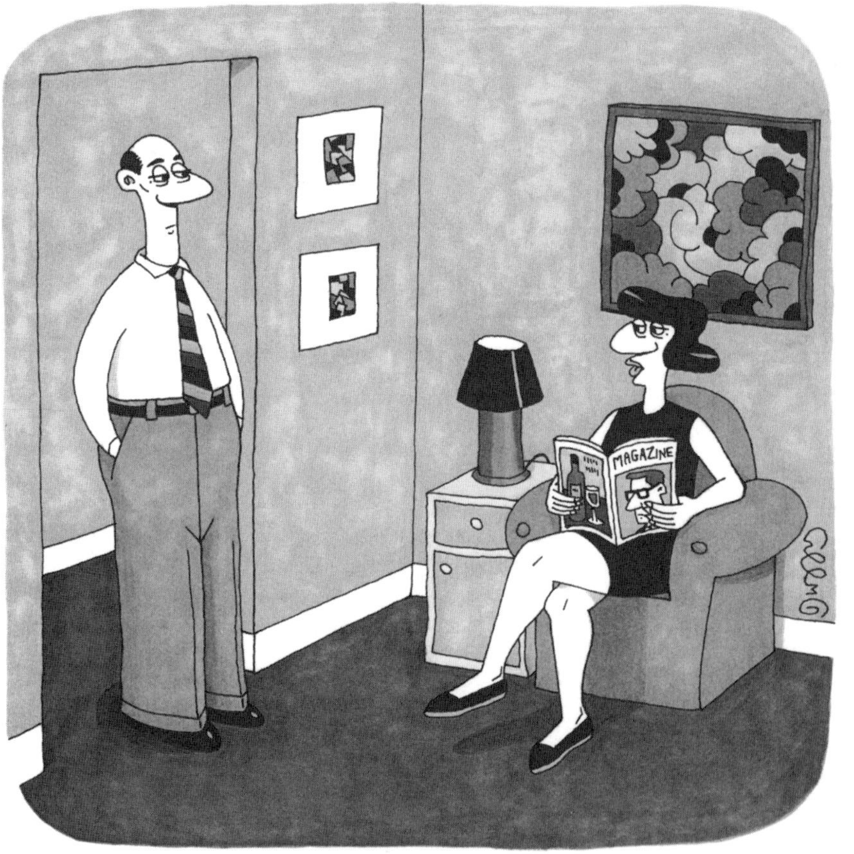
MAGAZINE

"I think your tailor has seriously miscalculated your rise, Herbert."

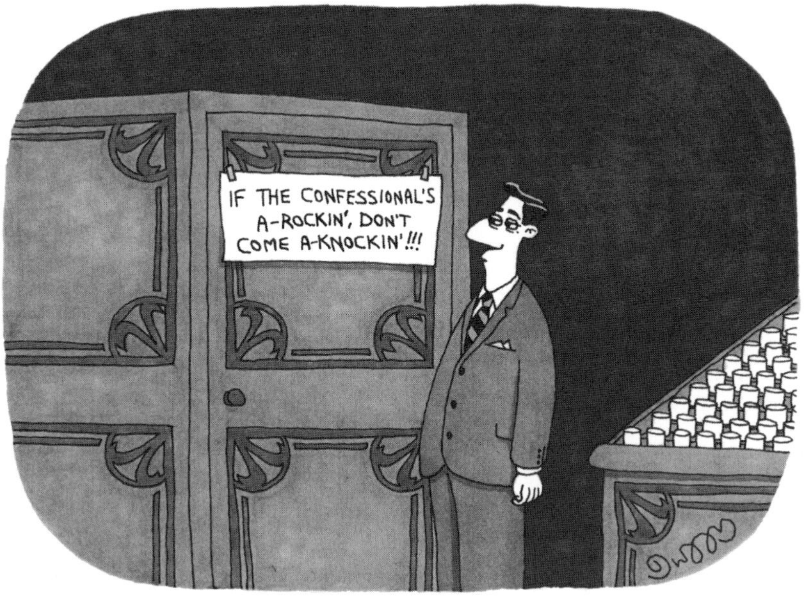
IF THE CONFESSIONAL'S
A-ROCKIN', DON'T
COME A-KNOCKIN'!!!

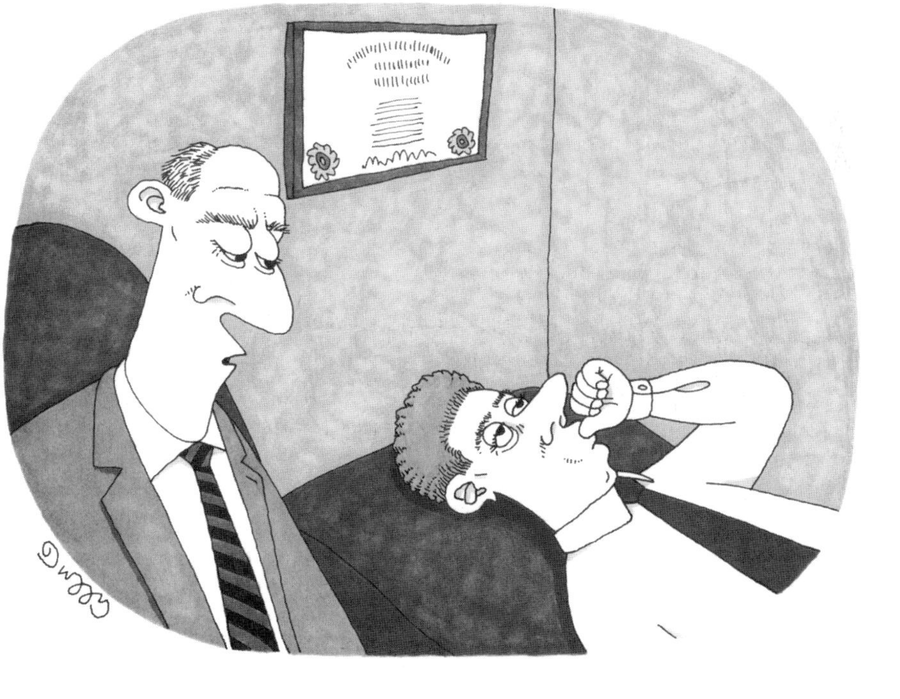

"Yes, Mr. Hargraves, thumb-sucking can be cured.
But first let's talk about what your other hand is doing."

"Could I do this with an imaginary friend?"

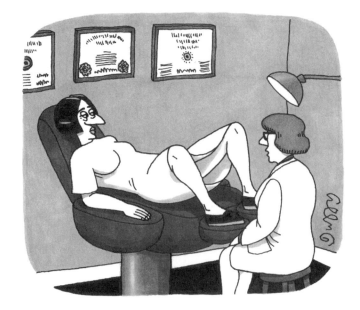

"I spy London, I spy France . . . neither of which rhymes with 'yeast infection.'"

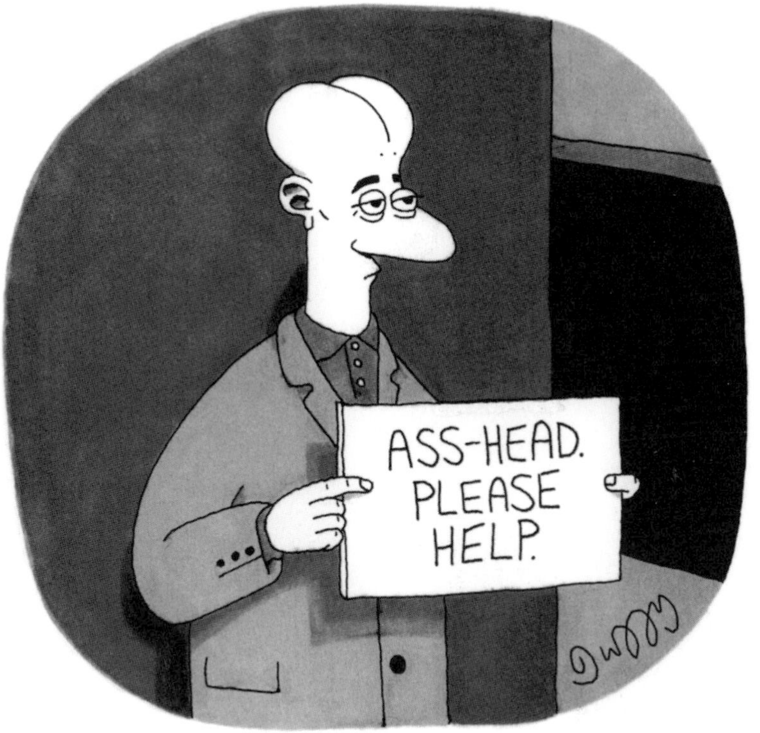
ASS-HEAD.
PLEASE
HELP.
DUFFY

"I never know what to do with my hands at a party."

"Waiter, there's a fly in my soup, and ironically, there's also a crouton in my shit."

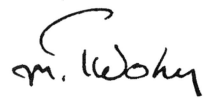

MIKE TWOHY

Frequently Asked Questions

■ Where do you get your ideas?
I think of them.

■ Which comes first, the picture or the caption?
A few random words and then doodling.

■ How'd you get started?
A guy asked me to draw up some gags he'd been carrying in his wallet for 30 years.

■ I admire . . .
Paul Klee, Dr. Seuss, Abraham Lincoln.

■ What are some things that make you laugh and why?
Political satire
Cauliflower ears
Bushisms
Pit toilets

■ How do you deal with rejection?

■ I've got a great idea for a cartoon—wanna hear it?
Sure—abuse me.

Infrequently Asked Questions

■ Have you mooned or *been* mooned more often in your life?
Hopefully, the Lord understands my mooning was always preemptive.

■ What would make a terrible pizza topping?
Scrabble tiles.

■ What might one expect to find at a really low-budget amusement park?
Sticky railings.

■ What did the shepherd say to the three-legged sheepdog?
Don't worry. Sheep can't count.

DENIAL

Yes-s-s! Another sale!!!

And Now for a Few More Questions . . .

■ What do you hate drawing?

Casts of thousands and detailed architecture.

■ Being as accurate as possible, how many desert island cartoons do you think you've come up with and submitted to *The New Yorker*?

Seven (five my first year).

■ What's the funniest thing that you witnessed, overheard, or came up with that you couldn't figure out how to use in a cartoon?

Numerous cartoons that other people did.

■ If you could ask Bob Mankoff, *The New Yorker* cartoon editor, one question, what would it be?

Do you laugh this hard at everyone's cartoons?

Naming Names

■ What name might you give to a mild-mannered, slightly overweight dental assistant in one of your cartoons?

Susan.

■ Other than Lance, what name would you give to a twenty-eight-year-old metrosexual entertainment lawyer who cycles on weekends?

Reg.

■ What would be a good name for a new, commercially unviable breakfast cereal?

Transfatty-Os.

■ Come up with a name for an unpleasant medical procedure.

They've all been invented.

■ If you used a pen name, what would it be?

2E.

Draw Something in This Space

. . . that will help us understand your childhood.

Complete the Pie Chart Below

. . . in a way that tells us something about your life or how you think.

"Underwear is aisle nine."

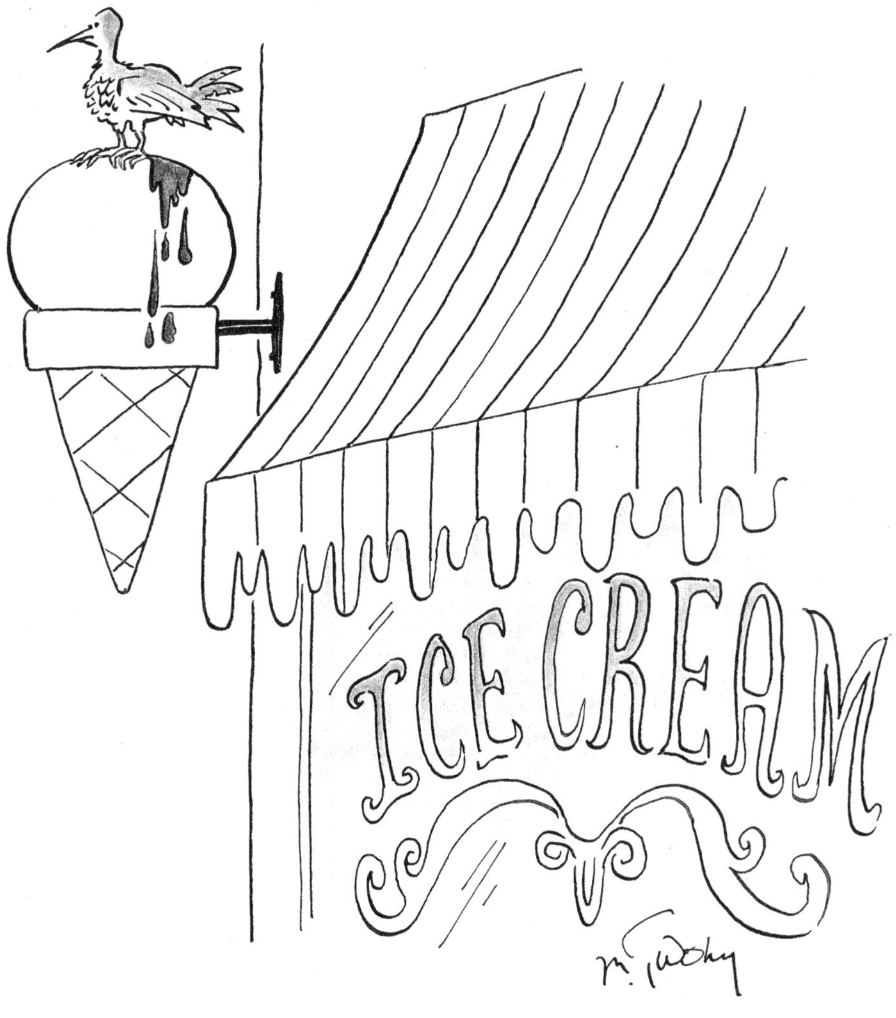
ICE CREAM
M. Twohy

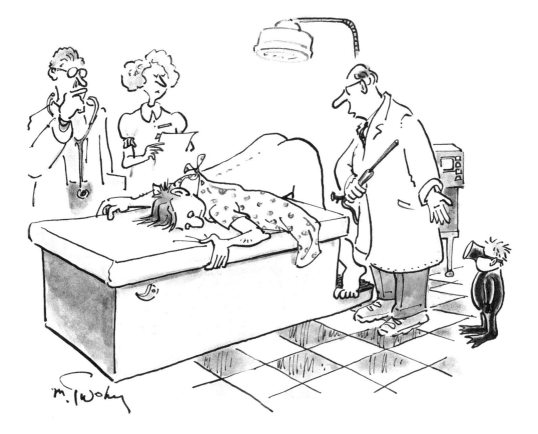

*"I'm afraid we can't see anything with the sigmoidoscope,
so we'll have to send in junior."*

"Anchored on the far side, we have the oldest ship in the fleet."

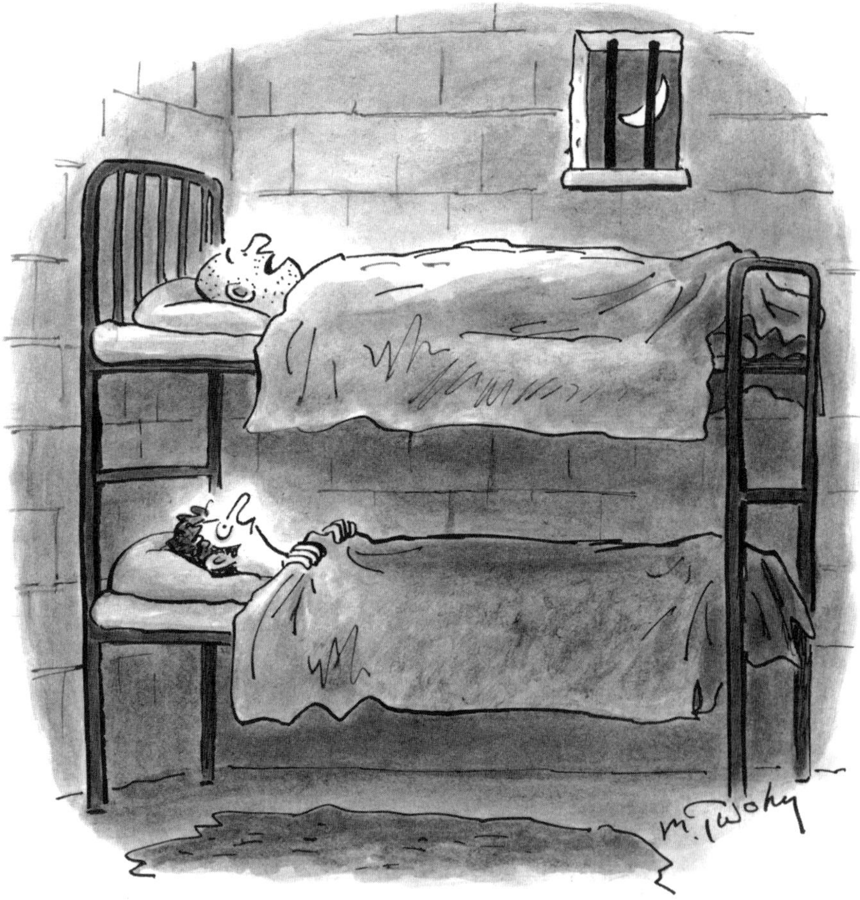
m. Twohy

"Nighty-night, sleep tight—don't let the bedbugs rape."

"You get the most accessories with the bi Kens."

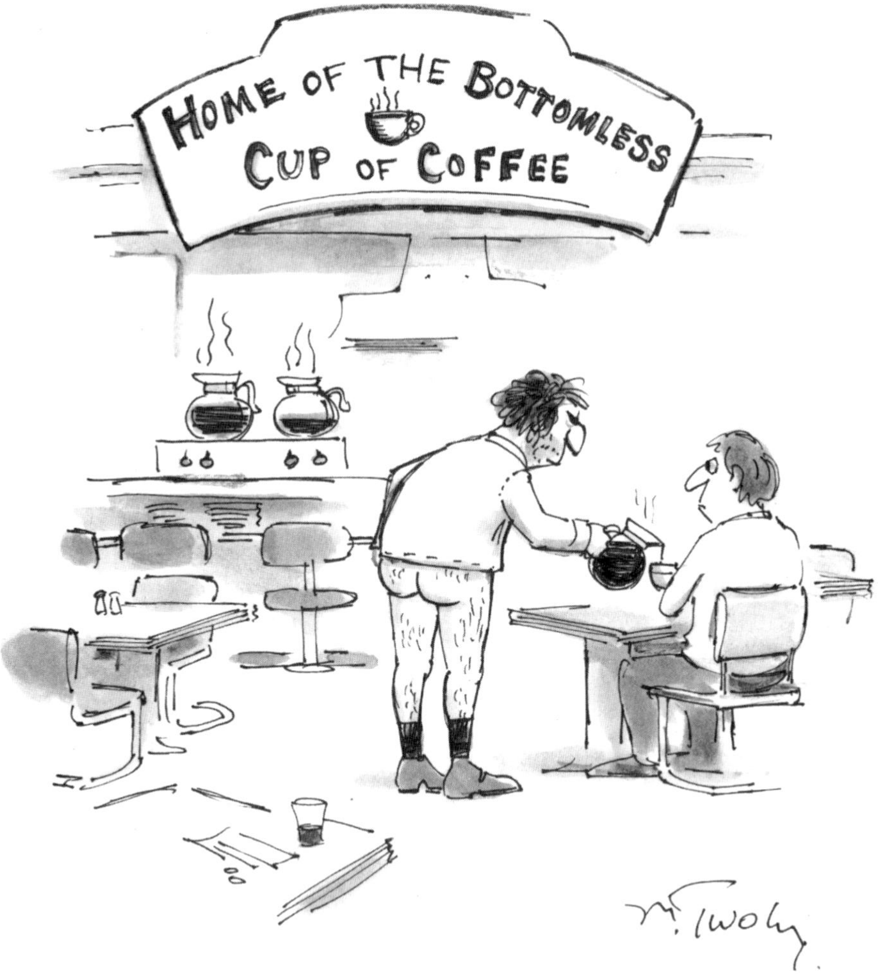
HOME OF THE BOTTOMLESS
CUP OF COFFEE

"And if nepotism exists, my brothers will root it out!"

GLEN LELIEVRE

LeLIEVRE

Frequently Asked Questions

■ Where do you get your ideas?

Southwest corner of East 62nd Street—facing north.

■ Which comes first, the picture or the caption?

The piction.

■ How'd you get started?

My dad had sex with my mom.

■ I admire . . .

Van Gogh. Anyone who'd cut off their ear and send it to a prostitute is a-okay in my book.

■ How do you deal with rejection?

Sacrifice a chicken over the magazine.

■ What are some things that make you laugh and why?

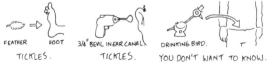

FEATHER ⇒ FOOT
TICKLES.

3/4" BEVL IN EAR CANAL
TICKLES.

DRINKING BIRD.
YOU DON'T WANT TO KNOW.

■ I've got a great idea for a cartoon—wanna hear it?

No.

■ I've got a great idea for a cartoon—wanna hear it?

NO!

■ I've got a great idea for a cartoon—wanna hear it?

NOOOO!

Infrequently Asked Questions

■ Have you mooned or *been* mooned more often in your life?

Avoiding both—lycanthropy.

■ What would make a terrible pizza topping?

New Jersey.

■ What might one expect to find at a really low-budget amusement park?

Escalator! The Ride!

■ What did the shepherd say to the three-legged sheepdog?

I've got a great idea for a cartoon—wanna hear it?

And Now for a Few More Questions . . .

- What do you hate drawing?

Boxes filled with hair.

- Being as accurate as possible, how many desert island cartoons do you think you've come up with and submitted to *The New Yorker*?

Five.

- What's the funniest thing that you witnessed, overheard, or came up with that you couldn't figure out how to use in a cartoon?

A desert island.

- If you could ask Bob Mankoff, *The New Yorker* cartoon editor, one question, what would it be?

Boxers or briefs?

Draw Some Sort of Doodle

. . . using the random lines below as a starting point.

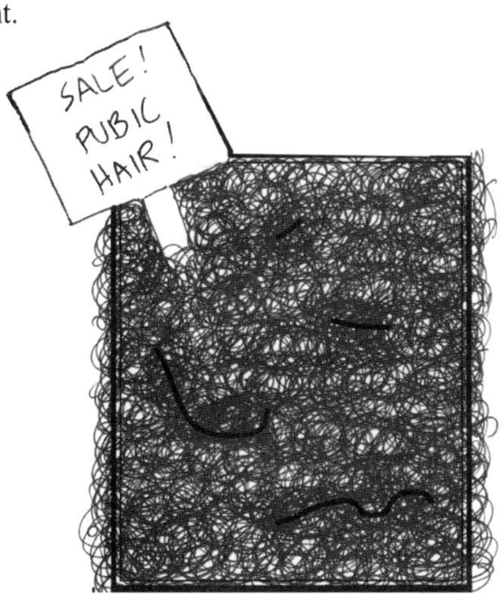
SALE!
PUBIC
HAIR!

Naming Names

- What name might you give to a mild-mannered, slightly overweight dental assistant in one of your cartoons?

Hey, you over there, in the corner.

- Other than Lance, what name would you give to a twenty-eight-year-old metrosexual entertainment lawyer who cycles on weekends?

Ian Denial.

- What would be a good name for a new, commercially unviable breakfast cereal?

Hair Ballios!

- Come up with a name for an unpleasant medical procedure.

Astralianization.

- If you used a pen name, what would it be?

Paper Mate.

Draw Something in This Space

. . . that will help us understand your childhood.

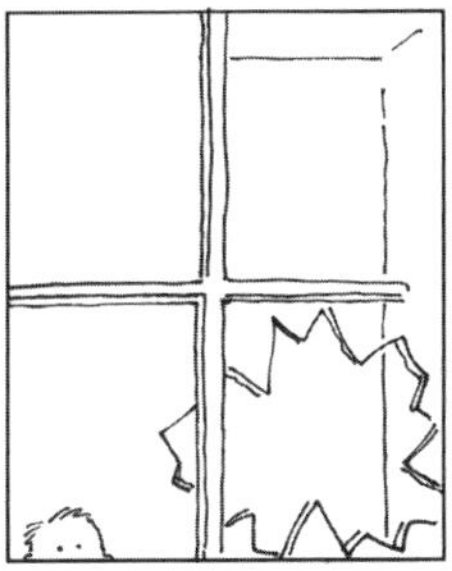

Complete the Pie Chart Below

. . . in a way that tells us something about your life or how you think.

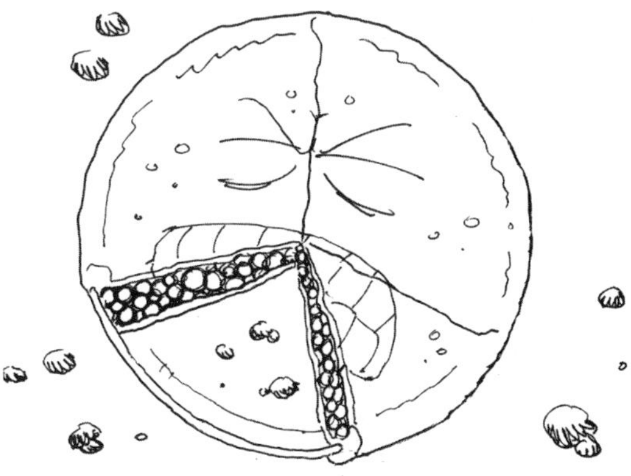

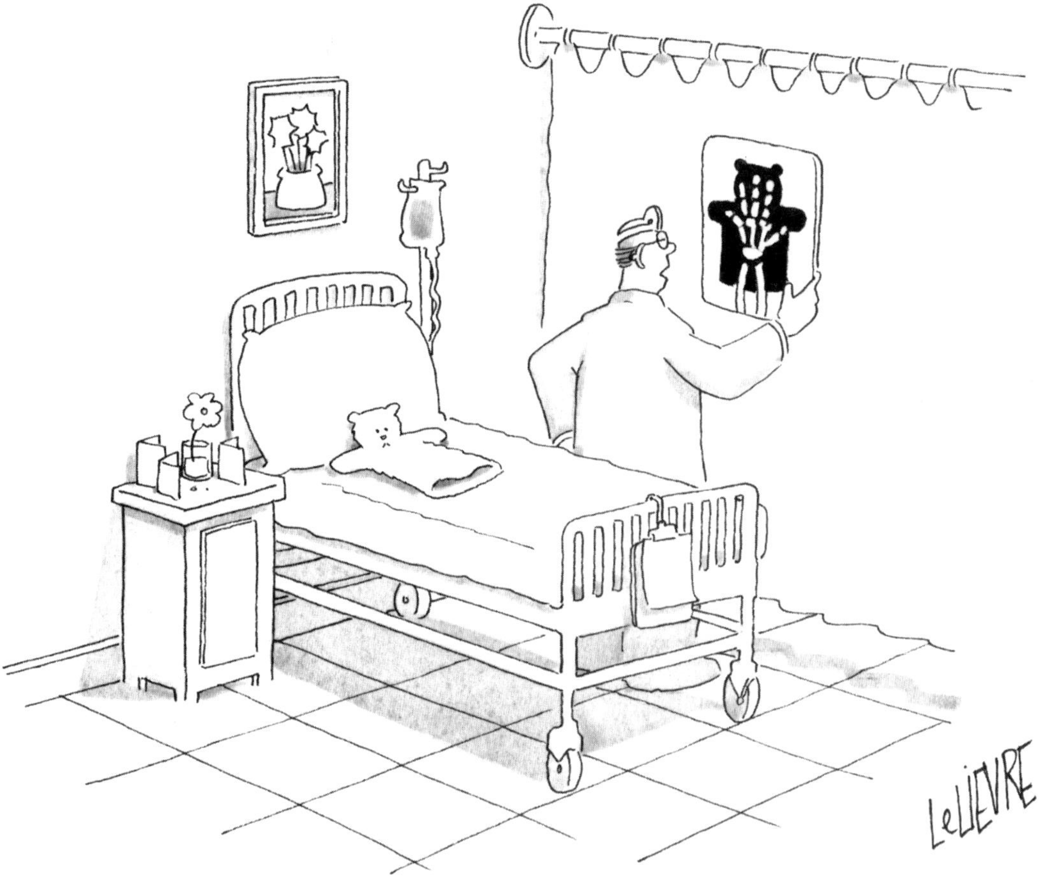
LeLIEVRE

"Well, we removed the growth, but the operation has left you paralyzed from the neck down."

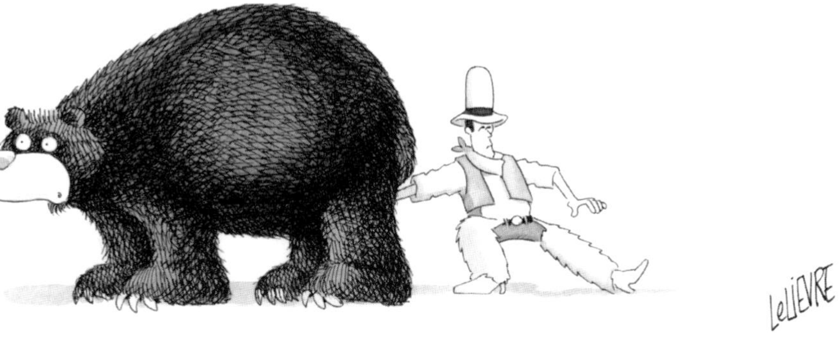
LELIEVRE

HIGH STAKES TEXAS HOLD 'EM.

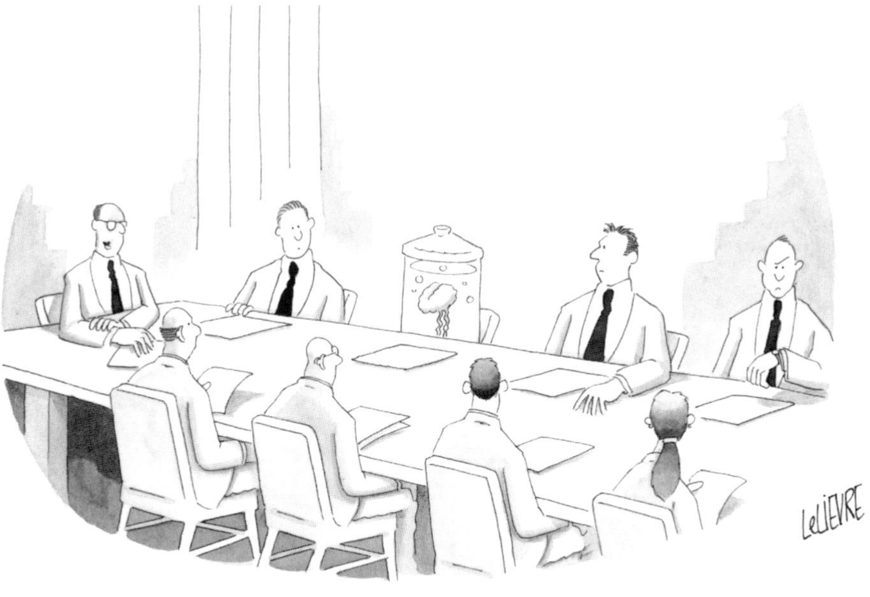
LELIEVRE

"But first let's all congratulate Ted on his return to work."

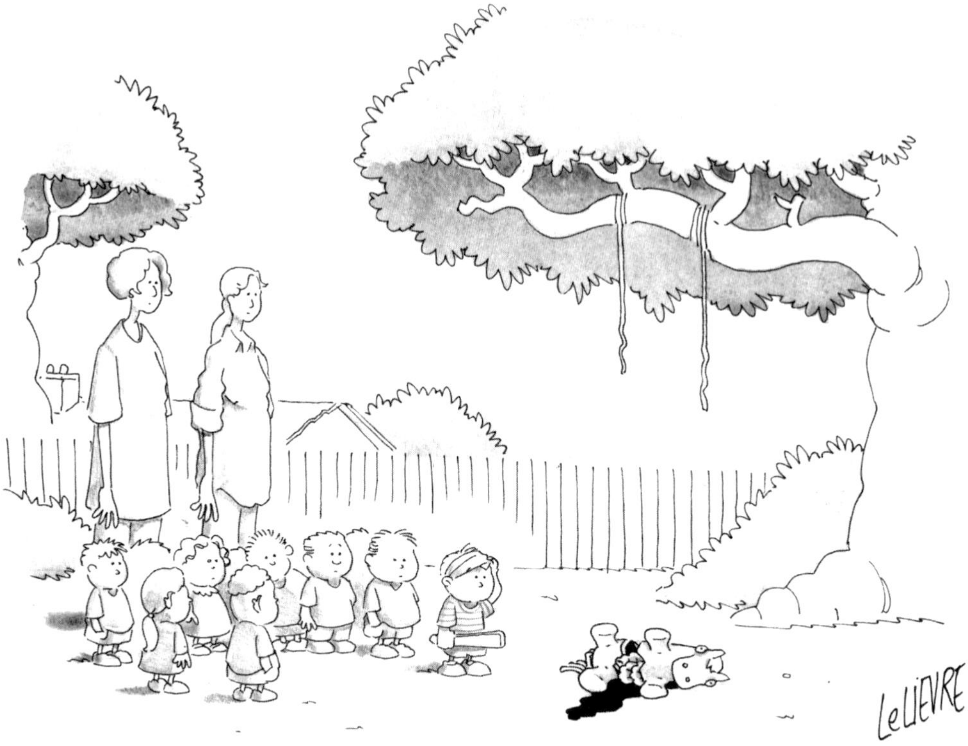
LeLIEVRE

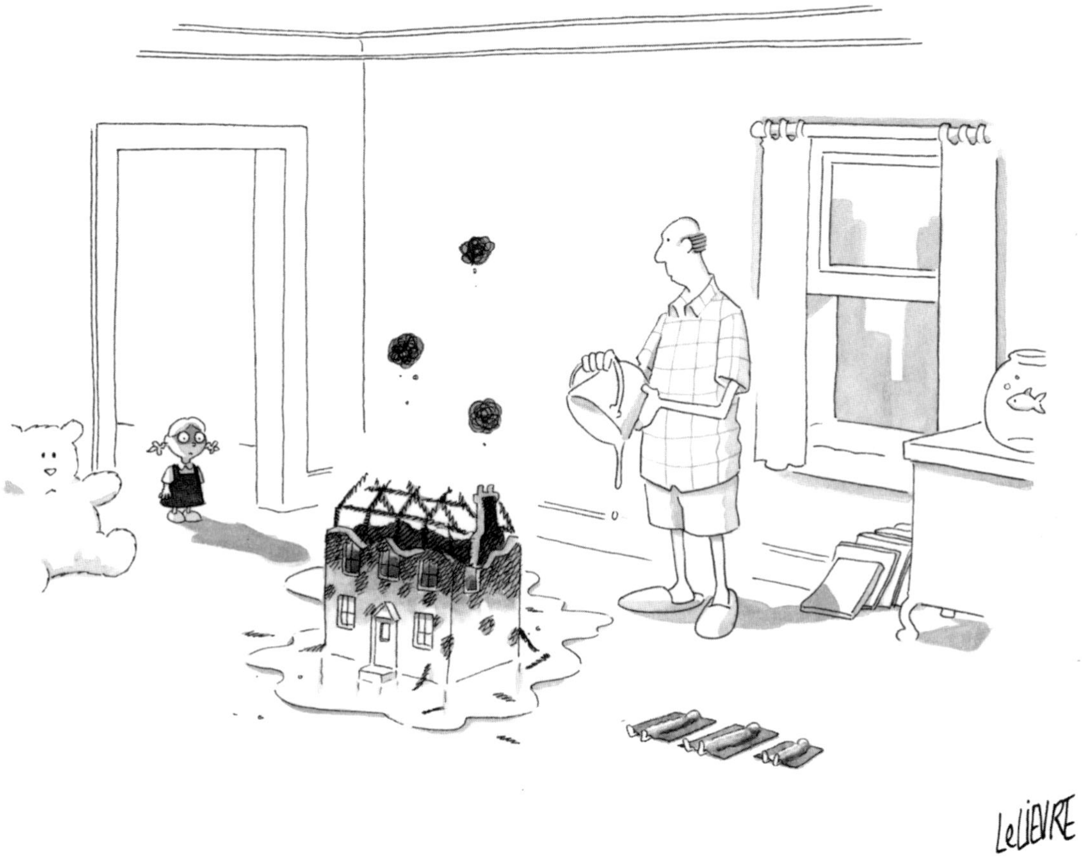
LeLIEVRE

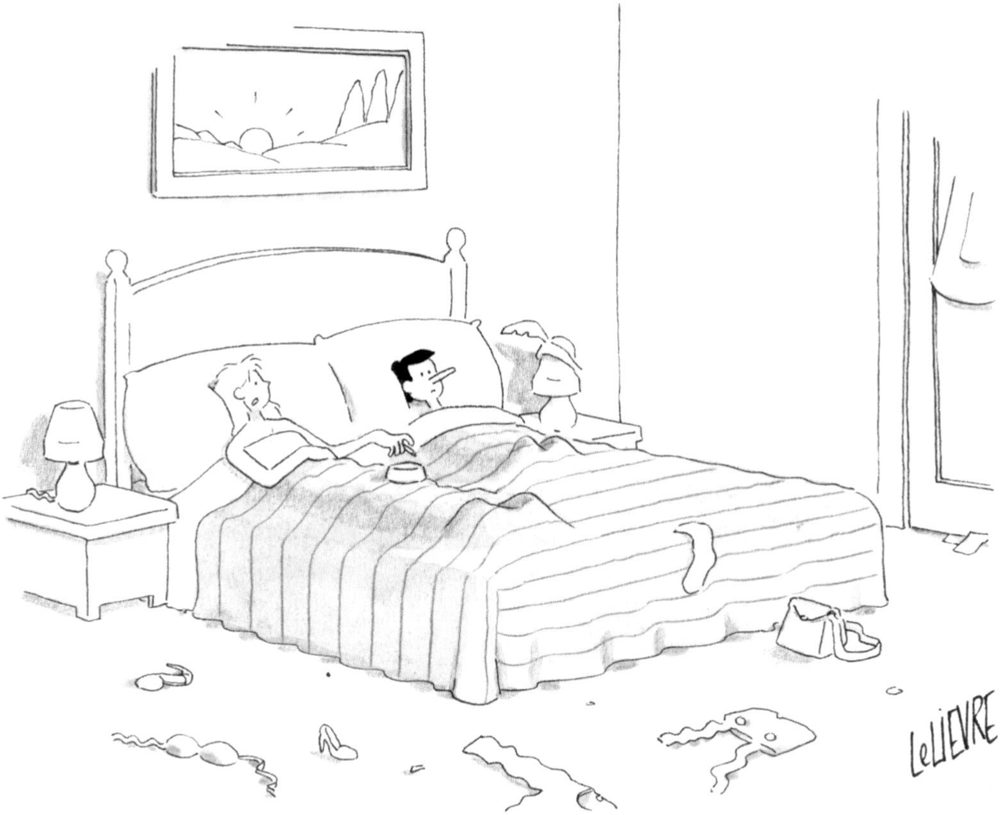
LeLIEVRE

"Lie to me again."

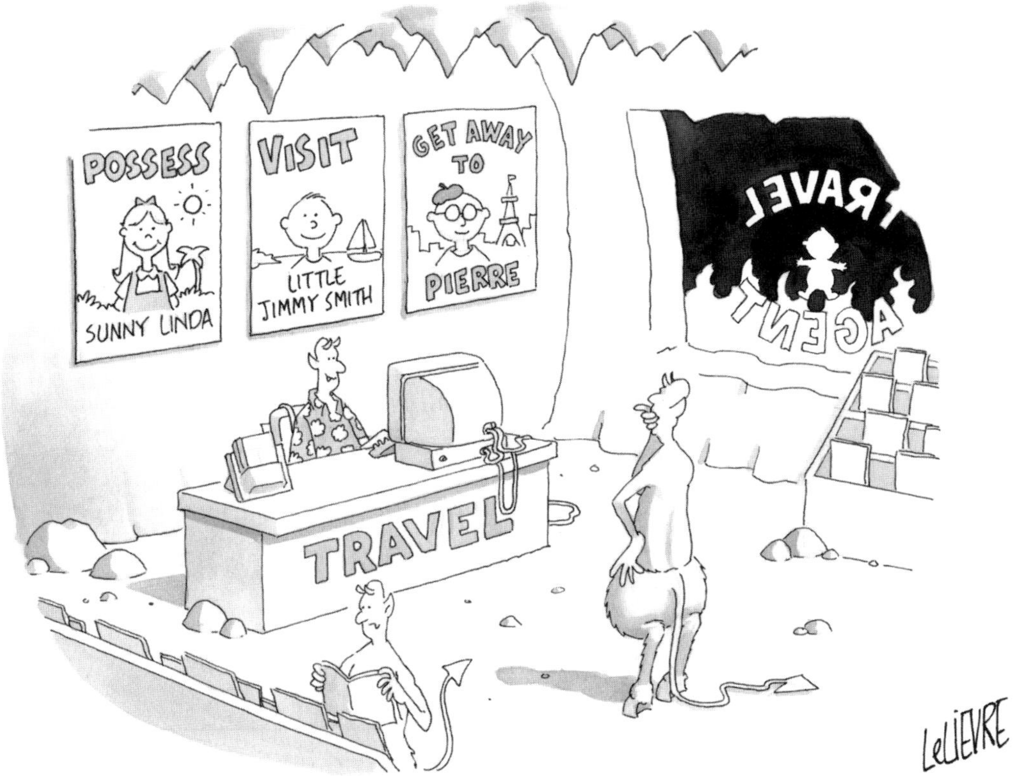
POSSESS
SUNNY LINDA
VISIT
LITTLE JIMMY SMITH
GET AWAY TO
PIERRE
TRAVEL
LELIEVRE

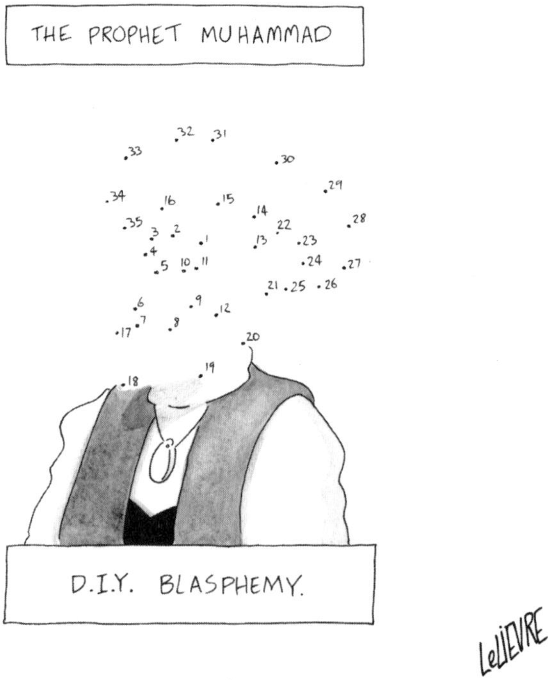
THE PROPHET MUHAMMAD
D.I.Y. BLASPHEMY.
LeLIEVRE

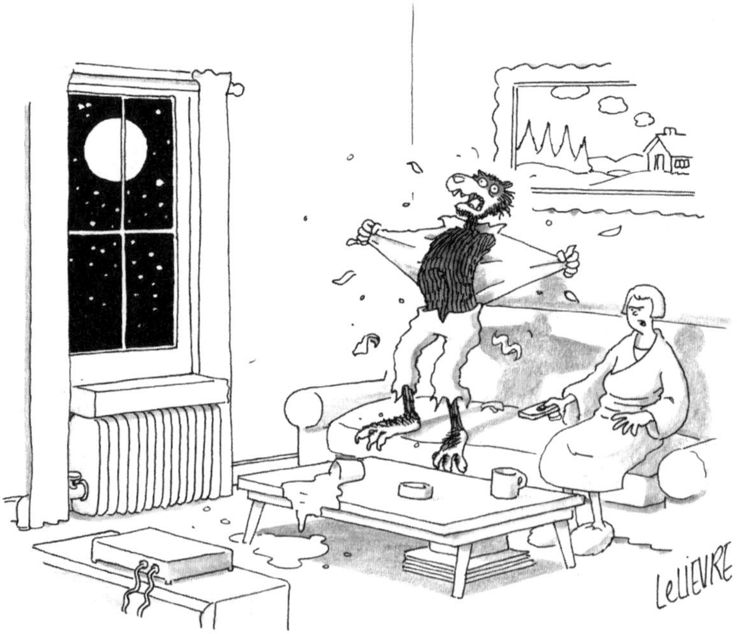
LeLIEVRE

"You're lucky. I'm turning into my mother."

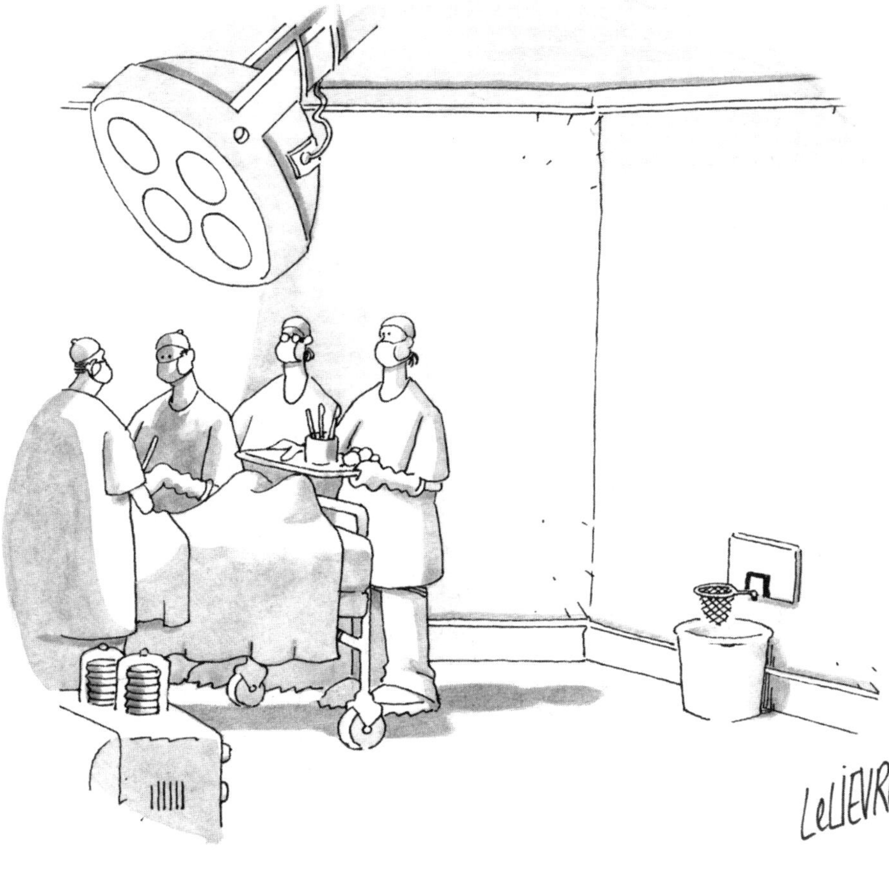
LeLIEVRE

MVELLER

P. S. MUELLER

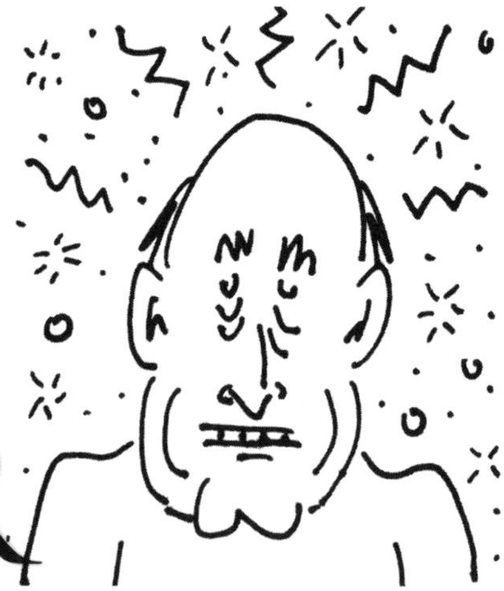

Frequently Asked Questions

Where do you get your ideas?
A secret place inside your head.

Which comes first, the picture or the caption?
The horror! The horror!

How'd you get started?
I was born in the sea. At first I just sort of floated around and absorbed sunlight, but after many years I slowly became a witless jellyfish, which was great until I found myself struggling in high school. Then peer pressure got to me, like, big time. Not long after that, I became a changeling mutant thing with a raging appetite for randomly acquired gene fragments to give my DNA some cool racing stripes. Eventually, however, despite my best efforts, I developed bilateral symmetry, eyes, facial hair, and a boyish grin, and then failed horribly in my attempt to master Chinese kick-farming, which gave me cauliflower feet. Perhaps not surprisingly, I was soon taken aboard a strange craft by mambo salad people from space. They were a crunchy race of aruguloids of crouton, which is about all I can remember before the experiments began. I woke up here utterly soaked in vinaigrette. And so, I suppose without any clear memory of my captors, I wander the streets of this grim dystopian megapolis, is that ok? Maybe there's a way out of this place. Perhaps my plankton friends will help. In closing, I'd just like to say evolution is a lie, and God was made by the oceans. Thanks.

I admire . . .
My own boundless capacity for coffee and my wife's patience.

How do you deal with rejection?
I tend to tell editors that, fine, I'll just take my MacArthur genius grant and go squat in a field somewhere in the former Yugoslavia, goddammit!

What are some things that make you laugh and why?
The Donald Rumsfeld squint—it's just flat out comical the way he brings it right to the edge of that crazy old man thing. And cats, always cats—because in the absence of prey they're quite happy to attack their own little charades.

- I've got a great idea for a cartoon—wanna hear it?

No. I'd rather taste it.

Infrequently Asked Questions

- Have you mooned or *been* mooned more often in your life?

Mooned much many moons ago.

- What would make a terrible pizza topping?

All those missing bees.

- What might one expect to find at a really low-budget amusement park?

Petting abattoir.

- What did the shepherd say to the three-legged sheepdog?

Where's lambie, you hideous freak?

And Now for a Few More Questions . . .

- What do you hate drawing?

Victims. I can't stand the way their eyes appear to follow you.

- Being as accurate as possible, how many desert island cartoons do you think you've come up with and submitted to *The New Yorker*?

20 or so. It's like an illness.

- What's the funniest thing that you witnessed, overheard, or came up with that you couldn't figure out how to use in a cartoon?

Once, when discussing spearfishing, a friend seriously asked about what kind of bait is placed on the point.

- If you could ask Bob Mankoff, *The New Yorker* cartoon editor, one question, what would it be?

Are the rumors true that you can bend foreign coins with your powerful mind?

Naming Names

- What name might you give to a mild-mannered, slightly overweight dental assistant in one of your cartoons?

Doris Bundt.

- Other than Lance, what name would you give to a twenty-eight-year-old metrosexual entertainment lawyer who cycles on weekends?

Matthew Diffee.

- What would be a good name for a new, commercially unviable breakfast cereal?

Floor Chex.

- Come up with a name for an unpleasant medical procedure.

Nastyplasty.

- If you used a pen name, what would it be?

Mr. Pen.

Complete the Pie Chart Below

. . . in a way that tells us something about your life or how you think.

APPLE PIE
CHERRY PIE
BLUEBERRY PIE
WHALE PIE

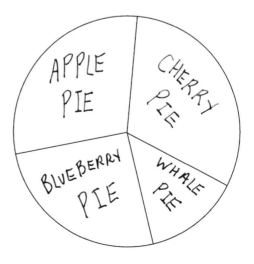

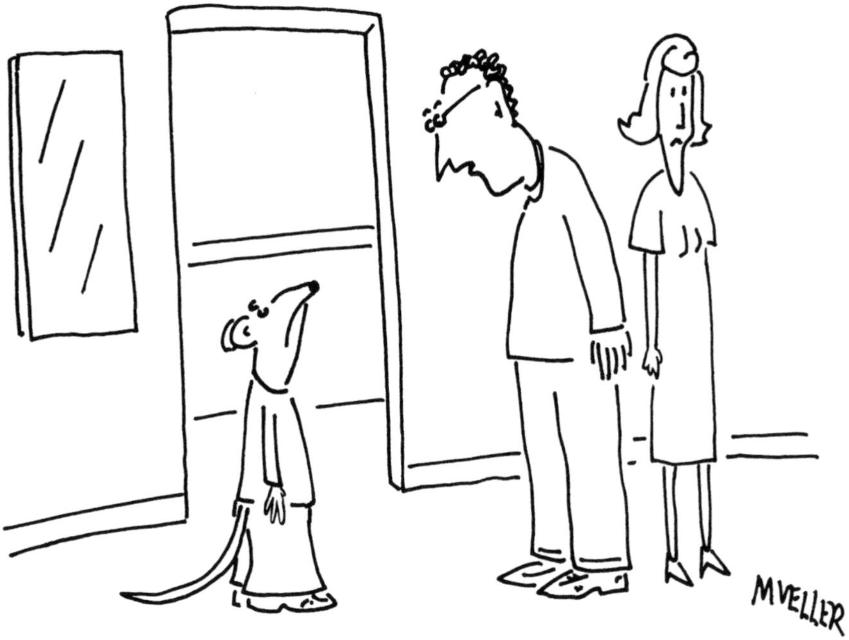
MUELLER

"I'm sorry, but the fact that your birth parents weren't married does appear to make you a rat bastard."

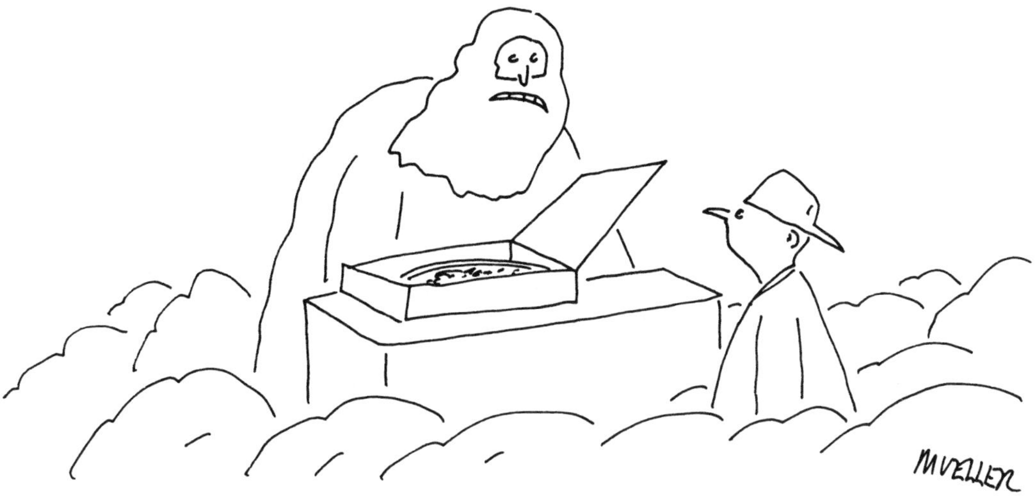
MUELLER

"It's got pineapple on it. You'll have to go to hell."

TITANIC ACTION FIGURES
MUELLER

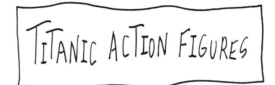

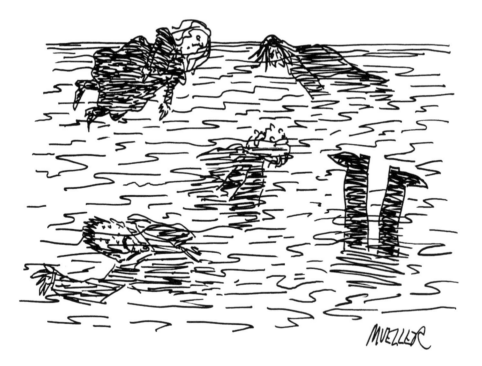

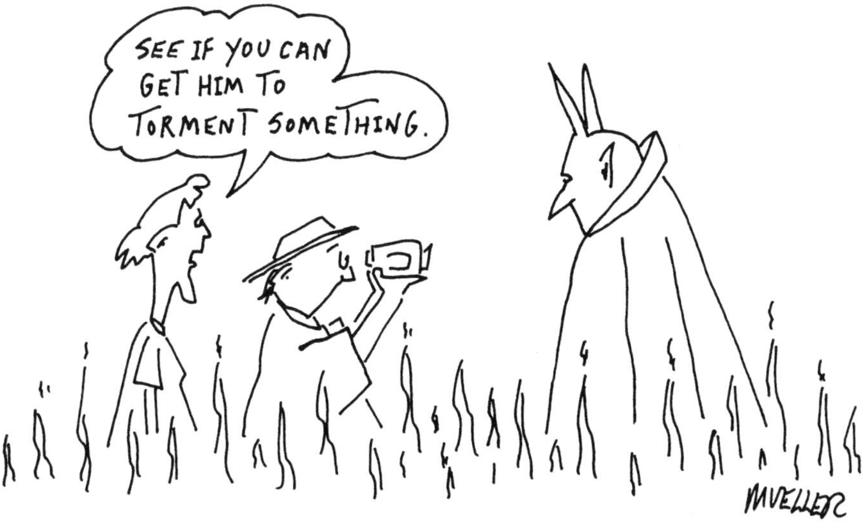
SEE IF YOU CAN
GET HIM TO
TORMENT SOMETHING.
MUELLER

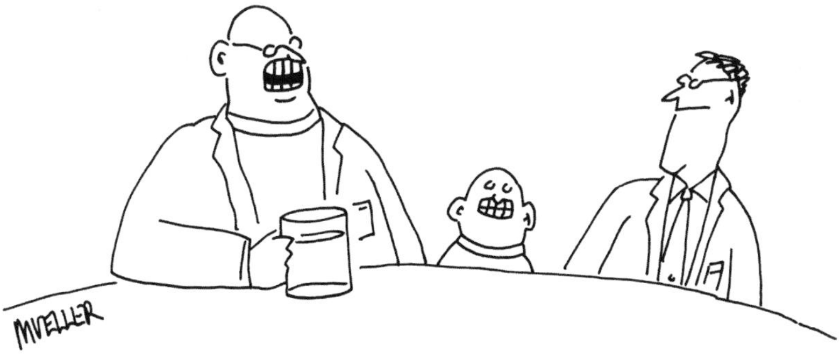
MUELLER

"Billy's going to be my new liver someday."

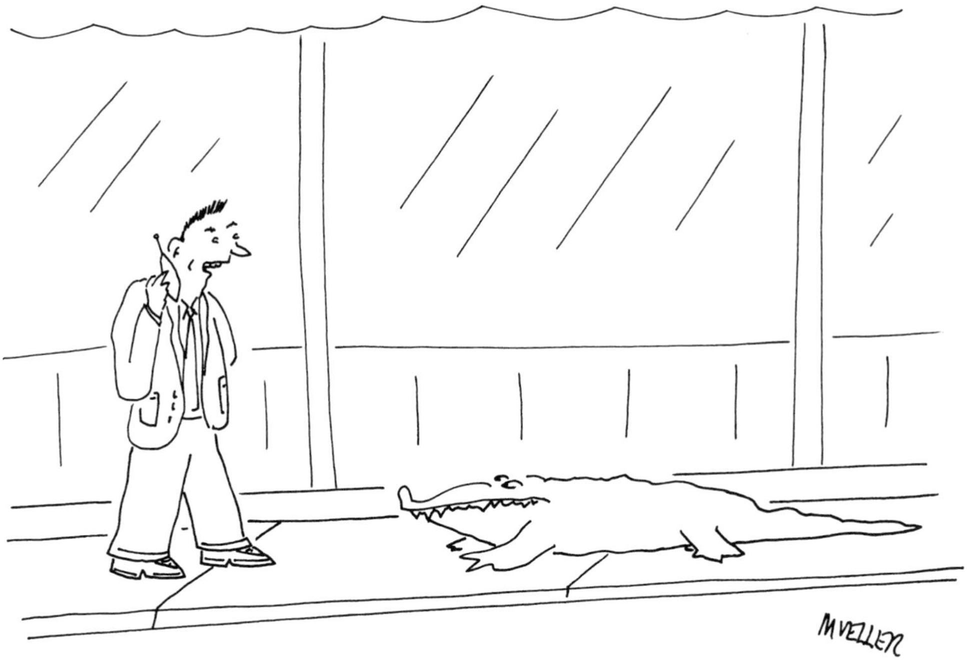
MUELLER

"I can't talk right now—I'm about to do something really stupid."

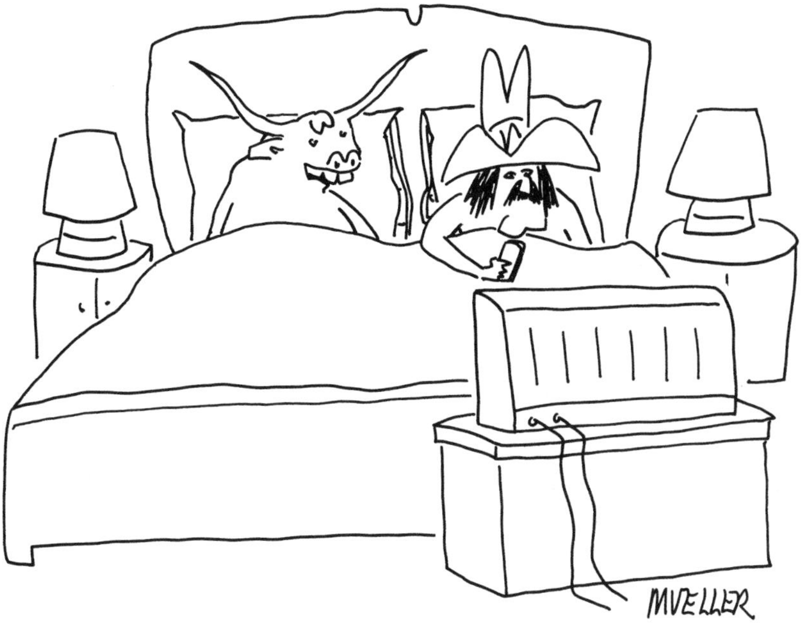
MUELLER

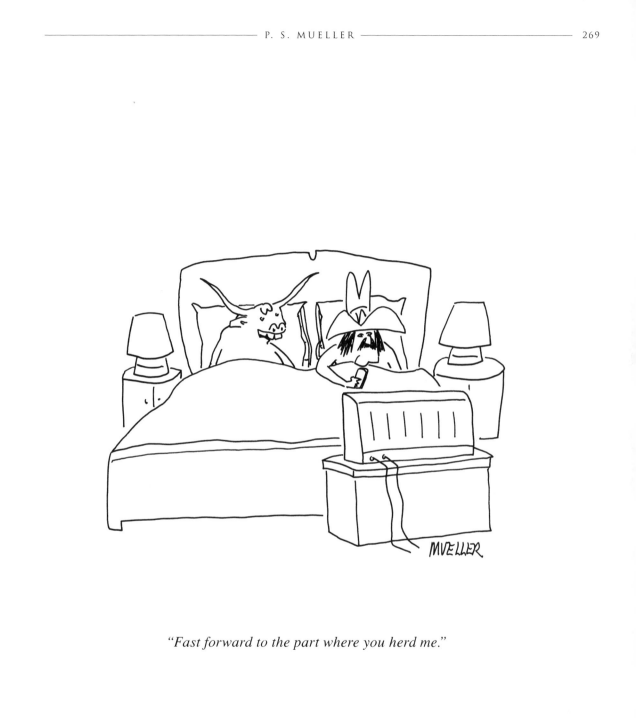

"Fast forward to the part where you herd me."

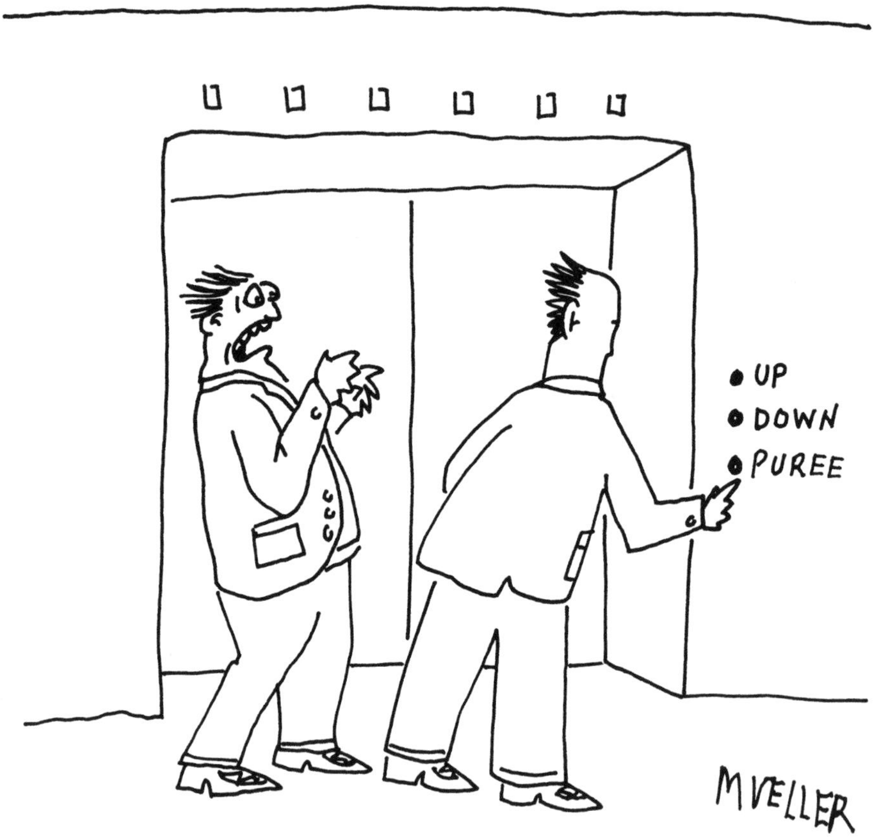
UP
DOWN
PUREE
MUELLER

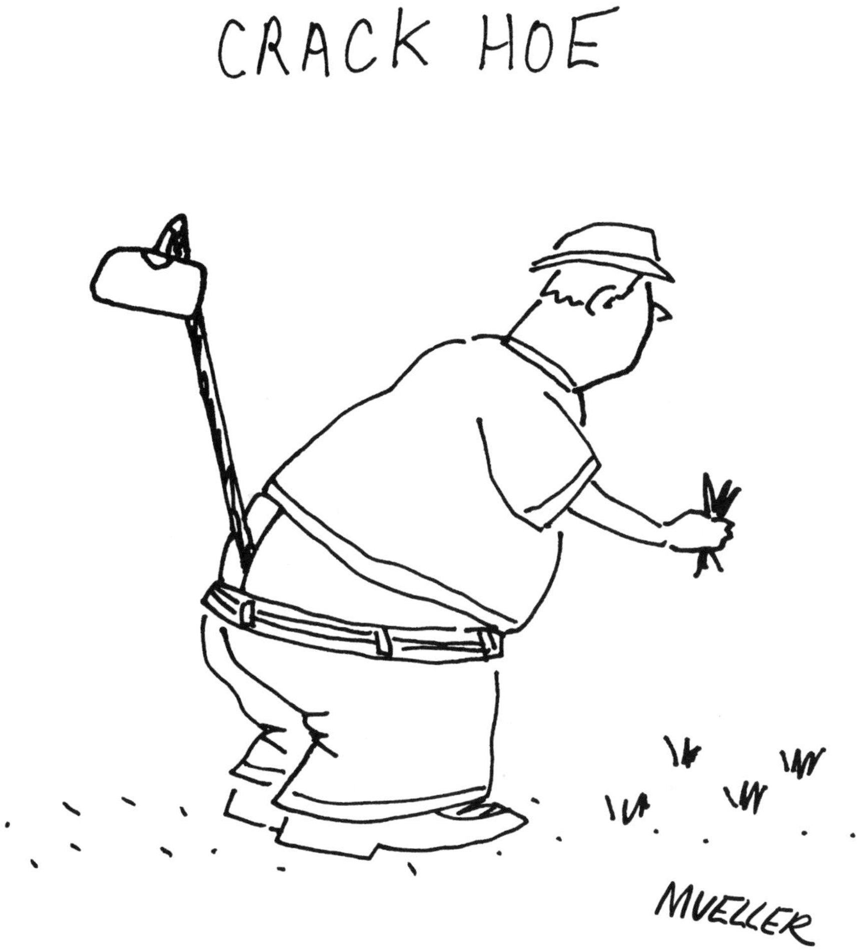
CRACK HOE
MUELLER

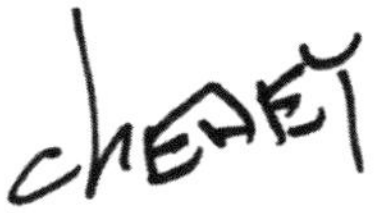
cheney

TOM CHENEY

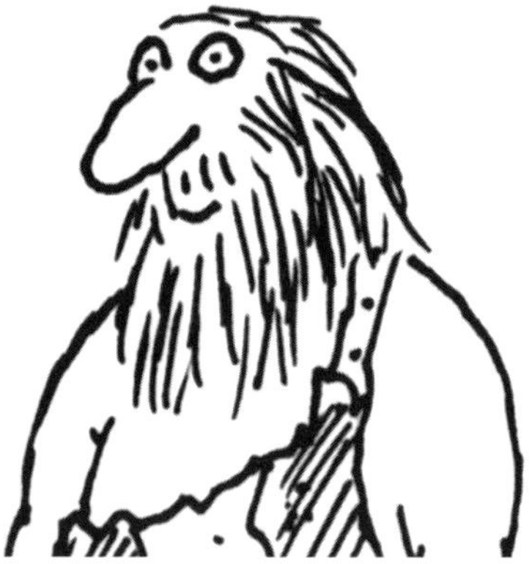

Frequently Asked Questions

- Where do you get your ideas?

  The produce section of the supermarket, and only if they're fresh.

- Which comes first, the picture or the caption?

  The picture, unless I overhear a couple of conservatives talking.

- How'd you get started?

  I got started the way all cartoonists do . . . one batch of submissions after another until I had enough rejection slips to contruct a small studio of my own.

- I admire . . .

  Lenny Bruce, George Carlin, and Richard Pryor.

- How do you deal with rejection?

  I regard it as the norm. Selling work is the exception. Even after 30 years in this business, I still think of each cartoon sale as a miracle.

- What are some things that make you laugh and why?

  People who take themselves very seriously—it seems the only thing they have going for them is their own importance, and that, in and of itself, is hysterical.

- I've got a great idea for a cartoon—wanna hear it?

  Yes, but only if you're willing to bet one thousand dollars that it's never been done before.

Infrequently Asked Questions

- Have you mooned or *been* mooned more often in your life?

  The mooner, but only in church.

- What would make a terrible pizza topping?

  Lake Erie.

- What might one expect to find at a really low-budget amusement park?

  The Bobbing for Piranha tub.

- What did the shepherd say to the three-legged sheepdog?

  Here, Tripod, c'mere, boy!

And Now for a Few More Questions . . .

- What do you hate drawing?

  Trees, badgers, baby elephants, marbles, and nude Eskimos.

- Being as accurate as possible, how many desert island cartoons do you think you've come up with and submitted to *The New Yorker*?

  Two, maybe three . . . oh, alright, about fifty.

- What's the funniest thing that you witnessed, overheard, or came up with that you couldn't figure out how to use in a cartoon?

  Watching an intoxicated man trying to find the coin return on a parking meter.

- If you could ask Bob Mankoff, *The New Yorker* cartoon editor, one question, what would it be?

  Have we really been at this for 35 years?

Draw Something in This Space

. . . that will help us understand your childhood.

Naming Names

- What name might you give to a mild-mannered, slightly overweight dental assistant in one of your cartoons?

  Yolanda Flench.

- Other than Lance, what name would you give to a twenty-eight-year-old metrosexual entertainment lawyer who cycles on weekends?

  Laird Bodine.

- What would be a good name for a new, commercially unviable breakfast cereal?

  Anchovy Puffs.

- Come up with a name for an unpleasant medical procedure.

  A colonoscopic tonsillectomy.

- If you used a pen name, what would it be?

  Dixon Ticonderoga.

Complete the Pie Chart Below

. . . in a way that tells us something about your life or how you think.

DRAWING
INTERRUPTIONS

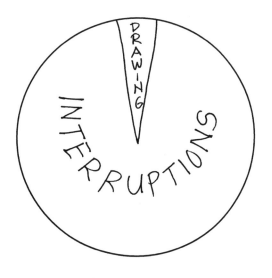

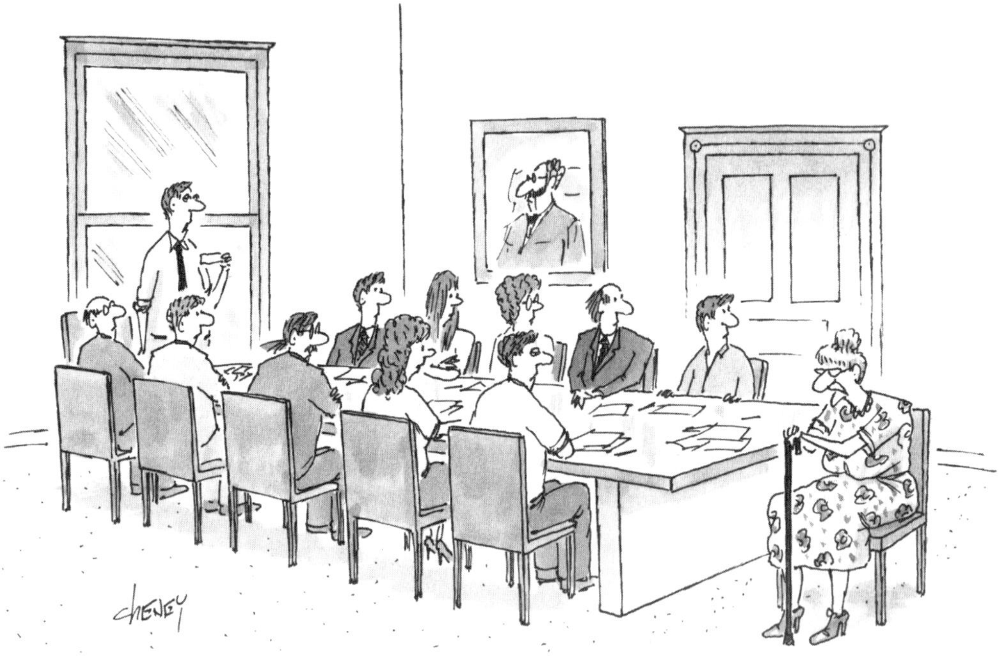
CHENEY

"We're going to be here awhile, folks—I count eleven 'not guilty's' and one 'fry the bastard.'"

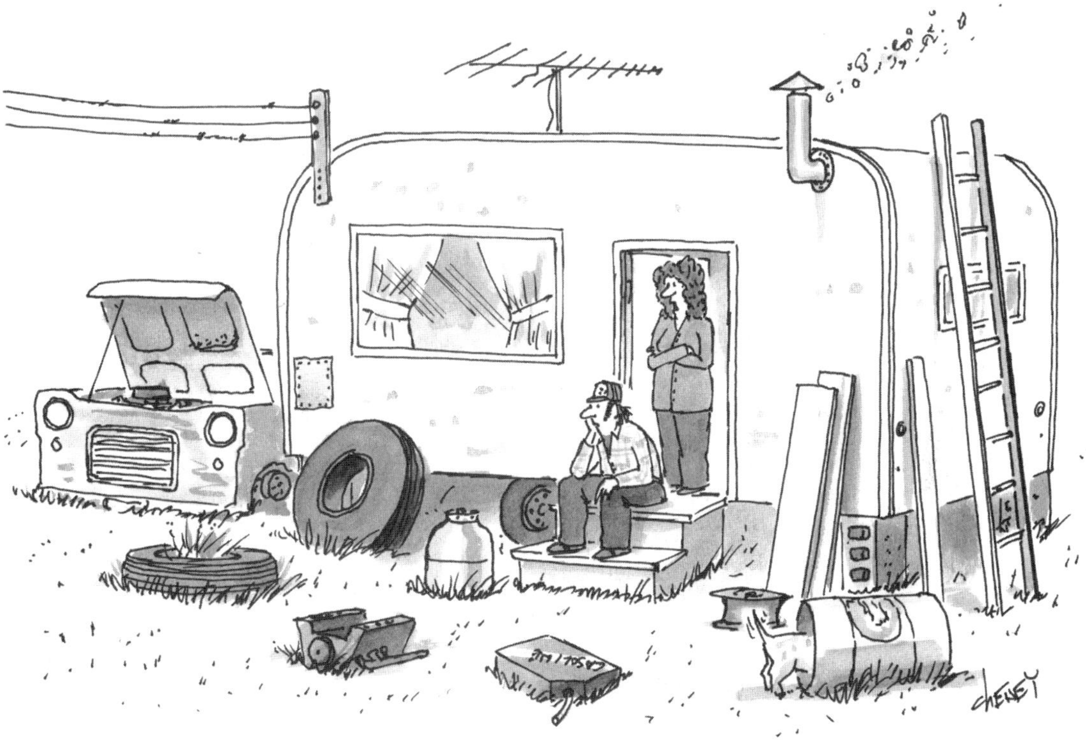
CHENEY

"What do you say we just kick back and let things slide for a while?"

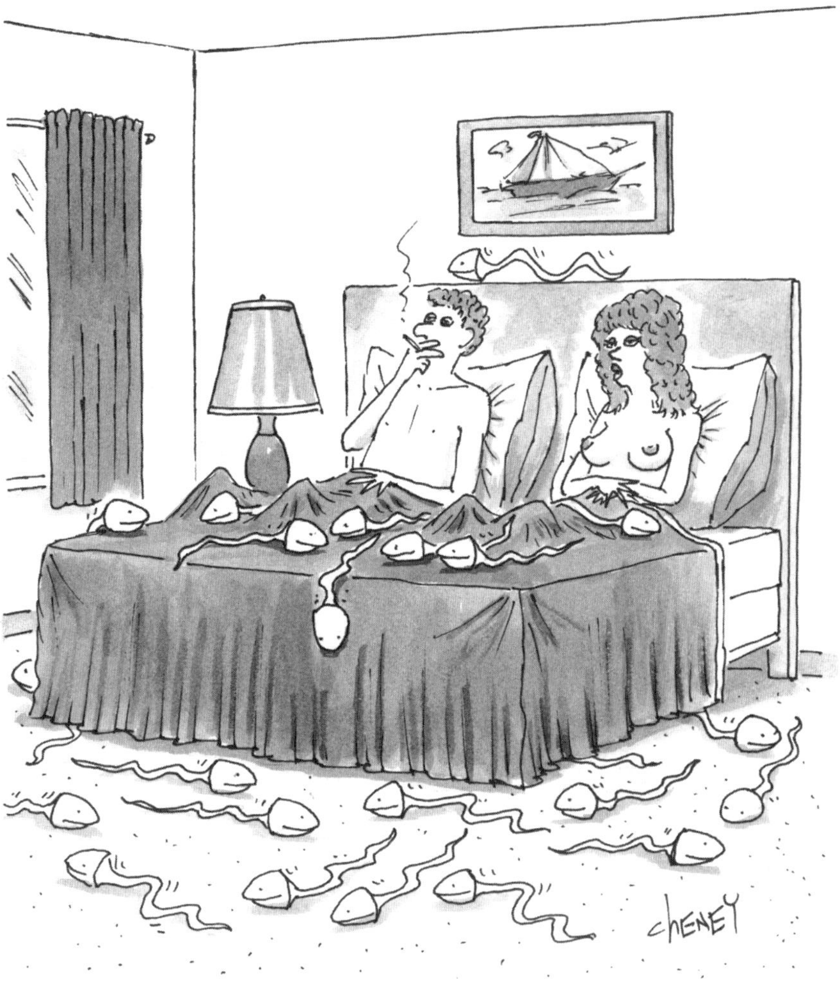
CHENEY

"So, how long have you been working at the plutonium plant?"

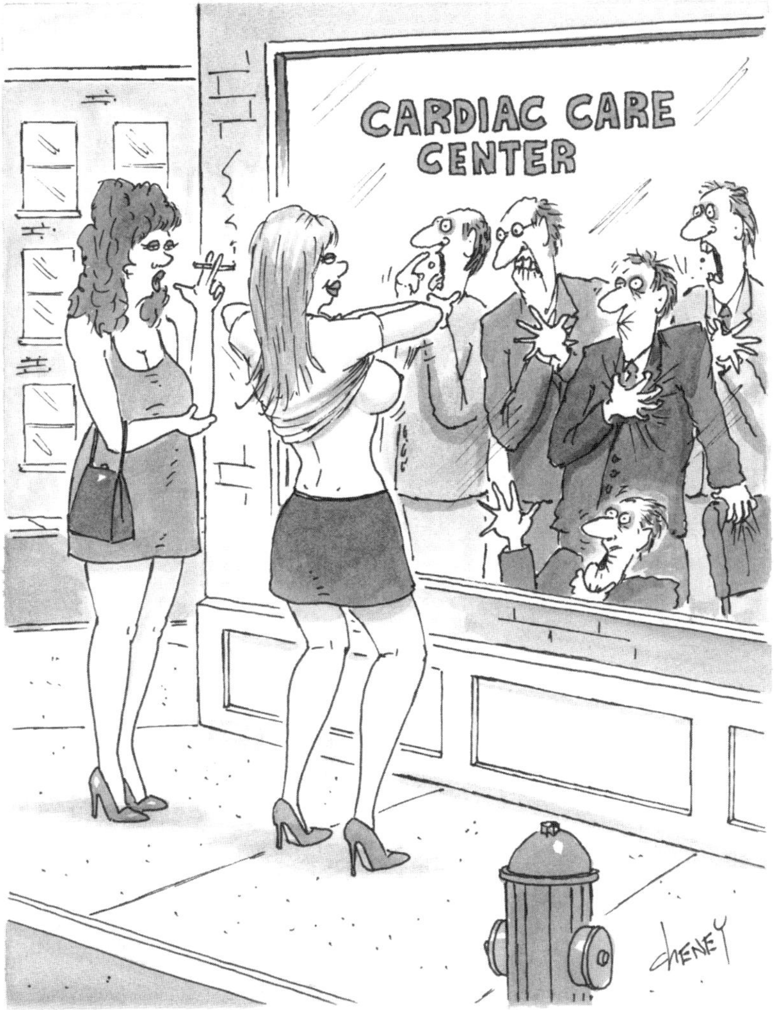
CARDIAC CARE
CENTER
CHENEY

"You're one sick puppy, Nadine."

PAUL
NOTH

PAUL NOTH

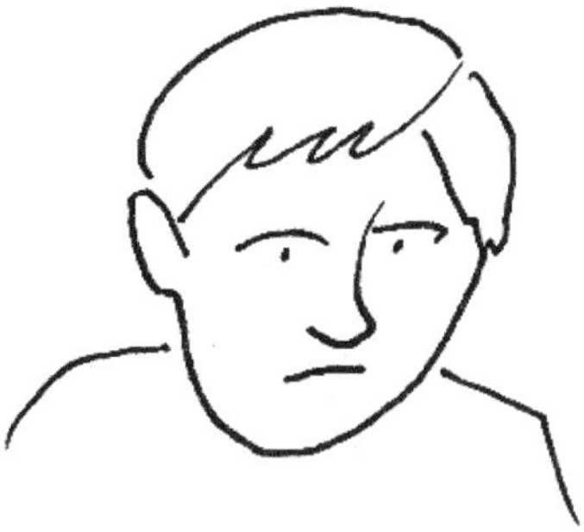

Frequently Asked Questions

- Where do you get your ideas?

  From a magical place called "Boredom."

- Which comes first, the picture or the caption?

  1. Mental image/idea
  2. Written caption (if necessary)
  3. Drawing

- How'd you get started?

  Sketchin' for nickels on the old Bert Levy Circuit.

- I admire . . .

  See self-portrait.

- How do you deal with rejection?

  Constantly.

- What are some things that make you laugh and why?

  My wife, Parnell—the funniester person in the world—Noths, Thiels, the best and worst cartoon, P. G. Wodehouse, Chuck Jones and Michael Maltese, Jack Handey, W. C. Fields, Woody Allen, Marx Brothers, etc., etc., etc.

- I've got a great idea for a cartoon—wanna hear it?

  How did you get into my basement?

Infrequently Asked Questions

- Have you mooned or *been* mooned more often in your life?

  I guess "been mooned." No, wait . . . Hold on a sec . . . Okay, make that "mooned."

- What would make a terrible pizza topping?

  Mike Wallace.

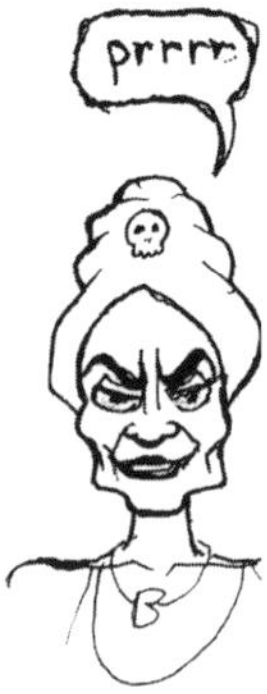
prrrr

- What might one expect to find at a really low-budget amusement park?

  The "Tilt-O-Merle."

- What did the shepherd say to the three-legged sheepdog?

  Something hilarious in Pashto.

And Now for a Few More Questions . . .

- What do you hate drawing?

WORDS and LETTERING

- Being as accurate as possible, how many desert island cartoons do you think you've come up with and submitted to *The New Yorker*?

  Five.

- What's the funniest thing that you witnessed, overheard, or came up with that you couldn't figure out how to use in a cartoon?

  That time I was stranded on a desert island.

- If you could ask Bob Mankoff, *The New Yorker* cartoon editor, one question, what would it be?

  I can and I don't.

Draw Some Sort of Doodle

. . . using the random lines below as a starting point.

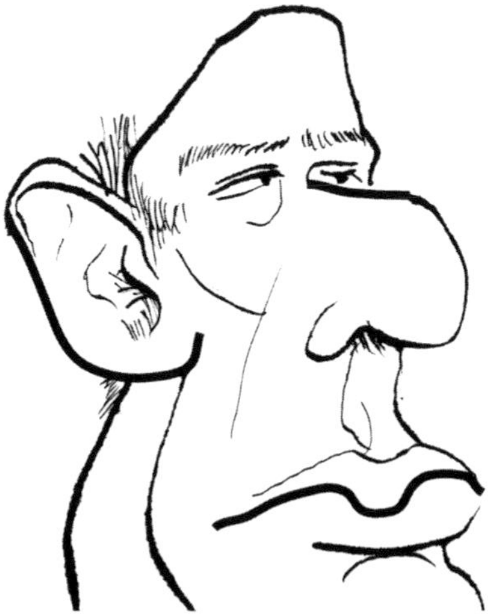

Naming Names

- What name might you give to a mild-mannered, slightly overweight dental assistant in one of your cartoons?

  Jenkins.

- Other than Lance, what name would you give to a twenty-eight-year-old metrosexual entertainment lawyer who cycles on weekends?

  Pierce.

- What would be a good name for a new, commercially unviable breakfast cereal?

  Swollen Bub-O's.

- Come up with a name for an unpleasant medical procedure.

  Swollen-Bubo-Lance-Pierce.

- If you used a pen name, what would it be?

  Jenkins.

Complete the Pie Chart Below

. . . in a way that tells us something about your life or how you think.

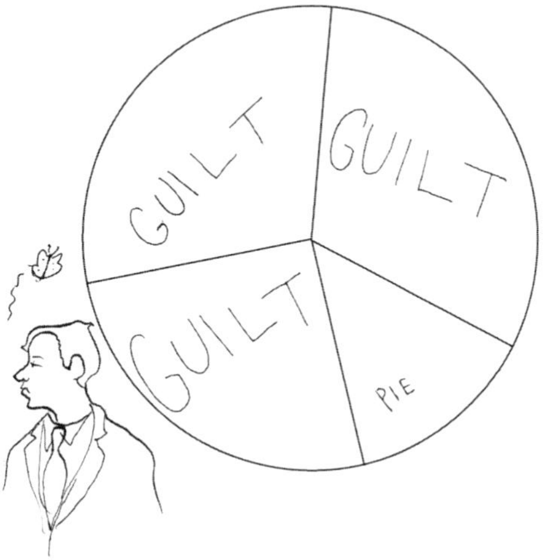
GUILT
GUILT
GUILT
PIE

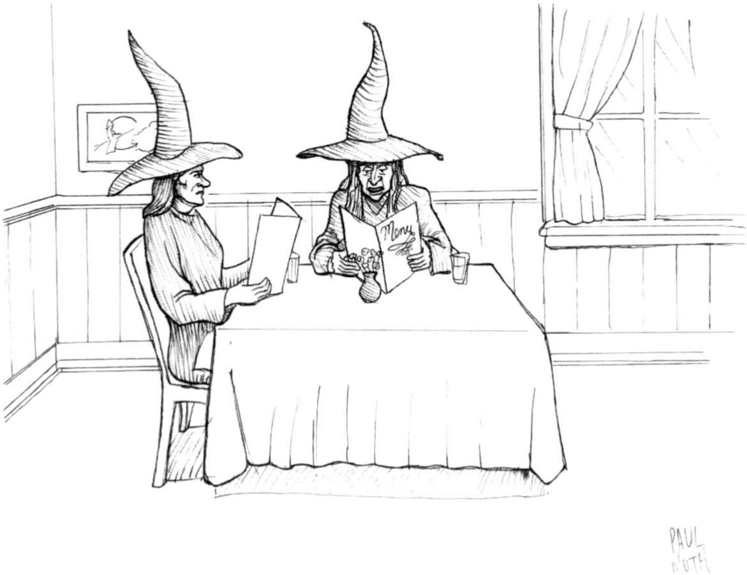
Menu
PAUL NOTH

"I'm thinking about having a child."

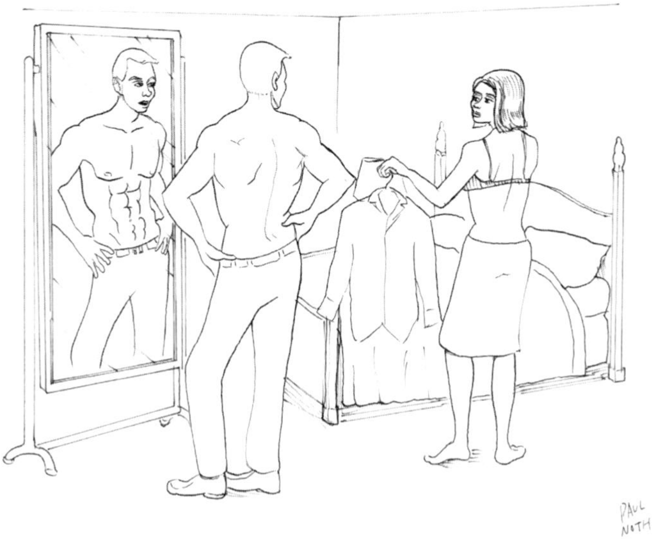
PAUL NOTH

"Do these abs make me look gay?"

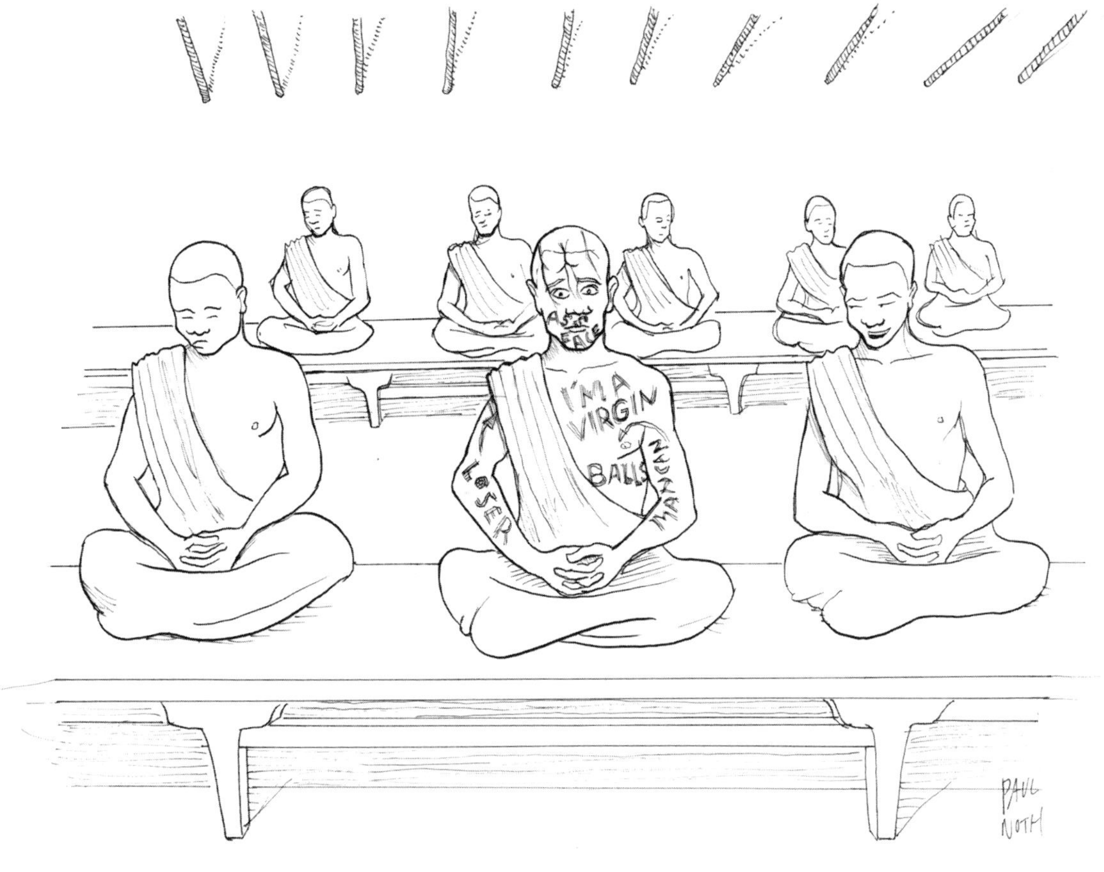
I'M A
VIRGIN
BALLS
LOSER
PAUL
NOTH

"Dude, you totally passed out."

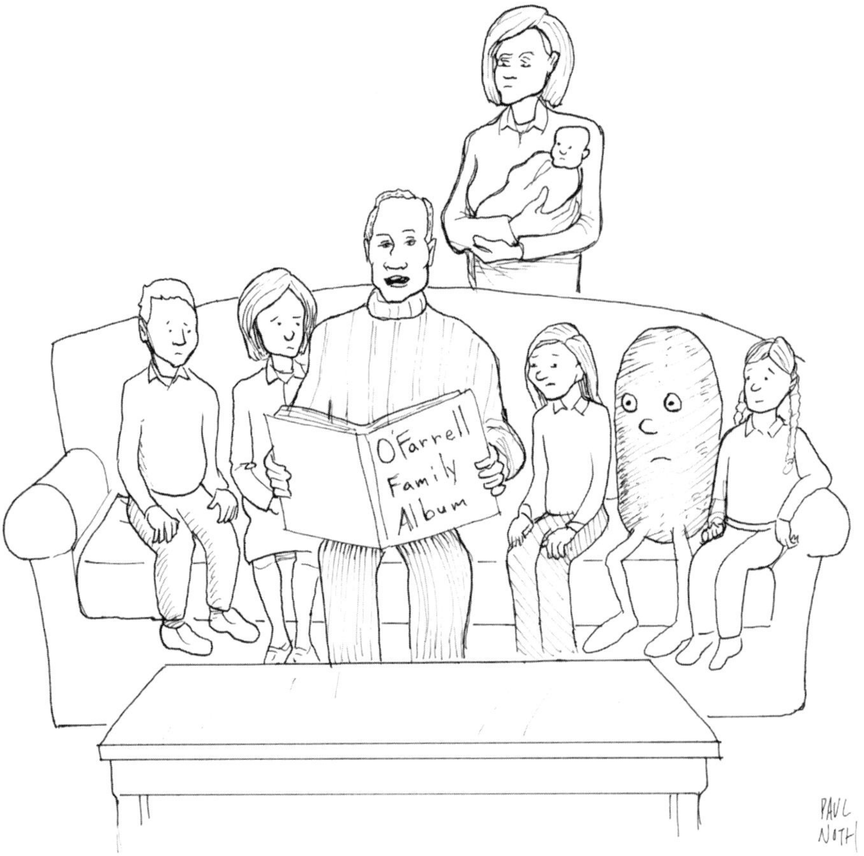
O'Farrell
Family
Album
PAUL
NOTH

"So, kids, you should all be thankful we don't live during a potato famine. Especially you, Jimmy."

"Wrong line, buddy."

S. GROSS

SAM GROSS

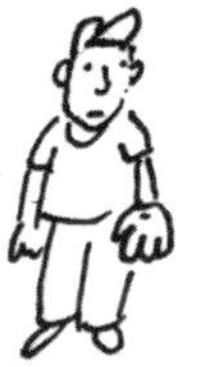

PLAYING RIGHT FIELD IN THE DIRT YARD IN THE BRONX.

Frequently Asked Questions

- Where do you get your ideas?
  funnycartoons@autocafé.com.

- Which comes first, the picture or the caption?
  The agony.

- How'd you get started?
  I have a button at the base of my spine.

- I admire . . .
  Lou Myers and Hap Kliban. They were working at a level that I'm trying to attain.

- How do you deal with rejection?
  It doesn't bother me at all.

- What are some things that make you laugh and why?
  Pretty much everything and I don't know why and I don't want to know why.

- I've got a great idea for a cartoon—wanna hear it?
  No, but I think Diffee has a need to.

Infrequently Asked Questions

- Have you mooned or *been* mooned more often in your life?
  I was once mooned by a starlet if that is at all possible.

- What would make a terrible pizza topping?
  Anything alive.

- What might one expect to find at a really low-budget amusement park?
  The Tunnel of Onan.

- What did the shepherd say to the three-legged sheepdog?
  A large erection will keep you from toppling over.

And Now for a Few More Questions . . .

- What do you hate drawing?
  Ten pins and horses. I've never done a cartoon of a horse bowling.

◼ Being as accurate as possible, how many desert island cartoons do you think you've come up with and submitted to *The New Yorker*?

All of my gags are desert island gags. Those that are bought are redrawn by the staff at *The New Yorker* so that they take place somewhere else.

◼ What's the funniest thing that you witnessed, overheard, or came up with that you couldn't figure out how to use in a cartoon?

It involved a naked 83-year-old diabetic grandmother and I can't go into any more detail.

◼ If you could ask Bob Mankoff, *The New Yorker* cartoon editor, one question, what would it be?

Why?

Draw Something in This Space

. . . that will help us understand your childhood.

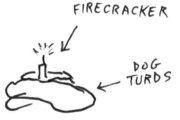

FIRECRACKER

DOG TURDS

Naming Names

◼ What name might you give to a mild-mannered, slightly overweight dental assistant in one of your cartoons?

Fiona.

◼ Other than Lance, what name would you give to a twenty-eight-year-old metrosexual entertainment lawyer who cycles on weekends?

Fiona.

◼ What would be a good name for a new, commercially unviable breakfast cereal?

Sugarturds.

◼ Come up with a name for an unpleasant medical procedure.

Endopancreatic lobar probe.

◼ If you used a pen name, what would it be?

Mont Blanc.

Complete the Pie Chart Below

. . . in a way that tells us something about your life or how you think.

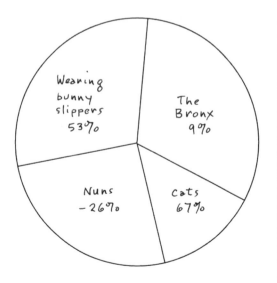

Wearing bunny slippers 53%

The Bronx 9%

Nuns −26%

Cats 67%

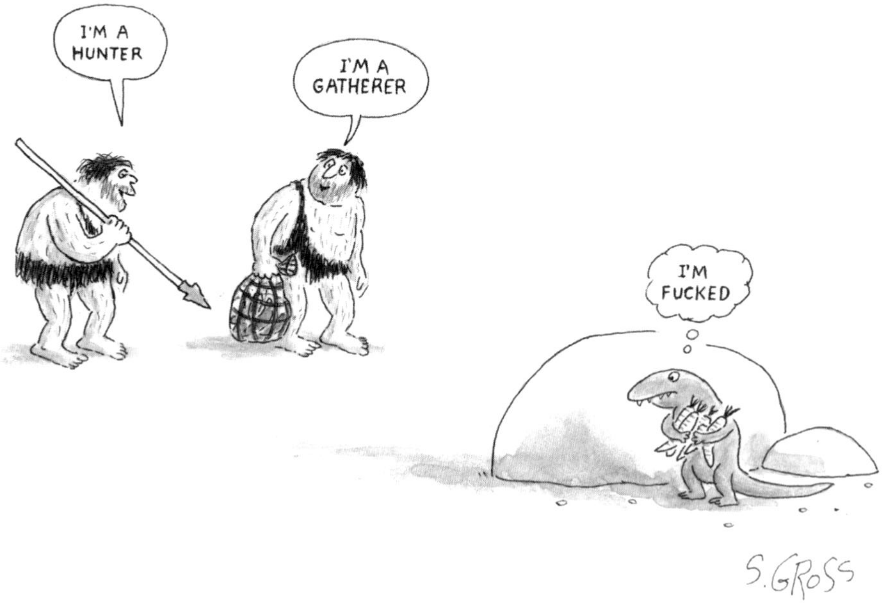
I'M A HUNTER
I'M A GATHERER
I'M FUCKED
S.GROSS

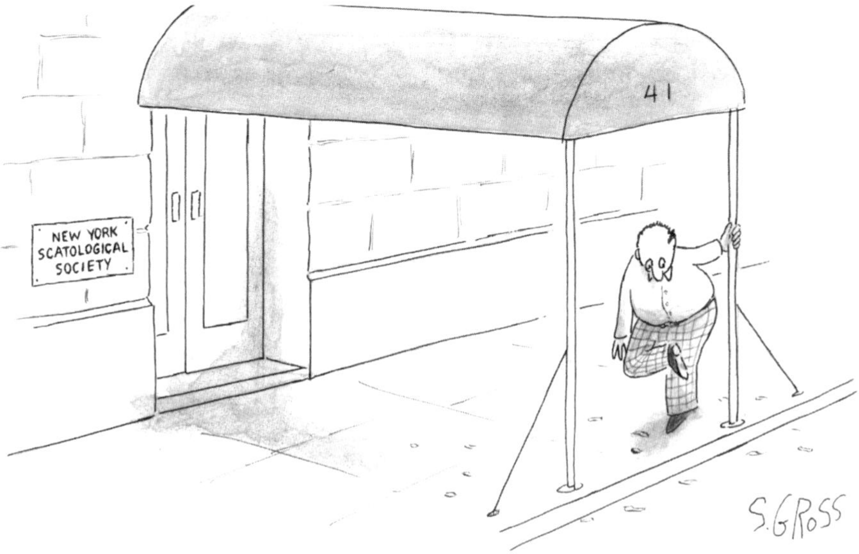
41
NEW YORK SCATOLOGICAL SOCIETY
S.GROSS

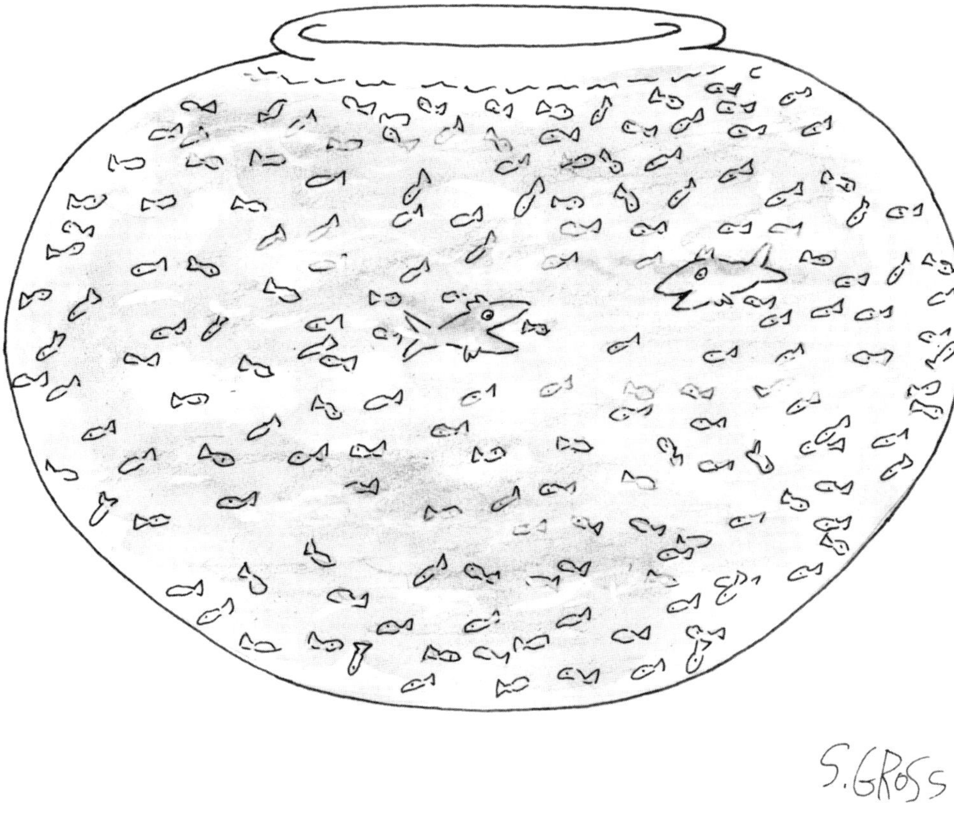
S. GROSS

"If I had the abortion we wouldn't be eating so good."

CHANGE
CHANGE
HIT MAN
PRO BOWL
INDY 500
FIND THE CLITORIS
S. GROSS

SQUEAK!
S. GROSS

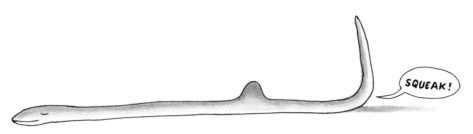

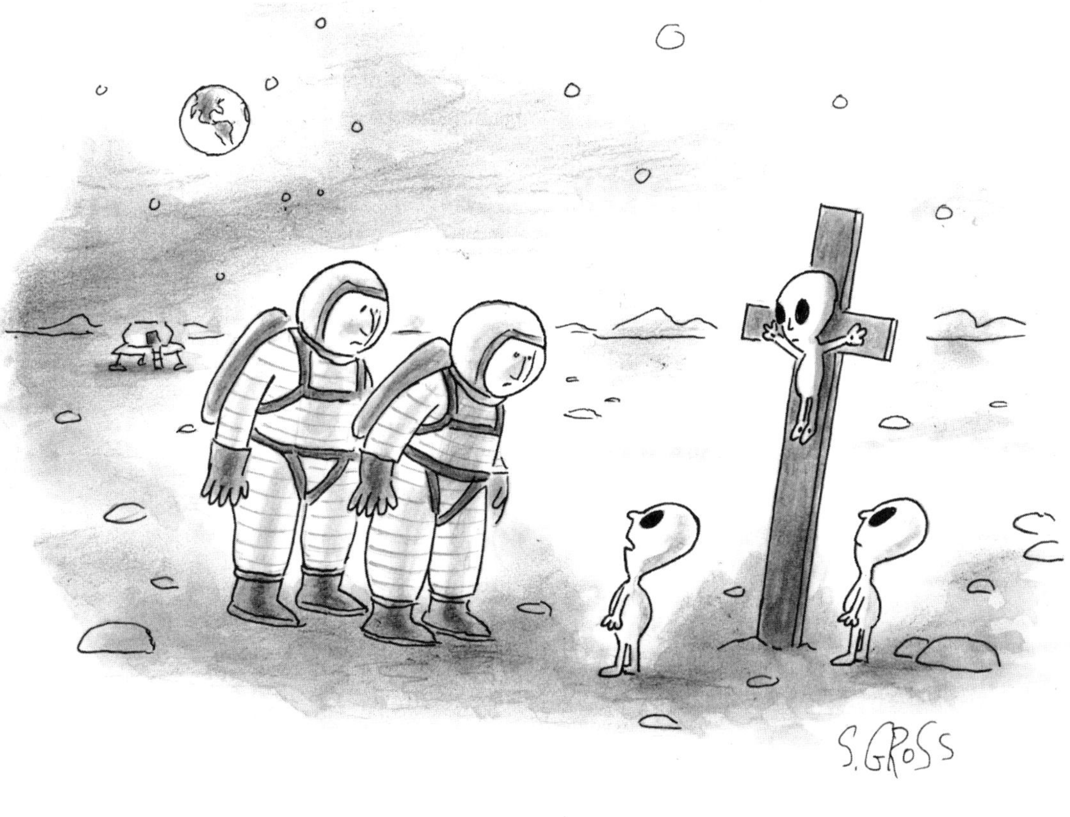
S. GROSS

"We've already blamed it on the Jews."

"Oh honey, I'm homo!"

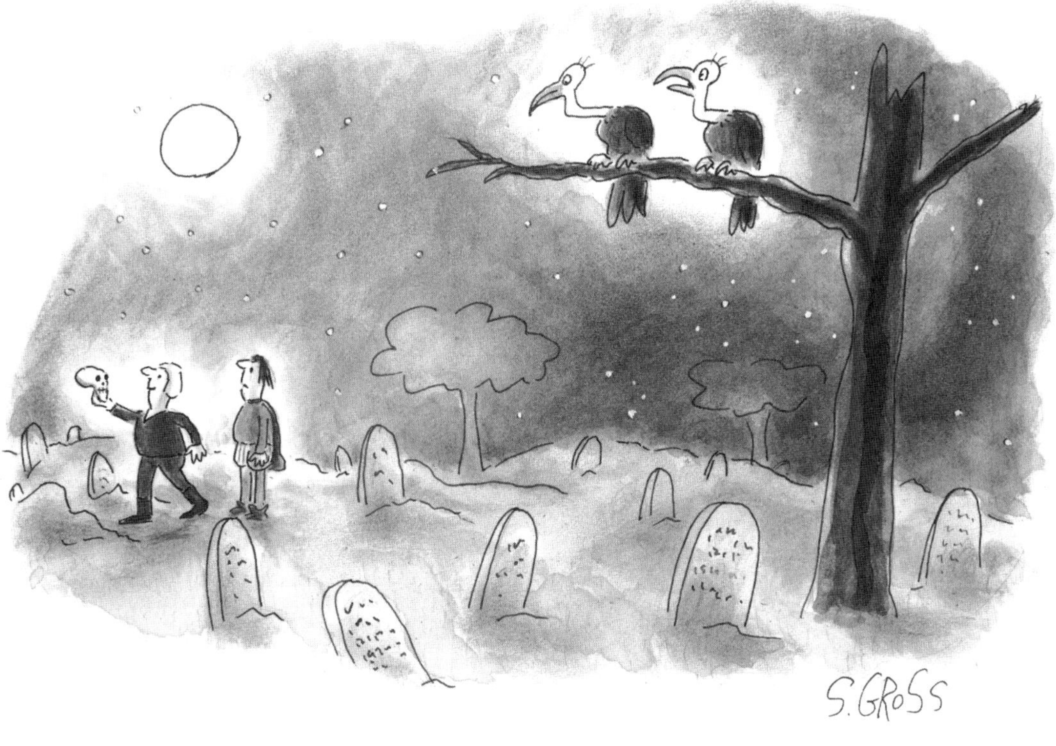
S. GROSS

"I knew Yorick also. He gave me diarrhea."

CHRISTOPHER WEYANT

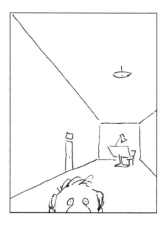

Frequently Asked Questions

■ Where do you get your ideas?

Deep in the heart of New Jersey, buried in an old abandoned mine there lies a trunk full of gags. Unfortunately, all about desert islands.

■ Which comes first, the picture or the caption?

The egg—wait—no, chicken.

■ How'd you get started?

Usually with a cup of coffee.

■ I admire . . .

In the cartoon world, I was raised on the perverse brilliance of Sam Gross and Gahan Wilson. Limitless imaginations. Bob Weber is stunning—I've learned so much from his lyrical line.

■ How do you deal with rejection?

I take a long *shvitz* in a 7-foot-long tub filled with scotch. Single malt if I feel particularly wounded.

■ What are some things that make you laugh and why?

Human relationships. That's all there is when you boil it all down. Husband and wife, diner and waiter, ventriloquist and dummy, lifeguard and drowning man, dog and cat, and so on. Relationships are never equal, always in conflict and therefore, forever funny. But ventriloquist and dummy is my favorite by far. . . .

■ I've got a great idea for a cartoon—wanna hear it?

That's the first three minutes of every cocktail party I've ever been to.

Draw Something in This Space

. . . that will help us understand your childhood.

Infrequently Asked Questions

- Have you mooned or *been* mooned more often in your life?

  I proudly refuse to write a Venus or Uranus joke here.

- What would make a terrible pizza topping?

  Cheese.

- What might one expect to find at a really low-budget amusement park?

  Most of my family. We're carny proud.

- What did the shepherd say to the three-legged sheepdog?

  Sit. Stay. Fall over.

And Now for a Few More Questions . . .

- What do you hate drawing?

  The shattered hopes and dreams of a generation. That, and walnuts.

- Being as accurate as possible, how many desert island cartoons do you think you've come up with and submitted to *The New Yorker*?

  Zero. Although strangely, some were published under my name.

- What's the funniest thing that you witnessed, overheard, or came up with that you couldn't figure out how to use in a cartoon?

  Once, there was this guy and he did this thing at this place and it was a riot!! You can't make that stuff up!!! Good times.

- If you could ask Bob Mankoff, *The New Yorker* cartoon editor, one question, what would it be?

  Bob, why do good things happen to bad people?

Naming Names

- What name might you give to a mild-mannered, slightly overweight dental assistant in one of your cartoons?

  Phil McCavities.

- Other than Lance, what name would you give to a twenty-eight-year-old metrosexual entertainment lawyer who cycles on weekends?

  Nancy.

- What would be a good name for a new, commercially unviable breakfast cereal?

  Hemorrhoids—now with Lil' Marshmallows!

- Come up with a name for an unpleasant medical procedure.

  Transnasalshmeckelectomy, with a twist.

- If you used a pen name, what would it be?

  Max Kensington or Karl Merriweather would be my nom de 'toon.

Complete the Pie Chart Below

. . . in a way that tells us something about your life or how you think.

APPLE
PECAN
MINCEMEAT
SCOTCH

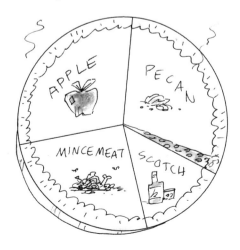

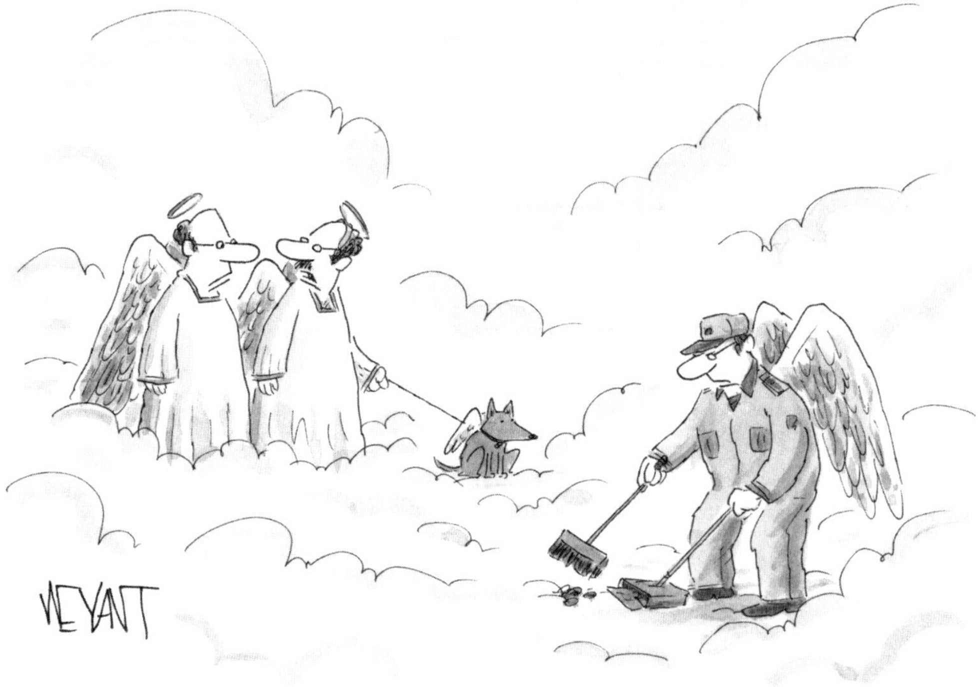
WEYANT

"Atheist."

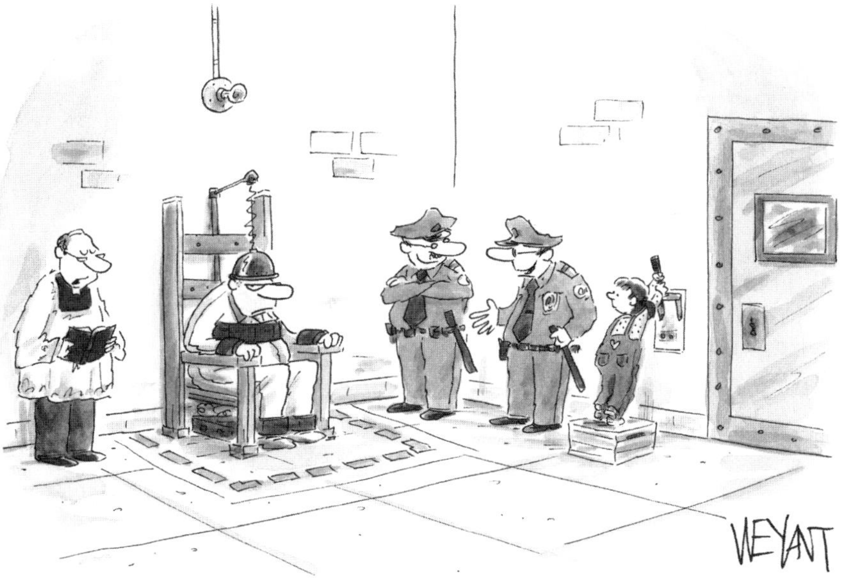
WEYANT

"I've got to admit, Bring Your Daughter to Work Day really adds a touch of home to the workplace."

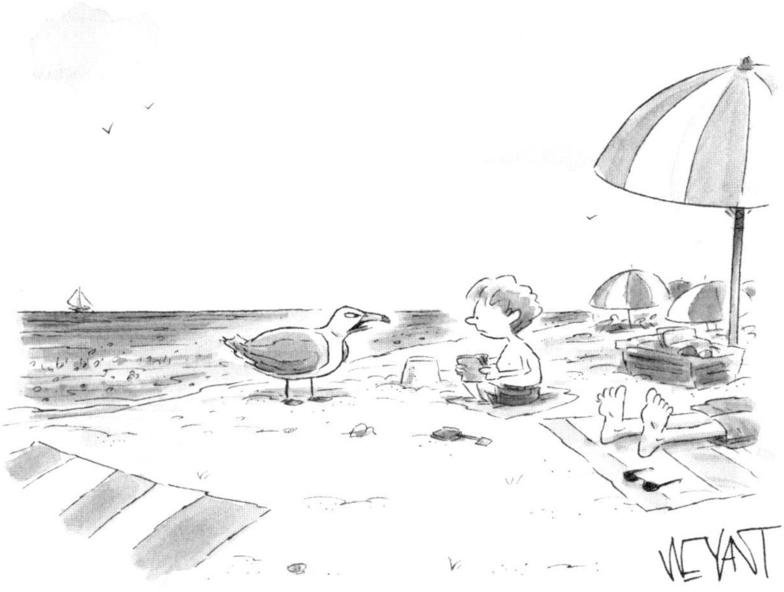
WEYANT

"Hand over the sandwich or I'll crap on your parents."

"Mostly, I just miss his hand."

"I told you I'm not into any kinky stuff."

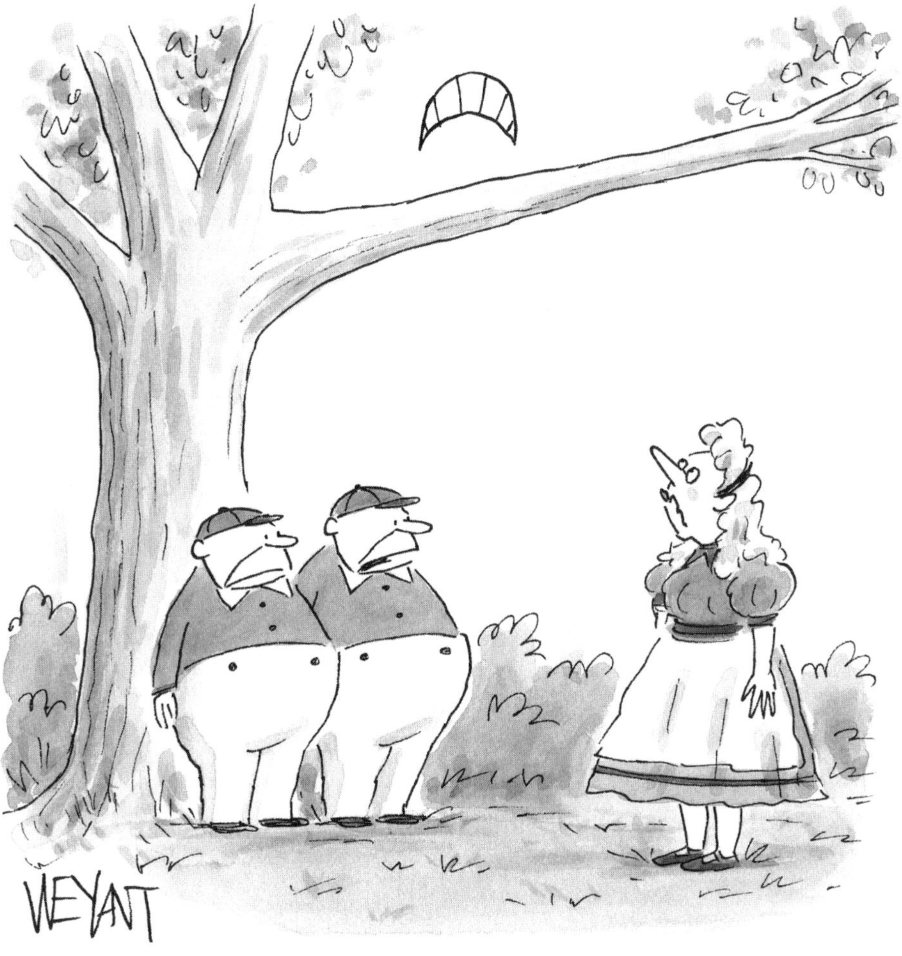
WEYANT

"We had him neutered."

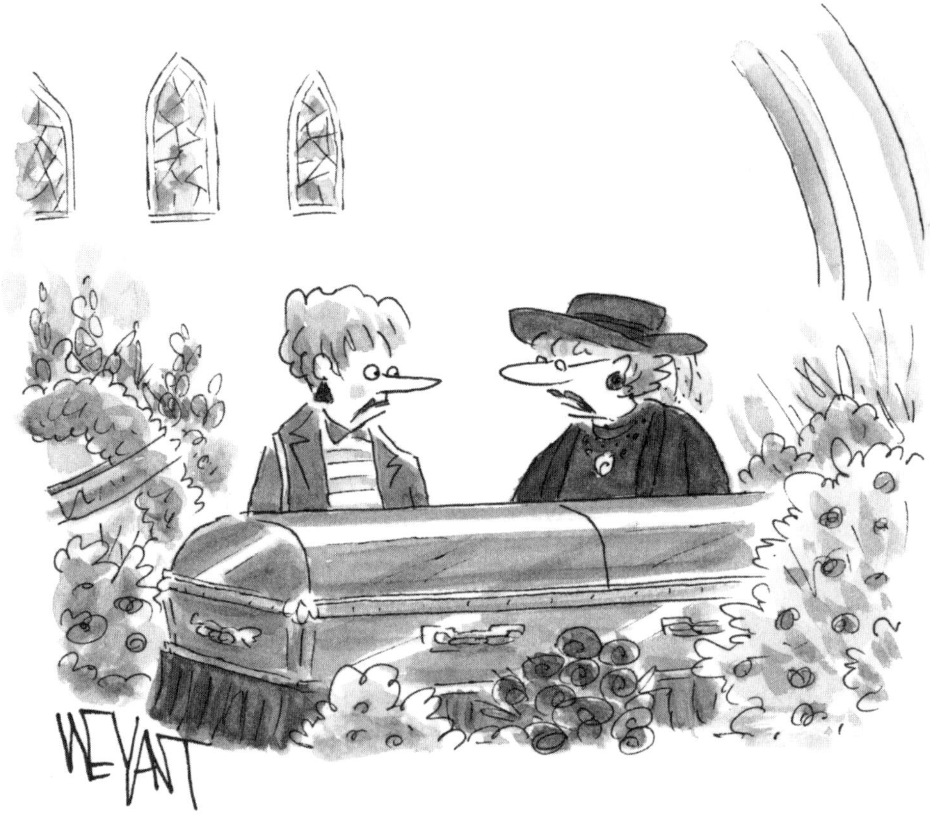
WEYANT

"It would have been an open casket, but he overdosed on Viagra."

"Richard, did you use all of the dental floss?"

—————— APPENDIX 1 ——————

"THE BUTT OF THE ICEBERG"

———————————

Cartoon Ideas the Cartoonists Have Rejected

Cartoonists get rejected a lot. I think we've gone over that, but we also on occasion get to do some rejecting of our own. In this section, I asked the cartoonists to sketch up any terrible ideas that had been pitched to them over the years by well-meaning friends, family, or strangers— in other words, ideas that the cartoonists have rejected and never even bothered to put on paper. Until now. If you know a cartoonist, there's a chance you might see one of your own ideas in the next few pages.

See, this is what happens: As soon as someone learns that you're a cartoonist, they'll say, "Oh, I've got a great cartoon idea for you." Then they proceed to tell you the idea (which is never great) and then they get a little miffed when you don't do cartwheels or guffawing spit-takes. It'd be like if you spent your whole life panning a short stretch of river for gold and some Cub Scout with a butterfly umbrella comes skipping along shouting "Hey, Mister. I found a gold nugget!" and then he holds up a piece of iron pyrite or more likely, a badger turd. It's cute, but come on!

David Sipress describes the scene perfectly in this strip.

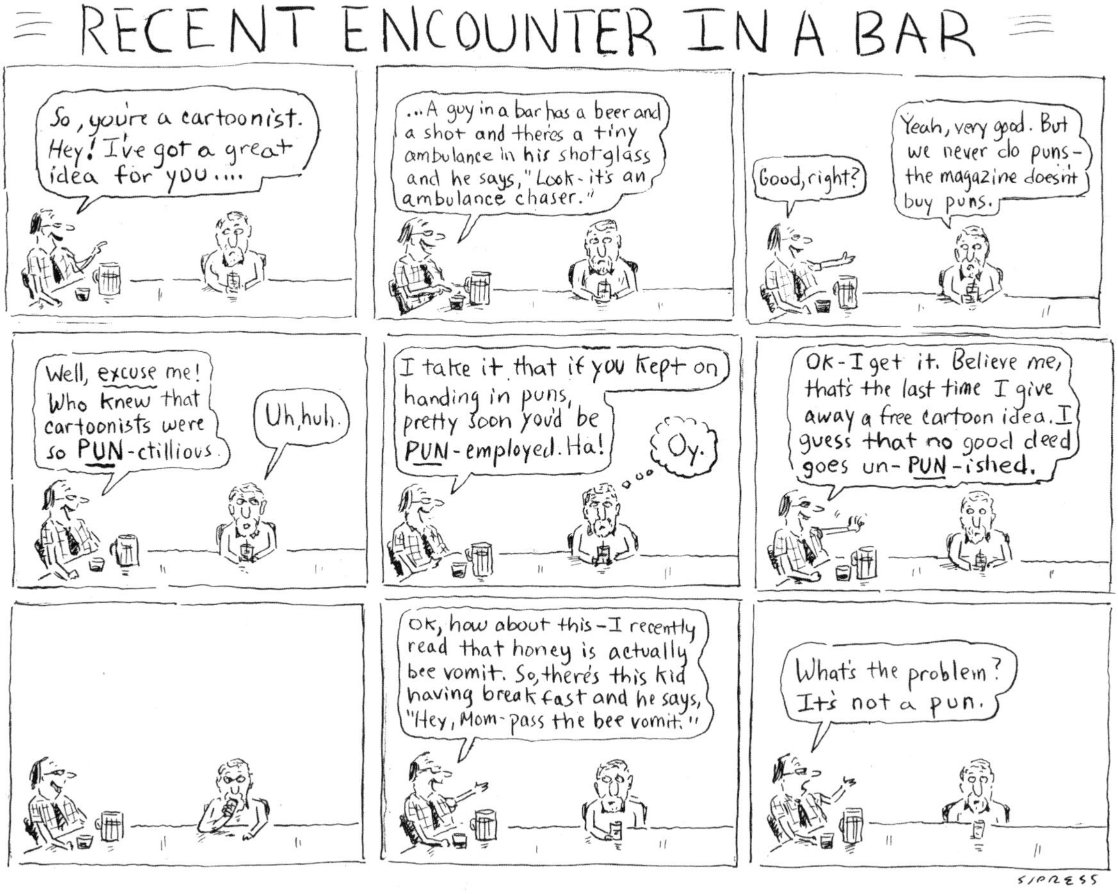
RECENT ENCOUNTER IN A BAR
So, you're a cartoonist. Hey! I've got a great idea for you....
...A guy in a bar has a beer and a shot and there's a tiny ambulance in his shot glass and he says, "Look - it's an ambulance chaser."
Good, right?
Yeah, very good. But we never do puns - the magazine doesn't buy puns.
Well, excuse me! Who knew that cartoonists were so PUN-ctillious.
Uh, huh.
I take it that if you kept on handing in puns, pretty soon you'd be PUN-employed. Ha!
Oy.
OK - I get it. Believe me, that's the last time I give away a free cartoon idea. I guess that no good deed goes un-PUN-ished.
OK, how about this - I recently read that honey is actually bee vomit. So, there's this kid having breakfast and he says, "Hey, Mom - pass the bee vomit."
What's the problem? It's not a pun.
SIPRESS

This is all probably making you think that we cartoonists are completely humorless, bitter people and that's not true. Some of us are only mildly bitter and partially humorless. The truth is we kind of enjoy these moments. It's nice to have a job that other people wish they had. It's also secretly enjoyable to see that other people can't do your job very well. So, let's have a little fun with this. We'll show you the cartoon and tell you where the idea came from and why we didn't go for it. I'll start with one of my own preemptive rejects.

- **Cartoonist who rejected this idea:**
  Matthew Diffee.

  Person who suggested this idea:
  The Reverend John DeLore. (He's a fantastic singer-songwriter and a not-that-fantastic gag man. And yes, he's an actual reverend, but unaffiliated, which means . . . um, I don't really know actually. Seems shady somehow.)

  Relationship to cartoonist:
  Friend.

  Reasons cartoonist rejected this idea:
  Well, it's terrible. What can I say? (Sorry, John.) I drew it just like he described it to me. It's clunky and punny. It's what some refer to as a "groaner," plus, as a Texan, I find it a little offensive. There are certain sacred things that we just don't joke about in Texas: Barbecue, Jesus, Chili, and above all, the Alamo. It just ain't done, Son.

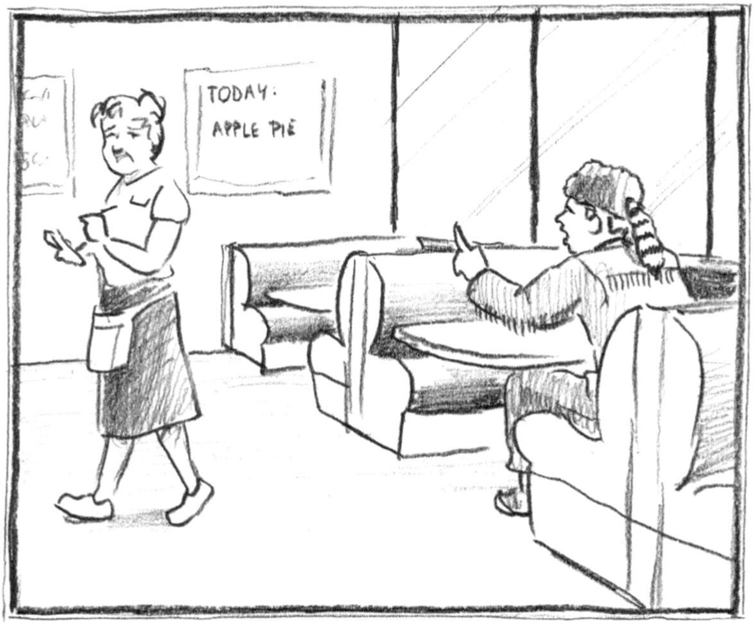
TODAY:
APPLE PIE

"Remember the a la Mode!"

- **Cartoonist who rejected this idea:**
  John O'Brien.

Person who suggested this idea:
Dr. Thomas McGuigan.

Relationship to cartoonist:
A close friend of more than 40 years, and my unofficial health-care provider. Does that make me cheap?

Reasons cartoonist rejected this idea:
I thought this one was a good representation of the scores of gag ideas regularly thrown at me by well-intentioned friends and acquaintances. Occasionally, I've been known to submit one. However, this one I didn't—I couldn't figure out how to draw an "ahead." Now that it's on paper, though, I find it strangely amusing. Does that make me weird?

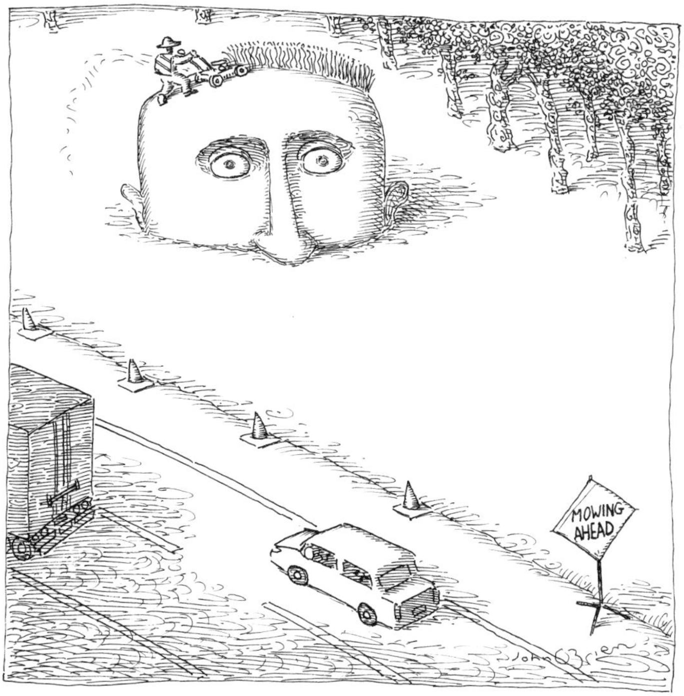
MOWING
AHEAD
JOHN O'BRIEN

■ **Cartoonist who rejected this idea:**

William Haefeli.

Person who suggested this idea:

A man who was trying to impress me
with his wit.

Relationship to cartoonist:

A man who failed to impress me with his wit.

Reasons cartoonist rejected this idea:

If you have to ask, I'm not going to tell you.

"I love to act. I'm a ham."

■ **Cartoonist who rejected this idea:**

Ariel Molvig.

Person who suggested this idea:

Eleanor.

Relationship to cartoonist:

My niece.

Reasons cartoonist rejected this idea:

The idea was ahead of its time.

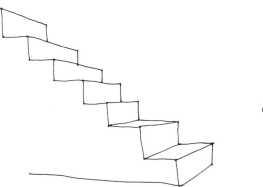

"Stop stairing at me."

- **Cartoonist who rejected this idea:**

  Tom Cheney.

  Person who suggested this idea:

  "Lani."

  Relationship to cartoonist:

  Bank teller.

  Reasons cartoonist rejected this idea:

  Not weird enough.

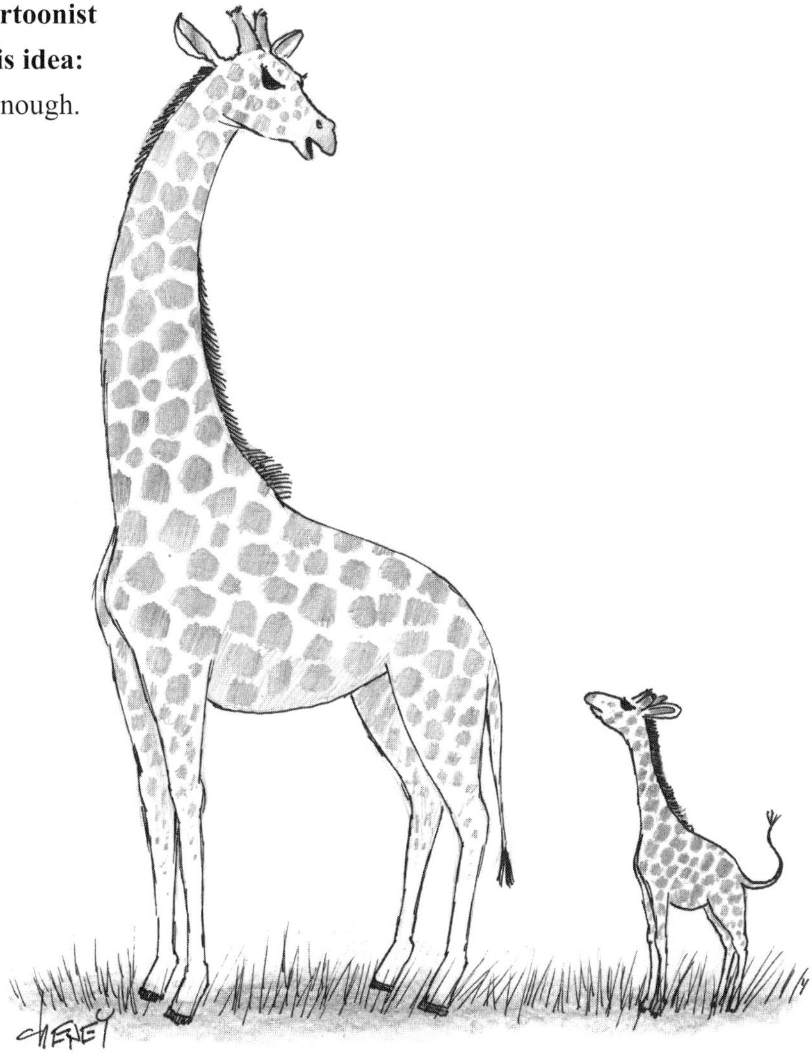
CHENEY

"Don't make me have to come down there."

- **Cartoonist who rejected this idea:**
  Marisa Acocella Marchetto.

  Person who suggested this idea:
  Bob Morris—he's actually brilliant. At least he cares about me enough to think of ideas.

  Relationship to cartoonist:
  BFF.

  Reasons cartoonist rejected this idea:
  I love topical, but this wasn't funny. Also, she's wearing something I totally *would* be caught dead in. When I told my friend Bob that *The Rejection Collection* was looking for cartoons cartoonists themselves have rejected, and his was perfect for that, HE rejected that idea and said, "oh no, give it to Mankoff." Well, I rejected that, obviously. So Matt, here ya go.

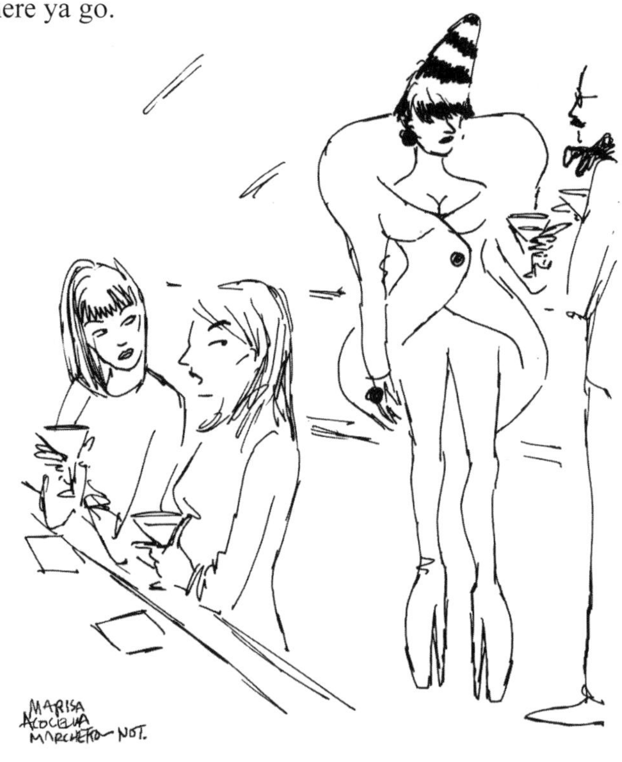
MARISA ACOCELLA MARCHETTO—NOT.

"Lady Gag-Gag"

- **Cartoonist who rejected this idea:**
  Pat Byrnes.

  Person who suggested this idea:
  My dreaming, sleepwalking, and—worse—sleep-*writing* self.

  Relationship to cartoonist:
  We share a body, a brain (allegedly), but clearly not a sense of humor.

  Reasons cartoonist rejected this idea:
  My unconscious self thought that this was hilarious enough to wake me up, force me out of bed in the middle of the night, and scrawl it down so I didn't forget it—regardless of the fact that it is utterly incomprehensible to any conscious human. Shame has (rightfully) prevented me from drawing it up. Until now.

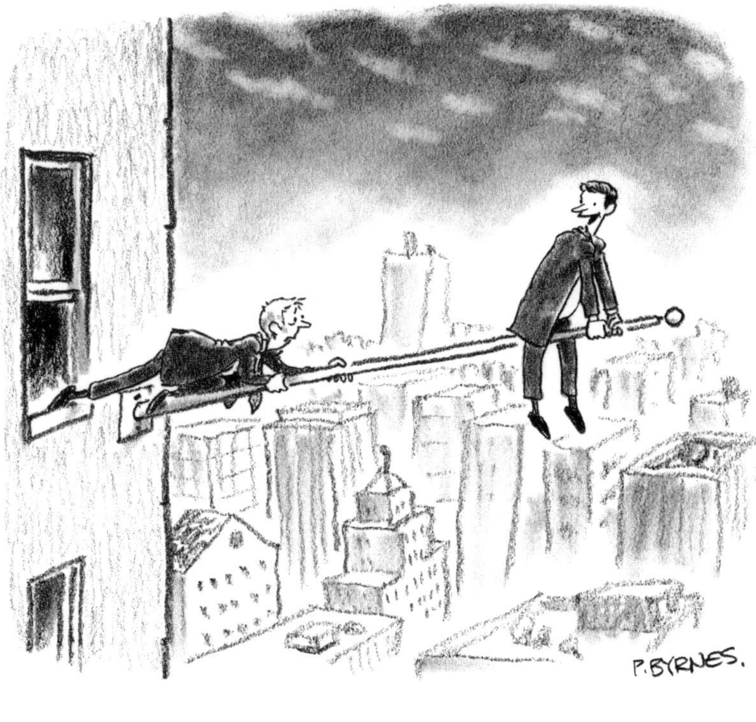
P.BYRNES.

"See? Aren't you glad you convinced them to deal me in?"

■ **Cartoonist who rejected this idea:**

Michael Crawford.

Person who suggested this idea/relationship to cartoonist:

A total stranger at a café in New Orleans, who said his name was
Ted and he was a "screenwriter."

Reasons cartoonist rejected this idea:

I complimented him with the always withering "cute!" and said thanks,
but for better or worse, I draw only my own "ideas." (Unless someone
forks over a ton of clams.)

"Ted, say 'Hi' to J.T.—he's from Alabama, too."

■ **Cartoonist who rejected this idea:**
Drew Dernavich.

Person who suggested this idea:
[name not so much redacted as forgotten]

Relationship to cartoonist:
The man who pinned me in a corner at a party hosted by an acquaintance of my wife.

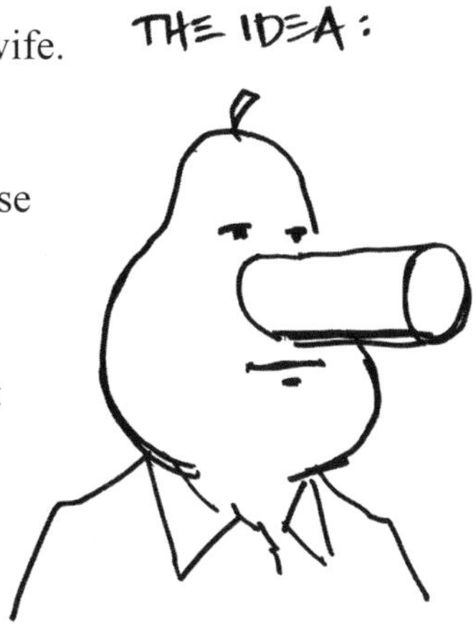
THE IDEA:

Reasons cartoonist rejected this idea:
I never actually rejected this idea, because it's not even really an idea yet. I'm still waiting for the rest of it. You can't send back your dinner if you're still staring at an empty plate, right? It could be really ahead of its time. Maybe in twenty years the other half of the idea will send me a postcard. Or even better, maybe this half-idea will be the code which unlocks the key to the language in some ancient scroll. So I'm keeping my options open on this one.

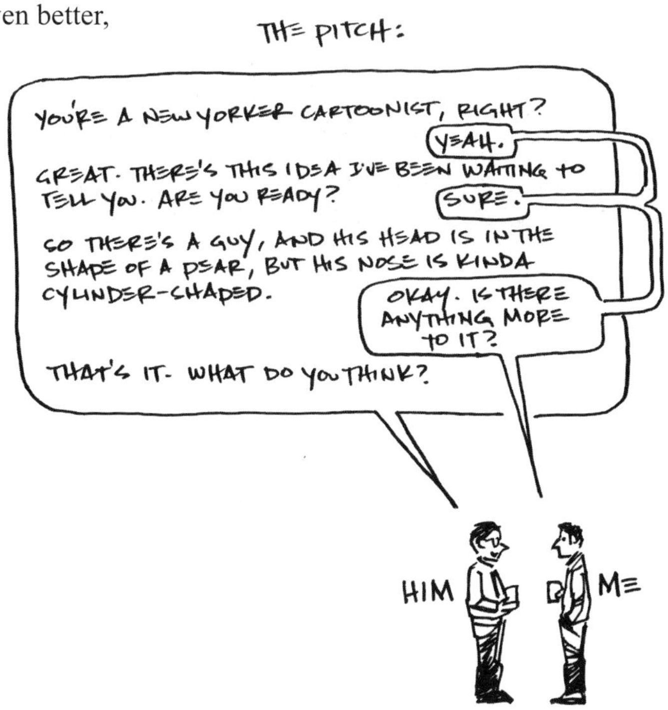
THE PITCH:
YOU'RE A NEW YORKER CARTOONIST, RIGHT?
YEAH.
GREAT. THERE'S THIS IDEA I'VE BEEN WAITING TO TELL YOU. ARE YOU READY?
SURE.
SO THERE'S A GUY, AND HIS HEAD IS IN THE SHAPE OF A PEAR, BUT HIS NOSE IS KINDA CYLINDER-SHAPED.
OKAY. IS THERE ANYTHING MORE TO IT?
THAT'S IT. WHAT DO YOU THINK?
HIM
ME

■ **Cartoonist who rejected this idea:**

Mort Gerberg.

Person who suggested this idea:

Dr. Jeffrey Goldstein.

Relationship to cartoonist:

My full-time dermatologist and one-time gag writer.

Reasons cartoonist rejected this idea:

1. I couldn't find any high-paying Axillary Hyperhidrosis magazines to sell it to.

2. Just the thought of Botox makes my drawings tighten up.

"Your Botox treatment for my axillary hyperhidrosis—
excessive sweating armpits—worked perfectly, except
now my ass sweats profusely instead."

- **Cartoonist who rejected this idea:**

  Sidney Harris.

  Who, what, and how:

  When Jackie Noodle tried to revive his stand-up career for the seventh time, he tried to get me to do a drawing to publicize his effort. He rented an elephant—only one, not three—came up with a Hannibal costume, hired a few retired Carthaginian soldiers, and set off. When the elephant, a nice, elderly grandmother named Elsebeth, realized she was on a bogus military operation, she refused to go on. They had only crossed one Catskill, and Noodle's career fizzled.

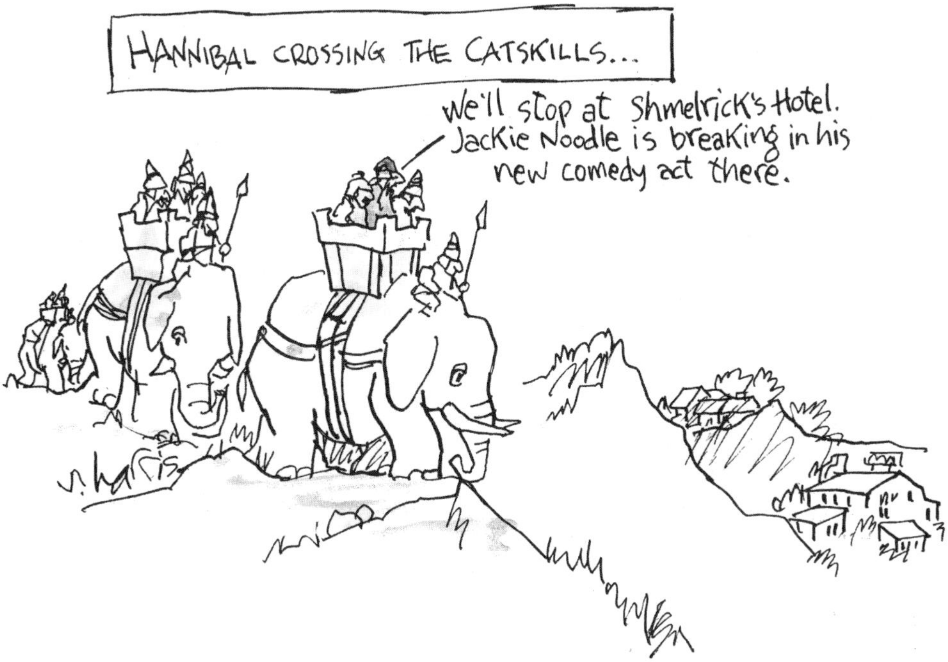
HANNIBAL CROSSING THE CATSKILLS...
We'll stop at Shmelrick's Hotel. Jackie Noodle is breaking in his new comedy act there.
S. Harris

- **Cartoonist who rejected this idea:**
  Carolita Johnson.

  Person who suggested this idea:
  A musician friend named Alex Battles.

  Relationship to cartoonist:
  Had to become friends with him after hearing him sing "Oiseau Libre" ("Freebird," in French) after Michael Crawford yelled "Skynrd!" at one of his gigs.

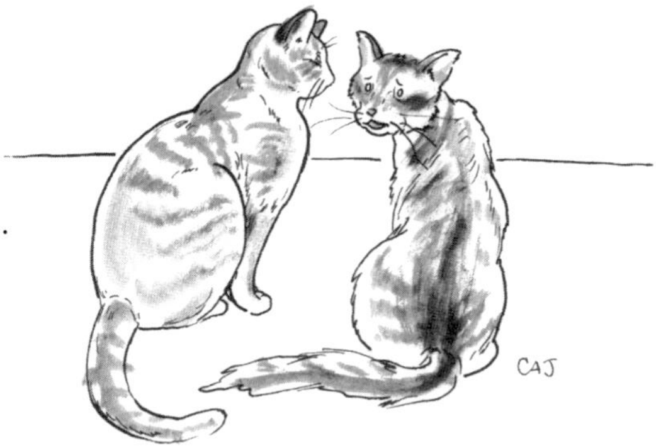
CAJ

"Seems like every time I hear the can opener it's not for me anymore."

  Reasons cartoonist rejected this idea:
  First it made me laugh, but then it made me cry. (I think I hadn't sold a cartoon in a while and it was too close to home!)

- **Cartoonist who rejected this idea:**
  Mick Stevens.

  Person who suggested this idea:
  A podiatrist.

  Relationship to cartoonist:
  Sat next to me at this little podiatrist bar I once went to in Miami Beach.

  Reasons cartoonist rejected this idea:
  Forgot it, until just now.

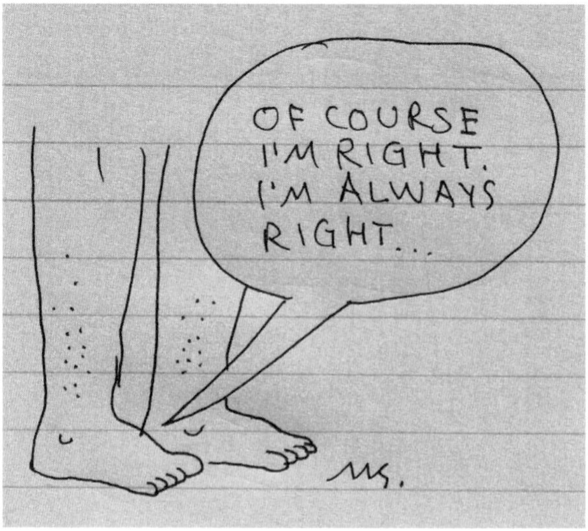
OF COURSE
I'M RIGHT.
I'M ALWAYS
RIGHT...
MS.

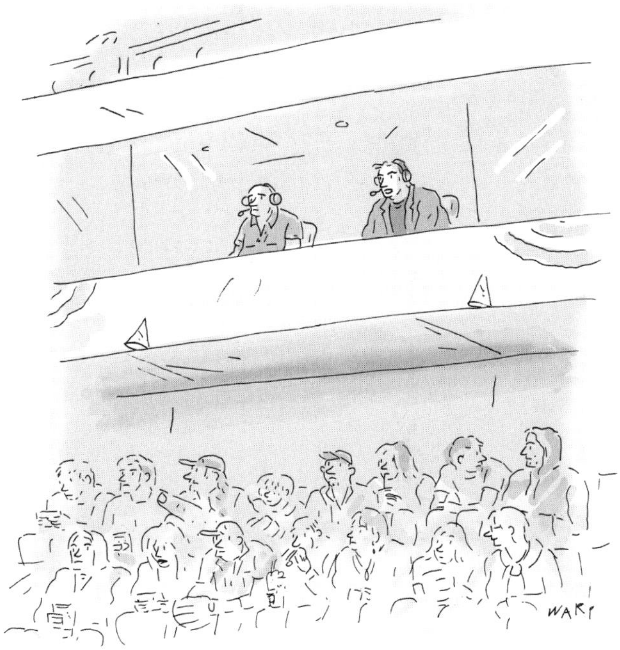
WARP

"During today's game, in honor of the tsunami victims, we ask that you refrain from doing the wave."

- **Cartoonist who rejected this idea:**
  Kim Warp.

  Person who suggested this idea:
  Alison Warp.

  Relationship to cartoonist:
  Sister.

  Reasons cartoonist rejected this idea:
  Okay, here's the deal. I can't remember ANY cartoon ideas. I have to write them all down immediately or they are gone with last week's grocery list. Moreover, if someone tells me a bad cartoon idea, I don't write it down at all or waste any remaining brain cells trying to remember it. I say something like "Okay, thanks Alison, I'm writing that down!" And forget it immediately. So, this is the only suggestion I can remember because I thought it was a good idea and it stuck in my brain somehow. I felt it's exactly the kind of thing we do in the face of feeling helpless at some horrific disaster. I rejected it because the tsunami was hugely tragic (this was after the Indian Ocean tsunami) and I didn't want to be perceived as making an unfeeling joke about it even though this wasn't an unfeeling joke. In my experience, subtleties like that get lost and I didn't want the e-mails. Plus, crowds are hard to draw.

- **Cartoonist who rejected this idea:**

  P. C. Vey.

  Person who suggested this idea:

  Some gal at a bar.

  Relationship to cartoonist:

  None.

  Reasons cartoonist rejected this idea:

  She had a hospital ID bracelet on her wrist.

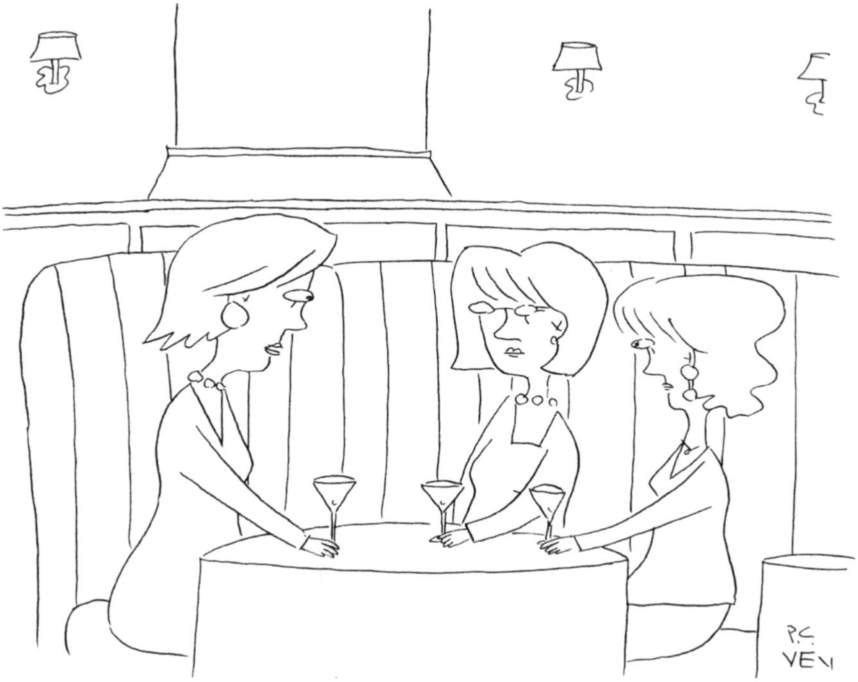
P.C.
VEY

"The new guy I'm seeing doesn't make a lot of 'cents' but he certainly makes a lot of dollars."

■ **Cartoonist who rejected this idea:**
Julia Suits.

Person who suggested this idea:
A certain teenager.

Relationship to cartoonist:
Son.

Reasons cartoonist rejected this idea:
A potato would have been a better choice than a pear. A potato has eyes.

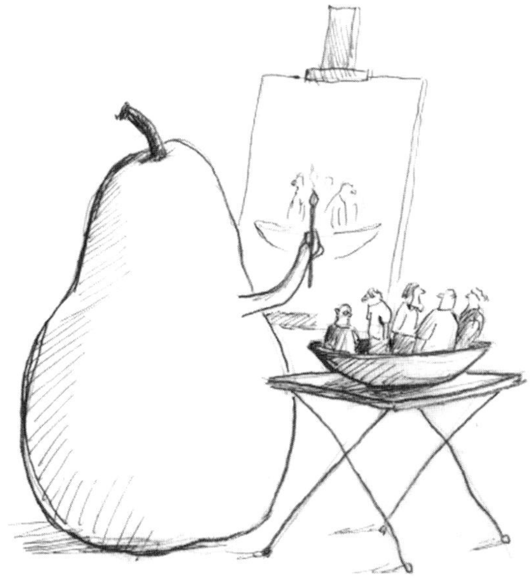

■ **Cartoonist who rejected this idea:**
Michael Shaw. (Unfortunately I didn't reject it—no concept is too odious to steal.)

Person who suggested this idea:
Patrick.

Relationship to cartoonist:
My twin brother.

Reasons cartoonist rejected this idea:
Growing up, we would play "Thurber 'n' White" instead of cops 'n' robbers. One day, when it was his turn to be Thurber, he passed an odious drawing of a nun with an oyster face and I dutifully inked it. The idea beautifully encompasses the holy trinity of awful cartooning: bad pun, organized religion, and raw seafood. Luckily, our younger sister did not want to play Ross.

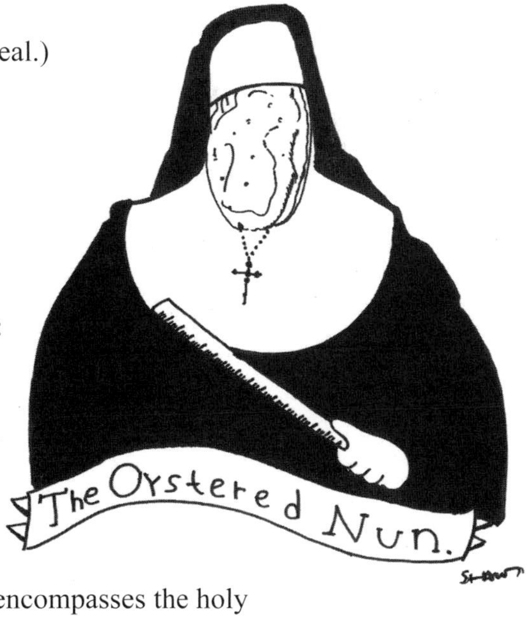
The Oystered Nun.

- **Cartoonist who rejected this idea:**
  Christopher Weyant.

  Person who suggested this idea:
  Anna Kang Weyant.

  Relationship to cartoonist:
  Wife and mother of my cartoon.

  Reasons cartoonist rejected this idea:
  I promised myself that if I publish another "tweet" cartoon, I will blow my brains out. Or become an accountant. I'm not sure which would be more punishing.

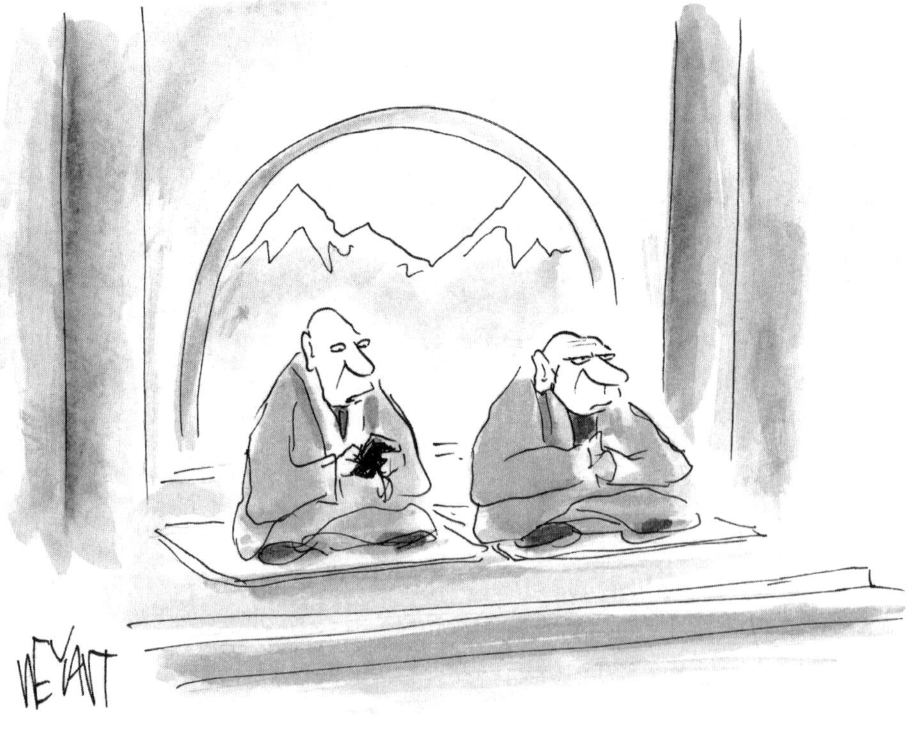
WEYANT

"Hold on a minute. I have to tweet my mantra."

- **Cartoonist who rejected this idea:**

  Glen LeLievre.

  Person who suggested this idea:

  Glen LeLievre.

  Relationship to cartoonist:

  Subconscious.

  Reasons cartoonist rejected this idea:

  Not enough blood.

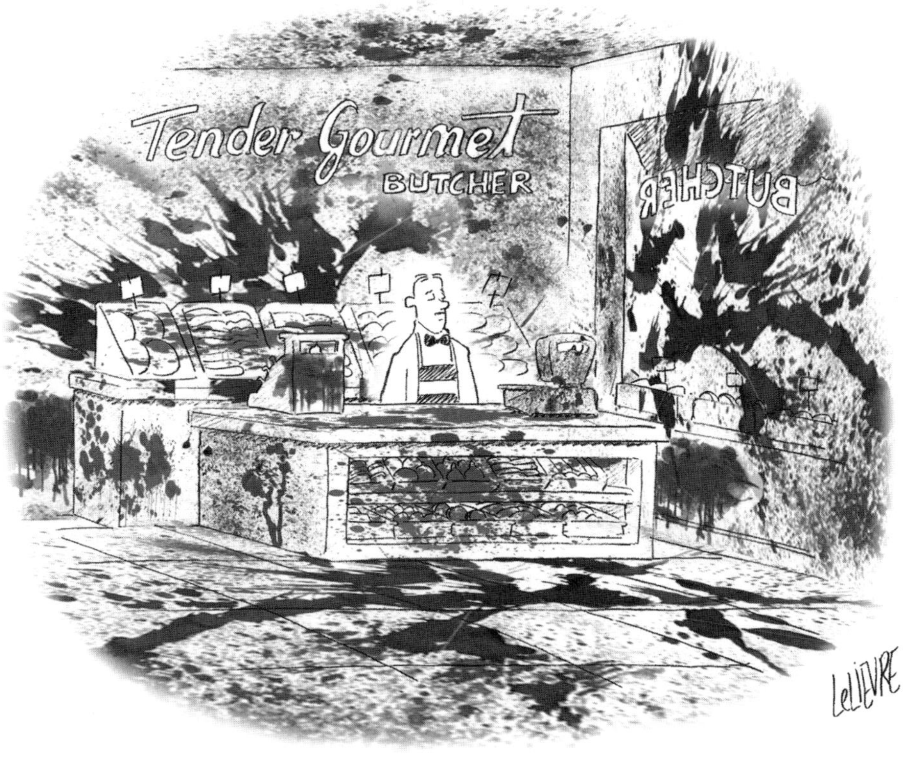
Tender Gourmet
BUTCHER
BUTCHER
LeLIEVRE

— A P P E N D I X   2 —

MANKOFF ANSWERS
THE TOUGH QUESTIONS

Paul Noth

I can and I don't.
He didn't so I won't.

Roz Chast

I just found this note on my desk that says, "Call Fred! Important! 2 P.M.!!" Do you know who this Fred is?
Roz, check out www.whoisfred.com.

J. C. Duffy

Was it something I said?
Not in so many words.

Marshall Hopkins

Is "never" good for you?
Neber has been berry berry good for me.

Alex Gregory

Why "Bob" and not "Rob"?
Hey, Alex, thanks for blowing my secret name.

Nick Downes

Who will be wearing what on Oscar night?
Personally, I'd like to see everyone in bright, orange Gitmo jumpsuits or boxer-thong combos.

William Haefeli

Where are you taking me to lunch?
On my calendar. Just bought the Lunchables.

Ariel Molvig

Why don't you wuv me?
Because love is blind, and then I'd have to ask everyone to submit Braille creations.

Glen LeLievre

Boxers or briefs?

Actually a combo with a boxer front and a thong back to show off my buns.

Robert Leighton

Get it?

Not really but I can fake it.

Mick Stevens

Why was my name on a gravestone in one of your earlier cartoons? I've been running scared ever since.

Silly boy. Just change your name.

Tom Cheney

Have we really been at this for 35 years?

Yes, time flies when you're in the heartbreaking business of being funny for money.

Julia Suits

Why dots?

Why nots?

David Sipress

Have you no sense of decency, sir? At long last, have you no sense of decency?

Not since I started wearing the boxer-thong combo.

Zachary Kanin

Where do you get your ideas?

Toledo.

Eric Lewis

Do you still love me?

How can I when you've treated me in such a cavalier and callous manner? I will have no more truck with you.

Barbara Smaller

Why, Bob, why?

Indeed. Not to mention who, what, where, and when.

Harry Bliss

Why don't we make love more than once a week?

Because your last name promises more than anyone could fulfill.

Mort Gerberg

Please, sir—may I have some more OKs?

Mort, all the OKs are going to China and India, so move.

Jason Patterson

Where can you get a good sandwich in Midtown?

My favorite is the Mid-Town Luncheonette, which is actually located in Toledo.

C. Covert Darbyshire

Could you please stop hitting on my wife?

Agreed, and you'll stop making those obscene phone calls to my potbellied Vietnamese pig.

Michael Shaw

Are you my real father?

No, your real father is that guy who is also the real father of Anna Nicole's baby.

Leo Cullum

Bob, may I ask you three questions?

Leo, I'm a busy man, so let's make that one question with three parts.

Carolita Johnson

Does it hurt you when I stick this pin in this little voodoo doll?

Yes, but it's a good hurt.

P. S. Mueller

Are the rumors true that you can bend foreign coins with your powerful mind?

More important, I can influence their exchange rates.

J. B. Handelsman

Why is *The New Yorker* prejudiced against me and/or my work?

We are not prejudiced against you, J. B. We are prejudiced against everyone.

Mike Twohy

Do you laugh this hard at everyone's cartoons?

Mike, I try to refrain from laughing at anyone's cartoons. It is a sign of ill breeding.

Sidney Harris

John O'Brien

What was wrong with that idea, eleventh from the bottom of that batch I sent on February 15, 2002?

The umlaut.

Jack Ziegler

Where did you get that haircut?

My hair was granted autonomy in 1986 and full independence with the fall of the Berlin Wall in 1989, so all questions such as this should be addressed to bobshair@gmail.com.

Robert Weber

Bob, are you sure this is something you really want to do?

No, but noblesse oblige.

Marisa Acocella Marchetto

Why are YOU always published?

Because I'm fair but not stupid.

Pat Byrnes

If a train leaves New York at 9:00 A.M., and another train leaves Albany at 9:30 A.M., and their speeds are, respectively, 50 mph and 42 mph . . .

Could we move on to the verbal portion of the test?

Michael Crawford

Could you supersize that for me, Sonny?

Yeah, in Toledo.

Gahan Wilson

What's the meaning of life, Bob?

I think I can best answer that with an analogy . . . color: spectrum as tone: scale.

P. C. Vey

When is the cartoonists' lounge going to be redecorated?

The new cartoonists' lounge will, when completed in the fourth quarter of 2013, fulfill every desire and exceed every expectation. It will be located in Toledo.

Christopher Weyant

Bob, why do good things happen to bad people?

Please see the analogy I gave Gahan.

Kim Warp

Have you ever laughed out loud at one of my cartoons? Smiled to yourself? Never mind.

Not only that, but I've passed gas as well.

Drew Dernavich

Why are you interested in coming to work for me, Mr. Mankoff?

Sometimes I think it's your hair, and other times I think it's your anaphylactic reactions to peanuts.

Danny Shanahan

Is it I, Lord?

Oh, you and your Shanahanigans.

Sam Gross

Why?

Because if a train leaves New York at 9:00 A.M., and another train leaves Albany at 9:30 A.M., one train has on it Harry Bliss, Robert Leighton, Roz Chast, David Sipress, Jack Ziegler, Leo Cullum, Mick Stevens, Gahan Wilson, P. C. Vey, Jason Patterson, Carolita Johnson, Michael Shaw, Alex Gregory, Robert Weber, Pat Byrnes, William Haefeli, Barbara Smaller, Drew Dernavich, Mort Gerberg , Julia Suits, C. Covert Darbyshire, Marshall Hopkins, and John O'Brien. And the other has Zachary Kanin, Danny Shanahan, J. B. Handelsman, Marisa Acocella Marchetto, Michael Crawford, Nick Downes, Ariel Molvig, Arnie Levin, Kim Warp, Eric Lewis, Sidney Harris, J. C. Duffy, Mike Twohy, Glen LeLievre, P. S. Mueller, Tom Cheney, Paul Noth, Sam Gross, and Christopher Weyant. Neither one of these trains is ever going to get to Toledo.

Arnie Levin

Bob, in no more than 5,000 words . . . ?

Finally, I'm stumped.

———— ACKNOWLEDGMENTS ————

A book is sorta like a freight train—one of those old-timey ones. Someone has to draw the plans and consult a map, someone has to build trestle bridges over rivers and blast tunnels through mountains, someone has to lay the track, connect all the cars, grease the wheels, collect tickets, check the pocket watch, shovel coal, and someone has to toot the horn. The horn-tooting was my job and all the rest was done by the following fine folks:

Tanya Erlach, David Kuhn, Billy Kingsland, my editor, Megan Nicolay and the rest of the crew at Workman Publishing, including Liz Davis, Peggy Gannon, Janet Vicario, Sue Macleod, and Peter Workman. Thanks also to Bob Mankoff, David Remnick, and especially the cartoonists themselves who came up with all the material, old and new that you see in here. If you see any of these people out anywhere, buy them something nice.

— COPYRIGHT INFORMATION —

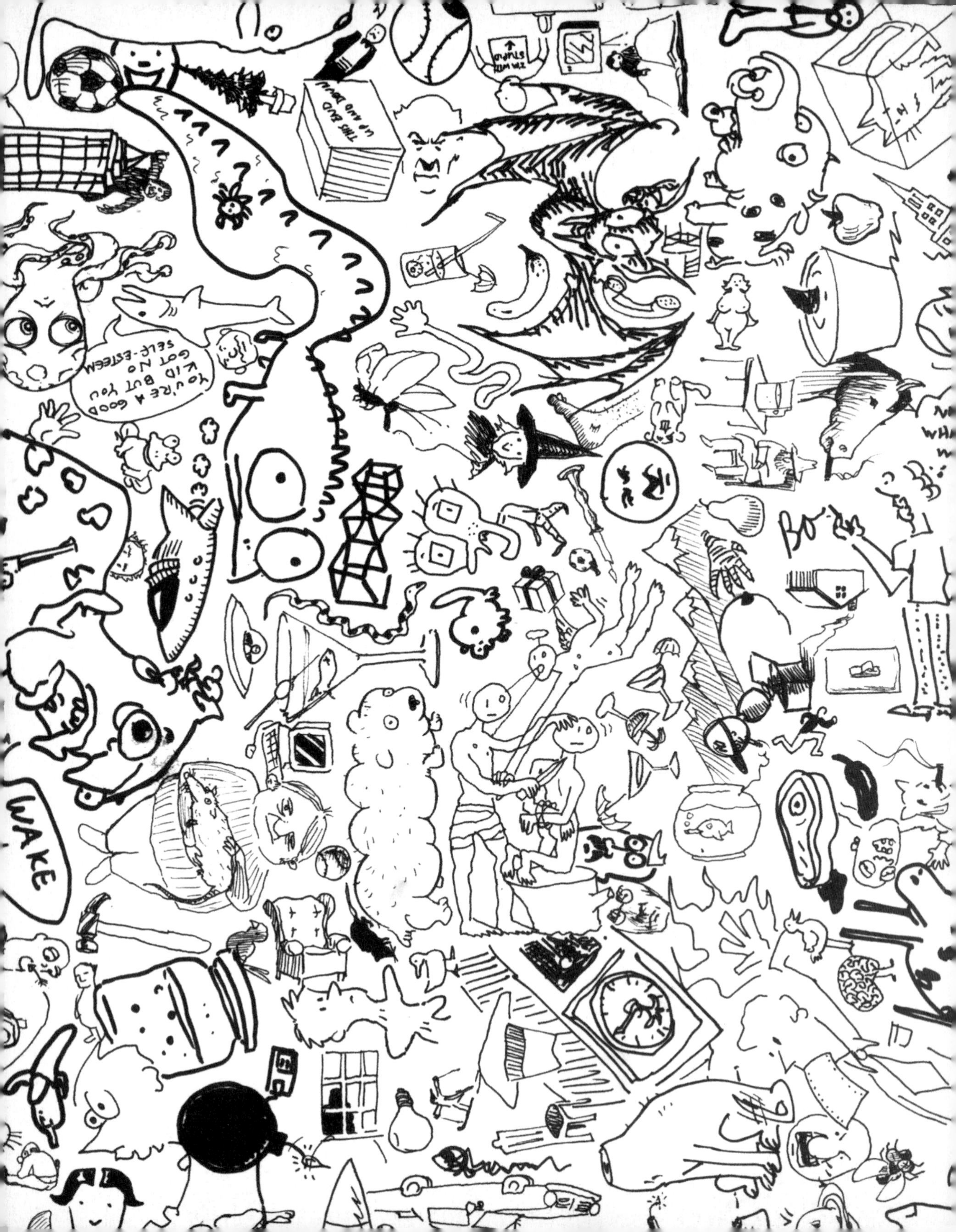
YOU'RE A GOOD KID BUT YOU GOT NO SELF-ESTEEM
WAKE